D1207139

THE MIRROR OF THE SELF

SHADI BARTSCH | The Mirror of the Self

Sexuality,

Self-Knowledge,

and the Gaze

in the Early

Roman Empire

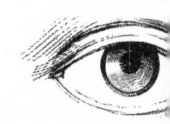

THE UNIVERSITY OF CHICAGO PRESS / CHICAGO & LONDON

SHADI BARTSCH is the Ann L. and Lawrence B. Buttenwieser
Professor of Classics at the University of Chicago. She is the
author of four books, most recently *Ideology in Cold Blood: A
Reading of Lucan's "Civil War,"* and coeditor of *Erotikon: Essays
on Eros, Ancient and Modern.*

The University of Chicago Press, Chicago 60637
The University of Chicago Press, Ltd., London
© 2006 by The University of Chicago
All rights reserved. Published 2006
Printed in the United States of America

15 14 13 12 11 10 09 08 07 06   1 2 3 4 5

ISBN: 0-226-03835-1 (cloth)

Library of Congress Cataloging-in-Publication Data

Bartsch, Shadi, 1966–
    The Mirror of the self : sexuality, self-knowledge, and the gaze
in the early Roman Empire / Shadi Bartsch.
        p. cm
    Includes bibliographical references and index.
    ISBN 0-226-03835-1 (cloth : alk. paper)
    1. Reflection (Philosophy)—History. 2. Self-knowledge, Theory
of—History. 3. Sex—History. 4. Philosophy, Ancient. I. Title.
    B105.R27B37 2006
    126.0937—dc22

                                        2005033447

CONTENTS

ACKNOWLEDGMENTS

Callimachus once said that a big book was a big evil. Not being a neoteric poet, I have reason to differ; but I do concede that a big book written over a long period of time generates an extensive list of scholars and friends who midwifed its tortoise-paced parturition. *Cui dono glaebula libri?* First, to the philosophers and literary critics who read all or most of the manuscript. Some (primarily philosophers) offered criticism that was both accurate and palatable; others (primarily literary critics) encouraged me by claiming the book had not put them to sleep. Their numbers include Christopher Gill, John Henderson, A. A. Long, Andrea Nightingale, and one very helpful but still anonymous press reader. To all, I am more grateful than they know: their expertise and generosity saved my offspring from some serious blemishes.

A number of colleagues and conference participants read or heard chapters of the volume in progress, and shared their suggestions: I would like to thank Catharine Edwards, Andrew Feldherr, Brad Inwood, James Ker, Glenn Most, Rob Nelson, Martha Nussbaum, Alessandro Schiesaro, and David Wray. And several scholars generously shared with me their unpublished manuscripts ahead of publication: Rachel Barney, Jaś Elsner, Christopher Gill, Brad Inwood, Brian Johnson, David Leitao, Andrea Nightingale, Niall Slater, and Christopher Star.

I would also like to briefly acknowledge the many people I have not mentioned so far whose comments or support deserve more than this scanty list of names indicates: Elizabeth Asmis, Sean Carroll, Page duBois, Jonathan Hall, John Kirby, Michael Putnam, Matthew Roller, Jonathan Sachs, Richard Saller, James Tatum, Chris Trinacty, and Froma Zeitlin, who supported the proposal before anyone else had seen it.

Who made it possible for me to unleash a volume about katoptricophal-losophia on the unsuspecting world? All recriminations should be addressed to the American Council of Learned Societies and the Franke Institute for the Humanities at the University of Chicago (which both supplied year-long fellow-ships), the Chicago Classics Department (which allowed me to accept them), and the University of Chicago Press (which published the result). Complain-ers will find a sympathetic ear in my mother, who lamented all my detours into the phallic. Further along, Geoffrey Huck at the Press took on the volume in embryo; Susan Bielstein saw it to adulthood and proved a wonderful interlocu-tor for conversations about this and other projects. Another editorial virtue: she always sprang for lunch (should I be concerned that we always ate at La Petite Folie?). My thanks also to Lys Ann Weiss, my sharp-eyed copyeditor.

I am getting to that doddering age at which one has earned those wonder-ful things, research assistants. At Berkeley and Chicago, I owe much to the help of Patricia Larash, Alex Gottesman, Linda Haddad, Jonathan Mannering, Stacie Raucci, and last, but definitely not least, Aaron Seider.

All translations are my own unless otherwise indicated; those of Plato have been consistently taken from John M. Cooper's 1997 edition of the complete works. I have restricted citations of the ancient texts in the original languages to instances when this has particular relevance. Finally, I note that parts of this volume have appeared elsewhere. A version of chapter 2 was published in *See-ing as Others Saw: Visuality before and beyond the Renaissance*, ed. Robert S. Nelson (Cambridge: Cambridge University Press, 2000), and part of chapter 4 was published in *Erotikon: Essays on Eros, Ancient and Modern*, ed. Shadi Bartsch and Thomas Bartscherer (Chicago: University of Chicago Press, 2005). I thank Cambridge University Press and the University of Chicago Press for allowing me to rework those articles.

This is a book about vision, sexuality, and self-knowledge in the ancient world, which, as topics for a single study, might seem an unlikely ménage à trois. One could reasonably justify combining any two of these terms as interdependent issues in classical antiquity: we could invoke the role of vision in sexual attraction in lyric and elegy, for example, or the way that the philosophical precept to "know thyself" is partially founded on a specular treatment of the gaze. But add the third term in each case, and the self-evident quality of any connection disappears. In the modern world in particular, where philosophers rarely publish on the ethical ramifications of various sex acts and ophthalmologists are unlikely to ask patients if they have been exposed to an envious neighbor's evil eye, it seems hard to imagine how these three discourses (one scientific, one risqué, the third abstractly philosophical) might, at their intersection, provide a space for conceptualizing selfhood. And yet the contention of this book is that such a space for thought did exist in ancient Greece and Rome; even further, that the interrelation of these three fields of discourse across the sweep of time has much to show us about how the ancients understood what it meant to be a person.

Theories of vision, cultural givens about sexuality, and the widespread valence of the philosophical injunction to "know thyself" provide this window into the ancient world because all three sought to explain how the individual was affected by his (I use the pronoun advisedly) relationship with his body, his relationship to his own judgments and passions, and his relationship to the broader ethical values of his community. These relationships were often mutually dependent; to cite a common example, ancient philosophical schools privileged control of the desires as part of their eudaemonist world view, while vision itself was treated both as a metaphor for knowledge and as a material sense that could physically affect the body of another. But their mutual dependence is perhaps most clearly graspable in and around the ancient treatment of the mirror, which was invoked both in accounts of self-discovery and in an erotic tradition of self-adornment. The literal and figural usage of the mirror, together with the concomitant idea of the gaze turned upon itself, provided in antiquity a central locus for discourses both about self-knowledge and about sexuality. For this reason the treatment of the mirror in both popular and philosophical texts opens up for us the important ways in which a complicated discourse first took form.

Chapter 1 of this study therefore starts from the act of self-speculation, which was figured in our Greek and Roman texts as an aid to self-improvement *or* as a decadent luxury, depending on which one of two main traditions was in force. In the latter case, the mirror—given its status as an object of self-cultivation used mostly by women, and an object of rarity and expense at that—often came to be associated (negatively) with luxury, effeminization, and a profitless love of self. A telling anecdote in Diogenes Laertius relates that the tyrant Aristodemus gave mirrors to the young men of the city of Cumae to dandify them and so keep their minds off politics (*Ant. Rom.* 7.9.4). The mirror also participated in a philosophical tradition with roots back to Plato and beyond. Here, the mirror was invoked (whether literally or figuratively) as providing a reflection of the self that could help the viewer come to a correct evaluation of what kind of person he or she was, or even spur an effort to reshape oneself into a better option. A surprising number of ancient sources cite Socrates or some other ancient "wise man" as the originator of this notion: as he supposedly advised, take a good look at yourself, and act according to what you see: if you resemble Quasimodo, you had better spruce up your behavior to counteract your unpromising appearance; if a paragon of beauty, be sure to live up to the high expectations thereby aroused.

There is not much that is metaphysical in this usage, in which the mirror was thought of as reflecting the expectations and the judgment of the community in which one lived, rather than as providing some kind of window into the world beyond. The popular texts and practices examined in chapter 1 make it clear that the self in the mirror was thought of as the self as seen by others; hence the instructive value of any specular revelation, and the normative ethical values the mirror reflected, sprang from the judgments of the community or of the communal subgroup to which one belonged—Athenian citizen, Roman senator, Homeric hero, *paterfamilias*.[1] This chapter also explores the complications of this idea in the (possibly pseudo-Platonic) *Alcibiades* I, in which the mirrored gaze becomes not a reflection of the judgment of the other, but a metaphor for our ability to see the divine in ourselves by seeing the divine in others. In general, however, it is clear that the notion of the self *as seen by others* was thought to provide the "truest" idea of who one is, a notion that survives in the Roman republic to be dramatically altered (for the elite classes, at least) by the philosophical developments of the early Roman empire.

The mirror tradition is thus twofold (at least) in its early attestations. But the full influence of this dual tradition, and especially its development in the Roman period, can only be fully understood against the backdrop of another treatment of vision—the ocular theories propagated by ancient treatises on optics, to which I turn in chapter 2. Schools of thought on optics in antiquity adhered to versions of several theories that we might roughly characterize as bounded on one end by extramission, on the other by intromission. Throughout, however, the common denominator seems to have been the tactile quality of "seeing." Here we find a significant difference from our own understanding of vision; theoretically informed or not, most of us do not think of seeing as a tactile phenomenon, and certainly not as an action that physically acts upon the thing seen (the store owner's caveat comes to mind: look, but don't touch).[2] Intromission theorists held that seeing was the result of a stream of discrete particles given off by the object and penetrating the eye; the school of extramission suggested instead the presence of a material effluence *from* the eye

---

1. I oversimplify here for the sake of clarity. Being a member of different ethical subcommunities at the same time is not only possible and likely, but the stuff of Greek tragedy and Roman declamation.

2. There are a few exceptions in our day. In quantum theory, for example, the distinction inherent in "Look, but don't touch" fails to hold. That is, it is a field in which looking can be said to affect the (subatomic) object seen. In a more general way, the harmful effects of an observer anthropologist upon a culture he or she has entered to study are well recognized; see, e.g., Ruby 1982.

that made contact with the thing seen. These notions diffused broadly enough into the educated classes to become themselves the object of play in the texts of philosophers, poets, novelists, and moralists in both Greece and Rome, often in a context that exploited the sexual possibilities latent in a gaze that could be said to penetrate or to grope. Plato's *Phaedrus*, for example, nods at optical theory in the discussion of the lovers' mutual gaze and their sublimation of sexuality into philosophy; Plutarch pooh-poohs the notion that such a gaze can only take place between males and invites women to join the party; Achilles Tatius, ever frisky, opines that this kind of mutual mirroring (and hence mutual ocular penetration) enables consummation of sex at a distance.[3] Less auspiciously, Greco-Roman culture understood the evil eye as another manifestation of the tactile force of the gaze; while the act of looking could spur love (and even sexual arousal), it could also harm its object by penetrating it with the equivalent of poisoned darts.

Where *eros* rather than ill-will is at issue, Roman texts as well as Greek ones often invoke self-knowledge and sexuality side by side. Two Roman accounts in particular—one literary, one from natural history—treat the failure of self-inspection as a tool for self-knowledge, a failure laid precisely at the door of the erotic possibilities represented by the mirror image. In these accounts, the mirror traditions (philosophical and cultural) that I examine in chapter 1 meet, first in Ovid's treatment of the myth Narcissus and then in Seneca's account of the hobby of one Hostius Quadra. Ovid's *Metamorphoses* is the first extant source to claim of Narcissus that he was doomed to die "when he should come to know himself," and indeed Narcissus' self-discovery in the mirroring waters of a pond (a discovery itself couched in terminology familiar from optical theory) is simultaneous with his death through frustrated self-love. Hostius, in contrast, knows well that mirrors were invented "so that man should know himself," but chooses carnal self-knowledge instead: rigging up magnifying mirrors all around his bedroom, he has orgies with partners of different sexes and thrills to see his body(-parts) thus enlarged. In both these accounts the joint play of mirrors and sexuality serves only to highlight their protagonists' deliberate rejection of specular self-knowledge.

These Roman texts provide a strong contrast to the claims of Plato's *Phaedrus*. Readers will recall the idea that the exchange of the gaze of the philosopher-lover

---

3. The possibilities here have not yet been picked up by the religious right.

and his younger male beloved is described there as a kind of mirroring of two looks that mutually arouses (in Plato's metaphor) the wings of the soul, and that spurs the sublimation of sexual desire into philosophical desire (the *Symposium* presents a related version of this argument). We see here both the sexual underpinning of the Platonic ascension tradition and an echo of the sexual potential in ancient optics; love, self-knowledge, the Good, ocular theory, and the mirrored gaze all play their part in this text. When we turn to our Roman texts, however, the same combination of elements is figured as a form of blindness rather than insight. Indeed, one of the arguments of this book is precisely that these three topics are transformed and separated in the transition from classical Greece to early imperial Rome. In the Roman inheritance of the philosophical tradition of self-knowledge initiated by Plato, acceptance of the sexual impetus to the drive for philosophy vanishes, and plays next to no part in the work of a Cicero or a Seneca (a development we take so much for granted that we would snicker at the idea of Cicero telling a would-be philosopher to gaze into the eyes of his male lover to initiate the search for the Good). The reasons for this are complex and varied, but I hope to have identified one, at least, in this volume: the very different attitudes toward same-sex sexuality between the elite Greeks whom Plato was addressing and the far more homophobic Romans.[4] It was conceivable for an Athenian citizen to discuss philosophy with a young adolescent pupil from his own class; inconceivable, however, for a Roman elite male to do the same thing with his own same-sex partner, who would almost invariably be a slave. Add to this that the Romans often disparaged philosophy itself as the study of Greeklings (and weaklings), and viewed self-declared Stoics and Cynics as bearded and unkempt bums on the outside, but effeminate pathics on the inside, and the death of the same-sex-loving philosopher is complete.[5]

---

4. The use of the term *homophobic* here is problematic for all the reasons laid out by scholars of ancient sexuality, such as Halperin (see especially his entry "Homosexuality" in the third edition of the *Oxford Classical Dictionary*), Williams (1999), and Cantarella (1992); given my agreement with Williams's arguments, a better term would be *pathophobic*. For arguments closer to an essentialist point of view, see Richlin 1993, Taylor 1997, and Lilja 1983.

5. Here, as throughout, I use the term *pathic* to designate the Roman grouping together of men who enjoyed being the "passive" partner in same-sex liaisons. The term conveys the normative Roman attitude toward such men, which was one of extreme disdain; please note that the contrast between active and passive, or penetrator and penetratee, is an ideological distinction that at Rome concealed and controlled the dangerous variety of lived experience.

Although it is curious that philosophers at Rome at the end of the first century CE should be compared to sexually deviant pathics, chapter 3 suggests that this phenomenon makes the most sense when considered against the Roman Stoic devaluation of the body. In reformulating the traditional idea of the inviolate male citizen body so that the locus of true liberty lay now in the inviolability of the Stoic mind, Seneca (and later Epictetus) was able to offer theoretical protection to an elite class that had lost its immunity to bodily punishment under the emperors. Exercises like the *meditatio* encouraged the formation of a mindset along the lines of "sticks and stones may break my bones, but no one can do anything to my *hegemonikon*." The Stoic's ability to ideally endure all sorts of bodily suffering without considering it an ill represented, then, a form of *patientia*, endurance, that was positively charged as a sign of the necessary detachment from one's physical circumstances. At the same time, however, *patientia* was itself a dangerously ambivalent term for the elite male; its other main referent was the sexually submissive role of a man who endured sexual penetration by his partner—the kind of penetration to which slaves especially were prey. The sexually suspect status of the Roman philosophers in some circles as bearded pathics in disguise suggests that the "endurance" on which the Stoics prided themselves struck other Romans, perhaps, as more revealing than the philosophers may have intended. At Rome, then, our extant texts suggest that the erotic impulse in philosophy goes astray, a deviance certainly well illustrated (if in different ways) by the accounts of Hostius and Narcissus, and by the suspicion that philosophers might be pathics in hiding.

Despite this tinge of sexual suspicion around the practitioners of philosophy, the visual component to philosophical self-knowledge survives well and strong in the Roman world, where in some ways it is more visible than ever before. Also in chapter 3, we turn to the "specular regime" of the Roman republic and review the connection between visibility and social values that lay at the basis of the elite performance of selfhood. Roman senators, consuls, generals, and even soldiers felt themselves called upon to provide models of behavior for what they perceived as a watchful society, and in this culture of exemplarity one repeatedly sought visual affirmation of one's ethical, military, or class standing—or even one's masculinity. The traditions and institutions of the Roman republic—from the throng of clients that accompanied a senator on his walk down to the forum and the competitive aspect of public oratory to the legends about figures such as Mucius Scaevola and the very office of the censor—can all be interpreted as partaking in this dynamic.

Less often studied than these basic givens about Roman public life are a series of rifts and contradictions in the integration of these visual aspects of self-performance with the mores and values of republican Rome as a whole— for example, with the sexually debased position of actors, the awareness of the aggressive capacities of the gaze, and the tension between exemplary subjectivity (the orator, the *triumphator*, the legendary Cato as models for their admiring audiences) and despised objectivity (again, the actor, the gladiator, the mime, there only for the pleasure of their viewers, occupiers of bodies that had limited protection against arbitrary physical or sexual violence). To be the cynosure of all eyes was to occupy a position with alarmingly bivalent possibilities. Yet, apart from the occasional caveat that the orator should not too much resemble the actor, these possibilities do not seem to have troubled the Roman elite to the extent we might expect—at least until the changing political situation of the empire shifted the power dynamics inherent in the public gaze, rendering the formerly exemplary senatorial class much less immune to the threat inherent in being the object of all eyes, especially when those eyes had their home in Nero's court.

Chapter 4 focuses more closely on the figure from whose work this shifting dynamic emerges the most clearly—Lucius Annaeus Seneca, philosopher, statesman, playwright, and (according to a few of his detractors) corruptor of young boys. As one of the most compromised figures of the period, a billionaire who pled the virtues of Stoic indifference to material goods, Seneca failed in his bid to become the Roman Socrates (Musonius Rufus, despite his comparative obscurity in modern classics, became that figure), but he did leave behind evidence of a striking overhaul of some of the basic givens of elite Roman selfhood. In an earlier work, *Actors in the Audience* (1994), I suggested that the performative quality of senatorial public life was distorted by the invasive gaze of emperors such as Nero, whom our sources figure as monitoring the senatorial elite so closely that they felt compelled to dissimulate their behavior and opinions to ensure their safety. One could say, then, that the public realm became a realm of inauthenticity, however dangerous it might be to use such a term in a culture that did not share our own tendency to assimilate the idea of the mask and of falsehood. The undermining of the naturally performative and visual nature of Roman elite selfhood by the senatorial sense that such performances were

now compelled in the interests of an emperor rather than voluntarily undertaken as part of civic life and in the interests of one's own name and status was
at least partially responsible for a striking shift in the source of self-validation.
It is indubitable that the contaminated nature of Roman public life fostered an
interest in the possibility of new, more internally generated standards for the
evaluation of the Roman elite by itself; the whys and wherefores of this change,
however, deserve far more attention than they have received.

This new interest is most evident in Seneca's letters, essays, and dramas, which
we can read as evidence of one man's solution to the compromised nature of
senatorial political agency and self-rule. His attempt to narrow down the audience for exemplary behavior from his peer group and Roman citizens in general
to a small selection of Stoically sanctioned individuals and even to just one
person—himself—provides a fascinating window in to the fortunes of the visual
paradigms underlying Roman republican politics. That most of Seneca's ideal
spectators are dead—Cato, for example, is a long defunct favorite—poses no
problem for our philosopher (one *pretends* they are watching). If the mirroring
of one's look upon the self was once used as a way of judging oneself from the
outside, it is now invoked as a way of *avoiding* community judgment and of con-
forming to a value-scheme generated solely by the abstract teachings of Stoicism
or the bygone deeds of its practitioners. As in Socrates' image of the mirror of the
soul in the *Alcibiades* I, here Seneca seems to appeal to a moral force that partakes
of the divine and that, in cultivating the best and most rational part of the soul,
can avoid leaning on societally sanctioned ideas of the Good. Or so the majority
of Seneca's writings and exhortations would indicate.

And yet, as always, there are tensions within this systematization of a
philosophical standard for everyday life. Seneca is not always consistent in
emphasizing the positive value of self-observation: at some junctures he
describes it as oppressive, at others impotent. Nor do his descriptions of ideal
Stoic behavior always cohere well with his observations elsewhere. It is not that
the values of Roman Stoicism per se are so different from the *mores* the
Romans themselves associated with heroism and civic responsibility. The problem, rather, is that the Stoic emphasis on self-control and self-monitoring even
in the most extreme circumstances eventually becomes tainted with the capitulation to those in power that the good Stoic is supposed to reject. Seneca's
unusual use of the term *persona* echoes this. In his writing, the term undergoes
a subtle shift, moving away from its uncharged republican sense of "a public

self" and instead returning to the metaphor of the theater, where it originally meant a mask. As a result, it comes in Seneca's usage to connote a political world in which the performance of the *persona* entailed the donning of a false surface rather than the manifestation of behavior appropriate to one's public office. The truth lies *beneath* the *persona* now—but the men who can see through to it are few indeed.

Chapter 5 turns to take account of what we might call the *dialogic* manifestation of the idea of self-mirroring or self-regulation—that is, the dialogue that the mirrored self holds with itself. It is possible to map the divided specular self onto the dialogic habits that Seneca recommends as the royal path to becoming a good Stoic: self-questioning, self-command, self-exhortation, and self-review are emphasized as elements of the Stoic *meditatio* that allow the self to bootstrap itself out of its prephilosophical state and advance toward wisdom. In these dialogues, an agent self will be the object of the scoldings or evaluations of an observer self, who might ask: "Why did you yield to anger this morning?" "What have you accomplished today?" or even "Why do you fear death, a state in which you can feel no pain?" It is arresting that one participant in this dialogue is conceived as already holding the keys to Stoic wisdom, and thus leading along his lagging partner, who is invariably less advanced, more prone to passion and to error, more in need of direct instruction. Socratic irony has certainly fallen by the wayside, and instead we find an internally hierarchical structure, with one interlocutor ethically superior to the other.

Such a division of the self seems to harken back to the divided self of the mirror discussed in chapter 1, in which the "objective" self illuminated in the reflecting surface has something to teach the misguided "observer" self—for example, that anger is disfiguring, or that one's handsome appearance needs living up to. The division can also be mapped onto the presence of the imaginary viewer discussed by Seneca—the corrective voice can be (and sometimes is) attributed to a Cato or an Epicurus rather than oneself. But a basic distinction from the earlier models we have considered—besides the oral component of Senecan self-correction—is, of course, that the mirror viewer is measuring himself by what he thinks his community judges him to be; the dialogically divided Senecan self is responsible to a higher authority (represented by one of the two internal interlocutors), and in fact the Stoic *proficiens* often abjures the opinions and judgments of his community.

This division of the self into moral superior and moral student is reminiscent (if the term can be used in chronological reverse) of the philosopher Harry Frankfurt's description of people in terms of first- and second-order selves, and I use his terminology as a partial aid to understanding what Seneca is about. Simply put, Frankfurt defines the human person as being characterized by an ability to make rational judgments about his or her desires, and, as a result, to form second-order desires (desires about which desires to have).[6] In a similar way, a would-be Stoic might criticize his own desire for fame or wealth or even a successful afternoon of oratory, and remind himself that these are not desirables in the way that emotional peace of mind might be. In both the Stoic model and the Frankfurtian one, the ethically superior observer self seems to evaluate the possibilities for action or emotion that are open to the less ethically advanced agent self, and to exhort that agent self to select options that are in line with ethically superior ideals. This is at the heart of what goes on during the Stoic *meditatio*, and for the Stoic, the wished-for endpoint of this process, after years of practice, is that the first-order and second-order perspectives should merge, so that there is never any internal struggle between a self that wants (say) to lie in bed all day and a self that exhorts it to rise, shine, and scribble bookish thoughts.[7] Instead, the unified individual springs up and rushes, coffeeless, to the desk.

Frankfurt's terminology is a useful tool, but it has certain shortcomings when applied to Senecan thought. A second, and complementary, perspective involves reconsidering the idea of *reflexivity* as essential to Senecan selfhood. This move attributes to Seneca a new development in thinking about the self: up to this point in the Greco-Roman world, I argue, reflexivity per se has not figured as a crucial component of thinking about the self. It is worth noting that many modern philosophers continue to deny it an important role in antiquity. They extend to Seneca and to Roman Stoicism in general the same cautions about post-Cartesian misreading that have proven well founded in the case of our Greek sources. In Seneca, however, the second-orderliness of self-judgment comes associated with forms of reflexive linguistic use that have

---

6. Frankfurt 1971. See similarly Taylor 1985, 75: "The human animal not only finds himself impelled from time to time to interpret himself and his goals, but . . . he is always already in some interpretation, constituted as human by this fact."

7. Not an autobiographical comment at all—cf. Pers., *Sat.* 3.

no parallel in earlier writers. Here for the first time, I argue, the relationship of the self to itself is stressed as an essential rather than incidental aspect of self-knowledge, even without the presence of a terminology for selfhood that neatly parallels our own.

Nonetheless, a discussion of self-knowledge as it is understood in the modern scholarship is not at issue here; I am concerned not with what self-knowledge "really" is, but with what Seneca and his predecessors thought it to be. At the same time, it is worth pointing out that my characterization of Seneca, in returning to the idea of reflexivity, does align his beliefs with the Cartesian notion that knowledge of one's own mental states is a particularly epistemologically secure form of knowledge. This is in sharp contrast to the better diffused ancient notion that a friend could see one's faults with greater ease than oneself (or that your peer community's view of you had more validity than your own). But Seneca's view is neither properly Cartesian nor, for that matter, properly Platonic (speaking here of the Plato of the *Alcibiades* I). Even with a stress on reflexivity, the Senecan self remains umbilically connected to an abstract ideal for self-formulation that has much more to do with the divine potential within the individual than with a radical critique of the knowability of what is outside the mind. Even with this emphasis on divine potential, the Senecan self privileges reflexivity in a way that is absent from the Platonic account of self-knowledge. It thus stands at the intersection of various discourses that are already familiar to us (including a Roman social one that stresses the visual and performative nature of selfhood), but is identical to none of them.

Foucault, rather than Frankfurt, is, of course, the name that one would most immediately associate with scholarship on "the care of the self" in antiquity, and part of chapter 5 is devoted to spelling out where he and I differ. Foucault's attention to the medical, philosophical, and sexual aspects of self-care in the Hellenistic and imperial periods sits oddly with his own prior work because it seems a movement away from the idea of the individual as a locus where power makes itself felt—the "repressive hypothesis." In addition, *The Care of the Self* argues that *pleasure* is generated by these attentions to the self, which are portrayed in a light that suggests creativity and volition rather than conformance to an abstract ideal and self-containment. Certainly where Senecan Stoicism is concerned, the sage would fit awkwardly into such a framework. If anything, it is what critics have had to say about Seneca's *dramatis personae*—Medea, for example—rather than the man himself that smacks the most of Foucauldian self-realization.

I would not agree with such a reading, but it is still striking that the most startling example of the unifying force of Stoic self-training in the entire Senecan corpus is not the abstemious Cato of Seneca's imagination (and certainly not Seneca himself, who stages his self-divisions for all his readers to see). It is in fact, his dramatic Medea. This is a peculiar claim, because Medea has so long been taken to show us precisely the self torn in two ways, the mother fighting the wife, and the wife the mother. And it is true that much of the play shows us this process in striking dialogic detail: to kill or not to kill is Medea's version of Hamlet's question, and she tortuously weighs her alternatives in soliloquies that show her vacillating between the two positions. At the end, however, her decision leaves her as triumphant as if she had overcome a weakness of will in making her awful choice; more important still, it is an end she has reached by a process that looks curiously like Stoic *meditatio*. What to make of this? At the very least, it offers a troublingly reversed mirror-image of the path to Stoic self-sufficiency.[8]

Even here, with Medea's passion-driven crimes of self-assertion, it seems that we have long since abandoned the last vestiges of the imbrication of sexuality with mirroring and self-knowledge (except where it is raised in its grossest form, only to be condemned, as with Hostius). The Stoic stance against *voluptas*, the jettisoning of the body as so much annoying baggage, the elimination of any erotic potential from the philosophical gaze all remind us that we could not be further from the Platonic system that made room for sexuality alongside self-knowledge and self-inspection. The failure of desire in this system is, I believe, one of the most striking developments in the Roman inheritance of Platonic thought, and together with the fortunes of specularity, self-knowledge, and the Roman "scopic regime," it provides one of the main strands of argument in this book.

Let me turn, in closing, to some of the issues with which this study does *not* grapple. Modern critics may perhaps be surprised to see that Lacan has not

---

8. I imagine that philosophers will be comparatively unperturbed by the prospect of such trouble-spots in Stoicism, since they generally point to the abstract tenability of philosophical ideas rather than to concrete examples of their distortion in the hands of nonideal individuals like Hostius, Medea, or even the failed Stoic on the street.

been wheeled in either as a piñata or a *deus ex machina*. I leave aside the vexed question of the use of concepts such as the mirror stage as tools for the interpretation of ancient texts and cultures, and will simply remark that incorporating the work of Lacan into this study would have given rise to a volume very different from the one I have produced. It would have had to situate the Lacanian response to psychoanalysis in a world unfamiliar with this kind of analysis, approach the notion of exemplarity in Roman culture in terms of the symbolic authority of the father, and overlay the Lacanian phallus (presumably) on the ancient phallus, both symbolic terms but not necessarily the same. While such a project would no doubt be interesting, I have chosen instead to apply interpretive tools that seem more or less familiar to the ancient cultures that generated them.

Absent for some of the same reasons is a treatment of contemporary film theory, with its emphasis on the gendered nature of the filmic gaze, and also its distinction (which originates in Lacan) between the gaze and the look. It could easily be argued that the stimulus of the act of seeing in an urge to emulate or to objectify is a quintessential facet of ancient visuality, while Laura Mulvey's early work on the voyeuristic and the narcissistic gazes could likewise be pressed into service as a lens through which to view the ancient world—as could earlier theoretical arguments that the filmic gaze is largely figured as male. Again, however, it would be clear that in so doing we were reading antiquity *for us*, and were reflecting, if anything, on how modern practice repeats-with-a-difference some very old problems and prejudices. I prefer to cling to the illusion that I am reading these elements of the ancient world *for them*.

A broader problem is that the scope of ancient texts and practices relevant to the topic of self-knowledge, sexuality, and vision extends far beyond the boundaries and the capacities of this volume. As a result, where authors and subjects in the ancient world have been capably dealt with by others, I have omitted extensive discussion (for example, Livy, Roman elegy, Lucan, Philostratus, and a host of others). Where the discussion would extend laughably beyond my own ability, I have chosen not to tread (I do not discuss the Church fathers, for example; Roman art gets short shrift; I have not attempted to read Ptolemy in the Arabic). Closer to home, even a detailed treatment of the Stoic Epictetus is lacking, though the related philosophizing of Seneca the younger occupies the last two chapters of this study. Epictetus, of course, was a freed slave rather than a once exiled senator, and as a result, I argue, felt formative emphases distinct from Seneca's. Finally, Persius deserves more attention than he receives here. In his work, too, the erotic, the philosophical, and the visual crop up in interdependent proximity, while the confusion of dialogic voices, the obsession with bodily boundaries (and their failure to hold), and the satirist's compromised position as critic suggest a questioning of normative Roman criteria for self-knowledge. It is an omission I hope to rectify in a forthcoming volume.

Builders of great systems, Kierkegaard once said, are like men who erect a great castle but live in a small hut next door. Seneca, in contrast, tried desperately to occupy his own castle, to use its equipment and abide by its truths. We will never know for sure, but his project probably ended in failure: not because of personal weakness, but because the demands of the system he helped construct were too great for anyone to fulfill. Nonetheless, I hope that Seneca's contributions to ancient thinking will emerge clearly from this book, which, in the end, is a study of the varied discourses that shaped thinking about ethical selfhood in antiquity—from the popular idea of the mirror of the self to the philosophical notion, in Seneca, that one can provide a mirror to one's own self.

1   The Mirror of Philosophy

Vision and knowledge have a long and intertwined history. If the act of seeing has been sometimes intimately linked to knowing—as the etymologies behind *theory, reflection, speculation,* and *enlightenment* make clear—at other times earthly sight has been criticized for blocking our vision of eternal verities. It was not only Kant or Descartes who thought that what we take for granted about our gaze on the world outside could undermine our ability to comprehend what that world really is; a philosophical sense of the precariousness of such an assumption has long roots in Greco-Roman antiquity, underlying, for example, the allegory of the cave in Plato's *Republic,* and informing aspects of the philosophical thought of figures as diverse as Aristotle, Seneca, and Augustine. Like Plato, Dante in the *Paradiso* saw the world as an inferior copy of the heavens, a mere *speculum inferius;* later, with the advent of perspectivalism in Renaissance painting, the mathematical qualities of linear perspective were deemed pure enough be related to the transcendental qualities of God's own sight.[1]

---

1. Plato, too, set mathematics above worldly phenomena in the divided line. For a summary of medieval and Renaissance ways of seeing, see Jay 1993, 21–82.

An interesting parallel is provided by modern quantum mechanics, in which our observations can never reveal the true nature of a physical object.

Despite the friction between seeing as blindness and seeing as insight, the idea of the gaze turned inward upon the self came to provide a lasting metaphor for the project of self-knowledge. John Locke's so-called observer model of reflection famously appealed to a subject's inner visual perception, which was directed toward his own mental operations as a method for self-knowledge, while René Descartes' notion that the mind inspects its ideas with an unwavering internal gaze provided, as some would claim, the fundamental ground of modern philosophy itself. As Rodolphe Gasché writes, "The philosophy of reflection is generally considered to have begun with Descartes' *prima philosophia*. . . . In Descartes the scholastic idea of the *reditus* [the inward turn] undergoes an epochal transformation, whereby reflection, instead of being merely the medium of metaphysics, becomes its very foundation" (1986, 17).[2]

This visual emphasis is present in ancient explorations of self-knowledge as well, and much of this book will focus on the intersection of vision and philosophy in classical formulations of coming to know the self. Nowhere in our ancient sources, however, do we encounter the idea of "the eye of the mind." There is no version here of Cartesian self-knowledge as the mind mirroring its own processes, or reflecting upon its capacity for reflection. Instead, ancient formulations of the epistemological power of self-regard stress the specular capacity of the actual gaze rather than the mind's eye— that is, its instructive potential when mirrored back upon the looking self. Indeed, the most common invocation of the possibility of self-knowledge thus holds that the mirror *itself* might help in the search for wisdom, and that the reflected image of the seeker after truth might have something to teach such a would-be philosopher. One might say that the mirror of philosophy had its most common instantiation in antiquity as the mirror *in* philosophy, and its invocation as a literal tool for use on the path to self-improvement was so common as to span the gamut of genres from sober treatises to impolite epigrams, and the run of authors from Plato to Martial—and beyond.

---

2. The reference is to Descartes' "Meditations on First Philosophy," first published in 1641.

The distinctive quality of the ancient mirror consisted, of course, in its then rare ability to reflect the viewer to himself, and far more accurately so than other available resources, such as still water or polished stone. What this meant in Greco-Roman thought, rather than in a modern philosophy steeped in the conceptual apparatus of reflexivity, will emerge from this work. And the mirror as cultural object, too, elicits different reactions in different eras. We moderns tend to take mirrors for granted: a cheap one can be bought for a few cents at any drugstore, and they surround us in our lives from the first bathroom stumbles of the morning. The ancient mirror, by contrast, was an object of comparative rarity and considerable expense. It was the subject of optical theorizing, magic beliefs, and most of all, of moralizing discourses that either praised it for its ability to render back an accurate reflection or damned it as a luxury and a tool of vanity. It lay, as we shall see, at the basis of a long tradition in which it appeared now as a means to truth, now as a fount of illusion. Most important for this book, the ancient reception of the mirror provides a way to understand the interrelation of such seemingly disparate discourses in antiquity as the nature of self-knowledge, the visual emphasis of ancient culture, and the interaction of eros and philosophy; the mirror allows us entry into all three topics of this study at once. Accordingly, this chapter approaches classical notions of selfhood by exploring ancient approaches to the mirror, before turning to such objects of study as prescriptive philosophizing, sociohistorical contexts, and the terminology of *sophrosyne* and *conscientia sui.*

The uses of the mirror laid out in this chapter will have continued significance throughout this volume. Some of the key terms and ideas introduced here—especially the contrast between the mirror of the community, the erotic mirror, and Plato's mirror—will recur in ways that offer startling insight into the cultural context in which they are produced. As we shall see, the Platonic gesture toward a mirror in which can be seen a divine perspective upon the self is partially recapitulated in the efforts of a Roman Stoic, Seneca the younger, to find ways of reflecting upon the self that might be independent of the judgment of one's fellow man; at the same time, the notion of a "mirror of the self," in all its permutations, beautifully elucidates the particular concerns of the elite of imperial Rome in the first century CE. In every case, the mirror illustrates the importance of the gaze *of* the subject, and *on* the subject, for the ethical development of the ancient self. For us too, then, as once for its Greek and Roman viewers, this implement will provide a view onto a larger picture.[3]

THE INCENTIVE TO VIRTUE

In late 158 or early 159 CE an unusual trial took place in the town of Sabratha in Roman North Africa. The defendant was Apuleius of Madaurus, the author of the *Metamorphoses* and a local philosopher and rhetorician of some prominence. The charge brought against Apuleius was that he was in fact a sorcerer who had put his magic skills to ill use by inducing a wealthy older woman to marry him. Accordingly, the accusers, headed by Apuleius' new stepson, Sicinius Pudens, and a troop of other relatives eager to defend family moneys from the interloper in their midst, summoned up a motley collection of evidence, including Apuleius' manufacture of tooth-powder and his purchase of various species of fish. But the prosecution also lingered on his appearance and *modus vivendi*: the long locks of hair, the love poems he wrote to young boys, and the discovery, in his house, of a mirror. These last items, they thought, hardly dovetailed with Apuleius' supposed dedication to the life of the mind; on the contrary, they marked him as a man very much lodged in the flesh.

In the end, Apuleius would carry the day, and partly so by denying the lascivious implications of the hair, the poems, and the mirror.[4] As he vigorously asserted in his rhetorical coup of a defense, his hair, far from the alluring

---

3. It bears remarking at the outset that there are topics this treatment will leave untouched. Most of these have been well covered in the secondary literature. Among the most important general studies on the mirror, see Grabes (1982) on medieval and Renaissance literature, Jonsson (1995) and Nolan (1990) on the Middle Ages, Hugedé (1957) for antiquity and the New Testament, Eco (1986) in semiotics, de Grummond (1982), Schefold (1940), and von Netoliczka (1935) on archeology, Balensiefen (1990) and Stewart (1996) on mirrors in ancient art, Elkisch (1957) on psychoanalysis, Lacan (1977) on the mirror stage, Frontisi-Ducroux (1995) on the history and anthropology of the mirror in Greece, Baltrusaitis (1978) with a more sweeping historical account, Gasché (1986) and Rorty (1979) on post-Cartesian reflexivity in philosophy, Konersmann (1991) on subjectivity and the mirror, Goldberg (1985) on mythology and technology, Simon (1988) on ancient optics, Siebers (1983) on narcissism and the evil eye. Most important, see Frontisi-Ducroux and Vernant (1997), Jonsson (1995), and McCarty (1989) on the history, theory, and anthropology of mirrors in classical antiquity, especially Greece.

4. Our Apuleius, we might suspect, bears passing resemblance to the Cynic philosopher in Lucian whose sack turns out to contain, not rustic bread and a book, but perfume, a razor, dice, and—a mirror (*Piscator* 45).

coiffure of a fop, could be seen to be a matted and dirty mess.[5] His love poems had a precedent in such eminent philosophers as Plato and Solon, and were less erotically explicit at that. As for the mirror, not only do all of us have an intrinsic affection for our own image, but even Socrates once avidly recommended its use to moral ends:

> Is not Socrates the philosopher reported to have enjoined upon his students to contemplate themselves frequently in a mirror [*crebro ut semet in speculo contemplarentur*], that so those among them who were self-satisfied with their beauty might above all else take care that they did not disfigure the attractiveness of their body by bad character traits, but those who thought they were less good-looking might take pains to conceal their ugliness with the praise of their virtue? To such a degree did the wisest of all men use the mirror for the inculcation of good character [*ad disciplinam morum*]. (*Apol.* 15.8–15)

Apuleius, then, met these charges head on by focusing on the ostensibly philosophical use of the mirror for moral self-improvement, and deduced the innocence of his own specular self-indulgence from a practice he ascribed to none other than the venerable Socrates himself. Further evidence of the mirror's utility, he added, could be seen in its scientific use to study the heavens, and even in its substitution for the judging eye of the other: Demosthenes, after all, rehearsed his orations in front of one *quasi ante magistrum*, as if before a teacher.[6]

Apuleius' self-defense was merely a late manifestation of a distinguished tradition that united the ethicist and the mirror in the exhortation to virtue. Socrates' dictum here, whether apocryphal or not, was quoted centuries earlier in Diogenes Laertius' *Lives of the Eminent Philosophers* (2.33), and is invoked at

---

5. Apuleius' speech of self-defense is commonly called the *Apology*, although the manuscripts identify it as *Apulei Madaurensis pro se de magia*. For an introduction and commentary to this work, including evidence for the historical reality of the trial itself, see Hunink 1997. On the dating of the trial, see Hijmans 1994, 1713. Apuleius' victory in the case is nowhere attested, but seems likely given his professional success later in life and the statues erected in his honor at Carthage and Madaurus.

6. Slater (1998) offers an interesting perspective on Apuleius' play with what is seen in the mirror in the Diana-Acteon sculpture of the *Metamorphoses*—in a scene in which Lucius notably fails to learn anything about himself.

the end of the first century CE, also with this attribution, in Plutarch's *Advice to Bride and Groom* (141d).[7] The later anthologist Stobaeus traces the recommendation to look in a mirror to a presocratic figure, Bias, who was one of the Seven Sages of Greek antiquity.[8] Elsewhere, the idea that looking in a mirror could impose ethical directives on one's behavior could be attributed to cultural authority figures such as the *paterfamilias*.[9] The first-century CE Roman freedman Phaedrus weaves the familiar elements of the anecdote into a short fable in which two siblings, looking in a mirror, discover a discrepancy in comeliness. The boy, reveling in his good looks, preens in delight, but his homely sister, upset and jealous, runs to their father to tell on her brother: although he's a boy, he's handled something that only belongs to women (*rem feminarum*)! The wise father hugs them both and tells them to look in the mirror every day: "*You*" (to the son) "so that you won't ruin your good looks with rotten deeds, but *you*" (to the daughter), "so that you can overcome that face of yours by your good character" (Phaedrus 3.8.14–16).[10] Phaedrus' introduction of the jealous sister to motivate the involvement of the father again draws attention to, and then dismisses, the negative connotations of such activity for the fable's audience—almost as if Phaedrus anticipated that they, too, might be perturbed by the thought of a good-looking young man admiring his own features in a mirror.

These anecdotes share an understanding of the reflection in the mirror as the motivating force that can appeal to an individual to alter his or her ethical behavior in order to reinforce, or alternatively to mitigate, the judgment of the community on that person's external appearance.[11] This reflection does not

---

7. It is interesting that in his retelling of the now familiar advice, Plutarch must acknowledge the same cultural bias against the male use of the mirror with which Apuleius had to reckon: the injunction to look in the mirror is pointedly directed at the new wife alone and not the husband. But for her to chat with herself whenever she holds her mirror in her hands is a fine thing indeed, and even the ugly wife has thus a chance to be loved for her good character.

8. Diels-Kranz I.10.73a.

9. The physician and philosopher Galen cites the advice simply as an "ancient precept" in his *Protrepticus* 8.

10. "Cotidie" inquit "speculo uos uti uolo, / tu formam ne corrumpas nequitiae malis, / tu faciem ut istam moribus uincas bonis."

11. Cf. also Bias' remark in Stob. *Flor.* 3.21.11: Θεώρει ὥσπερ ἐν κατόπτρῳ τὰς σαυτοῦ πράξεις, ἵνα τὰς μὲν καλὰς ἐπικοσμῇς, τὰς δὲ αἰσχρὰς καλύπτῃς. (The presence of the verb *kalupto* here argues against the emendation of Watson [1982] of Apuleius' *tegere* to *tergere* in *Apol.* 16.)

bring with it any form of subjective, uniquely self-generated insight, nor does it suggest that outside appearances are negligible in the face of character— only that they can be upheld or overcome. Indeed, our own expression "handsome is as handsome does" reverses the terms of this Greco-Roman polarity: for Socrates and Bias, an attractive face elicits the ethical injunction to uphold that *appearance* by matching your behavior to it, while "handsome is as handsome does" suggests that one's *behavior* is the true source of beauty. That this ancient impetus to self-improvement takes its origin from the visible features of the self-inspector, however they may be judged, is not surprising in face-to-face cultures such as Athens and Rome, in which personal appearance could be seen as an index of personal ethics.[12] After all, as many a pithy saying decreed, the face was the mirror of the soul. Cicero reminds the would-be orator of this: "imago animi vultus, indices oculi" (*De Or.* 3.221; cf. *Orat.* 60.5). The novelist Achilles Tatius has his hero Clitophon remark that "it does not seem correct to me to say that the mind is entirely invisible: it reveals itself, as if in a mirror, on the face" (*Clitophon and Leucippe* 6.6.2).[13] For Pliny the Elder, "in man alone is the brow an index of sadness, happiness, mercy, severity."[14] A common expression held that the eyes were the mirror of the soul.[15] Indeed, what you could read on a man's visage could tell you much about his character: "Qualem intus putas esse animum cuius extra imago tam foeda est?" as Seneca would remark of a man whose face was distorted with rage (*De ira* 2.35.4; cf. *Ep.* 52.12).[16]

If mirrors could be conceived of as encouraging forms of behavior that lived up to—or escaped the limitations of—the message of the face, another, equally widespread, strand of justification for the use of the mirror suggested that specular self-inspection could put a quick end to forms of *akrasia*, lapses in

---

12. For more on "face-to-face societies" and "shame cultures," see chapter 3.

13. ὁ γὰρ νοῦς οὔ μοι δοκεῖ λελέχθαι καλῶς ἀόρατος εἶναι τὸ παράπαν· φαίνεται γὰρ ἀκριβῶς ὡς ἐν κατόπτρῳ τῷ προσώπῳ.

14. "Sed homini tantum tristitiae, hilaritatis, clementiae, severitatis index," *HN* 11.138.

15. See, e.g., Pliny, *HN* 11.14; Philostr., *VA* 2.30; Achilles Tatius, *C&L* 6.2.2–3. On the face in ancient Greek society, see especially Frontisi-Ducroux 1995, 19–38; for Rome, see Bettini 2000 and Corbeill 1997, 112–23. On physiognomy in the Second Sophistic, see Gleason's (1995) study of rhetoric and masculinity in Polemo and Favorinus.

16. The practice of physiognomy in Greece went back to the fourth century BCE and perhaps beyond, and, as Maud Gleason remarks of the pseudo-Aristotelian treatise *Physiognomy*, "The argument of the whole depends on the premise that there exists a certain sympathy between the soul and the body" (1995, 29).

self-control; in other words, that the image in the mirror could cut short bad behavior as well as encourage good. Diogenes Laertius claims of Plato that he told drunkards to look in a mirror so that they would abandon this disfiguring habit, and the same idea, now applied to the irascible, occurs in Plutarch's essay on anger, where an interlocutor touts the merits of having a slave with a mirror follow him to catch him in moments of anger: "To see oneself looking so unnatural and all confused is no small step toward the discrediting of this ailment."[17] In a similar vein, Seneca's cure for a chronic bad temper is to catch your distorted face in a mirror, advice he attributes to Q. Sextius, the founder of an eclectic philosophical school at Rome: "As Sextius says, it has helped certain people while angry to have looked in a mirror: such a change in themselves disturbed them; drawn, as it were, to face reality, they did not recognize themselves. And how little of the actual deformity that reflected image in the mirror renders back! If the soul could be shown, if it could shine in any material, it would stun us as we looked—a thing black, diseased, seething, distorted, swollen!" (*De ira* 2.36.1–2).[18] More generally, Seneca opines that crimes hate sight of themselves ("scelera conspectum sui reformidant" [*Q Nat.* 1.16.4])—a harbinger of Tacitus' quip about the emperor Nero's distress upon hearing of his own criminal behavior: he was "as ready to commit crimes as he was unaccustomed to hearing about them."[19]

Again, these sayings seem to rely on a set of communal expectations about the relationship between behavior and appearance. In this case, it is the mirror's transformation of the viewer into a judging other—as in Apuleius' claim that Demosthenes orated while substituting a mirror for a teacher—that effects its ethical transformation in the subject.[20] For our hotheads and drunkards who do

---

17. Diog. Laert., *Lives of the Eminent Philosophers* 3.39; and Plut., *De cohibenda ira* 456b. Cf. Ov., *Ars Am.* 3.503–8. Plutarch, like Ovid, mentions the story that Athena, playing the flute and seeing herself in a river, was so disgusted by her distorted face that she threw the instrument away.

18. "Quibusdam, ut ait Sextius, iratis profuit aspexisse speculum. Perturbauit illos tanta mutatio sui; uelut in rem praesentem adducti non agnouerunt se: et quantulum ex uera deformitate imago illa speculo repercussa reddebat! Animus si ostendi et si in ulla materia perlucere posset, intuentis confunderet ater maculosusque et aestuans et distortus et tumidus." For further discussion of this passage, see chapter 4.

19. Tac., *Ann.* 15.67.14.

20. This anecdote, too, appears in earlier sources; Plutarch tells us in his *Life of Demosthenes* that the orator had a large looking-glass in his house, before which he would stand and go through his exercises (11.850e); see similarly Quint., *Inst.* 11.3.68: "Demosthenes grande quoddam intuens speculum componere actionem solebat."

not like what they see, the eyes of a self-as-audience show the mirror-gazer how he appears to others, so that the mirror-gazer is confronted with an "objective" judgment about his behavior—a judgment on the mirror-image's physiognomic fall from grace based on assumptions shared by the gazer and his community as a whole. This process is furthered when rage and inebriation are ugly enough to create estrangement from the self, a possibility that Ovid (like Seneca) evokes when he warns that an angry woman will scarcely recognize her reflected image.[21] Jean-Pierre Vernant (1991, 142) describes this notion, to which an entire gamut of ancient texts and varying genres make common appeal: "In seeing your face in the mirror you know yourself as others know you, face-to-face, in an exchange of glances. Access to the self is gained through an external projection of that self, through being objectified, as if one were an other."[22]

Accordingly, the mirror provides a tool for the splitting of the viewer into viewing subject and viewed object, judging "I" and judged-to-be-lacking "me." It does so in the weakest of senses, since none of these sources suggests that the momentary dislocation of self-identity leads to any permanent sense of self-spectatorship or self-judgment apart from the immediate resolution to forswear anger or alcohol. But since the figure who judges the mirror-image in disgust has taken on the role of a dispassionate audience, this use of the mirror does, suggestively, reflect upon the idea that a dislocation, or self-splitting, of the ego into judger and judged could have a part to play in formulations of the ethical self.[23] Such a dislocation could take visual or dialogic form; several of the mirror-viewers are urged to keep up a conversation with themselves as they

---

21. Ov., *Ars Am.* 3.507–8: "Vos quoque si media speculum spectetis in ira, / Cognoscat faciem vix satis ulla suam." An amusing version of this idea is applied to a boxer in *Anth. Pal.* 11.77: Although Odysseus' dog recognized his master after twenty years, after a mere four hours in the ring this boxer can't recognize *himself!*

22. Even Freud, in his 1914 essay *On Narcissism*, identifies as a potential object of narcissistic attachment not that which one is, but that which one would like to be—an ego ideal. McCarty (1989, 171–73) stresses the interactive nature of such exemplary mirroring. As he notes, the effort of self-discovery is also in part an act of self-creation based on what the mirror shows.

23. Schuller (1989, 4) is right to emphasize that the idea of self-improvement should not be immediately associated with self-knowledge or an inner world of the self: "The mirror, reflecting such physical attributes back to the person in front of the mirror, in fact reveals the point of view of an other, rather than yielding direct introspective insight. Thus what the mirror of self knowledge discloses in these examples from Seneca and Diogenes Laertius would be equally ascertainable for anyone looking at the person's face." However, as Schuller himself acknowledges, we should bear in mind that the clarity of this division between external behavior and internal selfhood is itself based on post-Cartesian ideas about selfhood that do not have exact parallels in the ancient world.

gaze at their likeness, such as the talkative wife in Plutarch's *Advice to Bride and Groom* (141d), who is encouraged to converse with herself about what she sees ("Nope, you're definitely not a looker. But how to make up for this?"), and so encourage herself to virtuous behavior.

In the texts we have considered so far, the view of the "other" upon the self in the mirror is itself in a sense indirect; for the self to judge itself, some part of it must identify with the judgment of a community and thus separate itself from the immediate perspective of the wrathful or the drunk, and what the mirror shows is therefore hidden from the subject.[24] As a result, any idea that these mirrors of self-improvement can generally be treated as mirrors of *introspection* runs into difficulty when we consider the social nature of the judgment that motivates change; the idea of specular insight as revealing something to the individual that is particularly personal and unique is absent.[25] This is not to suggest that the ancient self was only external in its manifestation, but simply to point out that our own sharp contrast between a hidden, private self and a visible exterior cannot be mapped onto these texts from antiquity.[26] Even more important, self-knowledge itself was not usually conceived of as any kind of specular turning of the mind upon itself. If we turn to the Apollonian command to "know thyself," *gnothi sauton*, which was inscribed (along with the saying *meden agan*, "nothing in excess") in the pronaos of the temple of Apollo at Delphi,[27] we see that it occurs first in a fragment of Heraclitus in conjunction with the verb "be prudent," *sophronein*: ἀνθρώποισι πᾶσι μέτεστι γινώσκειν ἑωυτοὺς καὶ σωφρονεῖν (to know oneself and to be prudent are [qualities] shared by all men).[28]

---

24. As Schuller (1989, 7) well observes.

25. So, for example, when Demas, in Terence's *Adelphoe*, is boasting to his slave Syrus about how he has brought up his son, his mention of a mirror only equates what one learns from it with what one learns from watching others (*Ad.* 414–19).

26. On the mirror and introspection, see the discussions in Cancik 1967, 43; Frontisi-Ducroux and Vernant 1997, 62; Hugedé 1957, 110–36; Jonsson 1995, 47–48; McCarty 1989, 168–69; Schuller 1989, 1–11. On the mirror and the lamp in the Romantic tradition, the one reflecting the outside world, the other illuminating it, see Abrams 1953. For more on interior and exterior as ancient and modern categories, see the discussion of "shame culture" in chapter 3 and that of *persona* in chapter 4.

27. There were several other inscriptions on the temple at Delphi; see Wilkins 1917, 1–11.

28. Diels-Kranz I.22.116. While many of the texts that refer to the ethical function of the mirror refer to self-improvement or self-control rather than explicitly evoking "self-knowledge," the matrix of ideas that tied together *sophrosyne*, self-knowledge, and self-mastery in Greek popular and philosophizing thought strips this distinction of much of its meaning.

The term *sophrosyne*, which is linked to the injunction to "know thyself" in a way that suggests that the two concepts are not sharply delimited from each other, seems to have been synonymous with "knowing one's limits," "knowing one's place in society." Although Eliza Wilkins, in her comprehensive study of ancient references to the maxim *gnothi sauton*, distinguishes some seven different interpretations of its meaning, all but one of these are closely linked to limits on behavior: know your measure, know what you can and cannot do, know your place, know the limits of your wisdom, know your faults, know you are mortal, and finally—but in classical Athens, only for the Socrates of the Platonic dialogues—know your own soul and its divine qualities. Pierre Courcelle's study likewise associates the ancient command with knowing one's own measure, knowing one is mortal.[29] In other words, although the idea of "self-knowledge" suggests, for us, a Romantic introspection into the hidden depths of the soul, or a Freudian uncovering of the unconscious desires of the id, the ancient notion of *sophrosyne* was directed toward moderation and control of the social behavior of the individual, toward the approbation of his peers rather than the flowering of an inner potential. This provides the crucial link between *sophrosyne* as a set of practices and the notion of self-knowledge in antiquity, and also explains why, for us, the employment of the mirror as a tool to those ends might seem empty or superficial, while for our Greco-Roman writers it provides a significant view onto the self. Even in the Platonic tradition, in which the divine takes a much greater role in self-knowledge, control over pleasures and desires, and mastery of the better half of the soul over the worse half, can still be defined as *sophrosyne*— or at least Socrates speaks this way in appealing to his interlocutors.[30] In the

---

29. The variations of the *gnothi sauton* studied by Wilkins (1917) and Courcelle (1974, 11–48) attest to the frequency of ancient discussions and evocations of the term, and also to the fact that its exact meaning was already a subject of some debate in antiquity. Several lost works, from Aristotle to Varro to Porphyry, are known to have treated the maxim in some detail; all that survives bearing the title *On the gnothi sauton* is a collection of quotations in Stobaeus, writing as late as the fifth century CE. For the identification of *sophrosyne* with the *gnothi sauton* in Plato, see *Alc.* 131b4, *Chrm.* 164d–e, *Ti.* 72a. On the reworking of the *gnothi sauton* by Plato, see Long 2001.

30. On *sophrosyne*, see Annas 1985; North 1966; Verene 1997, 75–76. On *gnothi sauton* in all its Greek and Roman manifestations, see Wilkins 1917, especially 100–103. In North's discussion, *sophrosyne* is conceived of as consisting partly of self-control, partly of self-knowledge. But this is confusing, because it returns us to the question of what self-knowledge is, to which the answer is again knowing your own affairs well—like a *sophron*. Annas clarifies (1985, 120–21), "The interpretation of *sophrosyne* as self-knowledge is more congenial to Socrates . . . than is its interpretation

Philebus, for example, the opposite of *gnothi sauton* is a form of ignorance that leads us to overestimate our wealth and personal appearance as well as our virtuousness.[31] Such texts render it conceivable that changes attributable to the image in the mirror—containing one's anger, abjuring drunkenness, living up to the expectations attached to one's appearance—could be seen as a step on the way to such prudent behavior or "self-knowledge," but not as a move toward a form of reflexivity, a form of the mind turned upon the mind, that did not involve, in some capacity, the judgment of the other.

The treatment of self-knowledge shares with that of the mirror precisely the absence of the idea of the mind's accurate reflection upon itself (and hence self-transparency) as standard of self-knowledge. We are familiar with the latter notion from Descartes, in whose thinking reflection is posited as the basis of metaphysical philosophy.[32] "No longer does the essence of the human being reside primarily in grounds ontologically and theologically independent of him; Descartes discovers it in the logically and ontologically prior phenomenon of the *cogito me cogitare*, in which the thinking self appears to itself as *me cogitare*. With the ego as *cogitans* becoming its own *cogitatum*, a major paradigm of reflection, and of the ensuing philosophy, is set forth" (Gasché 1986, 17). There are significant differences between such a model and the ethical applications of the mirror we have been considering in our Greco-Roman texts.[33] The ancient mirror is not a metaphor for the turning of the mind, pure *nous*, upon itself; what is mirrored is either the community or God. In this self-transparent mind, the gaze of the self on the self experiences no warping force, no importation of a culturally shaped or divine sense of self. Moreover, intimations of a kind of reflexivity that would be possible without intermediaries such as the (external) mirror, or without a division of whole into parts, are treated as problematic in the ancient texts that conceive of such a possibility. In Plato's *Charmides*, for

---

as self-control. . . . The self-knowledge that is *sophrosyne* has nothing to do with my subconscious and everything to do with what F. H. Bradley called 'my station and its duties.'"

31. *Phlb.* 48c–49a. For a more detailed discussion of this text and many others supporting the idea that the maxim is fundamentally about knowing one's limits, see Wilkins 1917.

32. See also Rushdy 1993, 83–84.

33. For arguments against the interpretation of ancient reflexivity as indicating a similar concept of personality to that of post-Cartesian thought, see Gill (forthcoming). I will argue in chapter 4 that a form of reflexivity is, in Seneca, significant in a novel way for the definition of the fully developed self, although here, too, modern ideas about "personality" cannot be backread into the texts.

example, Socrates and his interlocutor Critias come to the conclusion that there can be no kind of seeing that would be a seeing of itself (167c–d). Their dialogue had begun with a discussion of *sophrosyne*, which Critias eventually defined as self-knowledge according to the Delphic maxim (164c–165b). The next move Charmides made was to define such self-knowledge as knowledge of knowledge itself, and Socrates then points out the problems of such reflexivity: in his argument, knowledge must have a subject-matter distinct from itself.[34]

These very objections would be repeated by the philosopher-physician Sextus Empiricus in the early third century CE, in a passage worth quoting in full for its clarity:

> For if the mind apprehends itself, either it as a whole will apprehend itself, or it will do so not as a whole but employing for the purpose a part of itself. Now it will not be able as a whole to apprehend itself. For if as a whole it apprehends itself, it will be as a whole [both] apprehension and apprehending, and, the apprehending subject being the whole, the apprehended object will no longer be anything; but it is a thing most irrational that the apprehending subject should exist while the object of the apprehension does not exist. Nor, in fact, can the mind employ for this purpose a part of itself. For how does the part itself apprehend itself? If as a whole, the object thought will be nothing; while if with a part, how will that part in turn discern itself? And so on to infinity.[35]

The very self-splitting that for Sextus Empiricus is the main objection against the possibility of reflexive self-knowledge is, as I suggested earlier, the natural

---

34. See Annas 1985, 134–35; Bruell 1977; Rosen 1989, 87–98; and Wilkins 1917, 72–74. The problem of a thing knowing itself without internal division is also discussed in Arist., *De An.* 445b1–449b3.

35. Sext. Emp., *Against the Logicians* 310–12 (trans. R. G. Bury [Cambridge, Mass., 1957], 163–65). Explicit references to the *gnothi sauton* in the context of mirror usage are rare in the Greek texts, though it seems safe to observe that both the mirror tradition and that of the Delphic maxim focus largely on a concept of self-betterment mediated by community judgment and linked to ideas of limitation or propriety. A very late example occurs in Olympiodorus' commentary on *Alc.* 9.11–14. On the notion of the mirror of self-knowledge, see especially Wilkins 1917, 85–86; also Griswold 1986, 32; and Jonsson 1995, 47–48. On Plotinus' use of the mirror metaphor to speak of the human soul, see Jonsson 1995, 84–99. On the post-Cartesian mirror as the master metaphor of Western philosophy, see Rorty 1979 and Rushdy 1993.

effect of the viewer's evaluation of the self-image in the mirror from the perspective of his or her peers, where self-judgment relies on the verdict passed by the viewing agent upon the viewed object. Unremarked and unelaborated as it is in these texts, the notion of the self as judge and the question of the role of the community in that act of judgment will resonate powerfully in the philosophical thinking of the first century CE at Rome.

THE INDEX OF VANITY

We have focused so far on the ethical aspects of mirror use in antiquity. Yet this constitutes only one part of the ancient specular tradition, and for every invocation of the mirror of self-improvement, many more texts draw attention to the mirror's implication in luxury, illusion, and even perversion. The view that Apuleius offered in his defense was far removed from more severe, and more traditional, Roman judgments about men who used mirrors, as exemplified by Apuleius' prosecutors and by the satirist Juvenal just a few decades earlier; Juvenal had lambasted the emperor Otho as a *pathicus*, a man who enjoyed being sexually penetrated by others, just because he carried a mirror on campaign (*Sat.* 2.99–101). For Apuleius, the gaze turned upon itself was not the mark of deviant sexuality, but a practice that inculcated morals rather than undermined them.[36] His interpretation aligned itself with only one side of a longstanding cultural debate on the merits and demerits of the mirror — a debate both Greek and Roman, and one with roots in several of Plato's dialogues, as well as in Roman cultural prejudice against "Greek" self-dandification.

These associations were to some degree a pendant to the simple fact that in both Greece and Rome the mirror had its most common use in feminine self-adornment and self-inspection.[37] So it is that Anacreon wishes he were a mirror so that his love might gaze at him endlessly (*Anacreontea* 22.5–6 West), while Ovid bids would-be lovers not to be embarrassed to hold the mirror for their mistresses (*Ars Am.* 2.215–16); Roman funerary reliefs may even display the upper-class wife's toiletry articles or show her using her mirror. Elsewhere,

---

36. Deviant, that is, by Roman standards of normative sexual behavior. Later chapters will return to the topic of the *pathicus* and his role in the scopic culture of Rome.

37. See, e.g., in Ovid alone: *Am.* 1.14.36, 2.17.8–9; *Ars Am.* 1.305–7; *Tr.* 3.7.38; *Met.* 15.232. Also Plaut., *Mostell.* 248–51.

less surprisingly, ancient writers invoke the mirror as a sign of female vacuity and even of civic disruption; as Maria Wyke observes of the Plautine courtesan, "placed before her mirror, woman is defined and recognized as less than a male citizen and disruptive of his pursuits, irresponsibly frivolous and dangerously seductive."[38] There are countless epigrams and poems in both the Greek and Latin sources that mock female addiction to the mirror, mostly by suggesting that a given woman is really too ugly to enjoy the sight; others remark on mirrors dedicated by women as votive offerings—a great sacrifice.[39]

This connection with the feminine world is matched in the iconography of the actual mirrors we have. Small, convex, and circular, they are usually made from silver or bronze; the earliest ones are hand-held or mounted on a stand, but the most popular ones take the form of the "mirror box," a small lidded container, often with a chased top, containing a mirror as its base.[40] The scenes on these mirror boxes most often touch upon erotic topics: both the use of the mirror and its iconography were often associated with Aphrodite, and many Greek, Etruscan, and Roman mirror cases show figures such as Helen of Troy, Aphrodite, or Eros, thus reinforcing a connection between eros and mirroring that we shall see recur in a philosophical context as well as in literary fancies.[41] Venus' briny entourage in Apuleius' *Metamorphoses* includes a troop of Tritons not only making music on conch-shells and carrying a parasol but, of course, holding up the inevitable mirror for their mistress's eyes (*Met.* 4.31); a fourth-century CE bridal casket shows a semi-naked Venus being offered a mirror.[42] Particularly noteworthy in this context is the scene engraved on the back of a Roman bronze mirror from Flavian times, showing a couple having sex on a bed over which hangs a painting of yet another couple making love.[43] Simon

---

38. Wyke 1994, 136. Besides the texts collected here, see also *Dig.* 34.2.25.10: "mundus mulieris est, quo mulier mundior fit: continentur eo specula matulae unguenta uasa unguentaria et si qua similia dici possunt, ueluti lauatio riscus."

39. See, e.g., *Anth. Pal.* 6.18.210, 211, and 11.266; Mart. 9.16. On this topic, see Frontisi-Ducroux and Vernant 1997, 53–59; Rosati 1983, 16–17; Wyke 1994.

40. See Frontisi-Ducroux and Vernant 1997, 75–79.

41. On the erotic representations on mirror cases, see Bettini 2000, 113–14; Frontisi-Ducroux 1996, 98; Frontisi-Ducroux and Vernant 1997, 53–59; Jonsson 1995, 42–44; and Stewart 1996 and 1998, 22–29. For a list of texts associating mirrors with erotic subjects, see McCarty 1989, 167n11.

42. Wyke 1994, 143: London, British Museum, reproduced in Johns 1982, pl. 35.

43. See the excellent discussion in Myerowitz 1992, 145–50.

Goldhill reads this as creating the effect of a deconstructive *mise en abîme* that puts into question the seemingly self-contained quality of artistic reference (2001, 174); we might add, in a different vein, that the "mirroring" image over the bed points to the erotically pleasurable nature of self-speculation for the love-making couple (for *voluptas* is the common result of such gazing).[44] It also reminds us, the gazers upon this doubled scene, that we too are partaking in the dynamic of erotic viewing in which the mirror's occupants are already frozen.[45] And as Molly Myerowitz (1992) would argue of erotic paintings in Roman domestic interiors in general, this scene also forces those whose activity it mirrors to objectify themselves, to evaluate their appearance against an image.[46]

When used by men, however, the mirror could point to—or result in—more than an increase in vanity or an exhibition of the erotic. A broad range of texts from as early as fifth-century Athens testify to the idea that only the "effeminate" man—the passive homosexual, the eunuch, the hermaphrodite—would consult a mirror. We have already seen how the retellings of the Socratic maxim about mirrors in Plutarch and Phaedrus carefully neutralize the suggestion that such self-inspection is not appropriate in men. More explicitly, Orestes in Euripides' play by the same name criticizes perfumed Phrygian men from the feminine East as the sort to use mirrors (*Or.* 1111–12), while, according to Diogenes Laertius, the Stoic Zeno claimed that the reason a fop hates crossing muddy terrain is that he can't see his face in it (*Lives of the Eminent Philosophers* 7.17).[47] Dionysius Halicarnassus relates with horror that the tyrant Aristodemus gave mirrors to the young men of the city of Cumae to keep their minds off politics; Aristodemus' aim in distributing the mirrors

---

44. On the *voluptas* provided by the mirror, see, e.g., Sen., *Q Nat.* 1.16.1; Sen., *Clem.* 1.1.3; *Dig.* 33.7.12.16.

45. Myerowitz (1992, 145–47) calls it "a highly contextualized, constructed, artificial, and theatrical reflection of the self." See also Wyke 1994, 144.

46. In support of this, consider the figure of Circe in Petronius' *Satyricon*, whose response to erotic rejection is to examine her face in a mirror—and try out all the expressions that lovers put on (*Sat.* 128).

47. See Frontisi-Ducroux and Vernant 1997, 59–65; Stewart 1996; and McCarty 1989, 168n15 (list of texts linking the mirror to effeminacy or degeneracy). An exception seems to be the man at the barber (Plut., *De rec. rat. aud.* 42b); Augustus, too, asked for a mirror before he died so he could comb his hair and fix his falling jaw (Suet., *Aug.* 99). On a woman cross-dressing for the mirror, see Ov., *Her.* 9.115–19.

was precisely to effeminize (*ekthelunai*) those who looked in them (insidiously, combs and perfume were part of the package [*Ant. Rom.* 7.9.4]). As this story suggests, the mirror is credited with the potential to transform the virile man into an effeminate, an idea that Ovid's story of Hermaphroditus (*Met.* 4.285–388) in turn cleverly exploits: here the youth who refuses an amorous nymph but dares to step into the mirroring waters of her pond—Ovid stresses the water's reflective capacity—is transformed in that pond into a single body with twin sex organs (*duplex*, 4.378; *biformis*, 4.387). And forever after, this mirror-pool would render all who used it into *semiviri*, half-men (4.386).[48] We even find this tendency to effeminize the self-indulgent male gaze demonstrated in artistic representations of Narcissus, who, as he gazes winsomely at his image in the water in several Pompeiian wall-paintings, sprouts small but feminine breasts (fig. 1).[49]

A further "effeminizing" effect of the mirror was simply its cost: Roman mirrors in particular are implicated in moralizing discourse about the downhill path trodden by a hardy old breed once they learned to check for spinach in their teeth. At the end of the first book of the *Natural Questions*, Seneca vents part of his spleen on the atrocious expense of mirrors: the ones that people adorn with gems now, he says, could have supplied a woman's dowry in the good old days (1.17.8). This may have been especially true of the silver mirrors which were already extant, but rare, in classical Greece (bronze mirrors appeared earlier, in the middle of the sixth century), but whether silver or bronze, a mirror's value was only increased by having its polished surface covered (or backed) by silver or bronze of intricate workmanship.[50] And since, at Rome, *luxuria* was closely connected to an unmanly taste for the good life and even to ideas about sexual degeneracy, the mirror emerges as

---

48. As McCarty (1989, 181) puts it, "In Ovid's story of Hermaphroditus, catoptric vision leads directly and explicitly to emasculation." On Hermaphroditus, see Schickel 1961–62, 495; and the art-historical treatment in Balensiefen 1990, 53–54; also Nugent 1990, 160–85. Nugent emphasizes the catoptric elements of the story and the philosophic dialogue it enacts with the *Symposium*: "Salmacis' prayer for fusion [with Hermaphroditus] . . . expresses a desire remarkably similar to that state of erotic union which, in the Symposium's androgynous myth, Aristophanes posits as the *summum bonum* sought by all lovers" (1990, 178). Her success is brilliantly offset by Narcissus' failure; see chapter 2.

49. The effeminacy of the figure is still more clear in the Narcissus at the Pompeian house of M. Gavinius Rufus.

50. See Jonsson 1995, 42–46.

FIGURE 1 Painting of androgyne Narcissus from the House of
Loreius Tiburtinus, Pompeii (Photo by Leo C. Curran)

a guilty accomplice in moralizing tales about men all too interested in their
appearance.

The starkest illustration of the mirror's dual potential to corrupt and to
instruct emerges from Seneca's *Natural Questions*. Here Seneca introduces a
story of sexual degeneracy with some familiar material on the instructive

potential of the mirror, the discovery of which he attributes to the human drive for self-knowledge:[51]

> Mirrors were discovered in order that man might know himself [*ut homo ipse se nosset*] since he would gain much from this: first of all, knowledge of himself [*sui notitiam*], then, good judgment [*consilium*] for certain purposes: the handsome man, to avoid disgrace; the ugly, to know that he had to make up for his physical defects by means of his virtue; the young man, to be admonished by the bloom of his youth that it was the time for learning and for daring brave deeds; the old man, to abandon behavior unseemly for white hair, and to reflect a bit on death. For these purposes nature gave us the ability to actually see ourselves. (*Q Nat.* 1.17.4)

The word *consilium* suggests the advice of a friend or authority figure more than anything else, a notion paralleled by the idea that a friend and a mirror can share the same purpose, to tell you what you cannot see yourself.[52] Presumably one is to recognize one's friend's faults in oneself, and hence stop indulging in them.[53] In other words, the friend here plays the role of the mirror elsewhere, to aid in the acquisition of *sophrosyne* by the elimination of unbecoming behaviors, a process that in turn is linked with self-knowledge.

But Seneca soon moves from this positive mirror of self-knowledge to its

---

51. Apart from here, self-knowledge is explicitly associated with mirroring only, and briefly, in Ovid's story of Narcissus, *Met.* 3.339–510. See Cancik 1967, 47–48. Self-knowledge may also be associated with mirroring, although not explicitly, in Plaut., *Epidicus* 382–87, if we are to take the reference to contemplating one's "cor sapientiae" and past life in a mirror as anything like self-knowledge. The connection between the mirror and self-knowledge also occurs in some post-Senecan texts, including Lucian, *On Pantomime* 81. On the mirror of self-knowledge, see the discussions in Cancik 1967; Frontisi-Ducroux and Vernant 1997, 62; Hugedé 1957, 101–14; Jonsson 1995, 47–48; McCarty 1989, 168–69; Schuller 1989, 1–11.

52. Martial makes cruel fun of the friend-as-mirror when he tells the three-toothed Maxima not to smile, if she believes her mirror—and him ("si speculo mihique credis" [2.41.8]). On the word *speculum* as an adviser or a standard, see Callahan 1964. For more on the friend as mirror, see below, chapter 4.

53. One formulation of this idea appears in Schuller (1989, 11), who remarks that the mirror of self-knowledge "is part of the complex realm in which the individual meets the other: it is an instrument for the social inspection of the self. . . . [It is] not so much a metaphor for the mind as a simile for 'the other.'"

polar opposite, the mirror of *luxuria* and moral decay, which here appears as a chronological development of human mirror use itself. Although early man used the mirror sparingly, these days (he says) humans avidly open up the earth to find reflective metals "for the purpose of lust and soft living" (in libidinem luxumque [*Q Nat.* 1.17.5]). We have fallen far indeed:

> First, chance showed his own face to each man. Then, when innate love of self in mortals made the sight of one's own form sweet, they looked more often into surfaces in which they saw their reflections. . . . Then came other evils from the earth, whose smoothness presented a reflected image [*speciem suam*] to men otherwise occupied, an image which one man saw in a goblet, another in bronze bought for other uses. . . . Later, when luxury now ruled supreme over everything, full-size mirrors were chased in gold and silver, then adorned with gems. . . . Little by little, luxury has developed for the worse, invited by wealth itself, and vices have enjoyed a huge growth, and everything has become so indiscriminate through assorted practices that whatever used to be a female's cosmetic-kit is now the toiletry of a man: I mean all men, even soldiers. Is the mirror used now for the sake of orna-ment alone? For every single vice, it's a necessity. (*Q Nat.* 1.17.6, 8, 10)

Despite his earlier claim that mirrors were invented "in order that man might know himself" (*Q Nat.* 1.17.4), then, Seneca rather surprisingly finds in the desire for mirrors a new aetiology for the sense of cultural decay represented by the Roman lament, *O tempora, O mores*; elsewhere, the origin of such greed for luxury is more commonly attributed to Rome's imperial expansion and the conquest of Greece and Asia Minor in particular.

Despite Seneca's lambasting of gems and gold, most of the mirrors in circu-lation in Greco-Roman antiquity would have been made of bronze, as well as a smaller number in silver—first made (in Pliny's claim) by Pasiteles in the time of Pompey and much preferred to bronze (*HN* 33.128–30).[54] By the time of Pliny the Elder, by his own testimony, glass mirrors were just coming into use, although we have little information on their cost. It is also difficult to tell

---

54. References to silver mirrors also in, e.g., Plaut., *Mostell.* 311; Vitr., *De Arch.* 7.3.9; Pliny, *HN* 34.160; Sen., *Q Nat.* 1.17.8 (also gold); Apul., *Flor.* 15.14; Philostr., *Eikones* 1.6; *Dig.* 33.6.3. Pliny's dat-ing seems wrong, depending on how we interpret Plaut., *Mostell.* 265–67: Philolaches wants a stone so he can break Philematium's mirror, which would therefore seem to be made of glass.

how widespread the use of glass was; however, such mirrors are explicitly mentioned by Pausanias as well as Pliny.[55] Glass mirrors have been found in Germany and Austria in tombs of the Roman garrison from the end of the first century CE.[56] And of course, there was always water, the first, and cheapest, mirror of all.[57] And yet, whether glass, silver or bronze, what is most important here is that in the view of its ancient users, the image in the mirror was not conceived of as a distorting one. As McCarty (1989, 166) notes, modern scholars are incorrect to assume that "the use of the metaphor to represent distorted or derivative vision, as in Platonic thought, indicates the ancients' dissatisfaction with the optical quality of their mirror." On the contrary, the virtue of these mirrors for their users was their ability to present the most truthful possible representation of the face looking into them, and far more so than was possible in the plastic arts.[58] As Apuleius stressed:

> Of course, the work of creating images by hand takes time, and even so, there's no resemblance to match the mirror's. For vigor is lacking in those representations made from potter's clay, color is lacking in stone, solidity is missing from paintings, and motion is missing from them all, and motion is what represents an image most faithfully when an image is seen, reflected marvelously in the mirror, with likeness and motion responding to each nod of the man it portrays. . . . So greatly does that smart, smooth mirror, that marvelous artisan [*leuitas illa speculi fabra et splendor opifex*], outstrip the crafts in portraying a likeness. (*Apol.* 14.8)[59]

---

55. Pausanias 8.37.3 speaks of glass in a temple in Arcadia; Pliny, *HN* 36.193, tells us that Sidonians invented glass mirrors.

56. On Roman glass mirrors, see Lloyd-Morgan 1982, 47–48; von Netoliczka 1935, 44; Schefold 1940, 15–16; Pauly-Wissowa, cols. 30–31; and the bibliography in McCarty 1989, 167. For Etruscan mirrors, see de Grummond 1982. On the archeological data for ancient mirrors in general, see Jonsson 1995, 36–42; von Netoliczka 1935. De Grummond (1982, 39) argues for an increase in Roman mirror usage from the Augustan period onward. Pliny, *HN* 36.194–95, offers a recipe for glassmaking and explains how the art was banished under Tiberius but brought back under Nero. On archeological evidence from German tombs and Ptolemaic Egypt, see Pauly-Wissowa, "Katoptron," col. 44.

57. On the reflective surface of water as a parallel to the mirror, see the sources in Baltrusaitis 1978, 189; and von Netoliczka 1935, col. 29.

58. Hugedé 1957, 97–100.

59. For two smart analyses of Apuleius' treatment of mirroring and identity in the *Metamorphoses*, see Slater 1998 and Too 1996.

This perspective is repeatedly echoed in our ancient texts. Vitruvius speaks equally highly of the accuracy of silver mirrors (*De arch.* 7.3.9). Even as a metaphor the mirror stood for correct representation; Lucian, in his essay on the writing of history, invokes it as the paradigm of representational veridicality: "Above all, let the historian apply his judgment like a mirror, clear and glistening and accurately centered, and let him display the shapes of events just as he receives them, with nothing distorted, faded, or altered" (*Hist. Consc.* 51).[60] Plutarch prefaces his lives of Timoleon and Aemilianus Paulus by remarking that he is writing biography for his own sake, "trying somehow to beautify and make similar my own life in the face of their virtues by using history as a mirror; what happens is no different from our living and associating with each other."[61] And so on, in all manner of metaphor: Children are the mirror of nature, because they are so guileless.[62] The mirror of wine—*in vino veritas*—makes the drinker reveal himself, as does that of time.[63] Behavior, like the face, is the mirror of thought.[64] The wife is supposed to be a mirror to her spouse, which effectively means having no responses that do not mirror his.[65] Even a book can be the mirror of its author: Cicero comments of Piso that his adulteries are reflected in his verses, in which one can see his life as if in a mirror.[66] And in a more philosophical vein, as we have briefly seen, the metaphor of the mirror is applied to the function served by friends: they are aids to seeing the self as others see it.

This ancient stress on specular accuracy is important because it leads us to another charge raised against the mirror in antiquity: that in its ability to

---

60. See similarly Lucr., 4.166–67.

61. Plut., *Tim.* 1. On the mirror of epinician: Pind., *Nem.* 7.14; of epigram, Mart. 10.4.10–12; of epic, Alcid. apud Arist., *Rhet.* 1406b. On writing as a mirror in general, see the collection of texts at Too 1996, 306n26 and 306n27. On mirror titles in the Middle Ages and Renaissance, see Grabes 1982, 39–44.

62. Cic., *Fin.* 5.22.61: "pueri, in quibus ut in speculis natura cernitur."

63. On wine: Aesch., fr. 393 Nauck; and Alcaeus, fr. 104 Diehl. See also the suggestive comments of Frontisi-Ducroux 1989, 163; and Frontisi-Ducroux and Vernant 1997, 73, 114–16. As she discusses here, the painted image in the bottom of the wine cup offered a mirror of sorts to the reveler: sometimes it showed a banqueter, sometimes the grimacing mask of the Gorgon. On time as a mirror, see Eur., *Hipp.* 429–30; and Frontisi-Ducroux and Vernant 1997, 113. In this case, the confusion about who looks in the mirror of time, the sinner or his audience of collective spectators, is, I think, perfectly appropriate to the confusion of subject and object, viewer and viewed, for which the mirror can stand.

64. Plut., *Mor.* 172d.

65. Plut., *Conj. Praec.* 14.139–40.

66. "Adulteria denique eius delicatissimis versibus expresserit, in quibus, si qui velit, possit istius tamquam in speculo vitam intueri" (Cic., *Pis.* 7).

seemingly, but not actually, reproduce the material world, its function was an inherently deceptive one, promising something that literally was not there. As we have seen, our classical sources stressed the *accuracy* of their mirrors; if the specular image was condemned, it was because the image it supplied was *unreal*.[67] It is only from our perspective that the image in a slightly concave silver mirror seems unsatisfactory; to fail to understand this could lead us to misunderstand some of Plato's criticisms of the reflected image by emphasizing its visual rather than epistemological inferiority to *Realien*.[68] In the *Republic*, the discussion of the divided line in book 6 and the treatment of poetry and painting in book 10 both rely on the idea of the reflected image as an ontologically inferior version of the original. In Socrates' exposition of the divided line at *Resp.* 509d–511e, as is well known, a distinction is drawn between the visible world and the intelligible world, and each area is represented as a line divided into two unequal sections. The visible world is thus represented both by the material world around us and by shadows and reflections in water and in polished surfaces (509d–510a), and this fourth category is the furthest removed from truth and reality (511e); no praise, here, for the ethical or divinatory qualities of the reflected image.

Socrates later uses the example of the mirror to criticize the ontological status of the poetic and pictorial arts (*Resp.* 10.596d–e). As he professes (in dialogic form, of course) to his interlocutor Glaucon, the painter shares with the class of craftsmen the ability to produce what is not properly real but merely a reflection of the divine Forms:

> "Tell me, do you think that there's no way any craftsman could make all these things, or that in one way he could and in another he couldn't? Don't you see that there is a way in which you yourself could make all of them? . . . You could do it quickly and in lots of places, especially if you were willing to carry a mirror with you, for that's the quickest way of all. With it you can quickly make the sun, the things in the heavens, the earth, yourself, the other animals, manufactured items, plants, and everything else mentioned just now."

---

67. Jonsson 1995, 53.

68. On the ancient emphasis on the clarity and accuracy of their mirrors, see Baltrusaitis 1978, 75; Hugedé 1957, 37, 97–99, with treatment of Pauline and Christian texts as well; McCarty 1989, 169. Cf. Plut., *Conj. Praec.* 14.139–40.

"Yes, I could make them appear, but I couldn't make the things themselves as they truly are." (Trans. G. M. A. Grube, rev. C. D. C. Reeve)

Where the craftsman is one mimetic remove from the Forms, the painter is
twice an imitator; but both the artifacts created by man and the painted images
that reproduce them are no more real than the images one might create by
holding up a mirror to the heavens and the earth. Like the world around us,
what appears real in the mirror is an illusion. Similarly, in a restatement of the
principle of the divided line in the *Sophist*, the Stranger reminds Theaetetus
that the world around us is attended by unreal images—dream pictures,
shadows, the reflections in bright surfaces (*Soph.* 266c). To add to the illusory
nature of mirror images, it was well known—and a problematic fact for others besides Plato—that the mirror, purveyor of false visions, reversed these
images along the right/left axis. Thus Socrates compares the way this inverse
image affects the viewer to the formation of false opinion (*Tht.* 193c–d), and
the connection between the mirror image and false belief recurs elsewhere
(*Soph.* 239d–240a): when Theaetetus gropes for an answer to why one would
call a sophist (and purveyor of false opinions) an image-maker, he tries to
explain this negative use of the term *image* (*eidolon*) by reference to what one
sees in water, mirrors, painting, and sculpture. These references, however, are
not the whole (Platonic) story, as we shall see.[69]

Apart from these negative Platonic references to the mirror, numerous treatises, mostly lost, dealt with catoptric properties in antiquity, and with some
of the same distinctions between reality and illusion. Indeed, from Euclid in
the third century BCE to Ptolemy in the second century CE, the distinction
between direct vision and reflected vision was so fundamental as to demand
a distinct branch of study for the workings of the latter.[70] Hero of Alexandria
(fl. 80 CE) justified writing his *Catoptrica* precisely on such grounds.[71] Euclid

---

69. On left and right, see also *Ti.* 46a–b; *Tht.* 206d; Ptol., *Optica* 3.96; Lucr. 4.292–301. Apuleius,
too, marks the reversal of left and right for which mirrors are responsible (*Apol.* 16), but as Too
(1996, 142–44) would argue, for *this* philosopher the distortion is liberating. See on these texts
Hugedé 1957, 115–36.

70. As emphasized by Jonsson 1995, 51; and Simon 1988, 196–97.

71. "The study of catoptrics, however, is useful not merely in affording diverting spectacles but
also for necessary purposes" (quoted in Lindberg 1976, 14). Hero's text is available in William of
Moerbeke's Latin translation in *Opera quae supersunt omnia*, ed. Wilhelm Schmidt, Leo Nix et al.,
vol. 2., fasc. 1 (Stuttgart: Teubner, 1976), 310–65.

possibly authored a (lost) *Catoptrics* himself (and treats mirrored vision in *Optics* 19); we know of lost *Catoptrica* by Philip of Opus and Archimedes.[72] Ptolemy devotes the last three books of his *Optics* to the topic of mirrored vision.[73] As a corollary of the negative Platonic perspective, in these texts too the mirror represents a form of vision that is inferior: as Ptolemy points out, the rays that strike it bounce back and stream upon the viewer, generating in him the illusory notion that the image is where the mirror itself is; elsewhere the image the mirror produces is described as bent, deflected, and therefore vitiated.[74] Ptolemy stresses that the reflected image has no reality: as it does not appear *in* or *on* the mirror, there is, in fact, nothing in the mirror (*Optics* 3.3 in the Arabic text).[75] Gérard Simon (1987, 319–20) explains:

> What for us is a physical law presents itself to him [Ptolemy] as the cause of an error resting on a psychical law: we locate what we see within the extension of the initial direction of our gaze, even when an obstacle causes it to be deflected at a certain distance from our eye. Here resides the foundation of the illusion which the surfaces of mirrors, as well as that of refracting media, foist on us. . . . We must understand that the reflected or refracted image does not have any physical reality for him either. When we think about it, whether the image be real or virtual, it results from the propagation of a material entity, light, neither the existence nor the properties of which depend on what we are. In a theory of the visual ray, in the absence of a gazer, *the mirror reflects nothing that bears a relation to visibility.* The image has the status of a non-being which borrows the forms of being. . . . Consequently the entire study of mirrors and refracting surfaces is thought of as a *science of the false.*

Seneca puts it more simply still: "what is shown by the mirror isn't there" (non est enim in speculo quod ostenditur [*Q Nat.* 1.15.7]). As these thinkers

---

72. Philip of Opus, fl. before 330 BCE. See Diog. Laert., 3.25.37, 31.46.

73. On ancient theories of katoptrics, see Baltrusaitis 1978; Frontisi-Ducroux and Vernant 1997, 133–54; Jonsson 1995, 49–56; Lejeune 1948 and 1957; Lindberg 1976, 1–17; Simon 1988; and van Hoorn 1972, 42–107.

74. Explicit at Lucr., 4.150–58; Plut., *De gen.* 22.

75. In *L'Optique de Claude Ptolémée dans la version latine d'après l'arabe de l'émir Eugène de Sicile*, ed. A. Lejeune (Louvain, 1956).

were careful to point out in defense of this claim, the reflected image was an effect of the presence of a viewing subject alone, and without a viewer, it would vanish.[76]

Against these comments, we might expect the mirror to find a spirited defense among the ancient atomists from whom the notion of mirroring or reflection was made the foundation of the workings of vision itself. Their visual theory—at least as represented by Aristotle's comments on Democritus at *De sensu* 2.438a5–12—relied upon the mirroring capacity of the pupil to explain how it is that we see: Democritus believed that the image reflected on the cornea signified the presence of the image of the real object in the eye, and that this imprinting was the mechanism that enable us to see the object.[77] The later atomist Lucretius explained the image "in" the mirror itself by reference to the *simulacra* thrown off by bodies: the *simulacra*, bounced back swiftly and rapidly from the smooth, hard surface of the metal, produce a visible image, and no other visual theory would explain this.[78] But in the end, the implications of the mirror remained negative. Despite the importance of these specular studies for theories about the workings of sight in general, the image in the mirror, in this strain of the specular tradition, carried little authority: like the pronoun *I*, it only existed when a human presence was there

---

76. Simon (1988, 148–49, 196–97) stresses this point, remarking that "if the image can be designated a phantasm . . . , one cannot study it geometrically for itself, *since its proper quality is not having a physical existence*" (197; original emphasis). Jonsson (1995, 45–55) and Hardie (1988, 75) make a similar point. LaPenna (1997) offers an interesting discussion of Manilius' support of this view and anti-Lucretian perspective. For a modern take, see Eco 1986, 223–24: "If we compared mirror images to words, they would be like personal pronouns, like the pronoun *I* meaning Umberto Eco, if I pronounce it, and someone else, if someone else does so."

77. See the similar testimony at Arist., *Div. Somn.* 464a; Theophr., *De sensibus* 50–51; and Alexander, *De sensu* 24.14 = DK 67 A29. See also Brunschwig 1973, 24–25; Lindberg 1976, 3; and Frontisi-Ducroux and Vernant 1997, 144, who comment that "reflection is therefore situated at the center of the visual mechanism of the ancients." However, against this interpretation of atomist reflection, see Baldes 1975; and van Hoorn 1972, 74. For a more detailed treatment of Democritus' theory of vision, see chapter 2. Democritus' theory did not win universal adherence: Aristotle comments dryly that if Democritus' view were true, all reflective surfaces would presumably be able to "see" as well (*Sens.* 2.438a5–12).

78. "Nec ratione alia servari posse videntur / tanto opere ut similes reddantur cuique figure." See Lucr. 4.99–109.

to give it a false semblance of reality.[79] In truth, it was the equivalent of a sign with no referent. Seductive but empty, it had less to do with self-knowledge than self-deception.

THE MIRROR OF THE SOUL

These texts on mirroring provide us with an essential cultural backdrop of received ideas against which to consider the function of the mirror image in the culminating text of this chapter, the *Alcibiades* I.[80] Attributed to Plato in antiquity, this dialogue (according to the testimony of Diogenes Laertius [3.62]) was often placed at the head of collections of his works because it seemed to represent so many of Plato's arguments *in nuce*: as Forde (1987, 222) remarks, "The neo-Platonist Iamblichus wrote that the *Alcibiades* I contains the whole philosophy of Plato, as in a seed. The Islamic sage and Platonic commentator Alfarabi concurs, saying in effect that in the *Alcibiades* I all the Platonic questions are raised as if for the first time."[81] Despites the doubts voiced by Friedrich Schleiermacher in the introduction to his 1809 translation of the dialogue, modern consensus seems now to be building on the side of authenticity.[82] However, the question of authenticity is of limited significance for our purposes here: more important is that the dialogue was considered authentic in antiquity and certainly in the Roman imperial period. Indeed,

---

79. As pointed out by Eco 1986, 215–37; and Brenkman 1976, 312–13. As John Henderson points out to me, the fact that in Latin, but not Greek, "in" and "on" the mirror are covered by the same word, *in,* can lead to the playful conceit of Stat., *Silvae* 3.4: because Earinus' face is reflected *on* the mirror's surface, a Cupid snaps it shut to trap it *in* the mirror.

80. For discussion of the *Phaedrus*, which also uses the metaphor of the mirror, see chapter 2. It may seem odd to think of the *Alcibiades* I, probably written in the 350s BCE, as ringing the changes on a tradition that mostly postdated it. But this is not exactly what I am describing: it is simply that the ancient tradition of the *gnothi sauton* proved far more influential in the later texts we are considering than did the esoteric philosophical treatment accorded self-knowledge by the author of the *Alcibiades* I.

81. See also Pradeau 1999, 22–24, on the *Alcibiades* in antiquity. The most comprehensive treatment of its reception in antiquity, from Plotinus to Olympiodorus, is in A.-P. Segonds's introduction to Proclus' commentary on the *Alcibiades* (Paris, 1985–86), vol. 1, 10–125.

82. On the side of which are arrayed Annas 1985; Friedländer 1921, 2:28–29; Goldin 1993; and Pradeau 1999. See the useful summary of views in Pradeau 1999, 24–29.

even its doubters posit that it was composed immediately after Plato's death by a student of his school. It represents, accordingly, one strand in an intellectual tradition received as Platonic by later thinkers.

If its attribution to Plato is correct, the *Alcibiades* is likely be an early dialogue (as its frequent place at the head of the corpus, as well as some thematic similarities with the *Charmides,* might suggest), although its use of reflective terminology, which does not imply any borrowing from the concept of *theoria,* need not dictate its time of composition. In it, the cultural commonplaces about the use of the mirror with which we are now familiar are represented in an entirely different, innovating light. Just as the *gnothi sauton* is now taken to mean something beyond the idea of knowing the limits of one's abilities, so too the act of mirroring is no longer merely a reflection of standards of community judgment, but something that transcends what one's peers might have to say. As such, it echoes the altered concept of self-knowledge that informs Plato's dialogues from the *Phaedrus* on, what A. A. Long has called "Plato's extraordinary answer to the self-model question . . . : Make yourself as like as possible to God."[83] Long points out the influence of this new model on Hellenistic Stoicism. In my view the *Alcibiades* I is a neglected text that not only supports this proposition but repositions the reflected image at its center. In so doing, it provides a startling backdrop for the self-scrutinizing, self-watching Stoics of the early Roman imperial period, who grafted the seed represented by this dialogue onto an entirely different plant.

The *Alcibiades* I itself, however, cannot come under discussion without some regard for its own philosophical and scientific context. The mirror tradition in antiquity developed in a symbiotic process with the understanding of the workings of vision itself, and together these two discourses constituted what Martin Jay has called the "ocular-centric underpinnings of the philosophical tradition." Jay (1993, 21–82) traces the seeming ubiquity of the visual metaphor in the history of Western philosophy, from Plato's parable of the cave and Augustine's praise of divine light to Descartes' notion of the world reflected in a "steadfast mental gaze." Although Jay goes on to discuss the "detranscendentalization" of this tradition in the late nineteenth century, our

---

83. Long 2001, 21, who cites *Phdr.* 230a; *Tht.* 176a; *Ti.* 90b–d; and *Resp.* 10.613a.

eyes are nonetheless not uniformly "downcast" in the modern period, and we share some of the intellectual and metaphorical reflexes of this kind of thought—even on so commonplace a level as our daily use of such terms as *speculation, reflection,* and *illumination.*[84]

As others besides Jay have noted, the use of the visual metaphor in ancient philosophy from Parmenides to Plotinus is strikingly consistent, although less apparent in our remnants from the presocratics than in Plato, where it bursts (as it were) into sight.[85] Already Parmenides had bidden his readers to "[g]aze upon things which, even though absent, are still firmly present in the mind" (B4.1).[86] For Plato, however, truth itself—the Forms—are conceived of as properties seen with the eye of the mind, as they appear too in the doctrine of reminiscence (see, for example, *Meno* 82; *Phdr.* 247d–e). The sun, which enables seeing, is his metaphor for the Good; the activity of philosopher is characterized as *theoria,* a form of spectating; the intelligible is *contemplated* by dialectic (τὸ ὑπὸ τῆς τοῦ διαλέγεσθαι ἐπιστήμης τοῦ ὄντος τε καὶ νοητοῦ θεωρούμενον [*Resp.* 511c]). In the *Timaeus,* Plato goes so far as to locate the origin of philosophy in this contemplation of the heavens: "In my account, sight is the cause of the greatest benefit we have had, because none of the current explanations about the world would have been uttered if men had not seen the stars or the sun or the heavens." These phenomena, Timaeus continues, have given men the art of number and the notion of time, from which we have procured philosophy itself, and this, he claims, "is the greatest good benefit of the eyes" (*Ti.* 47a–b).

Most striking, in the parable of the cave the philosopher's ascent to knowledge of the Forms is couched throughout in visual terms (*Resp.* 7.514a–517c). In this allegory, in which Plato condemns the forms of vision shared by men who take shadows for reality, movement out and upward from this state to viewing the objects of the world outside the cave and, finally, to contemplation of the sun itself is an ascent "from a sight lost in an illusory realm of shadows and

---

84. And of course, the seeing/knowing relation is particularly marked in the relationship between *eidon* and *oida.* Snell (1953, 198) makes it explicit: "The *Nous* is the mind in its capacity as an absorber of images. . . . Knowledge (*eidenai*) is the state of having seen."

85. For a treatment of knowledge as vision in Plato, see Gosling 1973, 120–39, with important philosophical cautions about a consistently literal interpretation of model.

86. λεῦσσε δ' ὅμως ἀπεόντα νόωι παρεόντα βεβαίως.

reflections through a sight seduced by images and visible objects, and a higher sight drawn to the lights of the sky in which the divinities make themselves visible, to the moment, finally, of a glorious intellectual vision, a pure, disembodied contemplation, with the eye of the mind, of the Form of the Good, the invisible condition of all that is visible" (Levin 1997, 12).[87] Along these lines, Gosling (1973, 122) notes Plato's use of visual imagery "to illustrate the mind's progress in knowledge," his tendency to talk of the person with knowledge as looking at (*blepein*) the Forms, and his use of the word *gnosis* and cognates in certain crucial passages.[88] If Havelock (1963, 268) lamented Plato's contamination by visual imagery here—it brings the Forms back into the realm of the human, after all—Plato himself, as Andrea Nightingale would have it, "positively revels in it" (2004, 79).

This positive valence of the visual for the most part only extends to Plato's metaphorical language; as we have just seen, earthly seeing is for troglodytes.[89] Elsewhere in the *Republic* Socrates will underscore this point by setting up an analogy, again, between painting and poetry, themselves twice removed reflections of reality, and the deceptive qualities of what is seen with earthly vision, such as the partially submerged stick that tricks the eye into thinking it is bent (*Resp.* 10.602c). This is not a uniform criticism in the philosophical tradition, ancient or modern; we might rehearse one of the most famous defenses of vision, which occurs in the well-known passage that opens Aristotle's *Metaphysics*: "All men by nature desire to know. A sign of this is the fondness we have for our senses, for even apart from their usefulness they are loved for themselves—and above all the others, the sense of sight. For not only in order to take action, but even when we have no intention to act, we prefer seeing (so

---

87. On light as a metaphor for truth, see especially Blumenberg 1953. For this metaphor in Seneca specifically, see Waiblinger 1977, 68. It is worth noting that Oedipus' response to the gaining of self-knowledge—that is, knowledge of the limits he transgressed—is to blind himself, a form of punishment which in turn seems to be linked to the heightening of the capacities of the eye of the mind, as in Tiresias. For the sexual implications of this act, see chapter 2.

88. Gosling goes on to emphasize that this language does not mean that knowing *just is* mental viewing. And I have been careful to stress that my point here is about figural language, not about the actual nature of knowing.

89. And for Leontius, who, in *Resp.* 4.439e–440a, cannot resist the impulse of his eyes to glut themselves on the sight of corpses. Here the eyes are clearly aligned with the appetitive, rather than the noetic, part of the soul. On the philosophical belief in the unreliability of sight, see also Cic., *Acad.* 1.31.

to speak) over all the others. This is because of all the senses, sight especially makes possible knowledge and clarifies many differences" (*Metaph.* 980a). Nor is Plato unremittingly negative; in the *Timaeus*, for example, vision is called humanity's greatest gift from God, both for its earthly uses and for the higher purposes it fosters, since inquiries about the nature of time, the revolutions of the earth, and the universe, have given rise in turn to philosophy itself (*Ti.* 47a–b).[90] In general, however, a distinction must be drawn between the two forms of Platonic viewing.

Why is the ocular metaphor so powerful in ancient philosophy (and beyond)? Common sense might simply have it that vision is intuitively understandable as the most informative of our senses. Hans Jonas has suggested that of the senses, sight is ideally equipped for appropriation by the philosophical project of the search for truth, for at least three reasons. One is the simultaneity of the visual process: unlike, say, hearing, which takes place over a temporal span (however short), to look is to take in the objects of one's vision all at once. As Jonas argues, "The very contrast between eternity and temporality rests upon an idealization of 'present' experienced visually as the hold of stable contents against the fleeting succession of nonvisual sensation" (1982, 145). Hence the contrast between Being and Becoming. A second reason is what Jonas calls the "neutralization of causality": the objects of our gaze are present without drawing us into their presence, without seeming to impinge upon us in any way, an apparent neutrality that gives rise to the concept of objectivity itself—"the thing as it is in itself as distinct from the thing as it affects me" (147). Finally, the apparent unboundedness of sight's travel (as opposed to the limited range of smell, taste, and touch) is productive of the idea of infinity.

Jonas's arguments are extremely suggestive but cannot provide a complete answer to the question with which he engages, all the more so because his discussion of the "neutralization of causality" has limited practical application to the classical world. Although we moderns may well think of sight as the most antiseptic and ethereal of all the senses, ancient models for the workings of vision were remarkably tactile and, moreover, were implicated in the decidedly physical process of erotic arousal. There is no reason to believe, then, that ancient thinkers took for granted the "neutrality" of vision. Nor was the

---

90. See also the Athenian's remarks at Pl., *Leg.* 12.961d.

gaze always seen as finite. Aristotle explains the curious case of a man who saw himself facing himself as he walked about, by having recourse to the reflection of weak eye-rays back toward the viewer: they do not have the strength to travel through the blocking force of the opposing air (*Mete.* 3.4.373b).[91]

From a very different perspective, Andrea Nightingale in a fascinating recent article links the emergence of the conception of the philosopher as a "spectator" to the Athenian civic institution of *theoria*, which in its prephilosophical usages meant "spectating," in particular as the action of the state ambassadors sent to oracles or games. In Nightingale's account it is in the middle dialogues of Plato that we first find spectatorship employed as a metaphor for the project of approaching the truth (notwithstanding the later back-projections of writers such as Diogenes). As she argues,

> In the preplatonic thinkers, truth is something that is heard or spoken, not something that is seen. The philosophers who developed the "spectator theory of knowledge" in the fourth century were thus engaging in a novel enterprise which needed to be defined and defended. In the effort to both conceptualize and legitimize this new intellectual practice, these philosophers invoked a specific civic institution: that which the ancients called "*theoria*." . . . The defining feature of *theoria* in its traditional forms is a journey to a region outside the boundaries of one's own city for the purpose of seeing a spectacle or witnessing another kind of object or event. This activity emphasizes "autopsy" or seeing something for oneself: the *theoros* is an eyewitness whose experience is radically different from those who stay home and receive a mere report of the news. (2001, 29, 33)[92]

---

91. "Such was the case of a man whose sight was faint and indistinct. He always saw an image in front of him and facing him as he walked. This was because his sight was reflected back to him. Its morbid condition made it so weak and delicate that the air close by acted as a mirror, just as distant and condensed air normally does, and his sight could not push it back" (trans. E. M. Webster). The story is repeated by Sen., *Q Nat.* 1.3.7. Of course, the ancients did appreciate that one could see much farther than one could smell or hear; cf. Varro, *Ling.* 6.80: "Oculorum sensus vis usque pervenit ad stellas."

92. See now her paradigm-building book *Spectacles of Truth in Classical Greek Philosophy: Theoria in Its Cultural Context* (2004).

Nightingale builds here on Hannah Arendt's observation in *Life of the Mind* that the philosophical term *theoria* was derived from the same root as *theatai*, "spectators."[93] Nightingale turns to the *Republic* and to the parable of the Cave in particular to elucidate the force of the theoric metaphor behind the idea of the philosopher's ascension to, and return from, metaphysical viewing: "Whereas the 'lovers of spectacles' go to festivals to enjoy beautiful dramas and rituals, the philosopher 'goes and beholds beauty itself (476b–c).' The philosopher, then, is a new kind of *theoros*: a man who travels to the metaphysical realm to see the sacred sights in that region" (2001, 36). So too Diogenes Laertius in the third century CE makes the link between this form of spectatorship and the practice of the philosophers: "Pythagoras compared life to a festival: just as some go to it to compete, some for buying and selling, but the best men go as spectators [*theatai*], so in life the slavish ones, he said, are by nature hunters of fame and gain, but the philosophers of truth" (*Lives* 8.8).[94]

If seeing becomes the predominant Platonic metaphor for understanding atemporal realities, then it is all the more natural that seeing oneself seeing should furnish an appropriate metaphor for a form of self-knowledge that also transcends the temporal in this same philosophy. Just as vision becomes the figural underpinning of the mind's approach toward transcendent truth, so too the idea of reflected vision in the *Alcibiades* I is introduced as a simile to aid the process of grasping equally transcendent truths about the self. We have here for the first time an explicit connection between the mirrored gaze and a form of self-knowledge that seems to rely on no human intervention in the closed circle of the gaze: a form of knowledge that focuses, in the end, on knowledge of the godlike qualities of the soul rather than on knowledge of one's limits and abilities, one's status in social life, or the expectations aroused by one's appearance.

To return to the *Alcibiades*, then, Socrates opens the dialogue—set in 432 BCE, when the eighteen-year-old Alcibiades was on the eve of his political debut

---

93. Arendt 1971, 93.

94. Nightingale emphasizes that this particular appropriation of *theoria* was not shared by Aristotle and others. Nonetheless, her exposition illuminates, on the one hand, the distinction between common and philosophical "viewing" and, on the other hand, the way that Plato's innovations had their foundation in cultural, temporal constructs of the viewing experience.

in Athens—by pointing out that he alone of Alcibiades' suitors has persevered. Alcibiades' other admirers have long since fled, cowed by the young man's conviction that he stands above all men in his beauty, power, and wealth. His perseverance, says Socrates, is due to the fact that only he can help Alcibiades achieve his political goals; and he now proceeds to ask Alcibiades why he is so convinced he will make the best possible adviser for the *demos*. After a discussion that demonstrates that Alcibiades does not have the understanding of justice necessary to lead the state, Socrates finally leads him to acknowledge that self-knowledge too is a requirement for good leadership (and a prerequisite to the care of the self). But how then *is* one to observe the injunction of the Delphic oracle to take oneself as an object of knowledge? The divine command to *gnothi sauton* seems to call for Socratic exegesis because it confusingly requires that the soul be both the source and the goal of introspection, the subject and object of the same act of inquiry (treated as problematic, as we have seen, in the *Charmides* and elsewhere).[95] Socrates responds to this difficulty by appealing to the faculty of vision as a model, and to mirroring in particular: "I'll tell you what I suspect that inscription means, and what advice it's giving us. There may not be many examples of it, except in the case of sight. . . . If the inscription took our eyes to be men and advised them, 'See thyself,' how would we understand such advice? Shouldn't the eye be looking at something in which it could see itself?" (132d; trans. D. S. Hutchinson).[96] When Alcibiades is asked what sort of object lets us see both it and ourselves when we look at it, he answers at first, "Obviously, Socrates, you mean mirrors and that sort of thing." But Socrates prompts him to think beyond this traditional tool for seeing the self, and suggests that the eye as well as the mirror can play this role: "I'm sure you've noticed that when a man looks into an eye [*opsis*] his face appears in it, like in a mirror. We call this the 'pupil' [*kore*], for it's a sort of miniature [*eidolon*] of the man who's looking. . . . Then an eye will see itself if it observes an eye and looks at the best part of it, the part with which it can see" (133a; trans. D. S. Hutchinson).[97]

---

95. The issue of reflexivity that Socrates addresses here is also taken up in the *Parmenides* and in Aristotle's *De anima*, and later in Plotinus; see Wilkins 1917, 72–73; and, on Plotinus, Rappe 1997, 433–51.

96. The last clause reads: ἆρα οὐχὶ εἰς τοῦτο βλέπειν, εἰς ὅ βλέπων ὁ ὀφθαλμὸς ἔμελλεν αὐτὸν ἰδεῖν.

97. On the Greek text here, see Pradeau 1999, ad loc.

From this extraordinary image of the eye looking at itself in the eye of the other, a revolutionary recipe for self-knowledge emerges.[98] The reflected gaze here does not show a man how he appears to others; instead—and much as earthly forms of vision are consistently superseded in the Platonic dialogues— the idea of reflection is to be taken as a metaphor to help in the acquisition of true self-knowledge, which is the "reflection" (the metaphor is still visual) of a soul in another soul. "Then if the soul, Alcibiades, is to know itself [gnosesthai hauten], it must look at a soul, and especially at that region in which what makes a soul good, wisdom, occurs, and at anything else which is similar to it" (133b; trans. D. S. Hutchinson). Socrates here defines self-knowledge as a kind of fig- ural mirroring, specifically that of the best part of the soul—wisdom—in the best part of another's soul.[99] The mirroring potential of the pupil has allowed Socrates to invoke reflected vision as a model for the practice of introspec- tion.[100] The metaphor clearly depends on the ease with which seeing assimilates itself to knowing in Greek philosophy, which, as I pointed out, is well attested in Plato and Aristotle.[101] The soul, after all, is not said to *think* via another soul, or to *understand* via another soul, but to *see* via another soul; that is, although the eye looking at the eye does what is natural to the eye—namely, look—the soul looking at the soul borrows the terminology not of the activity natural for souls but of that natural for eyes (for surely what is natural to a soul is not seeing).

But what does the soul "see" reflected in the soul? And how are we meant to "cash out" this metaphor of mirroring—that is, what does the metaphor bring to our understanding of self-knowledge? Jean-François Pradeau (1999, 72–81)

---

98. I am reading *opsis* in this passage as "pupil," as most interpreters of this passage take it to be. See Brunschwig 1973; and Pradeau 1999, ad loc.; cf. Arist., *Top.* 1.17, 108a11. "Eye," a more common usage, would only slightly alter the sense of the passage.

99. Note the cautions of Griswold 1986, 2–4: Platonic self-knowledge should not be confused with any kind of psychological (in our sense) knowledge; it is the knowledge of what the soul really desires and should move toward, and thus involves a connection to the Ideas.

100. See similarly Pliny, *HN* 11.55.148: "Parva illa pupilla totam imaginem reddat hominis." Also Alexander of Aphrodisias, *De sensu* 42.10. For a detailed analysis of the paradigm of vision in the *Alcibiades*, see Soulez-Luccioni 1974, 196–222. On the image in the pupil, see Bettini 1999, 217. On the mirror and erotic reciprocity in this dialogue, see Brenkman 1977, 428–34; Goldhill 1998, 105–24; and Halperin 1986, 69. In general see Annas 1985; Brunschwig 1973 and 1996; Forde 1987; Goldin 1993; and Pradeau 1999, 9–81.

101. See also Denyer 2001, 230: "*Rep.* 507c–d itself points out that no other sense could provide the rich and detailed model for knowledge that is developed at 507b–509c. Aristotle (*Ptp.* Fr. 7 Ross) argues that vision is the clearest of all our senses, and thus the sense that is most akin to knowl- edge; 'for by comparison with the others, it simply is a sort of knowledge.'"

has suggested that since the eye sees itself with *less* clarity in another eye than it would in a mirror, Plato here is emphasizing the necessity of the eye's looking not so much into a mirror as into *that which resembles itself* before true self-recognition can take place. Translated to the soul, this language (Pradeau suggests) means that what the soul sees in another soul—that is, the best part of that soul—is its capacity for reflection (as thought, or *sophia*); understanding that he too has this (divine) capacity for reflection/thought leads the searcher to know himself. Now, there is no doubt, as Julia Annas (1985) and Owen Goldin (1993) have argued, that what is seen in the soul of the other is not any manifestation of individuality in the sense of the soul's unique characteristics, but rather the (shared) divine component of it; as Pradeau himself points out, the presence of the individual other is not important except as a medium to see what is essential in oneself. However, there is a movement in his account between reflection-as-thought and reflection-as-mirroring that seems a problematic basis for his argument that both reflexivity/thought and reflexivity/mirroring are the abilities one sees reflected in the soul of the other (for example, "to know a reflected soul is to know the subject of reflection in every soul, [namely] the intellect that is like the divine" [78]). There is no support for this play on reflection in Greek terminology, where there is no coincidence between the distinct terms for reflection-as-mirroring and reflection-as-thought.[102]

A less speculative answer to the question seems to be that the soul merely comes to see via this act of mirroring that the soul (which is identified with the intellect) is divine. This may be most clear in the suspect lines that continue the last passage cited above, where the imagery of the two souls is discounted as Socrates pronounces that just as mirrors are clearer than the eye, so too God is more luminous than the best part of the soul; we should therefore use God himself as an even better mirror of the soul (*Alc.* 133c8–17).[103] But the lines immediately before this text specify just the same that "[t]hen that region in it [which deals with knowledge] resembles the divine, and someone who looked at that and grasped everything divine—vision and understanding—would have the

---

102. Cf. *anaklasis, anatheoresis, emphasis, ennoia*, etc.

103. The lines, apparently a sequence of glosses, only appear in Euseb., *Praep. Evang.* 9.5.8–16, and Stob., *Flor.* 3.21.24. On the issue of their authenticity, see Annas 1985, 131–32; Goldin 1998, 15, 15n14; Pradeau 1999, 221–27. Part of the argument hinges on the appearance of the word *enoptron* in these lines, which is never used by Plato elsewhere.

best grasp of himself as well."[104] As Goldin writes (1993, 15), "even if we reject the disputed lines, we still have the finest part of the soul, that which thinks, labeled 'divine,' considered knowable, and such that knowledge of it provides access to knowledge of God and φρόνησις." In other words, to know God is to know yourself, because your soul sees that it too (like the object of its gaze) resembles the divine. On this reading, self-knowledge turns out to be, not awareness of the capacity for self-reflection in the mirroring sense, but a knowledge of the best part of the soul: that it, rather than worldly goods or reputation, is to be identified with the self; that it is divine; and that it should be the ruling element—even if earlier in the dialogue self-knowledge was more traditionally linked to Alcibiades' need to understand the possible limitations to his ambitions and his self-esteem.[105] Most important, Plato innovates on the popularizing uses of the mirror but still retains the idea of mirroring in an external body (here another's soul) as a necessary component of any search for self-knowledge. The mirror itself may be gone, but it has been used as a stepping-stone to a process of coming to know the self that takes its impetus not from within, but from without.[106]

A final note: "The self itself" is the most common translation of the Greek term *auto to auto* at *Alcibiades* 129b and 130c–d.[107] However, as Christopher Gill has clearly demonstrated, such a translation relies on the importation into the Greek of concepts and terminology that are not present here, and that do not have any parallels in Platonic philosophy. Instead, Gill translates the phrase as: "Come now, how might *the itself itself* be discovered? In this way we could

---

104. Τῷ θεῷ ἄρα τοῦτ᾽ ἔοικεν αὐτῆς, καί τις εἰς τοῦτο βλέπων καὶ πᾶν τὸ θεῖον γνούς, θεόν τε καὶ φρόνησιν, οὕτω καὶ ἑαυτὸν ἂν γνοίη μάλιστα.

105. Such a development is supported by the observation of Long 2001, 29: "*Sophrosyne* is often translated by self-control. But that translation anticipates the very idea that Plato in the *Gorgias* was probably the first to formulate explicitly—the difficult idea of conceptualizing the self in terms of a ruling principle (reason) and a set of otherwise unruly parts." On likeness to God in the Platonic dialogues, see Long 2001, 20–21, with bibliography in note 4; see also *Tht.* 176a; *Ti.* 90b–d; *Resp.* 10.613a.

106. Denyer (2001, 233) would agree: "Self-knowledge is gained, not by any inward-looking self-absorption, but by casting the mind outward." However, the outward gaze does not depend for its enlightenment on the view of the other; as Brunschwig (1996, 76) is correct to stress, the self that one comes to know is an *impersonalized* self.

107. See Allen 1962 and Annas 1985. Similarly, Pradeau (1999, 210–11) argues that the expression points to Plato's conversion of a reflexive pronoun into a substantive, the self. The discussion of the *Alcibiades* I in Foucault (2001, 32–40, 43–46, 49–54) takes *auto to auto* to mean "le soi-même soi-même," thereby falling into the same error. See similarly Foucault 1988. D. S. Hutchinson (the translator quoted above), however, translates this as "what 'itself' is, in itself."

perhaps discover what we ourselves are, but if we don't know this we never could" (129b).[108] As Gill notes, the unusual usage *auto to auto* underlines the question to hand, namely, what it means to characterize something as "itself" or in its essence; it "does not have a specifically psychological sense but simply conveys the general idea of 'the itself itself,' though that idea is raised here in connection with the idea that the psyche is 'what we ourselves are.'" It is not the "self itself" that we should focus on in our interpretation of this passage, but the soul (*psyche*) which, as Socrates says, can "see" (come to understand) itself.[109] Despite the clear reflexivity of this usage, then, there is no basis for reading into it any invocation of a "self" in its modern sense, nor is it the *fact* of this reflexivity that leads to an understanding of what we really are; reflexivity here is just a means. We are left with a definition of self-knowledge that cannot be pushed further than the soul's recognition that it is divine.

Significantly, the kind of mirroring that takes place here might be designated as vertical rather than horizontal: what it shows back to the viewer is the godlike quality of his own soul, rather than any social truth about himself or his visual partner. As Brunschwig (1999, 76) observes, "one provides oneself with the means of finally knowing oneself in a relationship which no longer has any symmetry in it, a relationship with a God whom one would not dream of asking to 'know' the soul which knows itself in him—any more than one would dream of asking a mirror to see the eye that sees itself in it." Contrast to this Aristotle's notion that one needs a friend for self-knowledge, because one can see one's own faults in a friend, and one can thereby stop indulging in them oneself.[110] This is a notion shared by the author of the *Magna moralia*, who remarks,

---

108. In Gill (forthcoming). Denyer (2001, ad loc.) suggests the same translation. The passage in Greek reads: Φέρε δή, τίν' ἂν τρόπον εὑρεθείη αὐτὸ ταὐτό; οὕτω μὲν γὰρ ἂν τάχ' εὕροιμεν τί ποτ' ἐσμὲν αὐτοί, τούτου δ' ἔτι ὄντες ἐν ἀγνοίᾳ ἀδύνατοί που. The similar usage at Alc. 130d reads: Ὁ ἄρτι οὕτω πως ἐρρήθη, ὅτι πρῶτον σκεπτέον εἴη αὐτὸ τὸ αὐτό.

109. This suggested reading finds different emphases in these passages from those supported by either Annas (1985) or Forde (1987), but is not exclusive of those interpretations. Forde, however, argues that what one sees in the eye of the other is not only the image of one's eye but of one's face and body as well (132e–133a). Accordingly, self-knowledge should likewise "include knowledge of how the parts of oneself, of soul and body and the parts of the soul within itself, are properly ordered around the rational center of the soul. . . . Self-knowledge seems to provide the avenue at least to knowledge of one's proper relations to 'possessions' more remote than one's body" (236).

110. One formulation of this idea appears in Schuller (1989, 11), who remarks that the mirror of self-knowledge "is part of the complex realm in which the individual meets the other: it is an instrument for the social inspection of the self. . . . [It is] not so much a metaphor for the mind as a simile for 'the other.'"

For it is the most difficult thing, as some of the wise have said, to know one-self, and also the most pleasant (for self-knowledge is pleasant). Yet we are not able to see ourselves from within ourselves (the fact that we cannot do so is clear because we criticize others for things that we do not notice when we do the same things ourselves. This happens through good will or passion; and this blinds many of us with regard to correct judgment). Just as, therefore, whenever we want to see our own face, we look at it by gazing into a mirror, in the same way, whenever we want to know ourselves, we can do by looking at a friend. For a friend, as we say, is a second "I." (2.15.1213a)

A. W. Price (1989, 122) suggests, of a similar concept in the *Eudemian Ethics*, that the presence of shared choice and action with a friend of similar character means for the viewing other that he thus becomes "explicitly aware of [himself] not just abstractly as an agent, but as an agent with a certain character, thereby achieving not a bare self-consciousness but a real self-knowledge." In other words, the friend in these texts plays the role of the (social) mirror elsewhere, aiding in the acquisition of *sophrosyne* by the elimination of unbecoming behaviors, a process linked with self-knowledge.[111]

How should we interpret the working of the Platonic "mirror" of the *Alcibiades* I in contrast to the other mirrors, literal and figural, into which we have been looking? First, we should remark that here literal mirroring (of the eye by the eye) does *not* promote self-knowledge: it serves instead as a simile, and the proper function of the mirror, to reflect accurately, is rejected in favor of the function of a less effective mirror (the pupil), which itself is only a conceptual stepping-stone to a different idea altogether. Nor does it seem likely that the Socrates we know would point to the values and norms of his society—for which the mirror usually stands—to provide a model of behavior to his interlocutors.[112] Second, the place of the friend-as-mirror has been

---

111. Aristotle treats the topic of the friend as a second self at *Eth. Nic.* 1169b–1170b and *Eth. Eud.* 1244b–1245a, passages that have generated much scholarship and whose philosophical intricacies are well treated in Price 1989, especially 120–24. See also Courcelle 1975, 21; and Wilkins 1917, 83–85. Aristotle's accounts are unique in stressing knowledge of our virtues rather than our faults. For the more traditional idea, see, e.g., Aesch., *Ag.* 839; Catull., *Carm.* 22.20–21; Cic., *Amic.* 23; Hor., *Sat.* 1.3.22–23, 2.3.298–99; Phaedrus, 4.9; Sen., *Vit. Beat.* 7.4–6; Plut., *De inim. util.* 5.

112. Napolitano Valditara (1994) sums up some of the themes of this chapter when she divides optical knowledge into two species, "etico-sociale" and "gnoseologico." But she would argue against

set aside in favor of a vertical form of mirroring in the divine—again a move away from the social norms of Plato's Athens. Third, this process of coming to know the soul may reflect on Socrates' famous claim to know nothing besides the fact of his knowing nothing; Socrates' function in the dialogues can be described as providing a "mirror" for his interlocutors, but one that does not possess any "content" of its own; it simply provides access to the divine.[113]

These formulations of the role of the mirror in antiquity, whether popular or Platonic, should prevent us from making a precipitous leap to any idea that self-mirroring, as described here, leads to any form of self-knowledge that we might recognize as the individual coming to terms with his or her uniqueness and individuality, or that the Greco-Roman mirror has much to do with the Cartesian idea of the mind turned upon itself, self-transparent, self-available for contemplation in its entirety. These texts, then, must throw doubt upon Willard McCarty's claim (1989, 166), in an otherwise excellent article, that "the use of mirroring to represent cognition itself, which we still call 'reflection,' was well established in classical times," a claim that seems to borrow from the modern notion of reflection rather than the ancient.[114] As Donald Verene (1997, 51–52) remarks:

---

the scholarly tendency to see the latter as Plato's main concern while the former typifies man's relationship with fellow man; for her, both come together under the heading of *metis*.

113. Griswold (1986, 28–29) argues that the Socrates of the *Phaedrus* acts out with mimetic irony the very flaws that hold back the young Phaedrus from self-knowledge: Socrates constructs a drama that "functions as a mirror in which Phaedrus is made to detach himself from himself and so observe himself." When Socrates professes intense desire to hear Phaedrus read Lysias' speech, for example, it is after being sarcastic about that same speech: he now imitates the gushing Phaedrus "in such a way as to both hold up the mirror to Phaedrus and show Phaedrus what he (Phaedrus) should look like." This analysis focuses on behavioral rather than ideational self-knowledge, which suggests that the innovations of the *Alcibiades* I did not preclude invocations of more traditional mirror usages elsewhere in Plato.

114. McCarty cites in defense of his claim four classical (pagan) passages, of which only one need detain us at any length. This is *Ti.* 71b–72d, in which we are told that the liver was made smooth and polished in order that it might reflect images, like a mirror. The liver's ability to receive images upon its surface renders it ideal for mantic purposes, and McCarty would suggest thus that it is "the inner mirror by which the mind perceives its own possibilities and prophesies in dreams what is to come" (1989, 166n9). But as the liver emphatically does *not* take part in *logos* or *phronesis* (*Ti.* 71d), its naturally prophetic capacity has nothing to do with the Cartesian "mirror of the mind." Note that although Gasché (1986, 43) claims that Cicero derives *speculatio* from *specularis*, I have not been able to substantiate this claim in Cicero's writing.

There is no cognate term in ancient Greek for the modern sense of *reflection* as a philosophical and psychological term. Image in the sense of *eidolon* or *eikon*, and *phantasia* as a power associated with images, is the subject of discussion in Greek philosophy, as are the physical phenomena of mirrors, the reflection of light, and the visual perception of objects. . . . As a classical Latin term, *reflectere* carries no meaning of the mind thinking itself. The philosophical meaning of reflection enters modern languages from late Latin.

Even the Platonic (or pseudo-Platonic) treatment in the *Alcibiades*, which borrows common cultural concepts and forces them into new uses, does not take us anywhere near an understanding of self-knowledge that puts any emphasis on "the individual" or on the role of unmediated reflexivity/self-thought per se in that understanding.

Where do the texts examined in this chapter leave us? For one, it is clear that the ancient mirror presents us with a paradox: it represents two remarkably contradictory strains of thought about the function of self-reflection, on the one hand as a tool for self-improvement, and on the other, as a sign of vanity, profligacy, and even emasculation.[115] This is true even of its metaphorical rather than literal usages, where the mirror is still the subject of a play of binary oppositions pointing to the beneficial or detrimental effect of the reflected image.[116] A third invocation of the mirror, extracted from the Platonic *Alcibiades* I, introduces the idea of reflection as an impersonal way for us to "see" the divine in all of us.[117] This notion will return in chapters 4 and 5 of this book, where it will serve as a necessary *comparandum* to Seneca's rethinking of the Platonic criteria for self-knowledge and his radical appropriation of

---

115. As Hubert Cancik remarks, "The mirror of knowledge is the mirror of vanity" (1967, 43).

116. These binary oppositions are nicely evoked by the treatment in Frontisi-Ducroux and Vernant (1997, 155–76), which covers "oneself and the other," "likeness and difference," "truth and falsehood," "positive and negative," "active and passive," "surface and depth," "shadow and light," and "seeing more, seeing less." On the catoptric metaphor in general, see Frontisi-Ducroux and Vernant 1997, 112–32; Jonsson 1995, 64–71; McCarty 1989.

117. I have often termed this usage "philosophical" in this chapter. This is not to be confused with "Platonic," but rather refers to a kind of popular ethics represented by figures from the Seven Sages onward.

self-splitting and self-speculation as the foundation of the ethical self. The first two strands of the tradition treated in this chapter, however, lead us straight into the material to which we now turn: a group of texts that show us how Roman elites took up and transformed the twin notions of specular self-improvement and specular self-emasculation in ways shaped by their own goals and prejudices.

2   The Eye of the Lover

When the Greek poet Sappho describes her physiological response to the sight of the person she loves—the trembling, the desire—her language makes intuitive sense to her modern readers, familiar as we are with the notion that the beauty of the loved one might have such an impact.[1] Similarly, when the Roman poet Propertius begins his first book of elegies with an emphasis on his "capture" by the eyes of his mistress, Cynthia, it does not seem strange to us that the power of her erotic gaze might weaken his knees.[2] But when the later novelist Achilles Tatius, penning his risqué work *Clitophon and Leucippe* in the second century CE, offers an explanation as to *why* gazing at the object of one's desire is so affecting, even the most intrepid oglers among us might have cause to balk. Viewing, it seems, is as physical and as intimate a process as its close cousin, sexual consummation: "Doing this is more pleasurable than actual consummation. For the eyes, mutually reflecting each other, receive *simulacra* of the body as in mirrors. This outward emanation of beauty, which flows

---

1. I refer, of course, to Sappho 31. Here see the suggestive work of duBois 1998.
2. On the erotic gaze in Roman elegy, see, e.g., Fredrick 1997; Greene 1995b; Greene 1998, 67–92; Hubbard 1984; and Raucci 2004.

through the eyes into the soul, is a kind of copulation between separated bodies, and it is not far from physical sex" (*C&L* 1.9.4–5).[3] This is the advice of the young Cleinias, offering consolation to his lovesick friend Clitophon: as if taking his cue from the *Alcibiades* I, Cleinias finds a path not to wisdom but to titillation from the reflection of one lover's eyes in the eyes of the other.[4] But this Cleinias is not, as we might suspect, a propounder of idiosyncrasies or a heretic of romantic love. On the contrary, the notion of the erotic penetration of the body by corpuscular bodies entering in through the eyes proves a remarkably consistent ancient paradigm for the workings of the gaze upon the soul and, as we shall see, has a distinguished heritage long before the second century CE.

In this discourse of love, the mirrored gaze thus has a role to play beyond the philosophical. We have already seen something of the erotic force of the mirror as an instrument: owning a mirror or using one carried with it a set of associations and assumptions that were hardly gender-neutral, and the mirror itself was a thing of vanity and *voluptas*. But in reflecting the desiring gaze back at the viewer, the mirror—and the mirroring eye, and even the still surface of a pond—entered into an visual exchange that effected physical changes in the body itself. The discourse of eros thus participated in a symbiotic relationship with another field of discourse altogether, that of ancient optical theory. I do not propose to inquire into the "chicken and the egg" question of causality— whether cultural beliefs about the permeability of the eye as a pathway into the body influenced scientific explanations about the workings of vision, or vice versa. But a consideration of ancient optics should illuminate Cleinias' odd (for us) disquisition and should illustrate, in so doing, why we may well be wrong to feel recognition at the visual language of ancient lovers—and perhaps even of ancient philosophers.

ANCIENT OPTICS

Sight, as Hans Jonas (1982) suggested, seems to us the most neutral and the most detached of all the senses: innocent of causality, boundless in its scope,

---

3. μείζονα τῶν ἔργων ἔχει τὴν ἡδονήν. ὀφθαλμοὶ γὰρ ἀλλήλοις ἀντανακλώμενοι ἀπομάττουσιν ὡς ἐν κατόπτρῳ τῶν σωμάτων τὰ εἴδωλα· ἡ δὲ τοῦ κάλλους ἀπορροή, δι' αὐτῶν εἰς τὴν ψυχὴν καταρρέουσα, ἔχει τινὰ μίξιν ἐν ἀποστάσει· καὶ ὀλίγον ἐστὶ τῆς τῶν σωμάτων μίξεως.

4. As Denyer (2001, 229) comments of the relevant passage in the *Alcibiades*, "Glaringly absent . . . is explicit mention of how erotic are looks from, or into, someone's eyes."

synchronous rather than diachronous in its workings. And yet this perspective has little to do with the understanding of the visual process in antiquity. Almost all the ancient schools of thought about optics, from the atomists to Plato, Euclid, and Ptolemy, put an emphasis on the tactile nature of sight, and several of them talk specifically in terms of penetration and touching in language that is literal, not metaphorical. For the purposes of this study, we can divide these major theories into five schools (intromission, extramission, Platonic, Aristotelian, Stoic), although such a grouping remains a slightly crude way of dealing with internal subdivisions and overlaps and with longstanding debates, both in antiquity and in the present, about the differences and simi-larities between the various schools of thought.[5] Many ancient thinkers them-selves chose to boil down the fine distinctions between these schools to a notion that vision simply involved a form of contact between the organ of sight and its object; as Galen would write of the two alternatives in the second century CE, "A body that is seen does one of two things: either it sends some-thing from itself to us and thereby gives an indication of its peculiar character, or, if it does not itself send something, it waits for some sensory power to come to it from us."[6]

These categories—the eye as active or passive participant in the process of seeing—shaped the debate about vision in general; the latter is associated with the ancient atomists and Epicurus, the former with a slew of theories extend-ing into the Middle Ages. Intromission theory, at least in its explication by Epicurus and Lucretius, held that objects emit tiny particles (in Greek, *eidola*; in Latin, *simulacra*) in the form of a film that retains the shape of the object. These *simulacra* impress themselves on the surface of the eye and then (by some accounts) enter in through the eyes and strike the soul, resulting in "seeing."[7] The theory is associated with the thinking of the atomists Leucippus of Miletus

---

5. For general treatments of ancient theories of sight and their reception, see Lindberg 1976, Park 1997, Rakoczy 1996, Simon 1988, and van Hoorn 1972.

6. Lindberg (1976, 219n59), citing *De placitis Hippocratis et Platonis* 7.5, trans. Philip De Lacy (Berlin: Akademie-Verlag, 1978–84), vol. 5, no. 4. See also Theophr., *De sensu* 7.6–10 on these alter-natives, with emphasis on the media that make them possible. Galen rejected the intromissive option, citing the impossibility of thereby seeing a mountain, which would have to shrink in order to fit into the pupil, and which also could not be seen by several viewers at once.

7. On intromission theory, see Baldes 1975; Burkert 1977; Jonsson 1995, 49–50; Lindberg 1976, 2–3; Rakoczy 1996, 25–28; Simon 1987; Simon 1988, 36–41; van Hoorn 1972, 49–57; and von Fritz 1953.

and his student Democritus, of whose work only fragments survive, often in hostile accounts; later, intromission is famously explained by Lucretius in book 4 of the *De rerum natura* and forms an important part of his accounts of erotic stimulation during sleep as well.

Crucial to our purpose here is that these films, or *simulacra*, emitted by objects were conceived of as corpuscular. This is clear in Epicurus' concise summary, in the *Letter to Herodotus*, of the views attributed to Democritus:

> For particles are continually streaming off from the surface of bodies, though no diminution of the bodies is observed, because other particles take their place. And those given off for a long time retain the position and arrangement which their atoms had when they formed part of the solid bodies, although occasionally they are thrown into confusion. . . . We must also consider that it is by the entrance of something coming from external objects that we see their shapes and think of them. For external things would not stamp on us their own nature of color and form through the medium of the air which is between them and us, or by means of rays of light or currents of any sort going from us to them, so well as by the entrance into our eyes or minds, to whichever their size is suitable, of films coming from the things themselves, these films or out-lines being of the same color and shape as the external things themselves. (Diog. Laert., *Lives* 10.48–49, trans. R. D. Hicks)

Even more explicitly, Aristotle criticizes Democritus for reducing all sensation to touch (*De sensu* 4.442a–b), while Lucretius would use a series of similes from nature to underscore the bodily character of these effluences:

> In the open, many things
> emit bodies [*mittunt corpora*]: some loosely diffused,
> the way wood gives off smoke and fire heat,
> and others more close-knit and condensed, as when
> cicadas put down their smooth skins in the summer,
> and when calves at birth discard the caul
> from their bodies' surface, and also when the slippery serpent
> sloughs off his skin among the thorns.
> (Lucr. 4.54–61)

As van Hoorn (1972, 52) comments, "Simple as the theory may sound, it is entirely consistent with the basic principle of atomic materialism, namely, that all perception is due to direct physical contact between perceiver and object perceived."

The atomist belief that these *simulacra* retained the shape of the original, as Epicurus notes, seems firmly established. When Lucretius invokes mirrors (4.98–109), he does so precisely to prove this theory, since the object's shape in the mirror is identical to the original. Alexander of Aphrodisias writes that Leucippus and Democritus "attributed sight to certain images of the same shape as the object, which were continually streaming off from the objects of sight and impinging on the eye" (Diels-Kranz, Leucippus A29–30). The further issues of whether these *simulacra* actually penetrated the eye or stopped after impressing themselves on its surface had ancient adherents and critics on each side. Epicurus' reference to things entering the eyes and mind supports a penetrative model, as does the account of Aetius (c. second century CE).[8] In contrast, Theophrastus in *De sensu* 50–55 problematizes this representation of the Democritean position by attesting to a more complicated original view that seems to have focused on air-imprints (*deikela*) rather than *simulacra*; on this account, these imprints (*emphases*) derive their shape from the efflux off the object and also from light (whose effect is to condense the air as well as to transport it), and the eye receives their effect and passes it to the soul.[9] This version in turn contradicts the account of Aristotle, *De An.* 419a, which treats air as an obstacle for atomist vision, while Theoprastus sees it as the enabler.[10] Further, even this most passive of theories seems to have attributed some form

---

8. See Lindberg 1976, 2.

9. Theophrastus' explanation of Democritus' view is that "the visual image does not arise directly in the pupil, but the air between the eye and the object of sight is contracted and stamped by the object seen and the seer; for from everything there is always a sort of effluence proceeding. So this air, which is solid and variously colored, appears in the eye." This, however, need not concern us too much; whatever Democritus really thought, it is the *reception* of Democritus' views that will prove significant here, especially the influence of Epicurus' version in the first and second centuries CE. For another second-century witness, see Bychkov (1999, 341) on Diogenes of Oenoanda, whose theories closely match those of Epicurus.

10. On the inconsistencies between Theophrastus' account of Democritus and other testimonia, see Burkert 1977, 102–9. For an attempt to resolve these differences without positing that Democritus held two theories of vision, see Baldes 1975.

of activity to "that which sees."[11] And in general, the obscurities of the atomist position caused several ancient critics to protest with worthy questions:
why don't we see the back of the object? And how could *simulacra* streaming off, say, a mountain, fit into my eye?[12]

Extramission theory, which seems to have been held in some form by Hero
(fl. 62 CE), Theon of Alexandria, and others, is similarly tactile, although here
the issue is not one of the entrance of *simulacra* via the eyes, but rather of
emanations *from* the eyes.[13] This theory was undoubtedly influenced by the
views of Empedocles and the Pythagoreans, who perceived the eye as an active
agent that emitted rays or a visual current toward the object of perception.[14]
Euclid based his work on optics on this assumption; although mostly geomet-
ric in its emphasis, this science too allowed for a tactile understanding of the
visual rays emitted by the eyes.[15] As David Lindberg (1976, 14–15) notes, "Hero,
like Euclid, could not avoid making statements with physical implications. . . .
He revealed his belief in the material nature of visual rays in his account of the
cause of reflection, pointing out that visual rays incident on unpolished mirrors
enter the porosities of the bodies and are not reflected. However, 'if these mirrors are polished by rubbing until the porosities are filled by a fine substance,
then the rays incident upon the compact surface are reflected.'" Hero follows up
with the analogy of a stone hurled against a wall or a soft body; in the former
case it rebounds, in the latter not. More graphic still is Hipparchus' comparison
of vision to a hand: "Hipparchus says that the rays from each of the eyes,
extended out to their limits as with the touch of the hands, grasp external bodies and return an apprehension of them to the sense of sight."[16] These "rays,"

---

11. Burkert (1977, 99) comments: "The third factor, some activity of 'that which sees' has
seemed to be suspiciously close to Plato's theory of the active eye; some tried to eliminate it by
altering the text. But the alternative or receptiveness or activity of the eye is not treated by the
Presocratics as strictly exclusive; Aristotle already blamed Empedocles for using 'effluxes' of the
objects and still comparing the eye to a lantern. . . . And Democritus explained the fact that owls
see at night by invoking the 'fire' in their eyes." See Arist., *Sens.* 2.6.437b–438a on Empedocles
(= Diels-Kranz B84); also Democritus (Diels-Kranz A157). Contra, however, see Baldes 1975.

12. See, e.g., Theophr., *Sens.* 53, Alexander, *Mantissa* 134–35.

13. See Jonsson 1995, 18–25; Lindberg 1976, 14–15; Simon 1988, 21–41, 57–82; van Hoorn 1972, 43–48.

14. For Empedocles' description of the eye as an emitter of light, see Diels-Kranz 1B.84.

15. For a more detailed account of Euclid's *Optics* and *Elements*, see Berryman 1998.

16. Ἵππαρχος δέ φησιν ἀκτῖνας ἀπὸ τῶν ὀφθαλμῶν ἀποτεινομένας τοῖς πέρασιν ἑαυτῶν
καθάπερ χειρῶν ἐπαφαῖς καθαπτούσας τοῖς ἐκτὸς σώμασι τὴν ἀντίληψιν αὐτῶν πρὸς τὸ ὁρατικὸν
ἀναδιδόναι. Aetius 4.13.8–12 in Diels 1965, 404. For bibliography on the nonmetaphorical character of Euclid's tactile language, see Lindberg 1976, 220n81.

then, should not be confused with their modern counterparts; they are not light rays, but forms of an emission—despite the occasional image of lightning from the eye as responsible for the birth of eros (see, for example, Soph., Fr. 474 Radt).

As for the Platonic view, it seems that Plato too drew from the theories of Empedocles and the Pythagorean school.[17] Like Empedocles, Plato offered a view that incorporated elements from both extramission and intromission, according to which a stream of light from the observer's eye combines with daylight and with an emanation from the object to produce "vision."[18] The *Timaeus* offers the best summary of this process:

> Now the pure fire inside us, cousin to that fire, [the gods] made to flow through the eyes: so they made the eyes—the eye as a whole but its middle in particular—close-textured, smooth and dense, to enable them to keep out all the other, coarser stuff, and let that kind of fire pass through pure by itself. Now whenever daylight surrounds the visual stream, like makes contact with like and coalesces with it to make up a single homogeneous body aligned with the direction of the eyes. This happens wherever the internal fire strikes and presses against an external object it has connected with. And because this body of fire has become uniform throughout and thus uniformly affected, it transmits the motions of whatever it comes in contact with as well as of whatever comes in contact with it, to and through the whole body until they reach the soul. This brings about the sensation we call "seeing." (*Ti.* 45b–d; trans. Donald J. Zeyl)

In this account too, tactile language is used to describe the temporary mingling of the internal fire from the eyes and the external daylight; these two form a body that touches (*ephaptetai*) objects at a distance. When the discussion of color enters the picture, it becomes clear that a kind of emanation from the

---

17. See Lindberg 1976, 3–6; and van Hoorn 1972, 43–48. On Platonic *aesthesis* as a noncognitive activity, see Silverman 1990.

18. On the confused account of Theophrastus (*De sensu* 26, Diels-Kranz A5), which may suggest that Alcmaeon of Croton incorporated emission theory into a theory of papillary images, see Lindberg 1976, 3–4. It also appears that Empedocles used the term *eidolon*, like Democritus, to describe a corpuscular emission from the object of vision, making both the eye and this object active participants in the process of viewing, but, unlike Plato, not stressing the role of daylight. For a good summary of the various views, with special attention to the skeptical critique of Euclid, see Berryman 1998.

object must play a part, since the color itself is described as a kind of fire and "an effluvium from shapes" (*Meno* 76d).[19]

Aristotle, in contrast, sometimes denies any analogy to touch. He identifies light as the medium between eye and object that bears the responsibility for enabling sight; because the pupil consists of water, and water and light share the quality of being a translucent medium, light can pass on its altered affect to the perceptive center within the eye (*Sens.* 2.438a–b).[20] Yet there are significant contradictions between these views expressed in *De anima* and *De sensu*, and several of Aristotle's other works. In the *De insomnis* 2.459b–460a, for example, he defines seeing as not only experiencing something inflicted by air, but also acting on it, a point he illustrates with a famously peculiar explanation involving menstruation: "It is clear from [the case of mirrors] that just as the eyes are acted upon, so too they do something. For in very clear mirrors, whenever menstruating women look into the mirror, the surface of the mirror becomes like a bloody cloud. . . . The reason is that, as I have said, the eyes are not only acted upon in some respect by air, but they also do something and move it."[21] In the *Meteorologica*, Aristotle systematically uses the theory of the extramission of visual rays; we have already seen the example of the man whose visual rays are rebounded back toward him by the air, and other examples occur at *Mete.* 2.9.370a–374b.[22] Accordingly, it seems mostly likely that, as Rakoczy (1996, 28–31) has argued, Aristotle simply fell back on traditional explanations of sight when he was not explicitly developing his own theories on the science of vision.[23]

---

19. ἔστιν γὰρ χρόα ἀπορροὴ σχημάτων ὄψει σύμμετρος καὶ αἰσθητός. See similarly at *Tht.* 156d–e, and, on the role of light, *Resp.* 6.507d–508c.

20. In this process, color plays a crucial part: "There is thus a continuous medium, the transparent, from the visible object all the way to the interior of the eye. The color of the visible object moves the medium, and the medium, 'being continuous, acts upon the sense organ'" (Lindberg 1976, 8). On the shared translucency of light and water, see similarly *De An.* 2.7.418b.

21. The elder Pliny voices a similar view in *HN* 7.64, saying that menstruating women dull mirrors. On this passage, see also Bettini 1999, 113–15.

22. All these observations rely on assumptions about the visual process that he has explicitly denied, and the ancient commentators themselves found cause to complain about his discrepancies, such as Alexander, *Mantissa* 136.30–138.2. On the apparent self-contradictions in Aristotle's treatment, see Lindberg 1976, 217–18; Rakoczy 1996, 134–40; and Simon 1988, 48–52.

23. Aristotle's novel views are taken up by his student Theophrastus, but otherwise seem to have had little influence during the classical period, especially compared with the powerful influence of the various forms of emissionist theory. For example, in Priscian's summary of Theophrastus' *De sensu*, we see the same treatment of the transparent as the crucial intra- and extra-ocular medium of vision (7.26–8.29), but we also see the same slippage into the language of activity and being-acted-upon, 5.21–6.16.

Where do the Stoics fit in all this? Are their views similarly tactile in nature? Our main sources are the peripatetic philosopher Alexander of Aphrodisias (early third century CE) and Aetius (second century CE?), about whom little is known; their testimonia and others are collected in von Arnim's *Stoicorum veterum fragmenta* (1964, 2:863–72).[24] According to these accounts, the Stoics ascribed vision to the *synentasis* (a stretching and tautening; Latin *intentio*) of the spirit or *pneuma* emitted by the eyes.[25] This visual *pneuma* extends from the pupil of the eye in a cone-shaped form with its base at the object of vision and the apex at the eye itself. Sight occurs when the *pneuma* strikes the mind, with which it has internal contact from the eye inward; in a striking—perhaps I should say stunning—simile, Chalcidius (*ad Timaeum* 237, *SVF* 2.863) compares the entire experience to that of someone who has been paralyzed by the touch of the torpedo-fish, whose effect travels up the fishing pole and penetrates through the body to one innermost sense.[26] Such imagery of a stick or rod (*bacteria*) is invoked several times to describe the working of the external *pneuma* that makes contact with the object: as Alexander writes, "There are some who say that seeing takes place through the *synentasis* of the air. For the air touching the pupil, being impinged upon by vision, takes shape into a cone. When this cone has been as it were stamped on its base by the visible objects, perception occurs, just as it does via actual touch, by means of a rod" (*De anima libri mant.* 130.14–17 Bruns, *SVF* 2.864).[27] The visual *pneuma*, then, creates the *synentasis* by its action upon the air and makes a cone-shaped extension that is compared to a stick.[28] This tensed air, when illuminated by the sun, makes contact with the object.[29] It sends the information necessary for seeing back to the *hegemonikon* (the governing part of the soul in Stoic philosophy), from which

---

24. On the Stoic theories of vision, see Gourinat 1996, 37–45; Ingenkamp 1971; Lindberg 1976, 9–10; Rakoczy 1996, 31; Simon 1988, 33–34; Todd 1974; Voelke 1973, 41–42.

25. This process is prior to the formation of *phantasia* by a stamping of the image on the soul. On Stoic *phantasia*, see especially Sandbach 1971, Watson 1988 and 1994.

26. "Similisque eius passio est eorum, qui marini piscis contagione torpent, siquidem per linum et harundinem perque manus serpat virus illud penetratque intimum sensum."

27. Εἰσὶν δέ τινες, οἳ διὰ τῆς τοῦ ἀέρος συνεντάσεως τὸ ὁρᾶν φασι γίνεσθαι. νυττόμενον γὰρ ὑπὸ τῆς ὄψεως τὸν συνάπτοντα τῇ κόρῃ ἀέρα σχηματίζεσθαι εἰς κῶνον. τούτου δὲ οἷον τυπουμένου κατὰ τὴν βάσιν ὑπὸ τῶν ὁρατῶν τὴν αἴσθησιν γίνεσθαι, καθάπερ καὶ τῇ ἀφῇ διὰ βακτηρίας.

28. Mentioned in three separate sources: Diog. Laert., *Lives*; Galen, *Plac. Hipp. et Plat.*; Alex. Aphr., *De an. libri mant.*

29. The role given to sunlight in the *synentasis* of the *pneuma* is treated by none of these sources; see Todd 1974 for details.

it has its physical origin.[30] Such is the view attributed to Chrysippus himself by, among others, Aetius (*SVF* 2.866): "Chrysippus says that we see via the *synentasis* of the air between [us and the object]; which air, being impinged upon by the optic *pneuma* (which extends from the *hegemonikon* up to the pupil), which stretches the air like a cone in accordance with the assault on the ambient air, whenever the air should be homogeneous. The fiery rays pour out from the organ of sight, not black and cloudy. Hence darkness is visible."[31]

The language of rays (*aktines*) used here by Aetius sounds suspiciously akin to the terminology of emission theory. A similar "contamination" is evident in other Roman imperial sources, in which Stoic theories of vision tend to be likewise interpreted with reference to rays emitted by the eyes. In the second century CE, for example, Aulus Gellius writes that "[t]he Stoics say that the causes of seeing are the emission of rays from the eyes onto visible objects and at the same time the intention of the air" (*NA* 5.16.2).[32] A century earlier, Seneca purported to be summarizing Aristotle's views when he wrote that "eyesight reflects its own rays from every smooth surface" and related once again the story of the man who saw his own mirror-image in front of himself: his weak vision could not penetrate the air in front of him (*Q Nat.* 1.3.7).[33] In a further example of the general valence of emissive theories of vision, Cicero too would endorse extramission theory. In his view, that we see clearly when we look through a narrow aperture works against the idea of intromission, since film of *eidola* coming off any object on the other side would be damaged if such an explanation of vision were true (*Att.* 2.3.2).[34] And we have already seen the ambiguous language of Seneca's contemporary, Hero, whose Euclidean perspective is nonetheless shot through with the tactile language of ocular emissions. Even Galen, with whom we began, would try to reconcile Stoic *pneuma* with the Aristotelian view in his own work—a syncretism typical of the period.[35]

---

30. Ingenkamp (1971) explores some of the complications here.

31. Aëtius, *Plac.* IV.15.3 (Diels 1965, p. 406, 4). For similar testimonia, see Galen, *Plac. Hipp. et Plat.* 7 (*SVF* 2.865); Diog. Laert., *Lives* 7.157 (*SVF* 2.867); Alex. Aphr., *De an. Libri mant.* 131.30 Bruns (*SVF* 2.868).

32. "Stoici causas esse uidendi dicunt radiorum ex oculis in ea, quae uideri queunt, emissionem aerisque simul intentionem."

33. "Ab omni, inquit, levitate acies radios suos replicat."

34. On this passage, see Keyser 1993.

35. Ingenkamp (1971) would argue that later understandings of Stoic teachings on vision are due to a misunderstanding on the part of Aetius and others who speak in terms similar to emis-

It bears repeating that the idea of an emission from the eyes as the source of vision, or, slightly less often, the idea that the eye is impinged upon by films of *simulacra* coming off the visible object, seems to have been far more influential in this period than the nontactile theories of Aristotle, however great his later impact within the history of optics. We have already seen Galen's simplification in *De placitis Hippocratis et Platonis* 7.5. Also in the first century CE, Apuleius sums up all the options in his discussion of mirror-images in the *Apology* 15 without deeming Aristotle worth a mention. Nor is he mentioned in Aulus Gellius' (second century CE) summary of the various theories of seeing, which ends by dismissing the finer points as not worth fussing over anyhow—a view for which my reader will have considerable sympathy at this point (*NA* 5.16). And when Seneca similarly theorized about the cause of the specular image, these three alternatives were reduced to two: extramission or intromission, rays emitted from the eyes or *simulacra* emitted from the body (*Q Nat.* 1.5.1).

EROS AND THE EYE

It might seem a far stretch to move from the tactility of ancient vision, and from theories of intromission or extramission in particular, to an eroticized notion of how sight works—even more so if one were to claim that such notions were a widespread element of ancient cultural attitudes toward sight. Yet several of our ancient sources are unequivocal in their association of sight with erotic penetration and even sexual arousal. It is not just that vision is reduced to a species of touch, as we have seen with theories of extramission and intromission alike, nor just that theorists of intromission offer some ground for believing that the eyes are physically penetrated by the *simulacra* emitted from the objects of sight. Nor does this connection between the gaze and arousal rely on merely metaphorical connections, or on the idea that eros itself is sparked by the sight of beauty, although this was a common notion in antiquity.[36] As Andrew Walker

---

sion theorists. This is coincident with my suggestion that the fine points of the different schools seem blurred in their reception in the early imperial period.

36. For the erotic impact of the sight of the beautiful in general, see the sources in Halperin 1986, 63n5; and Hubbard 2002, 267n32; along with MacLachlan 1993, 65–67; Pearson 1909, 255–57; Rohde 1876, 149n2; and, e.g., Hes., *Sc.* 7–8; Hom., *Il.* 14.294; Pind., *Nem.* 8.1–2; Pl., *Chrm.* 155d–e and *Phdr.* 251c. For the glance as erotic projectile (ray, spear, arrow), see Carson 1986, 20; Hubbard 2002, 266–71; and, e.g., Pind., fr. 123 S.-M. Some accounts of the erotic eye focus on the effect of interocular fire upon the victim; see Hubbard 2002, 269. For the scopophiliac gaze elicited by ancient

has noted, the tragic poet Agathon punned on the similarity between the Greek verb "to see," *horan*, and "to love," *eran*: "For human beings the source of erotic desire lies in an act of seeing."[37] This pun was in turn the subject of the sophist Philostratus' *Epistle* 52, a clever refutation of the idea that lovers are blind: if loving is seeing, then it is nonlovers who are blind.[38] But these popular ideas do not tell the whole story. On the contrary: Cleinias' theory of ocular copulation introduces us to a brave new world in which the laws of physics and those of love share an intimate connection.[39]

To return to our novel, our protagonist Clitophon himself has recourse to this theory when the smitten Melite is staring at him over dinner: "The pleasure of sight, flowing in through the eyes, settles in the chest. Drawing in constantly the image of the beloved, it impresses this image upon the mirror of the soul and moulds its [the soul's] shape. For the emanation given off by beauty, pulled via invisible rays to the lover's heart, imprints upon it its shadow-image" (*C&L* 5.13.4).[40] The language of the atomist (that is, intromissive) school is unmistakable in this sophistic lover's account, especially in the invocation of *eidola* and of the emanation (*aporrhoe*) from the object of sight, terminology that seems to occur already in Leucippus (Diels-Kranz 2.67, A29); as we know, the language of an image being stamped or imprinted upon the pupil was also present in Democritus (Diels-Kranz 2.68, A121 and A135).[41] In Achilles Tatius, however, this stamping occurs on the soul, conceived of as a mirror for the image of the beloved; with the syncretism typical to the period, this recalls the Platonic language of

artwork, see Fredrick 1995. For the gaze in the sex act in Greek vase painting, see Frontisi 1996, 90–93; and Hubbard 2002, 273–85. For a discussion of Freud on the relation between the sex drive and the desire to see, as well as on blindness and castration, the gaze of Medusa, and the mirror image, see Devereux 1973; Jay 1993, 329–37; and Siebers 1983, chap. 5.

37. Fr. 29 Nauck: ἐκ τοῦ γὰρ ἐσορᾶν γίγνετ' ἀνθρώποις ἐρᾶν.

38. As Walker (1992, 132) notes, "*Epistle* 52 provides a good example of the type of paradox that emerges when the notion of the lover's blindness is understood literally and pitted against the role that vision plays in the erotic experience."

39. In treating the connection between sexuality and sight I refer, of course, to a specific topos within the larger field of ancient visuality; readers interested in paradigm shifts over time in this larger field may consult Goldhill 1996, 15–28.

40. ἡ δὲ τῆς θέας ἡδονὴ διὰ τῶν ὀμμάτων εἰσρέουσα τοῖς στέρνοις ἐγκάθηται· ἕλκουσα δὲ τοῦ ἐρωμένου τὸ εἴδωλον ἀεί, ἐναπομάττεται τῷ τῆς ψυχῆς κατόπτρῳ καὶ ἀναπλάττει τὴν μορφήν· ἡ δὲ τοῦ κάλλους ἀπορροὴ δι' ἀφανῶν ἀκτίνων ἐπὶ τὴν ἐρωτικὴν ἑλκομένη καρδίαν ἐναποσφραγίζει κάτω τὴν σκιάν.

41. Bychkov (1999) and Goldhill (2001), respectively, trace the Epicurean and Stoic terminology of this passage.

sense impression as well as Stoic theories of *phantasia.* Indeed, the words *antanaklao* (reflect) and *apomatto* (take an impression of) used by Cleinias and Clitophon (*C&L* 1.9.4 and here) are borrowed from the discussion of vision in *Timaeus* 50e; Democritus, *Frag.* 135; and Alexander of Aphrodisias, *Problemata* 2.53.[42] It is worth pointing out that the penetrative model explicit in this account specifies that the *eidola* emitted by the beloved do not stop at the surface of the eye, but penetrate into the soul; they are also said to do so earlier in the novel, where we read that "beauty wounds more sharply than an arrow and penetrates through the eyes into the soul; for the eye is the pathway for the wound of love" (*C&L* 1.4.4). Achilles Tatius conceives of the visual effect of the object of love as one that penetrates the body of the observer in terms that are explicitly sexual, even as his language borrows from the optical theories of the atomists and the Stoics.

In another of the ancient romances, the later *Aethiopica* of Heliodorus, we find a similar eroticization of the penetrative and tactile force of vision. When the old sage Calasiris is called in to diagnose the ailment of the beautiful young Charicleia, he offers up at first a learned disquisition on the evil eye, which he claims can cause its victim to mysteriously waste away just as Charicleia is doing (3.7.5). But the true explanation in this case is entirely different: having set eyes upon the handsome Theagenes, Charicleia is in love. The vulnerability of the eyes to the *eidola* of the other eye is thus a deeply ambivalent boon, as the eyes function not only as an erogenous zone for the two lovers but also as the area of easiest bodily access for the malevolent force of an ill-wisher (*Aeth.* 3.8).[43] But the generation of love is a happier story:[44] as Calasiris explains, "The things we see result in the beginning of love by shooting the passionate feelings like arrows sent through our eyes into our souls. And reasonably so, for of all our bodily inroads and senses the most mobile and the warmest is our sight, which is the most receptive of effluences coming off bodies [*aporrhoias*], and by its fiery spirit [*pneuma*] attracts the migrations of erotic feeling." As in Achilles' account, this theory of love focuses on the intromissive workings of the vision of the beloved. And again,

---

42. Again, on the connection to Stoic *phantasia* see Goldhill 2001, 167–72.

43. On this whole passage, see the excellent discussion of Dickie (1991), who notes the absurdities of Calasiris' attempt to mislead his audience by underplaying the notion of Democritean influxes in favor of the (here) breath-borne evil eye.

44. On this passage, see Goldhill 1996, 25. Frontisi-Ducroux and Vernant (1997, 249) discuss the imbrication of sex and vision in ancient art: even during sex *a tergo*, heterosexual lovers turn to gaze into each other's eyes.

there is undoubtedly an element of sheer fun to these scientifically informed excuses lovers and scholars relied upon to explain their wretched state.

But it is Plutarch, in the late first century CE, who engages with the most powerful version of these claims for the erotic *and* the malignant power of the gaze. In his *Table-Talk* 5.7.680c–683b, Plutarch claims to report a dinner-party conversation on the evil eye at which he himself answered the scoffings of his host by explaining that bodily effluences (*aporrhoai*, again) and especially the emanations that pass out through the eye have a powerful impact upon other recipient beings. The eyes, then, are both active and passive; they give off and receive the most effluxes of all and are thus particularly suited for affecting others and for being affected themselves (681a). And, as we might expect, eros too relies on this double process of ocular emission and ocular penetration:

> Vision provides access to the first impulse to love, that most powerful and violent experience of the soul, and causes the lover to melt and be dissolved when he looks at those who are beautiful, as if he were pouring forth his whole being toward them. For this reason, we are entitled, I think, to be most surprised at anyone who believes that, while men are passively influenced and suffer harm through their eyes, they yet should not be able to influence others and inflict injury in the same way. The answering glances of the young and the beautiful and the stream of influence from their eyes, whether it be light [*phos*] or a current of particles [*rheuma*], melts the lovers and destroys them. . . . Neither by touch nor by hearing do they suffer so deep a wound as by seeing and being seen. Such are the diffusion of effluences and the kindling of passion through eyesight. (681a–c, trans. P. A. Clement)[45]

Familiar in this account, by now, are the vocabulary of effluences, the prominent role of the eyes, the notion of ocular penetration as a wound suffered by the receiver. However, Plutarch is impatient with the idea that one need pick either intromission or extramission as the sole explanation for the visual and tactile process that provides the impetus to love.[46] This is a striking enough

---

45. We will return later to the topic of the evil eye, which Plutarch also attributes to the twofold activity and passivity of the eye.

46. Stewart (1997, 19) remarks of extramission: "Such a glance was always tactile, always inflected, and always carried a libidinal supplement. Whether beneficent or maleficent, soothing or burning, erotic or debilitating, it was never neutral."

passage, but even more interesting is the account of intromissive arousal offered in his *Amatorius*, in an argument designed to prove the worthiness of women (as well as young men) to be objects of love. As Plutarch comments with some sarcasm: "As if it could be true that *eidola* flowing off boys and entering the lovers and running through them can arouse and titillate the bodily mass to the production of sperm [*kinein kai gargalizein ton ogkon eis sperma*], slipping along with the other atom-formations, but not so with the *eidola* flowing off women? And these beautiful and holy passions which we call recollections of the divine, and that true and Olympian beauty, with which the soul is winged—why should they not issue from maidens and women, as well as from boys and young men?" (*Amat.* 766e). Here we have not just erotic titillation but a stimulus to ejaculation as well.[47] Yet what is perhaps oddest in the eyes of modern readers here is that Plutarch feels bound to defend, not the hair-raising statement that *simulacra* stimulate the creation of seed, but that women, *as well as* men, can have this effect upon the (male) viewer![48]

A modern cultural critic might be tempted to attribute the incidence of all these passages in Plutarch, Philostratus, and the Greek novelists *only* to a form of generic play, a sophistic *topos* in lighthearted fiction that no ancient reader would take too seriously.[49] Yet their presence also points to cultural beliefs, such as the power of the evil eye, that were widespread and influential.

---

47. How *exactly* does sight produce semen? As Brown comments (1987, 181), "The mechanics of the process are unclear. It may be that particles of the eidola themselves are thought to spread from the perceptual organs throughout the body." Alternatively, it may be that "the direct action of the eidola is restricted to the pleasurable effect they have as they pass through the pores of the eyes or mind, perhaps leaving a residue which continues to reverberate within them. . . . This effect is then passed on to the whole body through the mediation of the soul atoms."

48. Note that Cleinias in the passage from Achilles Tatius cited above prefers the love of men to women, but, like Plutarch, uses the same paradigm of ocular penetration for heterosexual and homosexual love. On the *Amatorius*, see especially Brenk 1988; and Goldhill 1995, 144–61, with a critique of Foucault's reading.

49. Speaking of lighthearted, I cannot resist repeating here the observation Athenaeus attributes to one Clearchus in *Deipnosophistae* 9.389, who is quoted as uttering a protest on behalf of the aural, as well as the visual, power of the beloved: "Sparrows and partridges, and also roosters and quails ejaculate their semen not only when they see the females of the species, but even when they hear their call. The reason for this is the fantasy of union that arises in their soul. This is most obvious in mating-season, whenever you set a mirror down opposite them; for, running up close they are deceived by the reflection and ejaculate their sperm—except for the roosters. The sight of their reflection simply drives these ones to fight." One hopes that Aristotle's short-sighted man at *Mete.* 3.4.373b had some other options at his disposal.

Perhaps more significant still, Plutarch is here engaging with a tradition as old as Plato's *Phaedrus*, in which the ennobling effect of the erotic gaze is only discussed in the context of same-sex love. The presence of philosophical as well as literary and scientific treatments of the intromissive power of the form of the beloved is a significant rebuttal to the possibility of mere play in these texts, and in the philosophical context the role of the gaze in the causation of erotic love had ramifications that were neither playful nor lighthearted.

At one end of this tradition stands Plato; at the other (at least among non-Christian texts), Lucretius. When these two philosophers engaged with the topic of the eyes as an erotic medium—one in order to establish the mutual gaze of lovers as a foundational step in the process leading to self-knowledge, the other to stoutly deny that this medium, and the illusions that went with it, could ever make humankind happy—their treatment produced an unusual marriage of metaphysical questions with those of optics and erotic love. We shall examine some of these marriages, tracing in particular the influence of the ideas and imagery of Plato's *Phaedrus* on several late republican and early imperial writers at Rome. This dialogue, situated at the origin of the often playful passages on erotic vision in the first and second centuries CE, as well as the more serious treatments of vision and its role in knowledge in Lucretius and later Seneca, offers us a startling connection between the themes of this chapter and those of chapter 1 (love for the other, the role of the mirror, and the search for self-knowledge). In the end, however, the most interesting aspect of this text may be the parts that are not taken up by later philosophers; his trio of eros, self-speculation, and philosophical self-knowledge becomes diluted and fragmented in Seneca in particular. In Seneca's work the erotic force of gazing at the self provides an impediment to self-knowledge—and of course, for him, as for the other Romans of his day, the pederastic culture invoked by Socrates in the dialogues could not fail to strike a dissonant chord.

Let us start with Lucretius' "conspiracy of sight and semen," as Robert Brown (1987, 63) has described the poet-philosopher's treatment of *simulacra*, love, and sleep in book 4 of *De rerum natura*. When, in a well-known passage on the origin and workings of dream-images, Lucretius traces the cause of wet dreams in adolescence to the appearance of dream-images of beautiful bodies, his language too relies on the familiar physiognomic effects of the penetrating and titillating atomic films (4.1030–36), even though the *simulacra* cannot be external, but must emanate from a dianoetic image.[50]

> At this time, in men whose semen, for the first time, has slithered into the
>   channels
> Of their youth, when mature age has created it in their limbs,
> The *simulacra* gather from outside from some body—
> Those messengers of a fair face and a fine complexion—
> And they arouse and goad the places turgid with much semen,
> So that (as if the entire act were over), these men pour out
> The gushes of a massive stream and stain their clothes.[51]

The verb Lucretius uses for "stain" is *cruentent*, "bloody," which has occasionally struck commentators as odd. But it makes good sense on two grounds: it evokes the *topos* of the wound of love, and it reminds us that ocular penetration is, after all, a form of violation of the integrity of bodily boundaries.

Lucretius' treatment of the bloodied lover provides a transition to his treatment of human sexuality in general, and here the association between the penetrating *simulacra* and the idea of an actual wound in the eyes is made explicit. Explaining that only a human body can awaken the seed in another human body, Lucretius goes on to say (4.1045–56):

> The goaded places swell with semen, and there comes a desire
> To ejaculate it where the dread desire is striving,

---

50. For an Egyptian parallel, see Graziano (1997, 155–56), who notes that "the nexus of the eye, the phallus, and vital fluid has also generated substantial traditions relating eye emanations themselves (including the eye light of 'The Usher') to ejaculation. For the Egyptians the magical fluid *Sa* that flowed through the veins of the pharaoh was the gold of the sun's rays. The verb *sotpou* was used to describe the emission of *Sa*, but also denoted the shooting forth of water, flames, and arrows, as well as the ejaculation of semen."

51. "Tum quibus aetatis freta primitus insinuatur / semen, ubi ipsa dies membris matura creavit, / conveniunt simulacra foris e corpore quoque, / nuntia praeclari voltus pulchrique coloris, / qui ciet inritans loca turgida semine multo, / ut quasi transactis saepe omnibus rebus profundant / fluminis ingentis fluctus vestemque cruentent." In line 1036 K. Müller conjectures *seminis* for the reading of the OQ mss, *fluminis*. On the *simulacra* of line 1032, Brown (1987) comments ad loc.: "In Lucretius the word has a technical meaning, which injects a final scientific note (cf. 977, 996) into what has been a largely illustrative discussion of dreams and prepares for the important role assigned to images in the genesis of love. *Simulacrum* is the standard Lucretian translation of the Epicurean term εἴδωλον."

And the body seeks the cause of the mind's wounding by love.
For all men generally fall toward their wound, and we eject our blood
In the direction from which we were hit by the blow, and,
If fighting hand to hand, our red blood invades the enemy.
Thus, then, one who has received a wound of love,
Whether a boy with womanly limbs shoots him,
Or a woman emitting love from all her body,
He strives toward the source of the blow, and is eager
To join with it and to ejaculate into that body
The liquid drawn from his own:
For this voiceless desire foretells pleasure.[52]

The "wound" of love (perhaps this term had a physiological as well as a figural feel to it) is caused by the emissions "shot" at the victim (*iaculatur*).[53] The image of the wound is one sustained elsewhere in Lucretius' treatment of vision: in discussing why lions flee the sight of roosters, for example, he explains (4.714–21) that "there are particles (*semina*) in the bodies of roosters, which, when they invade [*immissa*] the eyes of lions, pierce [*interfodiunt*] their pupils and provide sharp pain." As Graver (1990, 97) comments, the verb *interfodire* seems to have been coined by Lucretius "to combine the ideas of piercing, *fodire*, with penetration, *inter*. It is as though daggers, and not atoms, were entering the animals' eyes."[54] In the case of Lucretius' wounded lover, the reactive process goes beyond the sensation of pain. Here, the intromissive particles emitted by the love object set up a corresponding reaction by which the wounded lover shoots back with his own bodily fluid, collected and ready (like blood) to spurt in the direction of the wounder. As Brown (1987, 180) sums up, "Semen . . . is dislodged by the external influence of another person (1037–40),

---

52. "Inritata tument loca semine fitque voluntas / eicere id quo se contendit dira lubido, / idque petit corpus, mens unde est saucia amore; / namque omnes plerumque cadunt in vulnus et iilla / emicat in partem sanguis, unde icimur ictu, / et si comminus est, hostem ruber occupat umor. / sic igitur Veneris qui telis accipit ictus, / sive puer membris muliebribus hunc iaculatur / seu mulier toto iactans e corpore amorem, / unde feritur, eo tendit gestitque coire / et iacere umorem in corpus de corpore ductum; / namque voluptatem praesagit muta cupido."

53. For similar imagery comparing the beautiful glance as a missile or lightning bolt, see chapter 3, and the sources collected in Brown 1987, ad loc.

54. Graver's fascinating article treats perceptual relativity in Lucretius: this is why lions may be hurt by the *simulacra* of roosters, but humans can gaze at the birds with impunity.

presumably through the influx of pleasurable simulacra into the eyes and a consequent effect upon the body." From the penetrated eye to seminal ejaculation; from the infliction of one form of penetration to the desire for another.

For Lucretius, this cycle is no joyous process, no foreplay to a union like that of the lovers Charicleia and Theagenes in Heliodorus' *Aethiopica*. Martha Nussbaum emphasizes the discrepancy between the physical and the idealized desire of the frustrated lover in this Epicurean text. Not only do the mutual influence of desire and perception mislead the lover (famously instantiated by Lucretius' list of the loving descriptions lavished on ugly girlfriends [4.1153–70]), but in any case the fusion with the loved one, which the lover so craves—and which causes him to bite and embrace the one whom he would absorb into himself, if he could—is an impossibility. As Nussbaum puts it, "the natural bodily function culminates in ejaculation into, whereas the wish of love is for a taking in from . . . Lucretius concludes that lovers must necessarily remain frustrated, feeding themselves on perceptions, and on these alone (1095–96)."[55] These passages, then, beautifully use atomic theory to highlight the paradox of the lover's quandary: not only is he misguided, but the form of union he craves is the opposite of what occurs naturally. Such a process may bring ejaculation, but that is not enough (although our friend Cleinias from Achilles Tatius' novel has no complaints). Romantic love is just one of the illusions we humans live with, and its absurdities are underscored by nature itself.[56]

As Philip Hardie has emphasized, the *simulacrum* emerges as a double-edged term in this text: it refers to the Epicurean explanation of vision as lying in the (nonillusory) emanation of films of corpuscular bodies off the surfaces of objects, but it may also refer to delusive and unreliable images, such as ghosts, warped representations (such as the ship stern that looks bent in water), dream-images, and the picture in the mirror. The final material on the errors of love "deals with a different type of *simulacrum*-based delusion, not one that mistakes the existence or shape of the original but one that falsely identifies an object of

---

55. Nussbaum 1990, 56–57; and see "Nil datur in corpus praeter simulacra frendum / tenvia" (Lucr., 4.1095–96). See also Hardie 1988, 182: "The lover is at the mercy of *simulacra*, atomic film-images coming from the object of his desire; his sexual appetite has no other object than these flimsy phantoms, and hence there is no possibility of ever satisfying the appetite."

56. On the interesting issue of why Lucretius begins the *De rerum natura* with an evocation of Venus, see the persuasive suggestions of Asmis (1982), arguing for Venus here as an allegorical rival to the Stoic Zeus.

appetite" (Hardie 1988, 72–73). So it is that mirrors, even as they are used to prove the existence of *simulacra* streaming off objects (Lucr., 4.98–109), are also the perpetrators of optical trickery that lead their viewers to false beliefs: for example, that the reflection in the mirror has agency of its own (Lucr., 4.318–31).

It is not surprising to find Lucretius reacting against the illusions fostered by the physiological effects of the sight of the loved one. Epicurus seems to have held similarly hostile views on erotic love, which emotion he defined as "[a]n intense desire for intercourse, accompanied by agony and distraction" (Usener 483).[57] In discussing his views, Nussbaum (1994, 151–53) suggests that sex itself was consigned to the category of "natural but not necessary," but that the influence of false belief rendered it into the more dangerous form, eros. And vision must play a role in this transformation; indeed, "Take away looking and association and daily encounters, and the passion of love is undone" is one cure attributed to Epicurus (*Vaticanae Sententiae* 18). Seeing is dangerous because its erotic effects feed our illusions about romantic love, which aid us in our mistranslation of the message of our body.

Lucretius may not be innovating here in terms of an Epicurean theory of love and *simulacra*, but set against the backdrop of a very different treatment, that of Plato's *Phaedrus*, his account lends itself to a rebuttal of any philosophy that would put an idealizing love at the basis of our movement away from illusion and toward metaphysical truth. The *Phaedrus* is our *ur*-story: not only the earliest extant treatment to bring together the elements of intromission, eros, and arousal, but also the source for the erudite borrowing and play we have seen in Plutarch, Achilles Tatius, and others. Moreover, long before these authors, the Socrates of the *Phaedrus* introduced into this constellation of the eye and the lover the question of the would-be philosopher himself, the figure who strives for self-knowledge and whose path is mediated and enabled, at least initially, by the very erotic striving that Lucretius would condemn as a futile dead end in the search for true love, and by the same mirroring process that Lucretius would treat as exemplary of the possibility of self-deception (for example, 4.342–45).

Socrates' response to the beautiful young Phaedrus, as to the beautiful Alcibiades before him, is a pedagogical one. It mirrors the content of the *Phaedrus*, a work that posits as the first step to self-knowledge the establishment

---

57. For accounts of Epicurus' (largely lost) teachings on love and sexual desire, see Brown 1987, 101–22; and Nussbaum 1994, 149–54.

of an erotic and mutually admiring relationship between the philosopher-citizen—a man who has some understanding of the Forms—and the young and freeborn adolescent male whom he has made the object of his attention.[58] This potential relationship, both erotic and educational in nature, is incubated in the exchange of the gaze.[59] As Socrates explains to Phaedrus:

> Vision, of course, is the sharpest of our bodily senses. . . . A recent initi-ate . . . , one who has seen much in heaven—when he sees a godlike face or bodily form that has captured Beauty well, first he shudders and a fear comes over him like those he felt at the earlier time. . . . Once he has looked at him, his chill gives way to sweating and a high fever, because the stream of beauty [*ten aporrhoen*] that pours into him through his eyes warms him up and waters the growth of his wings. Meanwhile, the heat warms him and melts the places where the wings once grew, places that were long ago closed off with hard scabs to keep the sprouts from coming back; but as nourishment flows in, the feather shafts swell and rush to grow from their roots beneath every part of the soul (long ago, you see, the entire soul had wings). Now the whole soul seethes and throbs in this condition. Like a child whose teeth are just starting to grow in, and its gums are all aching and itching—that is exactly how the soul feels when it begins to grow wings. It swells up and aches and tingles [*gargalizetai*] as it grows them. But when it looks upon the beauty of the boy and takes in the stream of parti-cles flowing into it from his beauty (that is why this is called "desire"), when it is watered and warmed by this, then all its pain subsides and is replaced by joy. (250d–251c, trans. Alexander Nehamas and Paul Woodruff)

The effluence of beauty that penetrates the philosopher-lover's eyes, the *apor-rhoe*, causes a rather astonishing response in the wings of his soul, which swell and grow from the root upward as part of the first step in the soul's ascension

---

58. The Platonic treatment of eros is complicated and context-driven, and the discussion of the *Phaedrus* in this chapter makes no claim to represent an inclusive account of his views. However, given that the Roman-period texts I discuss have this particular dialogue in mind (or so I would argue) when they in turn take up the topics of eros, speculation, and self-knowledge, narrowing our gaze to the *Phaedrus* (and to some degree, the *Symposium*) in particular should not be as misrepresentative as it would be under other circumstances.

59. For general studies of Greek pederasty, see Cantarella 1992, chaps. 2 and 3; Dover 1989, especially 81–110; and Percy 1996.

to the Form of the Beautiful.[60] The imagery of this passage, which has been much studied, is drawn from several different sources: the fields of horticulture, medical terminology (especially febrile), liquid imagery, and the biological arousal of what Anne Lebeck (1972, 274) euphemistically calls "an organic part of the body."[61] The eroticized language of this description of the impact of the beautiful is inescapable (and indeed, the liquid terminology is not incompatible with the movement of seminal fluid in the body).[62] Françoise Frontisi-Ducroux, not mincing words, suggests that the swelling psyche that looks at the beautiful object is, in effect, the phallus itself.[63] (An eyed phallus might seem odd to us, but not so to the Greeks, for whom the seeing phallus-birds and the one-eyed dildos represented on red-figure vases were a common visual motif.)[64]

We should acknowledge the familiar Democritean terminology of emanations from the object of vision and their ocular penetration of the spectator, a terminology that seems to coexist here with the extramissive idea of the eye as emitter of a ray. The idea of sight as a "piercing" force seems to support the latter, and the effluence of particles flowing off the body of the beloved, the former. Plato was no atomist, and his treatments of vision elsewhere rely on a different model from the one advanced here; once again, however, eros seems to pull into its orbit the popular assumption of our later texts and later Greco-Roman culture that arousal is caused by the internal effects of the *simulacra* that have entered in through the eyes.[65] So Achilles Tatius, Philostratus, and

---

60. Nightingale (2004, 163) notes that the beloved's body in the *Phaedrus* is termed an *agalma* (251a, 252d–e), which links it thereby to the statues of gods that were featured in religious festivals. These *agalmata* "were one of the most important 'spectacles' seen by the traditional *theoros.*" Phaedrus himself is thus figured as the kind of beautiful body that featured in the ritualized *theoriae* from which Plato took much of his optical imagery.

61. On the imagery of the *Phaedrus* passage cited here, see De Vries 1969, ad loc.; duBois 1985, 97; Halperin 1986; Lebeck 1972; Price 1989, 79; Rowe 1987, ad loc.; Van Sickle 1973–74.

62. Liquid imagery is not uncommon in treatments of eros; see Walker (1992, 138–39) on Philostr., *Epistles* 32 and 33, where the imagery is of eyes as fountains and the lover as a drinker. Plato (*Cra.* 420a–b) derives *eros* from that which flows in (*ersei*) through the eyes.

63. A view confirmed by the analyses of Dodds 1989, 162–65; duBois 1985, 97; Nussbaum 1995, 249. See also Kristeva 1987, 64.

64. Frontisi-Ducroux 1996, 95. For a further discussion of the eye, the phallus, and penetration, see chapter 3.

65. De Vries (1969), Lebeck (1972, 274), and Rowe (1987, ad 251b) all make a connection to Empedocles (Diels-Kranz B89) here because Plato uses the term *aporrhoe* rather than *eidola*. But Plato's account here does *not* support the idea of rays emanating from the eyes, and the term *aporrhoe/aporrhoia* occurs in atomist contexts as well; see Leucippus (Diels-Kranz 3.67, A29),

Plutarch read this passage: for their borrowing of Plato's specific vocabulary here shows that they had this passage in mind in formulating their own explanations of the genesis of arousal and love. When Plutarch, in the passage we have already seen, explains that "the *eidola*, entering into the amorous ones and coursing through them, arouse and titillate [*gargalizein*] the body to the production of seed" (*Amat.* 21.766e) he recalls the *gargalizein* of *Phaedrus* 251c; when Achilles Tatius uses the expression "the emanation of beauty" (*he tou kallous aporrhoe* [*C&L* 1.9.4–5 and 5.13.4]), he is recalling its only other occurrence at *Phaedrus* 251b.[66]

The sexual imagery here has parallels in Plato's language elsewhere. So it is that we read at *Republic* 501d that philosophers are *erastai*, "lovers," of the truth, and at 475e that they are lovers of the spectacle of truth.[67] One might say their affair is consummated when (in Plato's account) they have sexual intercourse with the really real and thereby give birth to intelligence (πλησιάσας καὶ μιγεὶς τῷ ὄντι ὄντως [*Resp.* 490b]). The erotic subtext can be quite explicit: for example, when Socrates proposes to interrogate the beautiful young Charmides in the dialogue of that name, he desires to *strip* his soul instead of his body (*Chrm.* 154e). And indeed, even the passage in the *Symposium* in which Socrates, recounting to Phaedrus and the rest what Diotima has told him about love and philosophy, repeats that the true vision of the Beautiful takes its stimulus from physical beauty, the tactility of this sight creeps into his language: in having such a vision, one *touches* not illusion but truth (τίκτειν οὐκ εἴδωλα ἀρετῆς, ἅτε οὐκ εἰδώλου ἐφαπτομένῳ, ἀλλὰ ἀληθῆ [212a]). The vision of beauty is *both* an erotically tactile phenomenon *and* a factor in the growth of self-knowledge, and for the beloved of the *Phaedrus* in particular, self-knowledge demands one step further: such a quest relies on a mirror through which you, as the seeking subject, are finally penetrated with

---

Epicurus 1 (p. 9 Usener), and of course Achilles Tatius. Even Democritus speaks of the *aporrhoe* of the *eidola* or *deikela* (Diels-Kranz 2.68, A135). Bychkov (1999) gets it right.

66. On these three occurrences of the phrase, see Bychkov 1999. For the continuing influence of this passage from the *Phaedrus*—and indeed the *Phaedrus* itself—into the imperial period, see Trapp 1990.

67. See also Price 1989, 51–52. Halperin (1986, 71) comments that "Plato, in certain passages at least, insists on using *eros*, not *philia*, as the basis for an ideal intellectual fellowship." Nightingale (2004, 114–16) discusses eros and *theoria*. For a survey of Plato's treatment of sexual desire, see Gaca 2003, 23–58.

the reflected rays of your eyes.[68] David Halperin (1986, 80) puts it well: "Plato refuses to separate—he actually identifies and fuses—the erotics of sexuality, the erotics of conversation, and the erotics of philosophical inquiry."[69]

Even more significant for our purposes, however, is that this passage in the *Phaedrus* takes place within the larger context of a dialogue devoted in part to self-knowledge and knowledge of the Forms. As Socrates propounds to Phaedrus, this sight of earthly beauty, by provoking the growth of the wings of the soul, provides for both the lover and the beloved the first step toward the ascension necessary to view the Forms. For the lover, a form of transference takes place as a result of his divinization of the beloved (*Phdr.* 253a); as Charles Griswold (1986, 126) explains, "The lover unconsciously transfers his own character-ideal to the beloved to whom he has taken a fancy, and then sees himself in the beloved. The role of the imagination is crucial here; the lover in effect fantasizes about the beloved and imposes the fantasy on the beloved, so externalizing his own self and thereby creating for himself a route to self-knowledge."[70]

For the beloved, however, this experience takes place only through the specular mediation of the lover:[71]

Now that he allows his lover to talk and spend time with him, and the man's good will is close at hand, the boy is amazed by it as he realizes that all the friendship he has from his other friends and relatives put together is nothing compared to that of this friend who is inspired by a god. After the lover has spent some time doing this, staying near the boy (and even touching him during sports and on other occasions), then the spring that feeds the stream Zeus named "Desire" when he was in love with Ganymede begins to flow mightily in the lover and is partly absorbed by him, and when he is filled it overflows and runs away outside him. Think

---

68. Would it be fair to say that the *Phaedrus'* closing image of the philosopher sowing truths in the soul (276c) is also based on a masculine, even ejaculatory, model? *Speiro* can certainly be used of procreation.

69. See Sheffield (2001) for a discussion of the language of pregnancy and parturition in the ascent passage in *Symp.* 201a–212a.

70. This is also why the nonlover simply won't do as a choice for the *eromenos*'s lover: however much he may be able to supply the young man with civic wisdom, he will not be able to help himself attain self-knowledge.

71. In Philostr., *Epistle* 56, and elsewhere—again in a play with the themes of the *Phaedrus*—human beauty causes the soul to fall away from the worship of philosophy; see Walker 1992, 135–36.

how a breeze or an echo bounces back from a smooth solid object to its source; that is how the stream of beauty goes back to the beautiful boy and sets him aflutter. It enters through his eyes, which are its natural route to the soul [οὕτω τὸ τοῦ κάλλους ῥεῦμα πάλιν εἰς τὸν καλὸν διὰ τῶν ὀμμάτων ἰόν]; there it waters the passages for the wings, starts the wings growing, and fills the soul of the loved one with love in return. Then the boy is in love, but has no idea what he loves. He does not understand, and cannot explain, what has happened to him. It is as if he had caught an eye disease from someone else, but could not identify the cause; he does not realize that he is seeing himself in the lover as in a mirror. So when the lover is near, the boy's pain is relieved just as the lover's is, and when they are apart he yearns as much as he is yearned for, because he has a mirror image of love in him—"backlove"—though he neither speaks nor thinks of it as love, but as friendship. Still, his desire is nearly the same as the lover's, though weaker: he wants to see, touch, kiss, and lie down with him; and of course, as you might expect, he acts on these desires soon after they occur. (*Phdr.* 255b–e; trans. Alexander Nehamas and Paul Woodruff)

The stream of beauty that comes from the beloved, passing through the eyes of the lover and then reflecting backward and outward toward the beloved again, acts like a film of *simulacra* hitting a mirror:[72] it shows the beloved's beauty back to him via the eyes of the lover, and there, in the beloved, this vision nurtures and increases the wings of his soul.[73] In short, his growth comes from the mirrored

---

72. This is one interpretation. It is also possible that Plato's terminology here borrows from extramissive theory, if we take the stream of beauty as passing out through the eyes of the beloved before being reflected back; and the analogy to a breeze (here suggestively called *pneuma*) would seem to strengthen such a reading. However, it is difficult to take the Greek this way, especially if the stream is simply *ion eis ton kalon*.

73. We have seen that the *eromenos* comes to wisdom only through his selection by, and mirroring in, the eye of the lover. Is his role then an essentially passive one, or does amatory reciprocity, as David Halperin (1986) has argued, provide a better understanding of Plato's paradigm? Halperin stresses that the beloved feels *anteros*, love in return, in the *Phaedrus*, and certainly in the *Symposium* Alcibiades is no shrinking violet to Socrates' sexual advances, complaining rather that it is he who has to make a frontal attack (217c); Socrates, on the other hand, rebuffs his young fans as if he were the haughty beloved (222b). Similarly at the end of the *Alcibiades* I, Alcibiades offers to be the pursuer rather than the pursued. On this topic, see also Brenkman 1977. For evidence supporting Halperin's thesis on the more active role of the *eromenoi* in Greek culture in general,

sight of *himself,* as reflected in his lover's eyes, and for the beloved, love—and the desire for self-betterment—arises from a reflected view of the self, lurking under the appearance of mutuality.[74] It is interesting, in this light, that we are told in *Republic* 500c–d that the path to virtue is to imitate the Forms and to fashion the self in their likeness—as if the Form of the Good, too, could be treated like a mirror into which one would look to become the best form of the self.[75]

Self-knowledge here, as in the *Alcibiades* I, can be traced back to the mirroring image of one soul's beauty (or most divine part) in another; although in the *Phaedrus* the first impetus to self-knowledge is the literal ocular mirroring that in the *Alcibiades* is merely a metaphor, these two passages have far more in common than other discussions of the social mirror of self-improvement.[76] Here too, the path to self-knowledge is not about social judgment but about the recognition of the divine; not about psychology, but about metaphysics.[77] As Griswold (1986, 98; original emphasis) reminds us, "*the desire of the wings,*

---

see Frontisi-Ducroux (1996) and DeVries (1997), arguing that the *eromenoi* were not always represented as "frigid." Certainly a number of sources claim that being loved causes one to love back willy-nilly; see *C&L* 1.9.6–7. Halperin (1990) and Price (1989, 86–88) intriguingly suggest that the mirrored self-love of the *eromenos* is one way of getting around the Greek taboo on an active role for the young beloved, who was expected to close his eyes and think of England.

74. "It seems clear that the beloved is enjoying here his own beauty, not the lover's beauty; in particular, the beloved's desire is aroused because the beloved is desired by the lover" (Griswold 1986, 126). For discussions of this passage, see DeVries 1997, ad loc; Frontisi-Ducroux 1997, 122–24; Griffith 1996–97, 31–40; Griswold 1986, 126–27; Halperin 1986, 62–63; Vlastos 1973, 38–42; and White 1990, 400–401. For those interested in Lacanian versions of this idea, see Lacan 1978, 268: "As a specular mirage, love is essentially deception"; and 253: "To love is, essentially, to wish to be loved," along with the treatment in Rushdy 1993, 95–96.

75. Alford (1988) offers a rather more radical version of this conclusion: for him the whole project of philosophical self-knowledge in Plato is entirely based on narcissistic self-love: "The object is attractive solely as a medium in which the lover may give birth to something beautiful out of himself." For Alford, this is a mature form of narcissism that wants to reconcile the ego and the ego ideal (that is, the ego wants to become worthy of an ideal). Self-love, according to Aristotle, *Eth. Nic.* 1168a–1169a, is the source of human action: an insight shared by Plato and Freud. For another, also positive, perspective on the narcissism of mirroring between polis and individual, see Lear 1994.

76. Cf. Grabes 1982, 10.

77. Griswold (1986, 2) wisely cautions (and we have already seen the importance of such caution in chapter 1): "The problem of self-knowledge must be approached with some care. . . . The word 'psyche' functions as the noun corresponding to our 'self.' In the *Phaedrus,* however, 'soul' does not necessarily have the connotation of 'substance' that came, during the history of philosophy, to be associated with 'self.' In this dialogue the 'soul' is fundamentally different from Descartes' *res cogitans,* as well as from Kant's 'transcendental ego.'"

and thereby of the whole soul, for 'divine qualities' is . . . a desire for one's true self. Since self-knowledge is the means for discovering what naturally satisfies desire, self-knowledge, the satisfaction of eros, and understanding one's soul as a whole all come to the same thing. To be oneself one must know oneself. This is the secret the philosopher understands." The would-be philosopher's rise to the contemplation of such wisdom and through this to self-knowledge (knowledge of the virtuous part of the soul) appears, then, to have its roots in the erotic impulse, and the perhaps surprising connection of self-knowledge to eros is accepted and then sublimated into desire for the Forms.[78]

This Platonic account, in invoking the familiar idea of the power of sight in matters of eros and incorporating, too, elements of both extramission and intromission, has added an element elided in other (later) erotic discussions: the mirrored vision of beauty leads to philosophic self-knowledge.[79] This treatment differs significantly from the ethical uses of the mirror we examined in chapter 1. It also introduces a far more positive role for earthly vision, and indeed for desire, than most of the Platonic corpus; as Griswold (1986, 121) notes, "Socrates explains desire as a low manifestation of the desire for wisdom. . . . Even physiological desire holds the promise of spiritual perfection *if* this desire is rightly understood."[80]

---

78. "Erotic reciprocity . . . mirrors the dynamic process of thought: it reflects and expresses the distinctive, self-generated motion of the rational soul," explains Halperin (1986, 79).

79. It is interesting to note that the erotic impact of the mirror seems to hold true even in the animal world: Columella tells the tale of a horse falling in love with his reflected image in a stream (*Agr.* 6.35), and we have already seen Clearchus' outlandish claim that a bird looking at his image in a mirror will ejaculate onto it (*Deipnosoph.* 9.389). But philosophy has yet to look into these matters.

80. How necessary is the *eromenos*, in all his individuality, in this process? As some scholars have suggested, the *Symposium* seems to correct the single love-object of the *Phaedrus*, introducing instead a progression from one beautiful boy to all beautiful boys, and thence to the Form of the Beautiful. Moore (1973) thus argues that the *Symposium* was meant as a correction of the *Phaedrus* (alluding back to it in its discussion of eros as a form of *hybris* or *mania*; in the *Symposium*, heterosexual love is treated with much greater respect, cf. 206c). The single love-object of the *Phaedrus* is transcended in the *Symposium*, in which the love of an individual is simply the first step on a ladder leading to the love of all beauty and through this to the love of the Beautiful. This has led to a scholarly debate on the role of the individual beloved on the path to wisdom: is he loved for himself, or as a rung to be discarded once the ladder has been mastered? Supporting the former view, see Nussbaum 1986b, 200–233; Price 1989, 21–92 (with whom I am in agreement); and White 1990. As Price notes, "A commitment to another person may fall inside a commitment to philosophy: philosophizing with and for another may be the only way of philosophizing oneself."

OVID'S NARCISSUS

Two texts from the early imperial period in Rome, one well known in its own right, the other a neglected oddity, engage with the philosophical implications of Socrates' teachings in the *Phaedrus*. One is the story of Narcissus as told in Ovid's *Metamorphoses*.[81] The other is a curious anecdote that closes the first book of Seneca's *Naturales quaestiones*: the tale of the pervert Hostius Quadra, who engaged in orgies in front of the magnifying and distorting mirrors that lined his bedroom. These texts are unique in responding to the full implications of the Platonic claim about eros, reflection, and self-knowledge; they invoke all three of these elements in their dual stories of reflection gone awry. It seems clear that both Roman authors had the *Phaedrus* in mind; both, in treating the triad of mirrors, eros, and self-knowledge, clearly had cause to reflect on a text whose popularity and influence are well documented for the centuries before and after.[82]

When Ovid's Narcissus, in book 3 of the *Metamorphoses*, looks into a still pool and is stricken with eros for his reflected image, he sets in motion a story of self-love that would come to stand for an entire pathology of the self: for Freud and his school, the mythical Narcissus was the point of origin for the diagnosis of such self-love as stunted and infertile relationship to the world.[83]

---

81. The literature on Narcissus is vast. Some excellent studies on the classical myth are the following: Bettini 1999, 94–108, 228–31; Borghini 1978; Brenkman 1976; Dietz 1970; DiSalvo 1980; Dörrie 1967; Eitrem 1935; Elsner 1996b and 2000; Frontisi-Ducroux and Vernant 1997, 200–241; Hardie 1998; Nicaise 1991; Nouvet 1991; Pellizer 1988; Rosati 1983; Vinge 1967; and Zanker 1966.

82. I hope that this chain of influence will become clear from the discussion that follows. Indeed, the *Phaedrus* seems to have left its imprints on very different texts from the early imperial period, from Ovid's *Metamorphoses* to Seneca's letter 116 discussing whether philosophers should be lovers. Trapp (1990, 141) calls it "deeply entrenched in the 'cultural syllabus' of Hellenic *paideia* by the second century C.E." References to it can be found in Dionysius of Halicarnassus, Cicero, Dio Chrysostomos, Xenophon of Ephesus, Plutarch, and others. Trapp (1990) offers a full list of citations. Nussbaum (1993, 443n5) points out that "Plato's *Phaedrus* is a work well known and much valued by Roman Stoics" and lists a number of Ciceronian references to this dialogue, as well as other passages in Posidonius, Arius Didymus, Plutarch, Philo, and Galen. Ovid also refers back to the *Phaedrus* in *Ars Am*. 2.493–502, where Apollo appears to tell the *praeceptor amoris* to lead his pupils to the shrine of Apollo at Delphi and thereby teach them that self-knowledge is necessary for correct behavior with the beloved: "Qui sibi notus erit, solus sapienter amabit." As Ovid continues, however, it becomes clear that this passage is a mockery of this notion rather than a serious endorsement of it: it encourages lovers to show off their best features (all except for declaimers and bad poets, who would do better keep their mouths shut).

83. See Freud 1957c, 145; Freud 1957a, 72–104; and Freud 1957b, 249.

And yet Narcissus comes not only at the beginning of a discourse devoted to understanding the workings of the self, but also toward the end of one. For as Ovid tells the story in the *Metamophoses*, several elements appear that seem to have had no place in its earlier versions. For Ovid, and Ovid alone, Narcissus' final realization that the mirrored image in the pond is himself represents a prophecy come true: he will live long, Tiresias has said earlier in his story, but only so long as he does not come to know himself.[84] Narcissus' fate thus seems to represent an Ovidian play on the longstanding injunction to "know thyself" that ran parallel to the mirror tradition in antiquity. It is a metamorphosis of this philosophical command, however, because it bears little resemblance to any of the stories of Narcissus we can retrieve, fragmented though they might be, from before Ovid's time. In Ovid's hands, and because of the uniquely Ovidian insertion of a prophecy about self-knowledge, the story becomes one that is not only about love, vision, and the self, but also about philosophy: if the story is erotic because the act of seeing leads to love, it is also philosophical because the gaze mirrored upon the self leads to what Ovid has chosen to call self-knowledge. And it functions as well as a warning, because when looking and loving meet up with knowing—that is, when Narcissus realizes that his specular double is himself—he dies there, by the side of the pond.[85]

Narcissus did not appear first in Ovid, although we know little about the earlier Hellenistic versions of the myth. Apart from the *Metamorphoses*, Narcissus' story is familiar to us from one contemporary source (Conon) and a number of later sources, ranging from Pausanias' *Description of Greece* and the art-critical texts of Philostratus and Callistratus to the *Enneads* of the neo-Platonist Plotinus.[86] Conon's tale is comparatively simple: Narcissus was a Boeotian youth (*pais*) who attracted male lovers (*erastai*) by his beauty (note the familiar Greek

---

84. "Fatidicus vates 'si se non noverit' inquit," *Met.* 3.348.

85. The whole Narcissus episode is treated in *Met.* 3.407–510. The scholarship on this episode is dense, although issues of subjectivity, psychology, intertextuality, and literary play, rather than the question of self-knowledge, have taken precedence in most readings. Among these, the most helpful are the following: Borghini 1978; Brenkman 1976; DiSalvo 1980; Elsner 1996b; Nouvet 1991; Rosati 1983; Vinge 1967; and Zanker 1966. An excellent reading that pays more attention to the philosophical tradition invoked in the passage is provided by Philip Hardie (1988, 71–89); and see Frontisi-Ducroux and Vernant 1997, 200–241; and McCarty 1989, 161–95. See below for a more complete discussion of Ovid's treatment of Narcissus.

86. See Pausanias, 9.31.7–8; Conon, frg. 24; Callistratus, 5; Philostr., *Imag.* 1.23; Plotinus, *Enn.* 1.6.8. On the history of the Narcissus myth, Eitrem (1935, 1721–33) and Vinge (1967, 19–38) are helpful.

pederastic underpinning of the love of a mature man for a beautiful freeborn boy). However, he disdained them all, and even sent the most persistent of them a sword. That suitor, Ameinias, took the hint and killed himself, but not before invoking the vengeance of the god of love. As a result, "Narcissus, seeing his own face and form appearing on the water of a spring, became the first and only paradoxical *erastes* of himself. In the end, at a loss and thinking that he was suffering what he deserved for scorning Ameinias' love, he killed himself" (*Diegesis* 24).[87] This is our earliest extant account. Pausanias, in contrast, seems to have a double tradition from which to draw. He relates two versions: in the first, Narcissus never realizes that the reflected image is his own, and dies of love at the spring. (Is this Pausanias' reading of the Conon strain of the story? It is hard to tell, as Conon gives us no direct information one way or the other on the question of Narcissus' self-recognition.) Pausanias rejects this story, thinking it nonsense that a man old enough to fall in love could fall prey to such an illusion. He then relates a second version, in which Narcissus, who had loved (romantically) and lost a twin sister, simply took pleasure in his reflection because it reminded him of her (9.31.7–8). In this second version, there are no male suitors at all, where Conon had a throng, and in the place of the tragic Narcissus from Ovid—who at first does not know himself, so outrageous a claim that Pausanias must euhemerize it as best he can—we have a rather Ovidian-sounding story of a boy in love with his sister.[88]

A knowing Narcissus and a naïve Narcissus: which is the original? The evidence, though thin, is in favor of Pausanias' duped youth, who dies without ever recognizing his face; this seems to be the main tradition against which Pausanias feels he must inveigh.[89] Which of the two do we find in Ovid? The answer—in what seems to be an innovation in the Hellenistic tradition—is both. This is because in Ovid alone, the story of Narcissus has been transformed into a story of *coming to know* the self, of moving from the naïve Narcissus to the knowing Narcissus: the presence of Tiresias' prophecy, the development of Narcissus' relationship with his specular other, and the emphasis

---

87. See Jacoby 1923, 197–98.

88. Pausanias' disbelief seems to me a little unmerited, given that Narcissus' own mother is a water-nymph. Presumably the prospect of meeting his significant other in an underwater setting seemed quite reasonable to the boy. For other explanations of his credulity, see the bibliography in Schuller 1989, 145nn21–24.

89. As argued by Rosati 1983, 12; and Zanker 1966.

on the moment of self-recognition seem to be uniquely Ovidian.[90] Narcissus first scornfully rejects the amorous advances of Echo, whose aurally reflective presence here probably represents another Ovidian innovation. He then looks into the spring and (bad Epicurean that he is) falls prey to the illusory capacity of the mirror to show what is not there, and thus takes its *simulacra* for reality (*Met.* 3.430–34):[91]

> He knows not what he sees, but he burns for what he sees,
> And the same delusion that deceives his eyes arouses them.
> Poor fool, why grasp in vain at fleeting images [*simulacra*]?
> What you seek is nowhere; what you love is lost if you but turn away;
> That shadow-form you see consists in a rebounded image.[92]

Not only do we have here a reference to the Lucretian discourse on mirrors and ghost-images in which *simulacra* can indeed be vain, but also a nod back to Lucretius' lover in book 4 of the *De rerum natura*, for whom the visual sight of the beloved was not enough. However, there is some ambiguity here, as in the *Phaedrus*, with regard to the kind of visual theory Ovid evokes. The language of *simulacra* and the play with deception are clearly Lucretian, but the difficult line *ista repercussae, quam cernis, imaginis umbra est* only makes proper sense if we take the *umbra*, the shadow or reflection in the water, to *consist in* the *repercussa imago*, the rebounded image. Have Narcissus' *simulacra* bounced off the water, then, or have the rays of his sight? Both readings are possible, although the line *atque oculos idem qui decipit incitat error* (431)

---

90. See, in agreement, Bömer 1969; Manuwald 1975.

91. On Ovid's introduction of Echo, see Hardie (1988, 74): "In favour of Ovidian innovation it has been pointed out that the intricate parallelism between the stories of Echo and Narcissus in *Metamorphoses* 3 is helped by the linguistic chance that allows Latin to use *imago* to mean 'echo' as well as 'visual image, reflection,' whereas in Greek εἰκών in this sense is very rare; Lucretius 4.570–71, *pars solidis allisa locis reiecta sonorem / reddit et interdum frustratur* imagine *verbi*, is cited as the first example of *imago* in the former sense. I would suggest that the Lucretian parallel extends further, and that Ovid has been led to the idea of combining echo and reflection by the parallel treatment of the two phenomena in *De Rerum Natura* 4." Hardie's wonderfully perceptive article is also the best general source for Ovid's use of Lucretius in this episode.

92. "Quid videat, nescit; sed quod videt, uritur illo, / atque oculos idem, qui decipit, incitat error. / credule, quid frustra simulacra fugacia captas? / quod petis, est nusquam; quod amas, avertere, perdes! / ista repercussae, quam cernis, imaginis umbra est."

seems intromissive if we are to think of an entering image "arousing" the eye (as in the Greek novelists).[93]

Here, as in Conon, this empty love is a punishment from the gods. It is not Echo who has brought down this punishment on his head, although she has been spurned. (And Narcissus takes her "reflections" of his own speech, just as with his water-reflection, to represent an independent subjectivity.) Rather it is another and unnamed lover, *aliquis despectus* (*Met.* 3.404), who has prayed for vengeance. In Ovid alone, however, the coming to fruition of this vengeance will specifically fulfill Tiresias' prophecy that Narcissus would lead a long life if he did not come to know himself.[94] When Narcissus finally realizes that the image in the water is his, when he cries out, *Iste ego sum*, I am he—that is when Tiresias' warning comes true.[95] This moment of specular self-recognition might remind us of distinct anecdotes in the mirror tradition: the Senecan irascibles who cannot recognize themselves and for whom such recognition brings a reassessment of the faults in their behavior; the boy in the fabulist Phaedrus' story who is delighted to see his beauty upon his first encounter with a mirror. But what goal does Narcissus' self-recognition serve? Like the Platonic *eromenos*, that other young boy of beauty on the path (willy-nilly) to self-knowledge, Narcissus has looked into the eyes of one who loves him—himself—and he has seen himself; but the process of discovery stops here, at the union of subject and predicate ("I am he!"). This process is mired in a circularity that—far from providing the impetus for change (the "social" mirror) or for progress toward the Forms (the "Platonic" mirror)—cannot escape beyond two pairs of mirroring eyes, one by the water and one in it. Such a story suggests that the dynamics of self-knowledge have been infected by those of catoptric seeing and those of the mirror of vanity: the "I" that such a search provides as the literal *or* metaphorical product of "reflection" offers only an *illusion* of referentiality, of informative and useful predication,

---

93. Knoespel (1985, 11) holds that "Ovid seems closest to an extramission theory which explained sight as the projection of a visual ray that excited the object in the field of vision and stimulated the return of the object's image to the eye."

94. "De quo consultus, an esset / tempora maturae visurus longa senectae, fatidicus vates 'si se non noverit' inquit" (3.346–48).

95. "Iste ego sum" has a rare variant, "in te ego sum," pointed out by Heinsius (cf. Schickel 1961–62, 491).

and at the same time it offers a catalyst for the destruction of self-love run amok.[96]

Ovid's apparent innovations here are significant.[97] All of them, I would argue, point directly back to the Platonic and Lucretian texts we have just considered and away from the Hellenistic tradition known to Conon and Pausanias.[98] As in Plato's account in the *Phaedrus*, Ovid's story here seems to borrow elements from both intromission and extramission theory; it also comments, whether seriously or ironically, on the dialectics of erotic reflection: *this* beloved sees himself reflected and, like Plato's, thinks he sees and loves someone else, when in fact he sees and loves himself.[99] Here too, in other words, the young beloved, the *eromenos* who has attracted the attentions of would-be lovers, has only fallen for his own beauty. And here too, the vision of the loved one collapses boundaries between the tactile and the visual, but with a twist. When Narcissus despairs, he weeps into the water, and destroys his own image by touching it even as he laments the absence of that touch (*Met.* 3.474–79):

He spoke, and mad with love returned to that same face
And roiled the water with his tears. The image was muddied
By the rippling water: when he saw it go away,

---

96. Cf. Kochhar-Lindgren (1993a, 1) on this "truncated symbolic dialectic." This whole episode is ripe for a Lacanian reading, given that the "mirror stage" itself consists in a construction of identity based on a misprision (*méconnaissance*) of the image in the mirror. As for Narcissus, it is the recognition of this image that leads to the moment of self-recognition: "during the mirror stage, the infant maps itself out spatially, introjecting and projecting a unified body surface or mirror image. . . . Through this enabling image, visible and invisible, container and contained, a whole and its part are structurally interrelated" (Freedman 1991, 33–34). But this understanding is flawed: the mirror misleads in its material wholeness, lying about the fragmentary and confused nature of the subject and also, at the very moment of this deception, forcing a split in the viewer between subject and object, between the *je* and the *moi*. For Freud's views on narcissism in particular, and the four object choices represented by this mentality (self-love, love for what one was, love for what one would like to be, love for someone who was a part of oneself), see Freud 1957a. On psychoanalysis, vision, and subjectivity, see especially Rose 1986; and Silverman 1992 and 1996.

97. Hardie (1988, 74–75) argues on the basis of Lucretian borrowings that "his reshaping of the material was very considerable," and this seems to be the scholarly consensus.

98. Other critics have also seen striking thematic similarities between the *Phaedrus* and the story of Narcissus: see Knoespel 1985, 11; and Pellizer 1988, 117–18.

99. Pellizer (1988, 117) suggests that the account in the *Phaedrus* serves "as an inventory of the elements that constitute the system of meaning on which is based the theme of Narcissus in all its variations and narrative manifestations."

He cried, "Where are you going? Stay, and don't abandon me,
who love you so! Since I cannot touch you, let me see you
And grant some nourishment to my unhappy frenzy!"[100]

In the most literal possible way, Narcissus enacts extramission: what emanates
from his eyes touches the loved one. But this time, erotic extramission destroys
the subject and the object of the gaze.[101] Narcissus' love for himself, for the
reflected image that he takes to be another, is not Platonic, does not lead him
to higher things.[102] Rather, it is sterile, and leads to the disappearance and
death of both *imago* and reality.[103]

In philosophical terms, then, Narcissus follows the Lucretian model, not that
of Plato in the *Phaedrus*, for whom specular mirroring leads on to higher
things.[104] The *simulacra* that come off the object of Narcissus' desire can be of no
assistance to him, and the watery "presence" of what he loves simply underscores
its actual absence: "What I desire is mine: but its abundance leaves me with nothing."[105] Hardie has eloquently expressed his plight: "Narcissus is condemned to
the insatiable gazing of the Lucretian lover (cf. Lucr. 4.1102), who can never get
past the surface, lured on by the *simulacra* that stream from the superficies of the
body." Moreover, Narcissus, like the deluded mirror-viewer in Lucretius, believes

---

100. "Dixit et ad faciem rediit male sanus eandem / et lacrimis turbavit aquas, obscuraque moto /
reddita forma lacu est; quam cum vidisset abire, / 'quo refugis? remane nec me, crudelis, amantem /
desere!' clamavit; 'liceat, quod tangere non est, / adspicere et misero praebere alimenta furori!'"

101. As Skinner (1965, 60) notes, "By touching the pool, Narcissus seeks to touch his reflection
and destroys it. He then seems to engage in a symbiotic and reciprocal process of self-destruction
with the pool, inflicting damage on his body that continues the disintegrative process begun in the
water." Kochhar-Lindgren (1993a, 9) remarks, "The myth of Narcissus narrates a dialectic of reflection that is internally disturbed by an obsessive desire for immediacy. It is a poetic narrative that
depicts a way of being that wants to destroy the surface of things, the appearances, in order to plunge
into the depth and shatter the reflecting mirror completely so that the other of love . . . might be
possessed. But a terrible paradox binds any desire that enters into this symbolic topos: If the appearances are destroyed, then the apparent object of love, the image of Narcissus, will also be destroyed."

102. With Echo, too, Narcissus' error is the same: he hears himself, and thinks it is another.

103. When Narcissus then does touch himself, it's to mangle his breast, the *sight* of which in the
pond further promotes his decline. Sight and touch are thus inextricably mixed in Ovid's treatment
of this story.

104. Borghini (1978) supports such an anti-Platonic reading of this Ovidian fable. Hardie
(1988, 86–87) also sees in this story a challenge to "the intellectual ethics of a Socrates" and suggests that the origins of this challenge lie in Greek tragedy, as in the story of Oedipus. I would
agree with this idea of a challenge to Socratic self-knowledge, but I believe that the role of *eros* in
such knowledge—for both Socrates and Narcissus—should not be overlooked.

105. "Quod cupio mecum est: inopem me copia fecit" (Lucr. 3.466).

for some time in the independent agency, even the reciprocity, of the figure in the water: Ovid introduces the illusion of a temporal gap between the movements of subject and mirrored object where it is impossible to rationalize that there could be any.[106] When Narcissus looks into the pond, he sees, of course, the *imago* of a young boy, not an actual *erastes* whose eyes mirror back the *eromenos*'s beauty. Nonetheless, the image seems to actively respond to Narcissus' love, a reciprocity that fills the young man with hope (*Met.* 3.457–63):

That friendly face holds out a certain promise to me,
And when I stretch out my arms to you, you do the same;
When I smile, you smile back, and I've often seen your tears
When I was crying; you tell me something with your nods,
And based on the movement of your beautiful mouth,
You're saying something—it's not coming to my ears!
He's me! I've realized it, and my reflection doesn't deceive me.[107]

Up to the moment of recognition, Narcissus' companion extends his arms in response, he "smiles back" ("cumque ego porrexi tibi brachia, porrigis ultro, / cum risi, adrides" [*Met.* 3.458–59]). And in the end, it is this reciprocity that actually leads to Narcissus' revelation: he cannot hear what his beloved is saying "back," and this first lapse in the capacity of his beloved to mirror his own longing provides the fatal clue.[108] His last cry, "nec mea fallit imago," is of course a supreme insider's joke: it is when Narcissus realizes that the reflection is just that (and not a real person) that he claims that it is *no longer* deceptive— just as it *becomes* deceptive, given that it is in the nature of the mirrored image to be unreal and thereby to deceive.

---

106. The reciprocity between Narcissus and his reflection is stressed in the later accounts of Philostratus and Callistratus as well: at Philostr., *Imag.* 1.23.4, for example (an ecphrasis of a painting of Narcissus), we are told that the figure thinks he is loved in return, since the reflection returns his amorous gaze. Philostratus even remarks, "Do you expect the pool to enter into conversation with you?" On this text, see the excellent discussion of Elsner 1996b.

107. "Spem mihi nescio quam vultu promittis amico, / cumque ego porrexi tibi bracchia, porrigis ultro, / cum risi, adrides; lacrimas quoque saepe notavi / me lacrimante tuas; nutu quoque signa remittis / et, quantum motu formosi suspicor oris, / verba refers aures non pervenientia nostras! / iste ego sum: sensi, nec me mea fallit imago."

108. This is correctly emphasized by Brenkman (1976), who draws out from this failure interesting suggestions on the relationship between subjectivity and the role of the speaking subject.

Ovid seems to grapple here with a uniquely Platonic twist on the pederastic relationship. David Halperin has recently argued that the figure of the Platonic *eromenos* who feels *anteros*, counter-love, for the *erastes* (*Phdr.* 255d), is a striking deviation from the norms of Athenian culture, in which the young beloved is supposed to tolerate, but not reciprocate, the passion of his older lover.[109] And yet, in Ovid, we have such reciprocity in its purest and most idealized form: the reflection in which you see and love yourself is a closed circle in which subject and object mirror each other and are literally collapsed into each other. The paradox is that this perfect reciprocity is also perfectly sterile: as Jaś Elsner has perceptively remarked, "Since his beloved is an object to be penetrated by the active *erastes*, Narcissus has turned himself as subject into a kind of object. His subjectivity objectified, Narcissus as subject loses all capacity for action, becomes feminized, infantilized, passive. His objectification of self turns the subject into an object and results in an absorbed paralysis of self, a self-absorption whose only end is death."[110] The only difference the *Phaedrus* can cite in its defense is its advocacy of the intervention of the older man, in whose presence, perhaps, this self-mirroring could not consume itself. Such a relationship would make little sense in the Roman world—unless to be parodied by such figures as Petronius' randy pseudo-philosopher, the Eumolpus of the *Satyricon*, and his still randier pupil.[111]

The perfect reciprocity of Narcissus' relationship with himself, with its invention of specular agency, its collapse of lover and beloved, its elimination of any difference in age or experience, and the active participation of both parties, is interesting for several further reasons. First, it invites us to reflect on the role played by subjectivity and desire in thinking that a particular love object is right for us, and might provide the best possible mirror for us to learn

---

109. Halperin (1986, 67). Griswold (1986, 255) asks a wonderful question: why does Plato never show us two mature philosophers engaging in dialectic together? Is it precisely because the erotic element would perforce be missing?

110. Elsner 1996b, 255. Willard McCarty (1989, 161–62) similarly argues that Narcissus' fate "suggests that instead of the regulated or fulfilled life, the pursuit of self-knowledge can lead to an intolerable, self-destructive vision." Nouvet (1991, 128) suggests that Narcissus' fate is "to recognize the self as a simulacrum, that is, as something other than a self"—an intolerable revelation. And note the story of Eutelidas in Plut., *Table-Talk* 5.7.4: he gives himself the evil eye by looking in a river.

111. A similar connection between sexuality, self-knowledge, and the gaze is at work in the drama of Oedipus, who blinds himself once he learns his true (social) identity. In particular, Oedipus' self-deoculation seems a response to his sexual transgression—and in this he recalls Tiresias, Phineus, and other mythical figures who were punished for the overstepping of sexual boundaries by blindness. See Graziano 1997, 134; Steiner 1995; Vlahogiannis 1998.

from. Indeed, the story seems a parable for how we remake the other according to the dictates of our desire (as Plato's *erastes* does). Second, this mirrored doubling is no use to Narcissus: in this case, the splitting of the self into viewer and viewed is not salutary.[112] Quite the contrary—one way of accounting for Narcissus' slow death by the river is to invoke the same explanation Plutarch offered for one Eutelidas who was also too interested in his water reflection: he gave himself the evil eye, falling prey to the fascinating power of his reflection.[113] Both Medusa's mirror and Narcissus' have the same effect: paralysis and death.[114]

Third, this story introduces the idea of the collapse between subject and object, between agent and acted-upon—a notion that was given a theoretical springboard in ancient theories of vision, which often stressed the similarity of the eye to the medium by means of which it saw. Theophrastus, for example, suggests that the sense-organs are homogeneous with their objects or the external substrata of these objects (*De sensu* 2.438a13–15); Galen in *De placitis Hippocratis et Platonis* 7.5.1 ascribes sight to the action of *pneuma* both in the air and in the optic nerve. Aristotle is the most explicit: "As the eye [in seeing] is affected [by the object seen], so also it produces a certain effect upon it. . . . In the act of sight there occurs not only a passion in the sense organ acted on by the polished surface, but the organ, as an agent, also produces an action, as is proper to a brilliant object" (*De somnis* 459–60; trans. John I. Beare). And the syncretism of the theories of extramission and intromission in Ovid's time also points in this direction: where sight is concerned, piercing and being pierced, being the actor or the agent, becomes an increasingly less important distinction. Gérard Simon goes so far as to suggest that "between a given sense and what is sensed, the presupposed similitude always renders possible the inversion of the roles of subject (agent) and object (acted upon). . . . Through the notion of the visual ray, ancient optics provides itself simultaneously with vision and what is visible, in an undividable and complementary pair."[115] And it is true that even the terminology for sight enacts this confusion

---

112. On the idea of the double in Greek thought, see Guidorizzi 1991, 36–38; Pellizer 1991, 15.

113. On the reflected image's ability to fascinate, see Plut., *Table Talk* 5.7.4; Barton 1993, 98–99.

114. Ovid was apparently the first author to add the element of a mirroring surface to the description of Perseus' decapitation of Medusa at *Met.* 4.783.

115. Simon 1988, 35, 52. As Socrates says (*Tht.* 157a), "The agent has no existence until united with the patient, and the patient has no existence until united with the agent; and that which by uniting with something becomes an agent, by meeting with some other thing is converted into a patient" (trans. B. Jowett). See also Soulez-Luccioni 1974, 205.

of active and passive: the Greek *opsis* is vision and the thing seen; *tuphlos* is what is blind or invisible; and similarly with the Latin terms *visio* and *caecus*.[116] Seeing *intrinsically* puts into confusion the status of the actor and the agent—categories that are gendered in the Roman world—and, once again, Narcissus is the embodiment of this confusion of agent and acted-upon, this collapse of boundaries.[117]

Narcissus is implicated in not one but both sides of the ancient mirror: Ovid has combined the traditions of the mirror as something that represents deceit, illusion, and vanity, and of the mirror as a tool for self-knowledge, for Narcissus is *both* deceived *and* comes to know himself via an image of extreme beauty. The philosophical tradition strove to keep these two mirrors apart: the Socratic enterprise of self-knowledge was not to be sullied by the treacherous waters of self-deceit, nor was the philosopher who took himself as the object of his (philosophical) gaze to be confused with the narcissist. Is so clear a division possible, at least where eros is involved? Ovid suggests not. Narcissus' mirror, even as it shows him himself, reminds us that his self-love has no room for any other.[118] Several modern, psychoanalytically oriented studies of this story have indeed seen ancient theories of self-knowledge as an attempt to harness man's inherent narcissism for the good.[119]

Ovid's story also gestures in the direction of a negative, rather than a positive, branch of the mirror tradition by its effeminization of the mirror-gazing Narcissus. In Ovid's text: "And while he grieved, he ripped his clothing from the edges / and beat his nude breast with his marble-white hands."[120] Fascinatingly, the iconographic tradition reflects this development. Lilian Balensiefen (1990, 50–54, 140–60) has made a comprehensive study of the great number of wall paintings of Narcissus preserved at Pompeii, which do not seem to be based on Hellenistic models. Dating from the reign of Nero up to 79 CE, these

116. As Frontisi-Ducroux and Vernant (1997, 140) and Simon (1988, 27) point out.

117. This is evocative of perspectives on love, whether ancient or modern, that see it as a response to *being* loved: consider Achilles Tatius 1.9.6–7; and Lacan's work in Miller 1977, 253. Eros is seen as reciprocal by nature.

118. Some readings of the story have suggested that his self-knowledge ultimately consists of a knowledge that his unattainability has caused pain, because now he feels it too. See Schuller 1989, 146. In an opposite reading, Nouvet (1991) stresses the dehumanizing need of the narcissistic subject to reduce all other subjectivities to the status of mere *simulacra*.

119. See Alford 1988. On the "phantasmatic character of a process essentially directed to the obsessive desire for an image," see the thoughtful comments of Agamben 1993.

120. "Dumque dolet, summa vestem deduxit ab ora / nudaque marmoreis percussit pectora palmis" (*Met.* 3.480–81).

pictures, as Balensiefen points out, coincide with the high point of mirror-portrayals in art, the fourth Pompeiian style.[121] One interesting feature of these is their willingness not only to engage in trompe-l'oeil perspectives within the painting (as is typical of third and fourth style painting) but also to confuse the boundaries separating the image and the real world around it; a painted Narcissus, for example, might be shown gazing into a real bowl of water (146).[122] Another iconographic reflection of the literary tradition appears in those Pompeian paintings in which Narcissus, gazing intently at his own image, has small but female breasts.[123] Indeed, as Paul Zanker (1966, 166) points out, paintings of Narcissus and Hermaphroditus on these walls employ the same *Bildtypen* and *Körperformen*: it is not always clear who is who. And even the straitlaced Pausanias could be read as offering support for yet another effeminization of Narcissus—in this case, not Narcissus-the-subject but Narcissus-the-object, the image in the pool which transforms, before the youth's desirous and longing gaze, into the picture of his long-lost sister and lover.

One final note remains on the literary Narcissus. Ovid's last innovation in our list is Echo: uniquely, the rejected suitor upon whom the text focuses attention is a *woman*.[124] Ovid devotes the central lines of the Narcissus episode to the story of this nymph, whose voice had been taken away by Juno and whose amatory approaches to Narcissus consisted thus in ambigious and tantalizing echoes of his own words.[125] Gone, however, is the beautiful

---

121. Interestingly, the painted mirrors in Pompeiian art reflect back to the viewer-in-the-picture the wrong side of his or her face: not the side turned toward the mirror, but the side turned toward us. We thus see in the mirror in the painting the same thing as we see in the painting itself—a curious doubling (Balensiefen 1990, 50–54, 83–84).

122. Rosati (1983) interestingly carries this a step further and sees the Narcissus story as a fable about the breaching of another boundary between art and reality, that between the reader and the text.

123. On this, see first Zanker 1966. For studies of the Pompeian wall paintings of Narcissus, see Elsner 2000.

124. On Ovid's innovation in adding Echo, see Cancik 1967; Dörrie 1967; and Vinge 1967, 11–12, 40–41. Here I do not discuss the other aspects of Ovid's apparent innovation in combining the stories of Narcissus and Echo, two characters linked by the theme of visual or vocal mirroring. On this topic, see especially Borghini 1978; Dörrie 1967, 67–68; and Skinner 1965.

125. I do not treat Echo's aural reflection here in any detail, but both in this account and in that of Narcissus, Ovid's language brilliantly reproduces the effect of reflective doubling by repetition, doubling, and chiastic structure. See especially Dörrie 1967, 67–68; Schickel 1961–62, 488–89; and Skinner 1965. The repeated verbs switch back and forth between active and passive (probat/probatur, petit/petitur, roger/rogem) enacting the same doubling with regard to agency as Narcissus himself, *erastes/eromenos*.

eromenos of Conon, who scorns his explicitly older male lovers. In Ovid, such
a male suitor survives only in the anonymous *aliquis despectus* who prays that
Narcissus may one day feel a similarly unattainable love (*Met.* 3.404). And
here, as in the tale of Hostius to which we will turn next, we might see an
implicit criticism of the *Phaedrus'* treatment of self-knowledge as dependent
upon an erotic and pederastic relationship: Narcissus has no such relationship, not only because he has rejected them all, but also because his passive
capitulation to an older *erastes* would cast his story in an altogether different
light for its Roman readers.

At Rome, as Michel Foucault, Ramsay MacMullen, and many others have
remarked, the young boy who served as sex-object for an older man (with the
older man playing a penetrating, rather than a recipient role) would be not a
free-born youth but a slave.[126] It is possible that MacMullen (1982, 490, 492)
overstates when he argues that it was "a disgrace to the community and an outrage to nature for an older man to press himself undesired on a younger man,
even a slave," and even "the man who accepted or requested . . . , without coer-
cing, submission to his sexual wishes was vulnerable to heavy reproach."[127]
Nonetheless, Roman attitudes toward freeborn men playing "passive" (that is,
recipient) roles in any sexual activity whatsoever, or using other freeborn men,
whether adult or youths, to be the passive partner to their lust, were unam-
biguously hostile; even a more idealized homoeroticism between social equals
and without physical acts seems rarely to have emerged into general discussion
at Rome.[128] As to the homoerotic relationships that did exist between the
Roman elite and their young male slaves, these were obviously not conducive

126. Williams (1999, 30–34) lists generally several examples of noncondemnatory language to
describe the use of male slaves for sex. Horace, Virgil, Augustus, Domitian—all had their *paidika.*
And it is on Roman pottery, not Greek (and on the republican-era Warren cup) that we see the anal
penetration of young slave boys (on the Warren cup, however, by a bearded figure who may be
intended to be Greek); see Williams 1999, 93–94; and Clarke 1998, 61–78.

127. One also wonders to what extent any generalizations about the sexual mores, and even
ideology, of an entire people can be upheld.

128. MacMullen 1982, 493. It is difficult to know how to treat the poetic idealizing of a Catullus or a Virgil. Note the argument of Makowski (1989–90), who suggests that Virgil's portrayal of
Nisus and Euryalus in book 9 of the *Aeneid,* and their chaste love, refers back to Plato's *Symposium.*
But in any case, Verstraete (1979–80, 235) has it right: "Unlike the classical Greeks, the Romans
never utilized the homoerotic bond between men to build and sustain their culture. . . . The taint
of slavery or service continued to cling to homosexuality."

to philosophical idealization: one does not practice self-knowledge with a *servus*.[129]

This general perspective has recently been confirmed in a comprehensive study by Craig Williams (1999, 32), whose conclusions are worth citing in full:

> Relationships on the Greek pederastic model (romantic and erotic relationships between freeborn adult men and freeborn adolescent males that were both publicly acknowledged and endowed with educational and sometimes specifically philosophical meanings) did not form a part of the Roman tradition, because any relations with freeborn Romans of either sex, other than one's spouse, constituted *stuprum*. Moreover, Roman men inherited a cultural patrimony that permitted, even encouraged, them to make sexual use of the slaves, of whatever sex and presumably also of whatever age. Thus it is not surprising that we find in the Roman sources few traces of a culturally encouraged pressure to dichotomize men's erotic objects into women and boys (as opposed to females and males), and less of a tendency to focus specifically on adolescents or boys as the only acceptable male objects of men's phallic desires.

Williams (1999, 120–24) also treats the shadowy evidence for a Lex Scantinia, first mentioned in two letters of Caelius Rufus (Cic., *Fam.* 8.12.3 and 8.14.4), which he interprets as a law to penalize *stuprum* as a whole rather than singling out pederastic variants.[130] If this is correct, the law could be invoked against the perpetrators of sexual violation of the free as well as those freeborn who played the receptive role.

---

129. This is not the place to enter into a long discussion of whether Roman same-sex eroticism should be understood in constructivist or essentialist terms, or of the question of the relationship between categories of behavior, sexual identity, and constructions of gender. As I believe that our term *homosexuality* cannot be mapped onto Roman ideologies of sexual behavior (whether or not the *cinaedus* was a category that defined an identity), I have avoided it throughout in this work. For the main texts on such issues, see Cantarella 1992, Edwards 1993, Fantham 1991, Foucault 1986, Gleason 1995, Halperin 1990 and 1998, Lilja 1983, MacMullen 1982, Richlin 1992b and 1993, Taylor 1996–97, Verstraete 1979–80, Veyne 1981, and of course the excellent work of Williams 1999. For the art-historical evidence, see in general Clarke 1998. For bibliography, see Verstraete 1982.

130. On *stuprum* and the Lex Scantinia see also Fantham 1991.

This is not to say that same-sex love did not occur at Rome even outside the approved boundaries; nor is it to say that Romans and Greeks had different forms of desire. But in terms of a publicly celebrated and condoned form of education, Greek pederasty did not have a parallel at Rome, and Roman philosophers did not make any claim that for them to erotically love adolescent boys would result in the latter's ethical improvement. The philosopher-lover so central to the *Phaedrus* goes undercover at Rome, where finding a young member of the Roman elite to mirror his loving eyes would simply be an act of *stuprum*.[131] It is possible that the Roman elite tradition in which younger men attached themselves to older experienced figures for the completion of their education and for an introduction to politics was close enough to the Athenian practice to make a distinction between the two all the more necessary.[132]

Indeed, the texts of the early empire (all in Greek) that do invoke the Platonic ideal for the relationship of lover and loved one—as well as texts that simply stress the sexual and penetrating power of the extramitted gaze— expand their discussion to include love between men and women as well. The whole question of which kind of love can better serve philosophical ends is explicitly debated in Plutarch, Ps.-Lucian, Achilles Tatius, and other figures writing in Greek during and after the late first century CE. To take one example: in *Amatorius* 766e, as we have seen, Plutarch argues that there is no reason why beautiful women, as well as beautiful youths, should not emit the *simulacra* that agitate the body to the production of seed; nor is there any reason why only *male* beauty and *male* virtue should provoke in their viewers the recollection of the Forms. Significantly, when Plutarch's father, speaking at 765c, revisits the role of erotic vision in philosophy, he explicitly rebuts the sexual language and imagery of the *Phaedrus*: the warmth of the gaze does *not* produce semen (οὐ σεισμόν, ὥς τις εἶπε, κινούσης ἐπὶ σπέρμα), but only a plantlike sap that predisposes the lover toward kindness.[133] Indeed, as the dialogue comes to an end, Plutarch himself seems to establish that it is the reciprocal love characteristic of

---

131. According to Williams (1999, 11), pederasty, but not homoeroticism in general, was felt to be a Greek borrowing. On this point he disagrees with MacMullen (1982) and a host of others, but is in agreement with Cantarella (1992) and Veyne (1981).

132. See Hadot 1969, 165–68; with Cic., *Orat.* 142, *Brut.* 306, and other references.

133. When Plutarch himself later seems to suggest that semen *is* produced (766e), he posits this in order to argue that the effect would be common to the sight of a beautiful woman as well as a boy.

marriage (rather than that of pedagogic pederasty) that can teach *sophrosyne* and self-control.[134] As Michel Foucault (1986, 205–6) remarks of Plutarch's language here, "He has borrowed from the erotics of boys its fundamental and traditional features in order to demonstrate that they can be applied, not to all forms of love, but to the conjugal relationship alone. . . . Pederasty can only be inadequate in view of the strongly marked difference between the *erastes* and the *eromenos*."[135]

In the early empire, then, something has gone astray with the *erotic impulse* in philosophy and in the quest for self-knowledge. It seems that in this period the Platonic perspective on self-knowledge, with its idealized basis in the *eromenos-erastes* relationship, was either under skeptical debate, or simply untenable, at Rome, from whatever perspective we look at it.[136] And in the end, the best confirmation of this is provided by the philosophers themselves. If we trace within a single school, that of the Stoics, the development in attitudes toward same-sex love from the Hellenistic period to early imperial Rome, a clear shift is visible from the tolerant, even encouraging doctrines of a Zeno or a Chrysippus to those of Musonius Rufus and Seneca, both Romans of the first century CE. Chryisippus and Zeno seem to have supported the "philosophic" love of boys. In examining the Hellenistic Stoic response to the

---

134. See similarly Plut., *Dinner of the Seven Sages* 156d; and Ps.-Lucian, *Affairs of the Heart* 27–28, where Charicles, arguing in favor of heterosexual love, stresses the equal enjoyment that obtains in heterosexual relationships. Even his opponent Callicratides wants to reduce the gap between the *erastes* and the *eromenos*, and borrows from Plato's *Phaedrus* the metaphor of a mirror to show how alike the two are.

135. Foucault 1986, 193–227; as he points out, a similar borrowing of imagery characterizes part of the discussion in the *Amatorius*, where the older woman who kidnaps a youth is described in the language normally used for the *erastes*. As Foucault notes, both in Plutarch's *Amatorius* and in the *Erotes* attributed to Lucian, the amorous reciprocity attributed to ἐρώμενος and ἐραστής by Plato is extended by one of the speakers to include, and favor, the heterosexual relationship and its capacity for true mutual benefit. Significantly, when Callicratidas, in (Ps.-)Lucian, *Erotes* 48, protests against this, he invokes the *mirror* to depict, once again, the ideal nature of homosexual love. The dialogue with Plato rages, but the pederastic relationship is clearly suffering ideological slippage. Foucault also discusses the Stoic perspectives of Musonius, Antipater of Tyre, Epictetus, and Hierocles along the same lines. See also Brenk 1988. For corrections and fine-tuning to Foucault's work on sexuality in antiquity, see the cautions of Cohen and Saller 1994.

136. Kristeva (1987, 110–15) grants Narcissus a crucial role in the history of Western subjectivity; partly because he figures in Plotinus, *Enn.* 5.8.2, as a figure for "a self-sufficient love that radiates in itself and for itself." As she would argue, he "set[s] in motion the internalization of reflection in order to transform Platonic ideality into speculative internality."

tensions present in philosophic homoeroticism, Martha Nussbaum has delineated the contrast between its beneficial or educational purposes and the fear of falling under the control of lust or losing oneself in love. Stoic doctrine held that all *pathe* (passions) should be extirpated, but also that the wise man could—and would—love virtuous and beautiful young men. This "love," however, was specified to be love of "friendship" rather than of "intercourse": "The wise man will love young men who show a propensity to virtue by means of their appearance, as say Zeno in his *Republic* and Chrysippus in the first book of *On Modes of Life*, and Apollodorus in his *Ethics*. Love, they say, is an attempt at creating friendship by means of the manifest beauty [of the beloved]. Its goal is not sex, but friendship" (Diog. Laert., 7.129–30).[137] Zeno seems to have defined friendship as involving intercrural sex (Ath. 563e) and suggested that an ideal city could be built around homoerotic ties, recalling Phaedrus' suggestions in Plato's *Symposium*. In such relationships, sexual exclusivity was not necessary (the better to avoid emotional engagement); all *pathe* were to be kept under control, and forms of erotic mania avoided. These Stoics, then, seem to have taken a stance similar to the Platonic one in focusing on the philosophical possibilities inherent in eros and in attempting to identify it with friendship.[138] However, "the *Phaedrus'* doctrine of reciprocal eros or *anteros* must be rejected by the Stoic sage, who must not comport himself in such a manner as to arouse such an intense feeling in a younger partner" (Nussbaum 1993, 261).[139]

This conflation of attitudes toward pedagogic pederasty did not receive a warm reception among its Roman inheritors, even those in the Stoic school themselves. Cicero, for one, would mock the Stoic *amor amicitiae* and the principles on which it stood:

---

137. See also *SVF* 3.650–53. This citation is repeated in Latin by Cicero at *Tusc.* 4.72.

138. See Babut 1963; Rist 1969, 65–68, 79–80.

139. Babut (1963) has several reservations about the gulf between Hellenistic and Roman Stoicism; he argues that there is a basic continuity between early and late Stoicism on matters of eros, because (a) in all periods, *eros* (homoerotic or heterosexual) is an *adiaphoron*, an indifferent, in Stoic philosophy, and (b) even Zeno, Chrysippus, and Apollodorus, who wrote in favor of the philosophic love of boys, held that the wise man should marry and have children (Diog. Laert., 7.121). Babut, however, completely elides the different valence of the "love of boys" in the Greek and Roman periods, and none of his points addresses the way Stoic theorizing shifted in its emphases to accommodate this change. For a more sensitive treatment of this issue, see Gaca 2003, 59–93.

And so we come to the teachers of virtue, the philosophers: who deny that love is a *stuprum*, and in this matter disagree with Epicurus—who in my opinion, is largely on track. For what is that so-called "love of friendship"? Why does no one love the ugly adolescent, or the handsome old man? To me, at least, this practice seems to have begun in the gymnasia of the Greeks, in which those kinds of love are free and allowed. We philosophers have risen up (with Plato as our authority, whom Dicaearchus rightly accuses) to assign authority to love. The Stoics, in fact, both say that the wise man will be a lover and also define love itself as "an attempt to create friendship out of the form of the beautiful." And if there is any such love in nature—without anxiety, without desire, without worry, without sighing—so be it. (*Tusc.* 33.70–71)

In other words, the identification of love and friendship on which the early Stoics rested their arguments seems to Cicero a sleight of hand, especially in its attention only to the beautiful and young. Plutarch, in an essay refuting some common conceptions of the Stoics, similarly acknowledges that Stoic views on love and philosophy are confusing to all; no one would bat an eyelid if they would simply call the chase a chase, but instead they waffle by calling friendship an activity that involves passion (*De comm. not.* 1072f–1073d).[140] Musonius Rufus, Seneca's contemporary, condemns male-male sex as *para phusin*, against nature.[141] He only endorses sex within marriage and for the propagation of children (86.4–10 Lutz).[142] Epictetus holds that only one's wife should look beautiful to her husband—no other women and no boys (*Discourses* 3.7.21; cf.

---

140. See Nussbaum (1995, 233) on 1072e. Lucian, *Dialogue of Courtesans* 10, includes mockery of such "philosophic" boy-love as well. Seneca's apparently negative stance toward the love of beauty strikes another non-Platonic tone; cf. Hieron., *Adv. Iovinian.* 1.49.

141. On this expression, see Williams 1999, 242. Seneca says the same of *virum pati* in letter 122.7; both, of course, are talking generally about homoerotic sex between males rather than between an older man and a boy. Williams (1999, 239) writes that "with this one pointed sentence, then, Seneca is suggesting that maleness itself is ideally incompatible with being penetrated," although, as Williams points out, it was not seen as unnatural to have the desire to be the active penetrator of young (slave) boys. However, Williams cannot be correct to see the origin of this sentiment—real men don't get penetrated—in Seneca's *philosophical* stance.

142. See Foucault (1986, 150–85) and Gaca (2003, 82–87) on the focus on marriage found in the Stoics writers of the imperial period. As Gaca points out, Musonius and Seneca are precisely *un*-Stoic in their strictures against unreproductive sex (111–13).

2.18.15–18, 3.22.13). Athenaeus remarks contemptuously of the whole school (563e): "You Stoics are oglers of boys." And the skeptic and philosopher Sextus Empiricus dismisses Zeno's teaching recommending sexual relations with boys as "having nothing to do with real choices in the real world, no more than intercourse with one's mother."[143]

Some of Seneca's writing engages still more directly with the erotic idealism of the *Phaedrus*, but again only to reject it.[144] In letter 116 he takes up the question of whether or not the wise man should fall in love in the first place. Panaetius, he says, gave wise advice to the young man who posed the question: "We'll see about the wise man later; but as for you and me, who are still far distant from the wise man, we should not allow ourselves to fall into a state that is unstable, uncontrolled, enslaved to another, and despicable to oneself" (*Ep.* 116.5).[145] More dramatically still, in *Ep.* 123 Seneca identifies as Stoic frauds those philosophers who *do* urge their followers to find young men for philosophical loving: "I believe that those men too damage us, who urge us to vices under the disguise of the Stoic school. This is what they propound: that only the wise man and the learned man is a lover. 'He alone has wisdom in this art; and the wise man is most experienced of all at drinking and feasting. Let's investigate up to what age young men are to be loved.' Let this be conceded to the Greeks' habits" (123.15). This is an explicit rejection of pedagogic pederasty and its idealist overtones, even as mouthed by men "pretending" (says Seneca) to be Stoics.[146] In short, even if we were to take the extreme case that all Stoic

---

143. Quoting MacMullen (1982, 500) on Sext. Emp., *Pyr.* 3.245.

144. The *Phaedrus* was well known to Roman Stoics. Cf. Nussbaum 1994, 443n5: Cicero shows his knowledge of it at *Tusc.* 1.5.3, while Seneca summarizes part of the dialogue at *Tranq.* 17.10. Further references occur in Plutarch, Galen, and others. See Inwood (1985, 462) for a discussion of other Stoic uses of the chariot and horses; see Trapp (1990) for second-century Greek evocations of the *Phaedrus*.

145. "'De sapiente,' inquit, 'videbimus; mihi et tibi, qui adhuc a sapiente longe absumus, non est committendum, ut incidamus in rem commotam, inpotentem, alteri emancupatam, vilem sibi.'" In *De brev.* 18.4 Seneca returns to the imagery of the *Phaedrus* when he portrays the *proficiens* (the Stoic on the path to virtue) as a horse, recalling the horses and charioteer from Plato's famous metaphor of the chariot. See Torre 1995, also on *Epistle* 76.20. This borrowing of imagery remains pertinent even if Seneca's position on the theory of the divided mind seems at times Platonic, at times not. Habinek (1992) underscores the erotic language Seneca uses to describe the irruptive impact of philosophy upon the *proficiens* in *Ep.* 90 and 94 here Seneca follows the *Phaedrus* in conceiving of self-knowledge as a form of sexually mediated foray into the soul even as he limits and proscribes elsewhere the place of eros in the philosophical project.

146. As Brown (1987, 86) says of Lucretius' writing, too, "There is no link between philosophy and *eros*."

language about boy-love is purely figural, Roman thinkers—including Roman Stoics such as Seneca and Musonius Rufus—explicitly reject this aspect of their doctrine.[147] The stain of the philosophers' heritage would continue to provide a source of ribaldry and outrage for early imperial satirists despite the best pleadings of several of the Stoics themselves.

HOSTIUS QUADRA

In closing, let us turn to a second Roman text in which love, mirrors, and self-knowledge conduct, like the antihero of the story itself, an unorthodox *ménage à trois.* This is Seneca's vitriolic story of the habits of one Hostius Quadra, inserted in what might seem an unlikely place at the end of book 1 of the *Naturales quaestiones.*[148] As Seneca describes him, Hostius is a man of unbounded sexual tastes and energies who conducts his private orgies in front of walls lined with magnifying mirrors.[149] Yet his story is set amid a discussion of meteorology and the benefits of the contemplation of the heavens. Book 1 of the *Naturales questiones* comprises, not an inventory of unsavory Romans, but an extensive treatment of the causation of such celestial phenomena as rainbows, sun streaks, *parhelia,* and *coronae,* which Seneca explains as illusions in the atmosphere, and all of which he attributes to the reflective effect of moist and hollow clouds, which produce distorted reflections of the sun in the sky.[150] Thanks to the mirroring surfaces of these phenomena, we can see things we could not gaze upon with the naked eye; as such they provide a useful means to achieve knowledge about the heavens.

---

147. Here I contradict Babut (1963, 62–63), who oddly claims that *at no point* could the Stoics be identified "among the partisans or adversaries of pederasty or of heterosexual love. This distinction never had any essential significance in their thought." This does not seem right: eros may an *adiaphoron,* but that status does not erase all distinctions within eros, at least not in practice. I also disagree with Babut's claim that the Roman Stoic texts we have do not advise against homoerotic "philosophical love."

148. On Seneca's treatment of Hostius Quadra, see Frontisi-Ducroux and Vernant 1997, 177–81; Jonsson 1995, 33–36, 51–52; Leitao 1998; Myerowitz 1992, 149–50; Solimano 1991, 77–78; Waiblinger 1977, 66–70. On the text, see Hine 1996.

149. Hostius, apparently, was not an original, if we are to believe the similar story about the poet Horace in the life by Suetonius: "nam specula in cubiculo scortans ita dicitur habuisse disposita, ut quocumque respexisset sibi imago coitus referretur" (*Vita Horatii* 40).

150. See similarly Arist. *Mete.* 372a–378b and *De An.* 2.8.419b.

Light and the sun itself, as Seneca makes clear both here and throughout his writing, are metaphors for true seeing (as indeed in Plato).[151] He reminds us at the outset of the *Naturales quaestiones* that our contemplation of the heavens is our path to the knowledge of God (*Q Nat.* 1.pr.13). But our vision of the sun is rarely direct; on the occasions on which we can see its glory, the sight is always mediated by various atmospheric phenomena. The high water-content of clouds, for example, is what lets them act as mirrors to the sun, reflecting distorted versions of celestial light; Seneca explains that the distortion here is readily understandable from the analogy of the broken appearance of an oar in the water (*Q Nat.* 1.3.9). Again we hear the echo of Plato, all the more so as Seneca's preface to this work generally contrasts the deceptive qualities of these earthly (or reflective) views of the sun with the truer wisdom to be gained by direct contemplation of the divine. As David Leitao (1998, 6) has put it, "The nature of lights observable on earth is bound up inextricably with man's morally and physically fallen existence on earth. For Seneca, too, worldly appearances are nothing in comparison with celestial truths, and, in studying the heavens, 'the mind at last learns what it has so long been seeking: there, it begins to know God.'"[152]

This celestial mirroring, Seneca feels, is ample proof of the utility of the mirror in the hands of the philosopher-scientist, the explorer of the heavens: it lets him see what would otherwise remain unknown.[153] Here we have an invocation of the benefits of the mirror that in some way strikes a new note—the ability to see beyond human ability. As a result, several modern discussions of the ancient mirror have associated this "indirect" usage of the mirror in scientific-astronomical inquiry with other attempts to use the mirror to see what is in some way dangerous to the direct gaze, and in turn set these apart from the ethical uses of the mirror we have seen so far.[154] Jonsson (1995, 56–60), for example, groups together the three main forms of "indirect vision" to include (a) using the mirror when direct vision is dangerous (to look at the sun or the Gorgon);[155] (b) using the mirror to

---

151. See, e.g., *Ep.* 115.6.
152. "Demum discit quod diu quaesit: illic incipit deum nosse" (*Q Nat.* 1.pr.13). For the relation between that knowledge and knowledge of the self, see *Q Nat.* 1.pr.7–10. For Senecan citations of the maxim of *gnothi sauton* throughout his work, see Wilkins 1917, 101, 103.
153. Cf. Sen., *Ep.* 88.27: "quae causa in speculo imagines exprimat sciet sapiens."
154. See Hugedé 1957, 115–36; Jonsson 1995, 56–60; McCarty 1989, 165–71.
155. On the mirroring frontal representations of vases showing Gorgon masks, see Frontisi-Ducroux 1989; on other frontal images, Frontisi-Ducroux 1995, 77–112; on Perseus and

see what is hidden or far (including catoptromantic uses);[156] and (c) using the
mirror to produce surprising or funny sights, including multiplications or distortions of the viewer.[157] These uses are contrasted to the "mirror of introspection,"
in which the image of the viewer that appears in the reflecting surface has a unique
relevance for self-knowledge.[158] This is a tidy way of dealing with the evidence, but
perhaps not an ideal categorization. For one, even distorted or multiplied images
have some role to play in ethical discourse about mirrors and the self, as Hostius'
story makes clear. Second, at least in Seneca, knowledge of the heavens (and thus
of God) is not unrelated to knowledge of the self. These two parts of philosophy,
he says, teach us what happens in the heavens and what should be done on earth
(Q Nat. 1.pr.2): gazing at the stars, "the mind, a curious spectator, examines the
details and seeks to know them: why should it not? It knows they pertain to itself"
(1.pr.12).[159] And finally, even the mirror of introspection is itself, in a way, a public
mirror—one that leads not to an "internal" self-knowledge but to a better understanding of one's "objective" character (as the community judges it).

In any case, Seneca's view of heavenly contemplation is already familiar to us
from the account of heavenly contemplation in the *Timaeus*, and it probably
reflects the influence, as well, of the fourth-century astronomer and student of
Plato, Philip of Opus, the author of a (lost) treatise on optics. The pseudo-
Platonic *Epinomis* is often attributed to Philip.[160] In it, the philosophical initiate
is described as an awed *theoros* of the stars' paths in the heavens, and he takes
from this study of the sky an eros for learning and for the contemplation of
the beautiful (986c–d). In Seneca's hands, however, these metaphysical and

---

Medea, see Vernant 1991. On the motif of the tigress tricked by her own image, see MacGregor
1989.

156. On the use of the mirror to see what is hidden, see, e.g., Lucr., 4.302–10; Paus., 7.21, 8.37.7.
For the catoptromantic use of the mirror in antiquity, see Baltrusaitis 1978, 189, 211; Delatte 1932,
133–54; McCarty 1989, 173.

157. As mentioned, e.g., at Plut., *De pyth. orac.* 404c–d; and Sen., *Q Nat.* 1.4.3, 1.5.5, 1.6.5, 1.15.8, etc.

158. For Jonsson (1995, 61), the distinction between the mirror's reflection of the gazing subject himself and its reflection of something *else* for him is the main principle of categorization; this appears to be
true of Hugedé (1957) as well, who similarly contrasts "vision indirecte" to "le miroir comme instrument
de la connaissance de soi." Grabes (1982, 39–44), discussing mirror titles in the Middle Ages and Renaissance, uses a different system of classification: (a) the mirror of the world (which reflects things are they
are); (b) the mirror of the way things should be (the exemplary mirror); (c) the mirror of the way things
will be (the prognostic mirror); and (d) the mirror that shows only what exists in the imagination.

159. "Curiosus spectator excutit singula et quaerit. Quidni quaerat? Scit illa ad se pertinere."

160. On this attribution, see Táran 1975. For a fuller discussion of Philip and the *theoria* of the
heavens, see now Nightingale 2004, 180–86.

meteorological matters seem to be a backdrop for the story of a most unphilo-sophical practice. Hence the *Naturales quaestiones* starts with the praise of celes-tial contemplation, but moves from this to an all-important question: why did nature supply us with materials that could reflect man's image? Because they allow us to look at the sun indirectly, without being blinded (*Q Nat.* 1.17.2–3), and in this way they provide us with a tool for both heavenly contemplation and self-knowledge. And from here we turn to the story of Hostius Quadra—no cheap diversion, then, but a rumination on the history of the mirror in human hands.

Hostius Quadra lives and sleeps amid self-reflection: his bedroom walls are lined with mirrors. These are not ordinary mirrors but magnifying ones; in them, the *imago* of a finger exceeds the length and thickness of an arm (*Q Nat.* 1.16.2).[161] And they have been put there for a purpose:

> Mirrors were set to face him on all sides, so that he could be the spectator of his own outrages and so that he could thrust upon his eyes, as well as into his mouth, the secret acts which oppress the conscience and which everyone denies he has done. But my God! even crimes shun the sight of themselves. . . . As if it weren't enough to submit to things unheard of and unknown, he summoned his eyes to help, and, not content to see how much he sinned, he surrounded himself with mirrors among which he might divide up and arrange his sex-acts. And because he couldn't watch as diligently when he had sunk his head and was glued to someone else's genitalia, he showed himself his handiwork through reflections. He watched that lusting of his own mouth; he watched men allowed into his body for every purpose alike; and sometimes, shared between a man and a woman and exposed to penetration in his whole body, he watched [in this position] the unspeakable goings-on. (*Q Nat.* 1.16.3–5)[162]

---

161. Myerowitz (1992, 150) lists other examples of trick mirrors producing an aggrandized sense of sexual self.

162. "Cum illi specula ab omni parte opponerentur, ut ipse flagitiorum suorum spectator esset et, quae secreta quoque conscientiam premunt quaeque sibi quisque fecisse se negat, non in os tan-tum sed in oculos suos ingereret. . . . Ille, quasi parum esset inaudita et incognita pati, oculos suos ad illa aduocauit nec quantum peccabat uidere contentus specula sibi per quae flagitia sua diuideret disponeretque circumdedit; et, quia non tam diligenter intueri poterat, cum caput merserat inguinibusque alienis obhaeserat, opus sibi suum per imagines offerebat. Spectabat illam libidinem oris sui; spectabat admissos sibi pariter in omnia uiros; nonnumquam inter marem et feminam distributus et toto corpore patientiae expositus spectabat nefanda."

In other words, Hostius, titillated by the distorting perspective on his person provided by his mirrors, holds orgies with both men and women in which
he plays both the passive and (possibly) the active part.[163] All the while he carefully keeps track of his reflection: sandwiched between a man and a woman,
every body part and orifice occupied, he avidly watches this monstrous coitus
in the mirror and "takes pleasure in the misleading size of his member as if it
were true" (*Q Nat.* 1.16.2).[164] Indeed, it is the reflected image that seems to offer
the man the most gratification: Seneca is careful to emphasize not the sex act
itself but its reflection as the source of Hostius' pleasure. "Let my eyes, too, have
a share in my lust," he says; "let them be witnesses and overseers of it. . . . Let
my lewdness see more than it can take in and admire what it undergoes"
(*Q Nat.* 1.16.7, 9).[165] If Narcissus represented the Platonic beloved, what we
have here would seem to be the opposite in every respect: a perverted older
man instead of the innocent *pais*, mirrors that distort rather than reflect back
truly, multiple lovers rather than one, self-congratulation rather than education, consummation rather than longing, disregard for reputation rather than

---

163. This depends on the meaning of the expression "marem exerceo" at 1.16.7. If we are to
understand it as "I do the work of a man, I use my virility," Hostius is active as well as passive. Elsewhere, however, he seems to be exclusively passive: "et virum et feminam patior." How might one
play the passive role with a woman, the reader might ask? Parker (1997) would argue that this
means to perform oral sex on a female partner, an act in which the man was felt to "submit" to the
woman; similarly Williams (1999, 204). On the text here, see Hine 1996, ad loc. The interpretation
"I use my virility" rather than "I keep a man busily employed" is that of Housman (1931, 405–6),
again with the support of Williams (1999, 204n252). Frontisi-Ducroux and Vernant (1997, 178),
however, remark of Hostius that "he is—as every mirror-usage is—sexually passive," and it is
certainly true that if Hostius is on the receiving end there is little he needs to do as he keeps his
partner hard at work. I have found only one other example of the term *marem exercere*, and
although it is not sexual in context it supports passivity than activity: Columella, *Rust.* 8.11.7,
writes, "Fere autem locis apricis ineundi cupiditas exercet marem cum Fauonii spirare coeperunt,
id est tempus ab Idibus Februariis ante Martium mensem." Here the expression clearly means
"exercises the man," not "use one's virility."

164. Based on what he says at *Q Nat.* 1.16.7, Hostius seems to be performing three roles simultaneously. He submits (*patior*) to a man and a woman: this would mean performing oral sex on
the woman while being penetrated by the man. But he also "acts the part of the man" (*marem
exerceo*) in penetrating another man. It is worth noting that the graphic paintings in Pompeian
bedrooms are not far removed in subject-matter from Hostius' escapades; and see Clarke (1998,
92–93) on literary references to such pictures. It is tempting to speculate that the connections
between vision and sexual activity would have made themselves felt for the self-conscious viewers
of these X-rated illustrations. On reflection in distorting mirrors, see books 3–5 of Ptolemy's
Optics. On the monstrous double, see Barton 1993, 139–43.

165. "Oculi quoque in partem libidinis veniant et testes eius exactoresque sint. . . . Obscenitas
mea plus quam capit videat et patientiam suam ipsa miretur."

concern for one's civic character, and an old goat unaffected by his knowledge of the self rather than a young hunter who dies from it—not to mention titillating farce rather than tragic narrative.

This account would stand for nothing more than a condemnation of one man's proclivities were it not for the philosophical and scientific context in which we have found it embedded. Both Leitao and Franz Waiblinger (1977, 66–70) have noted a striking parallelism in the mirroring terminology devoted to these atmospheric phenomena and to Hostius' own mirroring activity. As the echoes and repetitions in Seneca's account make clear, the reflections of the sun—the parhelia, streaks, and rainbows—are distorted much as Hostius' own mirror-images are. In both cases, some of these reflections are enlarged to monstrous proportion ("in portentuosam magnitudinem," such as the rainbow [1.6.2]); others have been multiplied into many copies ("totidem specula sunt," such as water droplets [1.3.8]). And like Hostius, the earthly gazer must divide and arrange the images he sees: "The curious spectator shakes out and investigates every detail" (curiosus spectator excutit singula et quaerit [1.pr.12]). In the end, Hostius' own magnified and multiplied images, viewed by this *curiosus spectator* with great diligence, are nothing other than a continuation of the theory that sees in earthly reflections the distorted images of the divine.[166] Hostius' story is thus the culminating point in an account that already sets the scene for a distinction between higher and lower forms of seeing and knowing, between the glory of the sun and the reflected and lesser forms in which that glory appears here on earth. Like Hostius, we all live among reflected images: they are the phenomena around us, and they reflect, dimly and bent, the true forms toward which we struggle in the search for greater self-understanding.

Seneca's discourse on celestial distorting mirrors as a model for the flawed quality of human ways of knowing might predispose us to see Hostius as a sort of Everyman: we too live among the distorting mirrors of the phenomenal world, and his is but an extreme case. But the all-too-earth(l)y Hostius is

---

166. Leitao (1998) makes this point and then goes on to suggest that Hostius represents for Seneca *both* an exemplum of bestiality and fallenness *and* a form of man that is unbounded, hence verging on divine. Hostius becomes emblematic of the convergence of god and beast at the moment of cosmic dissolution. This is a rich and fascinating suggestion to which these few lines cannot do justice. My own perspective on Hostius is somewhat different, however, as this discussion makes clear.

unlike the star-gazing Seneca in one important respect: although mirrors were invented so that man might know himself, as Seneca says in discussing Hostius' case ("inventa sunt specula ut homo ipse se nosset" [1.17.4]), and although the Senecan philosopher draws some such knowledge from his contemplation of heavenly light and its distortion in the mirrors of our atmosphere, our Hostius feels no impetus toward higher forms of knowledge, nor does he use the mirror for its God-given purpose. On the contrary, he is perfectly content as is: untormented by (Lucretian) emotional attachment, sexually fulfilled without (Platonic) philosophical strivings, unworried about the self-judgment his mirrors might impose, and, above all, completely aware of what he is doing and his manipulation of illusion. Hostius moves up the mirrors so he can even see what's normally hidden—so that "no one will think I don't know what I'm doing" (ne quis me putet nescire quid faciam [1.16.7]). As Molly Myerowitz has seen, this explanation "parallels almost parodically the philosopher's own explanation for the reason for the invention of mirrors."[167] And indeed, the moment of deliberation in front of the mirror seems oddly akin to the meditation of the dramatic hero—or the student of Stoicism—in the moment of his or her "quid faciam."[168] But Hostius does not crave further self-knowledge. He *likes* what he sees in the mirror, ugly though it might seem to other viewers; while he knows perfectly well it is deceptive, his blithe response is, "I will feast on the illusion" (mendacio pascar [1.16.9]). As Frontisi-Ducroux has commented, "The motif of the mirror of the philosopher thus correlates to the mirror of the debauched, which transforms introspection into a spectacular extrospection."[169] Like the philosopher, Hostius is sated on the spectacle ("satiatus spectaculo"; cf. *Cons. ad Marc.* 18.4) but the spectacle is all wrong,

---

167. Myerowitz 1991, 150. Here, as with Narcissus, there is ample material for a Lacanian reading. However, the scope of this discussion, defined as it has been by the erotic and visual thematics of ancient philosophy, cannot encompass an entire further school of thought on the formation of the subject by the internalization of a mirrored "other." The reader may wish to consult Kochhar-Lindgren (1993a). I have also not discussed the connection, in antiquity, between reading (taking in text with the eyes) and sexuality, a connection that suggests that we as readers are implicated in an erotic dynamic. See, for example, the perceptive comments of Fitzgerald (1995, 50), who cites the mischievous graffito, "he who reads this is buggered"; on the Greek side, see Svenbro 1993, 187–216.

168. Solimano (1991, 77–78) makes the comparison to the hero of epic or drama; I believe the passage also calls to mind Stoic self-dialogue, on which see chapter 4.

169. Frontisi-Ducroux and Vernant 1997, 179.

and the gazer on the heavens has become the gazer upon the unheavenly.[170] Moreover, when he asks himself, "Why should I sin only to the limit of nature?" he violates the original meaning of the gnothi sauton—know your limits— and does so both physically and ethically. The erotic gaze and the philosophical gaze clash in the mirror, where Hostius sees, not the judgment of his community or the reflection of his soul, but several exaggerated sets of genitalia. The illusory capacity of specular reflection has trumped its ethical use.[171]

That Hostius plays the passive part in front of his mirrors is fully appropriate: this story is not only a changeling of the philosophic project of self-reflection, but also addresses another cultural paradigm for the use of the mirror, one that is usually elided from the philosophical passages that evoke the mirror as a positive tool. We have seen how both in Greece and in Rome, a broad range of texts testified to the idea that only the "effeminate" man— the passive homosexual, the eunuch, the hermaphrodite—would consult a mirror; mirror-use could even be described as transforming the virile man into his opposite. Is the mirror of philosophy—the man's mirror—completely male? asks Frontisi-Ducroux.[172] The answer is no. Even the pupil in which the philosopher-lover sees himself reflected is—a kore, the Greek term for girl (and Latin pupilla, with the same double meaning). Hostius, in other words, represents the dubious effects of mirror-gazing even as he writhes in front of his reflection, for the hybrid beast that is Hostius in mid-orgy has,

---

170. "The eyes that perceive this scene are not only a means of knowledge, witnesses and critics of the act, but also stimulants, a vehicle with a synaesthetic effect, food for voluptas" (Solimano 1991, 78).

171. Seneca is not the only one to bring together celestial mirroring and earthly love. Plutarch compares the reflection of the sun in atmospheric phenomena to the way eros itself works: both are earthly versions of the vision of beauty: "What happens to our vision when we see a rainbow is, of course, refraction, which occurs whenever the sight encounters a slightly moist, but smooth and moderately thick cloud and has contact with the sun by refraction. Seeing the radiance in this way produces in us the illusion that the things we see is in the cloud. Now the devices and ruses of Love's operations on noble souls who love beauty are of the very same kind: he refracts their memories from the phenomena of this world, which are called beautiful, to the marvelous Beauty of that other world, that divine and blessed entity which is the real object of love. Yet most men, since they pursue in boys and women merely the mirrored image of Beauty, can attain by their groping nothing more solid than a pleasure mixed with pain" (Amat. 765e–f, trans. W. C. Helmbold). But Plutarch's account has no Hostius at its conclusion, and its mirrors, while not perfect, offer assistance in the vision of the divine. As a result, his version offers none of the challenges to self-knowledge provided by the happy antics of Hostius Quadra.

172. In Frontisi-Ducroux and Vernant 1997, 66.

like Hermaphroditus, the genitalia of both sexes: he is, as it were, a human sandwich.

Hostius' catoptric escapades also make a mockery of two other elements important in the Platonic tradition. Seneca's treatment of celestial and real mirrors in the *Naturales quaestiones* makes clear that he, like Ovid, is familiar with the varieties of optical theories: "There exist two opinions about mirrors. Some think that *simulacra* can be discerned in them, that is, the shapes of our bodies emitted and separated from our bodies; others think there are no images in the mirror but that the bodies themselves are seen once the ray of the eyes has been twisted back and bent on itself again. But it's irrelevant how we see what we see; in any case, a similar image has to be returned from the mirror" (*Q Nat.* 1.5.1–2).[173] Elsewhere in the *Naturales quaestiones* Seneca seems to rely on an extramission theory of optics that posits the reflection of ocular rays back from a smooth surface and into the eyes of the sender; water, for example, reflects because it stops our visual rays (*radii luminum nostrorum*), which cannot penetrate it (*Q Nat.* 1.3.7–8).[174] Hostius, then, as if enacting in the flesh the erotics of reflection, watches the penetration of his own body in the mirror as a grotesque fleshy parallel to the action of his own visual rays.[175] Like the *eromenos*, he sees himself reflected, but the sexual submission of the young boy—elided and idealized in Platonic pederasty—is here transformed into the unsightly penetration of an older man. It is almost as if Hostius strips philosophy bare and, in showing it a naked old goat, shows it the mirror-image it does not care to see—the most negative possible perspective, from the Roman point of view, on the philosopher who claims pederasty aids his progression to self-knowledge.[176] Or to put it less uncouthly, Hostius enacts the creation of a specular reflection that Plato did not care to address in his idealization of

173. "De speculis duae opiniones sunt. Alii enim in illis simulacra cerni putant, id est corporum nostrorum figuras a nostris corporibus emissas ac separatas; alii non imagines in speculo sed ipsa aspici corpora retorta oculorum acie et in se rursus reflexa. Nunc nihil ad rem pertinet quomodo uideamus quodcumque uidemus; sed, quae modo <est> imago, similis reddi debet e speculo."

174. See Jonsson 1995, 50–51.

175. Frontisi-Ducroux and Vernant (1997, 178) make a similar point: Hostius is both sexually passive qua user of a mirror, and literally pathic as well: "une passivité redoublée."

176. Frontisi-Ducroux (1989, 163) discusses a red-figure drinking cup illustrated with a mask that has, in the place of the pupils, two monstrous Gorgon-faces: the drinker sees, mirrored in these pupils, that he too is a monster.

the erotico-philosophical relationship: the self-mirroring of the older *lover* in the eye of his partner.[177]

Narcissus and Hostius also suggest that from the perspective of the Roman elite, philosophic *gaudium* and self-indulgent *voluptas* did not seem, perhaps, so clear-cut in their distinction, so easy to keep apart.[178] It is significant that Seneca, like Ovid, invokes both sides of the mirror tradition in the same text: although the mirror was created for man to know himself, in practice he abuses it, driven by the pleasure that comes with gazing upon the self (*dulcem aspectum formae suae*).[179] Even this phrase seems to stand as a warning about the philosophical as well as the catoptric practice of self-reflection.[180] When subject and object are one, and when vision is thus turned upon itself, with pleasure as the result, whence could come any impetus to change? Or to put it otherwise: could it be that for the already warped soul, like Hostius', the selection and approbation of inappropriate choices that appear to be in one's interest is unavoidable?[181] The reciprocal relationship between the subject and object, and the fact that the subject's choices for the object are already conditioned by the nature of that subject: these two conditions leave little room for the regulatory action of philosophy. As Griswold remarks already of the *Phaedrus* (1986, 32): "The problem, of course, is to find or construct . . . a reflection that will somehow cause one to move in the direction of self-knowledge

---

177. McGlathery (1998) sees a deliberate parody of the Platonic *erastes* in the tale of the Pergamene boy told by Eumolpus in Petron., *Sat.* 85–87. The old Eumolpus, with his eye for youth, poses as a sternly philosophical type and seduces his young pupil, only to have the tables turned when the boy discovers that pederasty is to his taste. Here, of course, the boy is a member of the local upper class—but the story is not set at Rome.

178. The Roman suspicion of philosophy as an appropriate activity for its citizens needs no documentation. The connection of philosophical inquiry with Greek intellectual "self-indulgence" and with *otium* rather than *negotium* had long made it the target of ethical and political criticism at Rome. On *voluptas*: the Epicureans used this term, as Seneca himself notes (*Vit. Beat.* 12.4), in a way that rendered it much closer to the Stoic notion of *virtus* than to the dissolute form of pleasure it so often indicates elsewhere. But there is no reason to think that Seneca has them in mind in his discussion of mirrors, or Hostius Quadra.

179. See Q *Nat.* 1.17.6. Jonsson (1995, 32–61) interprets the Hostius Quadra episode in terms of his own bipartite division of mirror usage. There is the mirror of self-knowledge, the reverse of which is the mirror of luxury; and the mirror of indirect vision, the reverse of which is the mirror of normally hidden body parts.

180. On letter 90 and the connection between philosophy and desire, see Habinek (1992, 203), who argues that the letter points to "the paradoxical sexual implications of the Senecan project," inasmuch as philosophy, too, is an irruptive force.

181. Long (1991, 113–15) lays out this ethical problem in a stimulating and important essay.

rather than a reflection that will simply mirror what one is already or what one would vainly like to think of oneself as already being." Hostius has selected the latter form of reflection. He thus provides us with a sobering counter-example to the exemplary mirror, the mirror of philosophic self-transformation. When Hostius looks in his mirrors, he sees a self that is *already* altered beyond recognition: it is magnified, just as he would have it, and there is no further change he cares to implement. True, Hostius' mirrors offer only distortions, rather than the accurate reflection for which the ancient mirror was praised. But the selection of such a distorting mirror was Hostius' own and wilful choice, and he is not deceived by its distortions, but rather takes pleasure in them. In other words, Hostius is exactly like the angry man described by Seneca in *De ira* 2.36.3, who derives pleasure from his twisted image and does not abjure it or forswear his rage: even in this philosophical text, there is room for Seneca to acknowledge that the mirrored self can provide the wrong impetus altogether.

Where, then, does the story of Hostius leave us? Not, of course, with a condemnation of the project of self-knowledge *tout court*. Seneca's entire corpus of letters and essays testifies to his continuing concern with what Foucault has called "le souci de soi" and with the Stoic cultivation of an interior space for meditation on the self.[182] Nor are we left with a condemnation of the role of visual self-monitoring and specularity in this larger project of self-knowledge and self-improvement. Instead, we have a fable in which the mirrored image is *literally* (rather than tropologically) tied to self-knowledge, but in a way that calls into question the ability of such an image to provide either a societal or a philosophical impetus to self-knowledge. More important still, we have here a fable in which a libidinous itch has replaced the driving role of eros in philosophical self-speculation. In this absence, I would suggest, we see what the narrative of Narcissus had already made clear: as *the* Roman representatives of specular self-knowledge gone astray, Narcissus and Hostius embody a negative and reactive development in the role of eros in the project of self-knowledge.

For the Romans of the first century CE, these issues were not merely raised in passing by two arguably playful treatments of reflection gone wrong. On the contrary, this particular cultural moment makes the difference in the centuries-old relationship between vision and self-knowledge. Much of the responsibility can be laid at the several doors of a rather complicated structure whose

---

182. See, e.g., Edwards 1997, 23–38; Foucault 1986, 39–68; Newman 1989; and Rappe 1997, 447.

elements included the different status of homosexuality between freeborn and freeborn at Rome, the shifting basis of political power between republic and empire, the enormous stress in elite Roman culture on the ramifications of seeing and being seen, and the new ethical questions being posed by Roman Stoicism under Nero.[183] The last three of these issues will occupy us in the following three chapters. But even the historical Hostius, with the happy-go-lucky philosophy that Seneca puts in his mouth, and the mythical Narcissus, whom Ovid turns into a play upon Lucretius and Plato, provide us already with an interesting reminder that how we see is both ethical and sexual in its implications, and that vision, ethics, and sexuality once clearly and openly existed in a symbiotic relationship with the subjects of ancient Greece and Rome.

---

183. Readers familiar with Foucault's theory of a new emphasis on sexual austerity in the texts of the first centuries CE may choose to see here an important and related factor in the splitting off of eros from philosophy. On Foucault's treatment of ancient sexuality, see Cohen and Saller 1994, 35–59.

3 Scopic Paradigms at Rome

To be at the center of the gaze: at Rome, there was no position more ideologically fraught, more riven with contradiction, more constitutive *and* destructive of male civic identity. It was the position of the general riding in a triumphal chariot through the streets of the city; it was also the position of the criminal marked for destruction by man or beast in the Colosseum. It was the site for the orator, as he addressed a jury and a corona of spectators in the Forum, and it was also the site for the actor, a man marked as *infamis* (without citizen rights) by the same citizenry that patronized his performance. These seemingly paradoxical and unstable positions imposed on the figures who came before the public eye relied nonetheless on a shared set of cultural beliefs about the nature of virtue, the power of the eye, and the importance of appearances. Despite the frequent invocation of the shibboleth *esse quam videri*, "to be rather than to seem," appearances and essences were closely enmeshed in Roman Republican public life.[1] Both *in melius* and *in deterius*, the gaze of one's

---

1. E.g., Cic. *Amic.* 98.5: "Virtute enim ipsa non tam multi praediti esse quam videri volunt" and countless other examples. That in Latin *video* means "to see," and *videor*, "to seem," provides a neat example of the link between visibility and public opinion. Contrast this with the sentiment of *Off.* 1.46, that even possessing the appearance (*imago*) of virtue is a praiseworthy accomplishment for the citizen.

fellow citizens and especially of the fellow elite were closely linked to self-worth, public worth, and ethical evaluation. Moreover, because the gaze could be aggressive as well as admiring, destructive as well as productive, one needed to have control over its motivation, origin, and direction in order to maintain control over its effects—a control that the Roman upper classes practiced with varying degrees of success.[2]

This chapter and the next will explore, first, the conflict between some basic Roman paradigms of viewing in the late republic and, second, the shifting parameters of this conflict in the early empire, with particular reference to the changing shape of *virtus* in the work of Seneca the younger, philosopher and politician. To understand the factors that eventually undermined the positive ethical valence of visual prominence in the Julio-Claudian period and beyond, we must recognize the ingrained cultural assumptions of the nobility in the late republic: that the origin of the gaze had an effect upon its ability to commend or to challenge its object; that some forms of the gaze itself were not physiologically neutral in their effects; that the aristocratic body had self-evident rights and defenses not shared by the urban lower classes.[3] These assumptions proved to be more fluid and more fragile than the elite class could have anticipated, and more dependent upon the political shifts and upheavals of the late republic and early empire.

This chapter takes as its starting point that the sexual and ethical concepts underlying the ancient understanding of vision necessarily interacted with the role of the gaze as a civic and political phenomenon.[4] In so doing, it will rehearse some well-known facts that are relevant enough to be repeated here, and will introduce others that will be less familiar. We have already seen that the emissive activity of the eyes, or, conversely, their conceptualization as the

---

2. As Barton (2002, 227) puts it: "The tension for the person of honor in ancient Rome had ever been the need to display him- or herself to others and, simultaneously, to preserve an inviolate and protected sphere." This chapter seeks to explore the possibilities and limitations of this dual purpose.

3. Rzepka (1986, 27) discusses similar phenomena in the case of Wordsworth, Coleridge, and Keats: "an abnormal fascination with and fear of the eye as an instrument of public self-confirmation and definition," and also as an instrument of objectification and alienation. At Rome, however, such a fear was not abnormal, but rather expected and assumed. For a modern distinction between *gaze* and *look* that draws on Lacan and film theory, see Silverman 1992, 125–56. (I am not using this terminology here.)

4. A sentiment anticipated in Fredrick (2002b, 237), who proposes to view "penetration" as "the concerted action of economics, politics, gender, and sexuality."

porous gateways to the psyche, carried the assumption that seeing was a tactile process that could evoke a physical reaction in the body. Even if we should wish to underplay as self-consciously exaggerated the penetrative sexual force with which vision is associated in ancient discourses on eros, it will prove impossible to dismiss as fanciful such attributions of effect in a culture that also worried about the damaging force of the evil eye and employed images and models of the phallus as a safeguard against it; or that drew parallels between a free man appearing on the stage and his submitting to the detested passive role in a homo-erotic tryst. These investigations should also lead us to ask why the dangers of the gaze are elided in some contexts and highlighted in others; why visual exposure is here to be desired, there to be shunned; why the senator who is the cynosure of all eyes need not fear the degradation of the actor—and also why the gulf between different forms of objectification at the focus of the gaze seems to have narrowed between the days of as late a republican as Cicero and the time of Seneca.

UNDER THE *IMAGO*

As recent scholarship has shown, republican Roman ethics were built on a foundation that was strongly informed by the elite's concern to provide visual and exemplary models for each other and for the lower classes as well. The institutions of the Roman republic—the Senate, the courts, the assemblies, the Forum, the retinues, the censors, even the games—were shaped by the judging force of a collective gaze, whether it emanated from the plebs or the senators, and these institutions both confirmed and helped to maintain the power of the elite in the Roman republic.[5] Indeed, the gaze that compelled the elite to exemplarity was felt to be everywhere: the gaze of the commoners upon the magistrates and the nobility; the gaze of the senators among themselves in the Curia or in the court; the gaze of noble ancestors upon generations of their progeny.[6]

---

5. As Dupont (1985, 29) puts it: "Each culture has its theater, each culture has its beliefs. At Rome, to know how to convince was to know how to render visible." See also Dupont (2000, 122), where she stresses the link between identity and the visible face. See also Solimano 1991, 35–36. For research on this culture of visibility, see especially Barton 2001; Beacham 1999, 1–44; Bell 1997; Bettini 2000; Dupont 2000; Feldherr 1998; Gregory 1994; Roller 2001a; and Solimano 1991.

6. As Solimano (1991, 35) puts it: "Rome appears as a city full of eyes that watch and desire, that spy . . . and evaluate."

Roman elite texts refer to the gaze repeatedly, making clear that its complex manifestations—threatening, sexual, regulatory, penetrating, shaming, controlling, admiring, imitative—shaped civic and personal identity as they fueled ethical, gendered, and hierarchical forms of the characterization of self and other in the Roman state.

This orientation toward the visible exemplum accounts for the number of spectacular displays that shaped defining moments of political life: the bustling morning retinue of clients and friends that followed a senator down to the Forum, the processional triumph that followed certain military victories, public trials before a jury of the fellow elite and a crowd of spectators, the magnificent funeral that recalled the dead man's civic and military service to the state, even the tiered hierarchies of the arena.[7] One's personal appearance was under similar scrutiny for signs of moral excellence or deviance; the orator, for example, had to keep in mind the way his body and his movements could be read for signs of "effeminacy" or lack of self-mastery. As Gunderson (2000, 70) puts it, "The body can and will be read against its bearer." Even such minutiae as how the folds of one's toga hung or the number of fingers with which one scratched one's head were interpreted as significant indices of manliness and hence political viability.[8] Seneca warned his readers about what we might call this transparency of the visible sign: "There are tell-tale signs [indicia] for everything, as long as they're noticed, and you can derive proof of character even from the smallest ones: the effeminate is given away by his gait and his hand-movement and sometimes by a single answer and moving his finger to his head and the shifting of his eye; laughter shows up the wicked man, his face and appearance the mad one. All of this comes out in public through visible characteristics [notas]" (Ep. 52.12).[9] In this "civilisation du spectacle," visibility, status, and judgment went hand in hand; one judged others and was judged in

---

7. On the production of Roman civic values by the seating arrangements of the arena, see Clavel-Lévêque 1986, Rawson 1987, and especially Gunderson 1996. Gunderson notes the explicitness of "the ideological representation to the subjects of their mutual relationship" (1996, 125).

8. On the toga specifically, see the famous comments of Sulla about Julius Caesar reported in Suet., Iul. 45.3: "He wore the toga with the broad stripe with fringes down to his hands, and he always wore a belt over it, but tied it rather loosely; this was the cause of Sulla's frequent warning to the optimates, that they should beware the badly belted boy." There are detailed instructions on its wearing in Quint., 11.3.138–39.

9. For an excellent discussion of Cicero's political manipulation of this "ideology of movement," see Corbeill 2002.

turn. One who could establish this outward display of self-worth, as measured by the traditional values of the elite, would find that his own judgment thereby carried more weight.[10]

Both in wartime and in peace, the figure in the spotlight could generate and give force to the visible *exemplum*, the exemplary act or the manifestation of model behavior that mimicked previous paradigms of military or civic virtue while providing a model to be imitated for senators and commoners alike. Roman history is full of such avatars of courage or brilliance, and their moments of glory are often described in terms of their immediate impact on a present audience (the army, the enemy, the *cives*) and their exhortatory force for the reading or listening audience. As Andrew Feldherr (1998, 3) has shown, the republican historian Livy conceived of his own work as a visually appealing re-presentation of these exemplary moments of history, and would "engage the gaze of his audience [to] allow his text to reproduce the political effects of the events described and thus to act upon the society of his own time."[11] Jane Chaplin's recent work on this Livian technique demonstrates the ubiquity of this practice, and its nuances, in Livy's work. The evocation of *exempla* is not limited to historical works; Cicero noted its efficacy for the orator's purposes as well, reminding his readers that "the evocation of antiquity and the citation of exemplary deeds provide the speech with authority and credibility together with the greatest delight" (*Orat.* 120).[12]

But the audience's role was not only to feel delight or admiration at the exploits, past or present, of their heroic countrymen; to some degree, their presence seems to have provided a necessary ratification of the exemplary power of those actions. This stress upon the role of the witness in the production of *virtus* meant that the exemplary quality of a deed was effectively felt to be lost without an audience. When Valerius Maximus spins out his exemplary accounts of Aemilius Lepidus, of Horatius Cocles, of the son of Cato the Elder, mention is often made of the admiring or fearful throngs who noted their behavior: Horatius, jumping into the Tiber with a full suit of armor, "though a

---

10. Roller 2001a, 20–27, an excellent work from which I have benefited greatly. See also Dupont 1985, 19–42; Feldherr 1998, 12–17.

11. See especially Feldherr 1998, chap. 2, "*Enargeia* and the Political Function of Spectacle."

12. "Commemoratio autem antiquitatis exemplorumque prolatio summa cum delectatione et auctoritatem orationi affert et fidem." The commons' urge to imitate the public behavior of their magistrates is illustrated by the anecdote about the procurator of Epirus told by Epict., *Disc.* 3.4.

single man, drew to himself the eyes of so many citizens and so many enemies, the former stunned with admiration, the latter caught between rejoicing and fear."[13] In epic and even in epigram, the spectator gives validity to the *exemplum*: when Lucan's Vulteius, urging his men on to suicide, tells them to be grateful they will not join the heaps of the dead in anonymity, this is because his soldiers have witnesses (*testes*) to see their fate; a noble death buried under a pile of bodies means nothing ("perit obruta virtus" [*BC* 4.488–99]).[14] Later, as Cato's men are dying of thirst and snake assault in the desert, their general's presence leads them to suppress their groans: they are ashamed to die *illo teste*, "with him as witness." As Lucan puts it, by serving as spectator, Cato is able to show that great pain has no power.[15] In a more gruesome account, the indomitable Mucius Scaevola is wittily described as his own spectator in Martial's *Epigrams* 1.21 and 8.30 ("Ipse sui spectator adest"): sticking his hand in the flames, he is there as an economical audience to his own *virtus*.[16]

Usually such moments of triumph and tragedy were staged for consumption by a larger audience than the family. I rehearse here very briefly the support for this view. Much attention has focused on what we know of the funeral processions of deceased senators, which were conducted as public events that re-created visually the magisterial history of an entire family line.[17] Amid the long chain of family members and officials in these processions, professional actors took part, wearing lifelike wax masks (*imagines*) of the dead senator and of all his noble ancestors. Accompanied by this throng and preceded by lictors, the dead man's body would be carried down to the civic space of the Forum;

---

13. "Unus itaque tot ciuium, tot hostium in se oculos conuertit, stupentis illos admiratione, hos inter laetitiam et metum haesitantis" (Val. Max., 3.2.1).

14. Eldred (2002) provides a strong reading of this scene in terms of the undercutting of the visual exemplarity at the heart of epic. See also Leigh 1997, 182–83. As Feldherr (1998, 135) notes, Livy conceives of Horatius' accumulated *virtus* as being able to "block out" the horror of his murder of his sister (1.25–26): "The word *obstabat* suggests that Horatius' honor, on visual display in the form of the spolia he bears, literally obstructs the viewer's contact with the scene of the murder." On the visibility of *virtus* in general, see Barton 2001, 34–38.

15. *BC* 9.886–89: "puduitque gementem / illo teste mori. quod ius habuisset in ipsum / ulla lues? casus alieno in pectore uincit / spectatorque docet magnos nil posse dolores."

16. In its reliance upon an audience, *virtus* could even be figured as a visible quality, a splendor or illumination cast by the hero: "the glory of one's ancestors is a kind of light for posterity" (Sall., *Iug.* 85.23). On the "light" of *virtus*, see Barton 2001, 34–38.

17. On this aspect of the Roman funeral, see Bodel 1999; Flower 1996, chap. 4; Gregory 1994; Versnel 1970, 115–29.

there, surrounded by simulated ancestors seated on ivory chairs, it was exhibited on the rostra, and a funeral eulogy delivered to the general public by a prominent descendant. So compelling was the impression this made on the audience that the historian Polybius claimed the ceremony itself functioned as a propaedeutic to virtue.[18] The triumphs celebrated by generals who had won a victory against Rome's enemies provided a similar combination of procession and pageant, and the two institutions were sometimes linked in the minds of the viewers.[19] As in the funeral, a processional made its way through the city displaying visual representations not only of the status of the great man but also of the absent sources of his glory: the booty, captives, even pictorial representations of the defeated nation. In a passage often cited by scholars of Roman culture, Polybius emphasizes the dramatic quality of the triumph and its staging for an audience of citizens: "The senate has the power to stage (*ektragodesai*) and magnify, or again to humble and render obscure, the successes of the leaders. For what they call triumphs, through which the vivid spectacle of deeds accomplished by the generals is brought before the eyes of the citizens—these they cannot administer as is fitting, and at times they cannot accomplish them at all, unless the senate agrees and provides the expenses for these things" (*Hist.* 6.15.8). The talk of staging and vividness is apparent in our Roman sources as well: Cicero stresses that the captives were only kept alive to provide "the most beautiful spectacle" for the audience of Roman citizens during the triumph, the end of which coincided with the end of the captives as well (*Verr.* 2.5.77.11). It was from this institution, the triumph, that, as Werner Eck comments, "[the] members of the Roman ruling stratum derived the highest kind of boost to their image and gained specific social prestige."[20]

---

18. Polyb., *History* 6.53.9–10. Polybius stresses such elements of the funeral as the conspicuity of the eulogized and the eulogizer, the size of the audience, the display of *imagines*, and the spectacle provided by the elite. Ancient sources for the Roman funeral include Pliny, *HN* 35.4; Polyb. 6.53–54; Livy 8.40.4; Cic., *Brut.* 62; Diod. Sic., 31.25.2; Suet., *Vesp.* 19. On the use of actors dressed in *imagines* and the garb befitting the dead, see Suet., *Vesp.* 19.2; and Diod. Sic., 31.25.2.

19. Seneca tells us that at the funeral of Livia's son, Drusus, the throng of citizens and officials who joined the procession gave it the dimensions of a triumph rather than a funeral (*Ad Marc.* 3.1). For further comparisons between the funeral and the triumph, see App., *Pun.* 66; App., *Mith.* 17.117; Val. Max. 2.10.3; Dion. Hal., *Ant. Rom.* 8.59.3; and the discussion in Versnel 1970, 115–29.

20. Eck 1984, 138, with Roman references to the prestige bestowed by the triumph. In general see Versnel 1970. For particularly spectacular triumphs, see, e.g., Livy, 34.52.4–5; Plut., *Aem.* 32–33; Pliny, *HN* 33.151.

Even in peacetime, the presence of an escort was the marker of the notable man. For magistrates, it was the lictors, given to all who held *imperium*, walking before them in single file, each carrying the fasces on their left shoulder; for those not in office, it was the daily *salutatio* by clients, and the retinue, or *comitatio*, that followed them down to the Forum. Q. Cicero's canvassing advice to his brother offered a reminder of the importance of a visible retinue of followers: "Take care to employ on every day men of every rank and order and age. For one can conjecture from those very numbers how much strength and opportunity you will have in the assembly. . . . A daily throng to lead you down to the Forum brings a great reputation and great authority."²¹ Other means of presenting oneself to the public eye had long had sanction in republican Rome. The Senate, in a practice that may have begun as early as the regal period, awarded honorific statues to great men of the state throughout the days of the republic—for Metellus Scipio, a whole troop of them on the Capitol (Cic., *Att.* 6.1.17).²² The erection of public buildings with honorific inscriptions, or the addition of such inscriptions to buildings, was another way to bring one's name, literally, before the public eye; Pompey's theater and the restorations carried out by Munatius Plancus for the Temple of Saturn and by Asinius Pollio for the *atrium libertatis* are just a few examples. And on display in the Forum of Augustus, after 2 BCE, was a collection of statues of *summi viri* with accompanying *tituli*—past heroes of the republic, arranged in turn around statues of Aeneas and Romulus in the northern and southern hemispheres.²³ The emperor Augustus himself, if we are to believe Suetonius' explanation, had erected these statues to provide a visual model of the standards he, Augustus himself, should maintain (*Aug.* 31.5). Such statues did hold an exemplary force for their viewers: Dio Cassius claims that it was the sight of the statue of his

---

21. *Commentariolum petitionis* 34–37. See Bell 1997, 9.

22. This practice "reached its apogee in the late Republic with individuals indiscriminately putting up statues of themselves and relatives" (Gregory 1994, 83), with the result that, for example, in 158 BCE the censors had to remove all the statues in the Forum that had not been set up by a resolution of the Senate or the people (Pliny, *HN* 34.30).

23. Kellum 1996; Zanker 1988, 210–13. As Roller (2001b) puts it, "The republican city was, from as early as we have evidence, awash in monuments—literary, plastic, topographical, anatomical, sartorial, and nomenclatorial, to name but a few types—that transmitted socially and ethically valued slivers of the past into the present for praise/blame and imitation/avoidance; the exemplary impulse was rooted broadly and clearly in the republican aristocracy, and was manifested in a great many cultural forms."

ancestor L. Iunius Brutus on the Capitol that inspired M. Brutus to undertake Caesar's assassination (43.45.3).

The presence of this same audience reminded the elite that their actions had weight, and clearly was felt to have a constraining and shaping effect upon such action: if Marcia was not allowed to grieve over her dead son because her dead father was watching (*Ad Marc.* 25.3), so Brutus, as Cicero reminded him on the occasion of the death of his wife, had to bear up under the impressionable gaze of his followers: "You must put yourself at the service of the people and the theater [*scaenae*], as it is said. For since the eyes not only of your army, but of all the citizens and almost of the entire world, are cast on you, it is not at all appropriate that he through whom we are all braver should himself seem weakened in mind" (*Ad Brut.* 1.9.2). Here too the collective gaze of the Romans turns Brutus' stance into a quasi-theatrical production of his values, in which he must not falter lest his exemplary status should be lost. Seneca borrows this argument a century later and puts it into play for Claudius' freedman and imperial secretary *a studiis* Polybius upon the death of his brother. "The consensus of mankind has imposed a great persona upon you: this you must guard [*tibi tuenda est*]. That whole throng of consolers surrounds you and looks into your mind and investigates how much strength it has against sorrow and whether you only know how to live well under happy circumstances or if you can bear adverse times like a man: your eyes are being watched" (*Cons. Polyb.* 6.1). And Dio Cassius has Maecenas remind Octavian of his duties in similar words: "You will live as it were in a theater with the whole world as spectators, and if you err it will be impossible to escape notice even for the briefest time" (*Hist.* 53.6.2).[24]

The face and its expressions, naturally enough, carried great weight in such a culture; this emerges sharply from Seneca's *De beneficiis*, in which the author repeatedly notes the mutual observation of the other's face that goes on during elite gift-exchange in order to assess the value of the gift and the gratitude owed in return.[25] It is interesting that as late as the seventh century CE Isidore of Seville would even derive *vultus*, "face or expression," from *voluntas*, "will,"

---

24. καθάπερ γὰρ ἐν ἑνί τινι τῆς ὅλης οἰκουμένης θεάτρῳ ζήσῃ, καὶ οὐχ οἷόν τέ σοι ἔσται οὐδὲ βραχύτατον ἁμαρτόντι διαλαθεῖν.

25. Cf. Carlin Barton's work on *dura frons* (2001, 55–58, 74–75).

because the one could throw light on the other (*Etym.* 11.34).[26] Quintilian (*Inst.* 11.3.76) offers up a long list of all the sorts of eyes one should never see on a true Roman's face: rigid, languid, dull, lascivious, watery, and so forth. But the *dead* face was endowed with cultural equal valence. As we have seen, the *imagines* were worn at funerals, where they cast an assessing gaze on the successor to the dead and provided for the audience an instantaneous visual genealogy of a noble old line, but their visibility and significance reached beyond their role in this specific institution. On display in the atrium, they reminded visitors of the nobility of the family: Horace mocks the presumed awe of the common people standing before the *imagines* and honorary inscriptions (*tituli*) of the nobility.[27] Their visual impact rendered them exploitable for political and legal ends as well. They could be employed as a crucial part of the appeal to the jury; Seneca the Elder reports declaimers imagining their physical deployment in the courtroom to make defendants weep and provoke pity (*Contr.* 2.3.6, 9.6.8, 9.6.11). And they reflected in turn upon those who took them as their models: the tribune of the plebs Sextus Titius could be accused of treason partially on the grounds that he had an *imago* of the turbulent tribune L. Appuleius Saturninus in his house (Cic., *Rab. Perd.* 9.24)—marking Sextus as one who had taken up an inappropriate exemplum for his gaze, as it were, and thus an immoral member of the state.[28]

In this culture that placed a premium upon living up to the judgment of an authoritative viewer, the *imagines* could even be conceived of as the spectators of the actions of their descendants. In his oration *Pro Murena*, for example, Cicero, as he tried to move the jurors to acquit a newly minted Roman consul, did not ask how the man could go home to face his living family if convicted,

---

26. "Vultus vero dictus, eo quod per eum animi voluntas ostenditur; secundum voluntatem enim in varios motus mutatur. Unde et differunt sibi utraque; nam facies simpliciter accipitur de uniuscujusque naturali aspectu, vultus autem animorum qualitates significant"; discussed in Bettini 2000.

27. *Sat.* 1.6.16: "qui stupet in titulis et imaginibus." To denigrate these *imagines* was to align oneself politically against the values of the elite; see Gregory (1994, 87): "When consul in 107 BC Marius is depicted by Plutarch as antagonizing the nobles by saying that he had wounds on his body that he could show the people, not 'monuments of the dead' (μνήμα νεκρῶν) or 'images' (εἰκόσι) of other men (Plut. *Mar.* 9.2). Marius' coarse bluntness or refreshing honesty (as you will) provides a strong contrast to the aristocratic/educated Roman idea of what objects such as the *imagines* were for and how they were to be responded to."

28. Flower (1996) provides the most comprehensive and up-to-date treatment of the *imagines* at Rome, and this discussion is indebted to her work.

but what he would say to the grieving mask of his distinguished father that awaited him as he entered (Cic., *Mur.* 88); Juventius Laterensis is similarly grilled about his potential response to the family *imagines* (Cic., *Planc.* 51). Elsewhere, Cicero introduces the dead Appius Claudius Caecus into his oration to ask his disreputable descendant, the libidinous Claudia, how she could ignore the *imagines* of her ancestors—including his (*Cael.* 34).[29] The sense that the *imagines* were there to be answered to or lived up to could motivate as well as reprove: Cicero, in a variation of Dio's story, would claim that the tyrannicide Brutus had been prompted to action by the *imago* of L. Iunius Brutus in his house (*Phil.* 2.26). The historian Sallust remarks on how such masks kindled an emulative zeal in their ancestors: "For I have often heard that Quintus Maximus, Publius Scipio, and besides them other renowned men of our state were accustomed to say that when they gazed upon the *imagines* of their ancestors, their spirit was powerfully fired for virtue, not of course because the wax or the likeness had so much force, but because the memory of their deeds fed a flame in the chests of outstanding men which could not be put out until their virtue had equaled their ancestors' fame and glory" (*Iug.* 4.5–6). The younger Pliny similarly commented on the way the *imagines* seemed to praise, exhort, and even *recognize* (*laudare, adhortari, et . . . agnoscere*) the descendants whose atria they occupied (*Ep.* 5.17.6). As Harriet Flower has justly concluded from this evidence, "For the aristocratic Roman the *imagines* played the role of an audience which reflected the norms of his 'honour group.'"[30]

Although little remarked, the multiplicity of meanings held by the word *imago* offers a suggestive link between the exemplary "mirror" presented to the citizens by such a man as Scipio and the notion that the *imagines* themselves represented visual models of behavior for their ancestors to emulate.[31] The earliest usages, in Plautus, refer to the *imago* as mask but stress also its similarity to the original. In the *Amphitruo*, one part of the plot turns on a *doppelgänger*, a character who by divine trickery has taken on the exact appearance of another. The slave Sosia comes face to face with Mercury, who looks exactly like him, and squawks in astonishment that someone else is wearing his *imago*. As Flower

---

29. See similarly Cic., *Leg. agr.* 2.100; Cic., *Planc.* 51; and Pliny, *Ep.* 3.3.6.
30. Flower 1996, 14. See also Gregory 1994, 90–91; and Penwill 1994 for further examples.
31. On these meanings, see especially Flower 1996, 34–35.

(1996, 47) notes, "the humour arises from the unexpected picture of a slave imagining a senatorial ancestor mask of himself. It also depends on the *imago* being a realistic representation, which could be imagined as someone's 'double.'" Indeed, the realism of the likeness provided by the mask is stressed in several sources, Plautine and otherwise.[32] The copy of the self and the model provided by the other thus seem conjoined fairly early in the usage, and in later developments the *imago* literally refers to the reflection in the mirror, the likeness from which one could learn to prune one's character into the necessary shape.

The term *imago*, like the mirror itself, thus provided a link between reflection and prescription, and came to be associated with a certain instructive potential.[33] Even one's life could function metaphorically as an *imago*—both a pattern, or model, to be followed, and, as it were, an ancestral mask bequeathed to younger generations for inspiration, emulation, and even surveillance. Seneca, for example, calls Cato the Younger the living *imago* of all the virtues ("Cato ille, virtutium viva imago" [*Ep.* 9.16.1]; cf. *Marc.* 18.1 and *Ben* 7.27.1, both *imagines vitae* with instructive impacts), and Cicero praises the Greek and Latin authors for passing down the inspiring pictures of brave men of old: "How many *imagines* of the bravest men—not only for viewing but even for imitating—have both the Greek and Roman authors fashioned and bequeathed to us! I always set these *imagines* before me in administering the republic and model my mind and thought through reflection upon these excellent men."[34] Most strikingly, in Tacitus' account of Seneca's suicide of 65 CE, the philosopher is attributed the dying boast that he is bequeathing to his followers his most precious possession, the *imago* of his own life; if they kept it present in their mind, they would attain the good character for which they strove (*Ann.* 15.62).[35] The several meanings of the word *imago* at play here imply that Seneca is leaving behind an image that can both keep an eye on posterity (as we have seen of the *imago*'s role elsewhere) and offer a represen-

---

32. See, e.g., *Men.* 1063 ("Tuast imago, tam consimilest quam potes") and *Mil. Glor.* 151; Diod. Sic., 31.25.2; Polyb., 6.53.5; Pliny, *HN* 35.4.

33. Just like the simile, also called *imago*. Seneca comments that even in prose, such similes are a necessary means for the instruction of weaker intellects (*Ep.* 59.6).

34. Cic., *Arch.* 6.14. For a similar usage, see *Tusc.* 3.3. Val. Max., 5.4, describes a painted *imago* carrying an ethical charge.

35. "Quod unum iam et tamen pulcherrimum habeat, imaginem vitae suae relinquere testatur, cuius si memores essent, bonarum artium famam fructum constantis amicitiae laturos."

tational model for it as well.[36] *Imago* and human viewers provide a mutual audience, and ideally the actions of the latter should be shaped by the imaginary gaze of the former. Moreover, Seneca's death was itself an *imago*, a reflection of a prior and more famous death: that of Socrates in the *Phaedo*.[37] In this case, the chain of exemplarity stretched back into the Greek world, taking its origin (atypically) from a source that was not a hero from the Roman past.[38]

Where the term does refer specifically to ancestor masks, its invocation, as Raimund Daut (1975, 142) has pointed out, was to ethical rather than aesthetic ends, at least throughout the republic: "the *imago* was not invoked to comment on its artistic merits, but rather to provide a linkage to social and moral value-judgments, and its goal, always, was the production of memory in those who gazed upon it: *posteritatis memoria*." This interpretation is supported by Pliny the Elder's contrast between the decadent forms of portraiture in vogue in his day and the *imagines* (*HN* 35.4–7). The painted *imagines* of the ancestors have disappeared from the houses of the nobility, killed off by the indolence and *luxuria* of their owners, who prize instead the use precious materials and the interchangeability of statuary heads: "as a result, no one's likeness lives, and they leave behind *imagines* of money rather than of themselves" (*HN* 35.5).[39] In this move to perverted artistry, as Georges Didi-Huberman (1996, 122) has shown, lies the ruin of generational resemblance, and with it the ruin of tradi-tional ethical standards: "Resemblance via permutation is illegitimate; it derails both natural law and juridical institution."[40]

---

36. See Solimano 1991, 62. Other examples of the *imagines* as a potential audience: Cic., *Cael.* 34; Cic., *Leg. Agr.* 2.100; Pliny, *Pan.* 56.8.

37. On his death, see Griffin 1976, 365–88.

38. More abstractly, and without the language of craft associated with the mask itself (*expressas*, in the example from Cicero), exemplary moments in history could also be described as *imagines*, as in Sen., *Ep.* 120.8. And so could the images provided by nature: Cic., *Rep.* 2.39.66. On the visual quality of exempla in Seneca, see Solimano 1991, 43–44.

39. "Itaque nullius effigie vivente imagines pecuniae, non suas, reliquunt." On the term *imago* in Roman art, see Daut 1975; and Lahusen 1982. It is used only of the human form in art until Lucr., 2.609, 6.420, which Daut ascribes to the poet's philosophical program. As a result, both scholars speculate that this original meaning might have been the ancestor mask.

40. See the comments of Flower 1996, 34. The misapprehension that the masks were not painted seems to have led astray other commentators on this passage; Didi-Huberman's (1996) defense of the opposing position seems to me convincing, as does his demonstration that *imaginum pictura* cannot refer to portraiture.

The *imago* had a philosophical application as well—in fact, several. It could be invoked to describe the mental image by means of which the striver after virtue encouraged himself or herself to follow a praiseworthy path of action. Seneca was struck by such an *imago*, in this case a simile, in the writings of the Augustan Stoic Q. Sextius: "So, I am reading Sextius right now; a sharp man, one who philosophizes in Greek but with the character of a Roman. I was moved by a simile [*imago*] he used: an army is marching in a hollow square, in a place where the enemy is expected from every side, and ready for battle. 'This,' he said, 'is exactly what the wise man should do; he should deploy all his strengths on every side, so that a hostile force may spring up, his protections will be prepared in that place, and will respond to the general's sign without confusion'" (*Ep.* 59.7). But the *imago* could be a simple mental image as well, part of the Stoic's self-preparation in building up a kind of emotional immunity to possible future unpleasantness (torture, shipwreck, penury, and the like) or in keeping horror at bay if any such event befell him. Seneca often exhorts his interlocutors to set such pictures before their minds' eye.[41] In contrast, Cicero's discussant in the *Tusculan Disputations* makes fun of such exhortatory invocations of the virtues in Stoic philosophy. Expressing his disagreement with the Stoic dictum that the wise man is always happy, even when stretched out on the rack, he remarks:

> Those arguments don't move me at all; not only because they're hackneyed, but much more because those Stoic principles, like certain light wines which lose their body in water, offer more pleasure when tasted rather than drunk down. Similarly, that troop of virtues of yours, when laid on the rack, sets before the eyes *imagines* of the greatest dignity, as if the happy life seemed about to come to their aid soon and not to allow them to be abandoned by itself; however, when you wrench your mind from that picture and the images of the virtues [*ab ista pictura imaginibusque virtutum*] to actuality and the truth, this bare question is left: can anyone be happy while he's being tortured? (*Tusc.* 5.5.13–14)

---

41. See, e.g., Sen., *Ep.* 74.7: "Set this picture before your mind: that Fortune is putting on games, and is showering among this mortal throng honors, riches, influence, of which some are torn to pieces among the hands of those snatching at them, some are divided up by an impious partnership, and some are seized to the great detriment of those who receive them."

Here it is the virtues themselves that have been stretched out to suffer, and are imagined as consoling themselves with the *imagines* that dance before their eyes. This whole image itself is then called an *imago*; both the virtues looking at the *imagines*, and we looking at the *imago* of the virtues, are participating in an exemplary viewing of the sort encouraged by Stoic philosophy; but neither of us—or so claims the speaker—could really bear up under actual torture once we had ceased gratifying ourselves with this noble but self-deceptive picture. Here the philosophers' claims for the exemplary qualities of the *imago* held up before the mind are explicitly mocked; Cicero seems to doubt that the force of the ancestral *imagines*, which he himself has acknowledged at *Pro Murena* 88.6, can be transferred to the imaginary constructs of the Stoics, given their gulf from truth and their lack of foundation in any real political or genealogical reality.

These abstract images of the virtues and the kind of mental exercises the Stoics practiced to inure themselves to future eventualities find an interesting counterpart in the literal *imagines* of the founders of various philosophical sects that their followers wore on rings. This seems to have been particularly common in Epicurus' camp, where the image of the founder presumably provided a constant reminder to his students of the behavioral standards and philosophical values to which they were supposed to adhere. Atticus confessed to wearing a ring with an engraved image of the philosopher, as well as owning several pictures of him and carrying images of him in his pocket; his friends, he said, did the same—as a result, no chance of forgetting the fellow (Cic., *Fin.* 5.3). Seneca too kept around *imagines* of the great men who were his teachers: both Catos, Laelius, Socrates and Plato, Zeno and Cleanthes (*Ep.* 64.9).[42] For him, these were the great leaders of the past, a group who only partially coincided with the more traditional Roman exemplars; this latter throng included military heroes as well as statesmen and philosophers, so we are not surprised to find Fabius Cunctator or various Metelli invoked in such a work as Valerius Maximus' collection of exemplary anecdotes, the *Facta ac dicta memorabilia*.

Finally, the *imago* could be the image in the mirror as well. Such an emphasis on the seen quality of the exemplum and the ratifying force of its audience returns us to the mirror metaphor of chapter 1: this attitude, in its emphasis on

---

42. On this practice in general, see also Zanker 1995, 205–8; and Pliny, *HN* 35.2. Some Roman villas even had portrait galleries with images of intellectuals and philosophers.

public, visible accomplishment over (say) mental states and unrealized intentions, allowed for the description of the virtuous individual as precisely a mirror for his fellow citizens, a glass in which they could see an idealized self-potential, and try to emulate or live up to it. Scipio Africanus, who defeated Hannibal at Zama in 202 BCE, cuts such a figure in Cicero's *De republica*, where he himself, in turn, offers a definition of the ideal statesman that relies upon the intersection of visibility and exemplarity: a man who "should never cease to gaze at and contemplate himself, should call others to emulate himself, and should provide a mirror, as it were, to the citizens, by the splendor of his soul and his life" (*Rep.* 2.69).[43] The ideal statesman thus bridges the gap between self-contemplation and the contemplation afforded him by others; in looking at himself, presumably once again through the critical eyes of the (right-minded) members of his audience, he sees how he may improve himself according to their standards, and in so doing, he becomes a mirror and a model to others, who are now called to remake themselves according to the image that stands before them. Several kinds of visual judgment are at work here, and all contribute to the surprisingly powerful visual component in Roman ethics, in which we can see a process involving self-contemplation in the mirror of the community, contemplation of the exemplary other by his fellow citizens, and then a mirroring process of self-judgment by that audience, which tries to measure up to the model in the mirror.

As with Scipio, the mirror of self-improvement, in the specular world of Roman politics, could be another man, and the figure one lived up to or belied could be supplied, not by the beautiful or ugly image in one's own mirror, but by the potential reflected in one by the virtuous other. The sentiment is echoed by Plutarch in his essay on how to make progress in virtue: let those who would improve themselves set before their eyes good men of the present or past, and reflect on what Plato would have done, or Epameinondas, or Agesilaus, "adorning themselves before such mirrors, as it were, or remodeling [*metarrhuthmizontas*] themselves, or checking ignoble utterances or resisting some passion" (*De prof. virt.* 15.87a–b). The lost *Imagines* of M. Terentius Varro, containing

---

43. "Ut numquam a se ipso intuendo contemplandoque discedat, ut ad imitationem sui vocet alios, ut sese splendore animi et vitae suae sicut speculum praebeat civibus." This usage of *speculum* to mean "model" occurs earlier in Plaut., *Epidicus* 382–84 (discussed in chapter 1). On *speculum* in its meaning as "model," see Callahan 1964.

seven hundred or so illustrated biographies of famous Greeks and Romans, presumably contained similar models for its readers—and perhaps played on its own title in so doing.

Not all Roman philosophizing in the first centuries BCE and CE shared this positive assessment of the potential role of the *imago*, of course. Lucretius in the *De rerum natura* had already commented in negative terms on this use of the terminology and ideology of the political *imago*. In Lucretius' startlingly un-Roman assessment of the goals of life, the statesman's desire to provide a model for future generations is skeptically equated with "a cloak for the pursuit of wealth and power" (5.1120–35), and, as J. L. Penwill (1994, 81) underscores, Lucretius' evocations of Homer, Epicurus, Democritus, and others are meant to provide, not an incitement to political action and imitation, but a reminder of the inevitability of death. Lucretius' *imago* is the image in the mirror in its most deceptive sense: in Roman ideology, as on the reflective surface of a piece of silver plate, there is no there there.[44]

My point here is not to ascribe causal or temporal relationships to different meanings of the word, but to show that a complicated web of associations (as well as the repeated use of the word *imago* itself) linked the mirror-image, the exemplum, the double, and the ancestor mask—and linked these, in turn, to the thing seen, which had the potential to stir the viewer to virtue. The gaze upon the other, at least among the Roman elite, for whom we have the best sources of literary and historical evidence, was thus a source for judging and assessing the other, a witness to his *virtus*. However, no senator or equestrian occupied purely the subject position as the issuer of this gaze; rather, all in turn judged and were judged, all occupied the position of both subject and object. The very exemplarity of those in the spotlight also rendered them more vulnerable to the scrutiny of those who looked up to them. The polyvalence of the *imago* itself—an object worn at elite funerals to impress spectators with the dead man's ancestors, but also enforcing the mores of those ancestors in their descendants, or a sign of the importance and/or the emptiness of Roman political ambition, or even the image that stared back from the mirror—

---

44. As Penwill (1994, 80–81) continues, "In this sense the traditional Roman response to the *imagines* of the dead, whether at funerals or in the works of national poets and historians, is revealed as a monumental act of self-deception, turning the past into a source of ideology for the present."

connected a string of meanings, associations, and traditions which, it bears repeating, were purely Roman in their interrelation (the Greeks had no *imagines*). The power of the assessing gaze at Rome brings us to the topic of the "shame culture," which has been the focus of renewed study. Scholars of antiquity such as Bernard Williams and Douglas Cairns have sought to place this societal stress on the controlling and exemplary force of the visual in the context of a shame culture, and they have shown the value of such a notion. In the simplest and most sweeping formulations of the distinction between shame and guilt, applied by E. R. Dodds (1951), Ruth Benedict (1947), and others, "guilt cultures" were defined as relying upon the Judaeo-Christian religious tradition and notions of conscience and the internalization of divine law, while shame cultures derived their sense of right and wrong from the force of public opinion and from external sanctions upon behavior. In Benedict's (1947, 233) classic definition, "true shame cultures rely on external sanctions for good behavior, not, as true guilt cultures do, on an internalized conviction of sin. Shame is a reaction to other people's criticism. A man is shamed either by being openly ridiculed and rejected or by fantasying to himself that he has been made ridiculous. In either case it is a potent sanction. But it requires an audience or at least a man's fantasy of an audience. Guilt does not. In a nation where honor means living up to one's own picture of oneself, a man may suffer from guilt though no man knows of his misdeed and a man's feelings of guilt may actually be relieved by confessing his sin." As Williams, Cairns, and others have pointed out, this distinction between external sanctions (or external audiences) and internal convictions (or "conscience") is not sustainable. The production of shame can easily rely upon an *internalized* viewer present only in the mind of the wrongdoer, and as a result, it is difficult to argue for clear-cut separation from the notion of an inner judge and conscience—indeed, one could characterize the latter as having lost awareness of the internalized watching divine figure. In such case, the "inherently moral" behavior that conscience seems to adjudicate is not quite so private as one would think. Even in a "shame culture," then, such an internalized viewer can take precedence over external viewers who represent a community whose judgment carries less force.[45]

---

45. On the internalization of community standards, see especially Cairns 1993, 14–18; Williams 1993, 81–85. Creighton (1990) would argue that Benedict, while wrong to use the internal/external criterion to distinguish guilt from shame, did not mean to affix value judgments to these two terms.

Another problem is that detailed investigations into ancient "shame" (often, but not always, translatable by *aidos* and *pudor*) reveal that its main distinction from our notion of guilt is one of degree rather than quality: "no distinction in terms of external versus internal sanctions; no exclusion of the phenomenon of conscience; and no denial of the existence of personally endorsed moral standards" can be maintained as clear markers of the difference between guilt and shame (Cairns 1993, 45). Cairns (21–22) also cautions against too readily accepting the distinction that guilt relates to what one has done to the other, while shame looks to who one is; self *simpliciter* and self as agent cannot always be clearly separated.

Nonetheless, it is clear that while we can no longer maintain a simple division between internal "guilt" and external "shame" in ancient *or* modern cultures, the cultures we used to identify as "shame cultures" can still be distinguished by a shared emphasis on concern about reputation, public persona, one's peers as a source of moral authority; they are small-scale societies that tend "to construe obligation in personal rather than abstract terms" (Cairns 1993, 49).[46] Visual metaphors and visual references are particularly common in such cultures, which Cairns would therefore rename "face cultures"; as he notes (1993, 18), "references to the audience . . . and metaphors of 'eyes' and 'being seen' indicate the essential role of the detached observer in shame." Bernard Williams (1993, 75–102) develops the same idea when he remarks that in cases of shaming, the victim wants to sink through the floor and get away from all those eyes; with guilt, it wouldn't matter if he did, because he would feel he took the guilt with him.[47] This gaze, again, does not have to be understood in any literal sense: shame can also be the product of an internalized viewer that embodies the judgments of the community, and the "other" who watches can be so internalized that one can be an observer of oneself. As Matthew Roller (2001a, 22) puts it, "When the agent himself endorses and subscribes to those [communal] values, when he judges himself as he foresees being judged by

---

46. Cairns (1993) stresses, however, that the significance of these features should not be taken as suggesting a psychological differentiation between the ancient and the modern world. The nature of this redefinition and fine-tuning of the work on shame culture does nothing to vitiate the important discussions that focus exactly on such issues as reputation and honor in ancient Greece and Rome; see, e.g., Barton 2001, 202–70; Cohen 1991, 35–97; Dover 1974, 236–42.

47. Williams is, of course, discussing classical Athens, but I am not the first to find his perspective equally illuminating for aspects of the Roman world.

others and as he would judge them in turn, then this community-oriented value can also exist internally."[48] Moreover, one's sensitivity to opinion is capable of being represented as a sensitivity to an ideal built on the hypothetical judgment of others, which leads Cairns (1993, 17–18) to formulate the role of the audience in a face-culture as bringing "a previously unconsidered interpretation of the agent's action or situation to his or her attention." Accordingly, "to consider the hypothetical judgment of a fantasy audience is to see oneself in a different light, to step back from self-absorption and take a detached view."[49]

It is interesting to note that the ancients themselves were so conscious of this connection between ethical behavior and the sense of being seen that a few of them derived the origin of religion accordingly. The fifth-century Athenian Critias suggested that when it was clear to primitive man that human laws prevented men from committing acts of violence in the open, but not so in secret, some psychologically astute ruler invented the gods and warned that they could see and punish acts which no mortals could.[50] This strain in sophist thought recurs in other contexts as well. In Hesiod's *Works and Days*, for example, Zeus is figured as the all-seeing enforcer of morals; his eye, which marks the forms of justice in the city, is assisted in this project by "ten thousand spirits, watchers of mortal men" (cf. 248–73).[51] Such stories offer us a political origin for religion, but at the same time stress the role of the sensation of feeling watched in this origin; the ubiquitous judge gazing on

---

48. Cf. Williams 1993, 82: "Even if shame and its motivations always involve in some way or other an idea of the gaze of another, it is important that for many of its operations the imagined gaze of another will do." Barton (2001, 202–70) brings together many striking examples of the link between shame and vision at Rome. On the regulating force of the community as source of moral value, see also Earl 1961, 18–27; Habinek 1998, 45–59; Kaster 1997; Williams 1993; and Roller 2001a, 64–126 (with further bibliography at 22n10).

49. For a similar view, see Kaster 1997, 5: "People feel *pudor* not only because they are seen, or fear being seen, but because they see themselves and know that their present behavior falls short of their past or ideal selves."

50. In his satyr play *Sisyphus*, *TGF* fr. 25.9f, Diels-Kranz B25. On the topic of "doing wrong in secret," see Williams 1993, 360–70.

51. As Andrew Stewart (1997, 16) put it, "Hesiod insists that man's emergence as a uniquely moral being is predicated on the gaze, which he personifies as that of All-Seeing Zeus and his mysterious, omnipresent Watchers. . . . The archaic Greek scopic regime was thus created by Zeus to civilize mankind."

one's actions stands at the origin of the moral self.[52] Fifth- and fourth-century Greek interest in this topic is also well represented in the literature, where the constraining presence of a viewer is often posited as the cause of moral behavior even when the audience is mortal; in Soph., *Trach.* 596–7, and Eur., *Hipp.* 403–4, Deianeira and Phaedra, respectively, point out that shameful deeds that have no witnesses bring no disgrace, and the Corinthians in Thuc., 1.37.2, charge the Corcyreans with avoiding alliances so they could proceed with their crimes without witnesses. In a philosophical context Glaucon, in Pl., *Resp.* 2, tells the story of how the Lydian Gyges found a ring to make him invisible and merrily proceeded to a life of crime (359c–360d).[53] Glaucon uses the story to support his opinion that if any man, no matter how just, were able to be invisible, freed of the constraint of the community's gaze, he would steal, rape, and commit murder. The truth of this was a matter of some debate, not only in the Platonic corpus, but also in an important Democritean fragment suggesting that shame before the self is more important than shame before others, and that the same standards should be maintained with or without an external audience (Diels-Kranz B264).[54]

At Rome, too, ethical behavior could be attributed to the presence of a watching audience; this is precisely what the emperor Tiberius breaks free of when, having retreated to Capreae in 26 CE and cast aside the reins of empire, he is said to capitalize on his removal from public view by yielding to a life of sexual depravity (Suet., *Tib.* 42.1).[55] What the rumors definitely reveal is not so much whether Tiberius had a kinky side, but that removing oneself from

---

52. See Maier (1997, 132, 133) for Christian versions of this notion of the divine eye; in this literature, we repeatedly find "actors under God's eye whose deepest thoughts and most secret activities are visible to the divine *spectator* or surveillant. . . . Both formal apocalypses and literature that draws upon apocalyptic themes more generally stage a divine gaze in a textual theater in which audiences encounter themselves stripped and dressed to play various roles and thus to embrace the ideals of the apocalypticist."

53. Hdt., 1.8–12, offers a different version of the story, but one in which it is precisely through Gyges' *being seen* in an initial transgression of *nomos* that leads to his murder of the Lydian king Candaules.

54. μηδέν τι μᾶλλον τοὺς ἀνθρώπους αἰδεῖσθαι ἑωυτοῦ μηδέ τι μᾶλλον ἐξεργάζεσθαι κακόν, εἰ μέλλει μηδεὶς εἰδήσειν ἢ οἱ πάντες ἄνθρωποι· ἀλλ' ἑωυτὸν μάλιστα αἰδεῖσθαι, καὶ τοῦτον νόμον τῆι ψυχῆι καθεστάναι, ὥστε μηδὲν ποιεῖν ἀνεπιτήδειον.

55. "Ceterum secreti licentiam nanctus et quasi ciuitatis oculis remotis, cuncta simul uitia male diu dissimulata tandem profudit."

public view itself may produce such allegations![56] Certainly at Rome the position of the watcher had long been institutionalized in an office not shared by the Athenian polis: that of the censor, elected every five years to revise the senatorial and equestrian rolls for immorality or incompetent administration. Dionysius of Halicarnassus commented admiringly on this elite self-subjection to the gaze in his *Roman Antiquities*:

> The Romans, opening up every house and extending the jurisdiction of the censors even to the bedroom, made them the watcher and guardian of everything that happened in the house, feeling that neither should a master be harsh in punishing his slaves, nor a father cruel or soft beyond measure in the upbringing of his children, nor a husband unjust in his fellowship with his wedded wife, nor children disobedient of their elderly parents; nor should legitimate brothers pursue more than what was fair; nor should there be all-night drinking and banquets, nor licentiousness and the corruption of young men, nor abandonment of the ancestral honors of sacrifices and burials, nor any other of the things done against propriety and the benefit of the city. (20.13.3)

So strict was the gaze the censor turned upon his fellow Romans that Cato the Elder notoriously expelled one Manilius from the Senate for kissing his own wife in public (Plut., *Cat. Mai.* 17.6); not for nothing did Cicero call this office the guardian of the citizens' *pudor* (*Rep.* 5.6).[57] As censor, Scipio Africanus threatened a perjured equestrian with his ability to act as accuser, witness, and judge all at once (Val. Max., 4.1.10). The censor provided only the most official source of the gaze. It was a function that ideally every citizen should undertake, like Cicero's evocation of men on the watchtowers across the country, carefully focusing their gaze on the behavior of the senatorial members of Verres' jury (*Verr.* 1.1.46).[58]

The regulatory force of the gaze under discussion here might remind us of Jeremy Bentham's panopticon, the innovative prison design discussed by Foucault in *Discipline and Punish* (1979). In this imaginary circular prison in which

---

56. As Christopher Gill points out to me.

57. These two passages from Plutarch and Dionysius are already cited together in the brief discussion by Barton 2001, 21.

58. For further examples on the regulating force of *pudor*, see Barton 2001, 18–23; and Kaster 1997.

every inmate, sitting in his lighted glass cell, can be seen by a warden located in a central tower, it is "the fact of being constantly seen, of being always able to be seen, that maintains the disciplined individual in his subjection" (187). Foucault calls this form of visually abetted control the "disciplinary gaze," and in its linking of the visual sphere with the production of a societally prescribed form of behavior—or, in negative terms, with the suppression of societally proscribed behavior—it resembles the community gaze we have been examining at Rome. As with Foucault's general understanding of the working of power, the Roman gaze is generative as well as repressive; it produces behaviors that conform to definitions of *virtus* and in so doing contributes to the entire Roman machinery of literary and philosophical self-shaping. But the differences are perhaps more striking than the similarities. For one, the panopticon relies on the policing force of a single and authoritative individual, the warden in his central tower, whose constant gaze upon the circle of inmates—a potential, rather than an actuality, of course—is their sole source of behavioral modification. Foucault identifies this arrangement as "a machine for dissociating the see/being seen dyad: in the peripheric ring, one is totally seen, without ever seeing; in the central tower, one sees everything without being seen" (1979, 201–2). There is, in short, no reciprocity of the gaze, no symbiosis in the enforcement of societal mores and the simultaneous production of power, while in republican Rome entire social groups are engaged in reciprocal acts of watching and evaluating, with the stakes highest (and most evident in our sources) at the highest levels of the political hierarchy: "In a true republic no citizen monopolized the public gaze."[59] Second, Bentham's panopticon is specifically an institution for convicts, not for the elite, who are presumably conceived of as sufficiently self-policing under normal social conditions; and it is, of course, one institution rather than a web of institutions and practices. Finally, the panoptic gaze is purely assessing, purely judgmental. There is no sense of glory in being the object of its focus, no room for triumph or for the display of family lineage, no assignment of exemplarity to be handed down for posterity. At Rome, these were the rewards for subscribing to the shared values of the community and performing them in the flesh—at least during the republican period. One of the most salient aspects of the transition to empire was

---

59. Bell 1997, 8.

precisely the breakdown of these rewards and the breakdown, too, of the reciprocity of the gaze. Along with this went a breakdown in the distinction between safe and unsafe forms of visibility.

THE PENETRATING GAZE

An attempt to apply a panoptical metaphor to Roman ways of seeing would run into difficulties more fundamental still than those laid out above. The models of vision we have examined so far have had to do with exemplary or ethical constructions of the gaze—its use in the transmission of local and historical values concerning elite behavior. Within such models, the member of the elite on whom the community's gaze was trained—whether specifically, as in the Forum, or generally, in everyday political life—felt himself monitored in a way that could only (re)produce societally sanctioned and approved forms of action; he was thus simultaneously pupil and pedagogue, supplying the gaze with behaviors resulting from this impetus to correct action and with further fodder for the continued transmission of the values he enacted. For this symbiotic relationship, the *imago* is probably itself the best image: the ancestral face that gazes and is gazed upon, that incites exemplary behavior by providing a model and a sense, however fanciful, of a present witness. These ethical models for the workings of the gaze, however, seem to have had little to do with the sexual and philosophical ramification of the gaze and its physiological workings that we examined in chapter 2. Did these aspects of visual theory drop from popular awareness altogether in daily life at Rome, and remain merely the province of writers such as Lucretius and Ovid?

The answer, of course, is no. The crucial factor in setting apart Foucauldian ideas about vision and power from the beliefs and cultural practices is the more sinister role vision has to play in interpersonal dynamics among both the elite and commoners at Rome. Another manifestation of this gaze brought with it vulnerability rather than glory. The individual on display could suffer the debilitating effects of the evil rather than the emulatory eye, of aggression or *Schadenfreude* rather than admiration. This form of the gaze could be figured as a weapon, and was sometimes imagined as penetrating its human object, or else feeding itself on the sight of suffering. In such a case, if the conditions were right, one might expect that the result of exposure to an audience would be a weakening of one's authority, a lessening of one's political impermeability.

Certainly in the extreme case of someone who mounted the stage, the demeaning and emasculating effects of such self-display were keenly felt: to present oneself to the collective gaze of a theater crowd proves to have been a most uncomfortable subject position. Contrary to what we might expect, the spectator's position was not always one of authority or judgment with regard to the figure on whom he trained his eyes, for some sights could damage or corrupt the viewer even as he basked in the pleasure of the spectacle. Context was everything: and as the dynamics of particular contexts changed in the political transition from republic to empire, the comparatively clear-cut division between these two forms of viewing, emulatory and aggressive, came under question as well. By the mid-first century CE, some of elite Rome's habitual forms of viewing became subject to reconceptualization and reevaluation.

A graphic, and immediate, illustration of the permeating force of the hostile gaze readily emerges from the consideration of some of the most striking images to have survived from ancient Rome and its provinces in Asia Minor and North Africa, many showing us strange representations of the human eye under attack from other humans or from animals and weapons. That the eye is itself in danger of violation in these images might suggest that they illustrate the vulnerability of this organ to external attack, and indeed, we saw in chapter 2 how the eye was conceived of as the most immediate gateway to the body. But the meaning of these images is quite the contrary, and points instead to a variety of graphic defenses *against* the eye's potential to harm. For example, a small terracotta figurine dating to the first century CE shows a large, disembodied eyeball being sawn in two by a pair of little men shaped like phalluses (fig. 2). In a thematically similar image dated to 150–200 CE and discovered in a villa in Jekmejeh, near Antioch, a mosaic eye is under attack from a variety of beasts and weapons—a trident, a dagger, a scorpion, a snake, a dog, a centipede, a leopard, and a crow (fig. 3). Most oddly, once again phallic imagery enters the picture; the phallus of the dwarf who is turned away from the eye seems to be trying to enter into the attack as well. A Roman panel shows the eye being stabbed by a spear; above it sits an owl and around it a similar menagerie of attackers—snake, scorpion, leopard, bull, goat, and others (fig. 4). A mosaic threshold in Mokenine shows a heavy-lidded eye surrounded by an oval enclosure made by two snakes against which presses the tip of a pisciform penis that points down on it from above (fig. 5). A startling terracotta found in Cairo from the Hellenistic or Roman period shows a skeletal man with a hugely

FIGURE 2 Terracotta figure showing eyeball being sawn in half by two phallus-men (Collection of the British Museum 1865, 11-18.78. Photo © The Trustees of The British Museum.)

FIGURE 3 Floor mosaic of eye under attack by dwarf and animals, from House of the Evil Eye, Antioch (Antioch Expedition Archives. Photo courtesy of Research Photographs, Department of Art and Archeology, Princeton University)

FIGURE 4 Roman floor mosaic panel of an eye stabbed by a spear. An owl sits atop the eye, and a menagerie of attackers—snake, scorpion, leopard, bull, goat—are ranged around. (Photo from M. E. Blake, *Roman Mosaics of the Second Century in Italy*, Memoirs of the American Academy at Rome 13, p. 158, pl. 38.2; courtesy of the American Academy at Rome.)

distended phallus pointing down to the eyeball he is standing upon. Finally, the reverse of an amulet shows an isolated eye under attack. The assailants in this case are three daggers, two lions, a scorpion, a snake, and a long-beaked bird— creatures and implements that can readily breach the body's integrity, if not in the precise manner of the phallus (fig. 6).

These images present us with what seems to be a iconographic assault on the disembodied eye, which is repeatedly shown with various objects whose main power is that of penetrating or piercing the human body.[60] Part of the puzzle behind these representations finds an answer in the work of anthropologists of Roman culture, who have long since shown that the images are visual

---

60. On these images, see Clarke 1996; Dunbabin 1978, 161–62; and Johns 1982, chap. 4.

FIGURE 5 Mosaic threshold, Mokenine, showing an eye surrounded by an oval enclosure made of two snakes, with the tip of a pisciform penis pressing down from above. (Photo by Katherine M. Dunbabin)

FIGURE 6 Reverse of amulet from the Schlumberger collection, showing a disembodied eye under attack by three daggers, two lions, a scorpion, a snake, and a long-beaked bird (Photo by Katherine M. Dunbabin)

versions of apotropaic efforts against the evil eye, a phenomenon described in a broad variety of literary and doxographical texts in antiquity. Such images combining the phallus and the eye, or aggressive animals and the eye, were apparently believed to turn away or defeat the force of any ill-intentioned wielder of the evil eye in their presence; hence their frequent presence in the threshold images of houses, and, in one case the inscription in Greek *kai su*: "You, too (mind this message)." Other images also believed effective against the evil eye include the ithyphallic representations of men in Roman baths (fig. 7), as well as the presence of phallic symbols such as the amulet, or *fascinum*, worn

FIGURE 7 Mosaic pavement from House of the Menander, Pompeii, I.10.4, entryway to *caldarium* with ithyphallic black man (Photo by Michael Larvey)

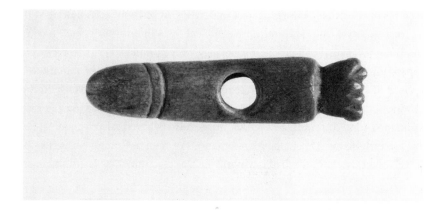

FIGURE 8 A fascinum, or amulet to ward off the evil eye, in the shape of a phallus (Collection of the British Museum 1974, 7-8.1. Photo © The Trustees of The British Museum.)

around the neck by young Roman boys, who were believed to be particularly susceptible to the evil eye of strangers (fig. 8).[61]

This interpretation is upheld by the literary sources of the early empire, which also repeatedly refer to the use of the phallus to avert the evil eye, most often in the form of a *fascinum*, or phallic amulet (also known as a *bulla* for the round leather sachet in which it was enclosed), that was hung around the necks of young boys for their protection (cf. Pliny, *HN* 28.29; Varro, *Ling.* 7.97; also Plaut., *Mil. Glor.* 1399). The same phallic *fascinum* was also attached to the underside of the chariot of the triumphing general, again to protect him in his moment of supreme glory from the invidious looks of others (Pliny, *HN* 28.29; Macrob., *Sat* 1.6.9). In general, what Pliny calls *saturica signa*, "lewd emblems," were considered efficacious for this use "in the garden and in the Forum"

---

61. Barton 1993, 95–96. On the connection between the evil eye and the penis that averts it, both called *fascinum* in Latin, see also Graziano 1997, 154–56, with bibliography. As Graziano remarks, "The nexus of the eye, the phallus, and vital fluid has also generated substantial traditions relating eye emanations themselves . . . to ejaculation"; he cites examples from ancient Egypt to modern Greece. See also Fredrick 1995, 285. Graziano remarks (1997, 89) on the erotic *causation* of the punishment of death-by-reflection doled out to both Narcissus and Echo in Ovid: Echo's sin is covering up for Jupiter's adultery, Narcissus' is the rejection of all his suitors. Cf. Freud's explanation of Oedipus' self-blinding as symbolic castration, discussed in Graziano 1997, 134. On the connection between the evil eye and intromission, see Dodds 1973, 162–63.

(*HN* 19.50), perhaps referring in the first case to the ithyphallic statues of Priapus erected against garden trespassers and in the latter case to the phalluses carved in the stones of the Forum.[62]

The phallic component in such imagery, however, remains to be explained. Whence the emphasis on the penis as an apotropaic device, rather than on the other solutions and apotropaic measures familiar still in Mediterranean cultures—the Hand of God or the Hand of Fatima (with an eye in its center), a clove of garlic, the application of henna to the hands, and so forth?[63] The answer may lie in how the Romans explained the working of the evil eye. As we will recall, one prominent optical theory in antiquity explained vision as a form of ocular penetration by minuscule bodies sent out by the object under view; another, as the result of rays emitted by the eyes and making contact with what is "seen." The special case of the evil eye illustrates how these views percolated into the general culture without much concern for the niceties of which theory was being evoked. In the scientific literature, there are long discussions in Pliny the Elder (*HN* 7.17), Plutarch (*Quaest. Conv.* 5.7), the Aristotelian commentator Alexander of Aphrodisias (*Prob.* 2.42), and elsewhere that explain in detail the physics of the evil eye in terms that rely predominantly on the extramissive idea of the *eidola* or *corpuscula*, the little bodies sent out by the eye. That is, the ill effects of the evil eye are caused by *eidola* emanating from the eyes of an envious viewer (even without his own knowledge or consent); these particles penetrate the body of the victim through his pores, and especially through his eyes (in focusing on the eyes as a pathway as well as a source of emissions, the explanation borrows from intromission), and throw into disarray the body's internal balance.

Plutarch's interlocutors in *Quaest. Conv.* 5.7 go so far as to offer differing explanations for the nature of the phenomenon and, in so doing, invoke rival theories of vision. The host, Mestrius Florus, suggests a contagion theory of the evil eye; the glance, breath, or speech of people with the evil eye, upon contact with others, infects them as well (680f).[64] Plutarch himself then

62. On this, see Kellum 1996. On the evil eye in general, Pliny, *HN* 7.17; Aul. Gell., 9.4.7–8; Plut., *Quaest. Rom.* 288a.

63. Pliny, *HN* 28.39, describes how a nurse might spit in the face of a sleeping infant to avert the evil eye from it. Some herbs were also considered effective remedies. See, e.g., Pers., 2.31–34.

64. For the infectious quality of the eye, see also Ov., *Rem. Am.* 615; and the sources listed in Rakoczy 1996, 185.

congratulates Florus on hitting the crucial fact: effluences from bodies (*apor-roias*) are the answer, and "this is especially likely to happen via the eyes; for sight, being extremely prone to movement, broadly sows a wondrous force, a fiery ray, as the *pneuma* is sent out; man both experiences this and inflicts many things through it." According to this extramissive and Platonizing account (a few lines later Plutarch leaves it open as to whether the emission is light [*phos*] or a stream of particles [*rheuma*]), love is the most obvious example of this, and those who fall in love suffer a far deeper wound by see-ing and being seen than by touch or hearing (681a, b).[65] Plutarch goes on to explain that the ill effects of the eye upon its victim are caused by the trans-mission of envy from the mind to the eyes of the ill-wisher; at that point, the eyes attack the victim "as if with poisoned darts" (681e). When yet another member of the company, Gaius, jumps in to express his astonishment that Plutarch invokes *pneuma* but not Democritean *eidola*, which must be the real answer to the problem, Plutarch explains that this is precisely what he meant, but that he stopped short of attributing agency to these *eidola* as Gaius does.[66] It is interesting that in his own discussion of the evil eye, our later source Heliodorus seems to adopt the "contagion" theory, which he puts in the mouth of the wise seer Cal-asiris.[67] Although Calasiris accordingly stresses the role of circumambient air in transmitting the infection through the body, he subsequently adds that his proof for this comes from the gene-sis of love, in which the recep-tive eye of the beloved takes in the emanations of the body of the lover (*Aethiopica* 3.7)—as if he were here representing, and reconciling, both sides of the argument in Plutarch's *Quaest. Conv.*[68] In both these examples, we have a perfect example of the syncretism of the period: *pneuma*, *eidola*, extramission, intromission, emanations from eyes

---

65. That the evocation of *pneuma* is here Platonizing rather than Stoicizing seems to be indi-cated by Plutarch's stance at *Quaest. Conv.* 626c.

66. On the evil eye in antiquity, see Barton 1993, chap. 3; Dickie 1991, 17–29; Dunbabin 1978, 161–62; Goldhill 1996, 25; Kellum 1996, 172–73; Rakoczy 1996, 186–216, with sequential discussions of Plutarch, Heliodorus, and Ps.-Alexander of Aphrodisias.

67. For an excellent comparison of the two accounts of Plutarch and Heliodorus, see Dickie 1991.

68. Ovid similarly combines contagion and vision at *Rem. Am.* 613–15: "If you love, but do not want to, make sure to shun contagion; often, this can even harm beasts. When the eyes see those who are afflicted, they are afflicted themselves."

and into eyes. Most im-portant seems to be the notion that the evil eye involves the penetration of the body by a visually directed force from the exterior.

If we now think about those several apotropaic images involving phalluses, we might be ready to offer a hypothesis as to why in some cases the eye is shown being pierced and why in general the phallus should be involved. Since the eye itself is thought to have the ability to transgress the boundaries of the body, especially when its gaze is malevolent, here it is its own penetrative action being turned against it. Accordingly, the phallus may have come into use against the evil eye at least partially via homeopathic reasoning: against something that penetrates, use something else that penetrates.[69] The eye, in other words, is figured in its effects in terms borrowed from or assimilated to the workings of the phallus, the penetrative instrument par excellence.[70] Again, the connection between the eye and the phallus is not quite as alien an idea to the modern world as we might think, in the light of Freud's claim—in chapter 6 of *The Interpretation of Dreams*—that Oedipus' self-blinding repre-sented a symbolic castration because he had slept with his mother.[71] Indeed, some three hundred years before this observation Francis Bacon had made the connection more explicit still by claiming that the gaze of the envious viewer produced an "ejaculation" from the eye—a reversal of the Greco-Roman

---

69. Such thinking may be supported by the graphic links between the eye and phallus found in ancient art; consider, for example, the strange *olisboi*, or dildos, painted on Greek black-figure vases: these ancient phalluses are themselves endowed with eyes. See also Aesch., *PV* 654, on the "eye" of Zeus. Devereux (1973, 42n36) lists monuments that show phalluses with eyes. In her own analysis, Frontisi-Ducroux (1996, 93–95) prefers to emphasize the paradoxical reciprocity of the gaze in this case: the sex organ not only draws the eye's attention, but also "looks back" at it.

70. Walter Burkert (1982, 40) suggests of Greek herms that "they stand in front of the house, in the market place, at crossroads, and at the frontiers. . . . Thus we are left with the 'apotropaic' meaning; but who is to be kept away by such means, and why? The indecencies rather catch the sight—and this is why they avert the evil eye, Plutarch suggested." Burkert goes on to acknowledge that he cannot find any "real explanation" other than one provided by ethology: certain species of monkey have males sitting at the outposts of their territory facing outward and sporting "their erect genital organ." The citation of Plutarch is from *Quaest. Conv.* 681f–682a; while it is the only place I can find this suggestion, there is no reason it should not exist as a simultaneous and parallel aetiology for the defensive phallus.

71. Devereux (1973) explores precisely this connection, with a collection of data linking sexual trespass to blinding.

attribution of the phallus to the defensive, rather than the offensive, side in this particular discussion.[72]

Contexts that have to do with erotic looking or aggressive looking also meld the languages of vision and of wounding to describe the effect of being the object of the gaze, even without invocation of the idea of the evil eye. In erotic looking, the most common conceit is that the image of the beloved is what penetrates the eye, so that wounding and gazing become linked with the eye not as aggressor, but as victim; in other contexts, the eye is once again figured as the source of damaging emissions that penetrate or attack the body on which they are trained. Thus Lucretius (4.1030–36), Plutarch (*Quaest. Conv.* 5.7), and many other authors evoke the notion of an erotic wound caused by the rays of beauty from the body of the beloved, which pierce through the eyes into the soul. Indeed, the eye as the path for the erotic wound is so common a trope as to barely need instantiation.[73] The projectile metaphor is combined with a liquid one in Achilles Tatius, *Clitophon and Leucippe* 1.4.4, where the beauty of the beloved is sharper than arrows and causes the "erotic wound" by flowing into the soul via the eyes.[74]

This rings the changes on the Lucretian passage already cited in chapter 2, which equates the irruption of the erotic *simulacra* of the beloved with the blow of a weapon on the battlefield, which causes a bloody ejaculate (4.1045–56). As R. D. Brown (1987, 63) comments, "The theory [of desire] is summed up in the ironic analogy of wounding, which equates the expulsion of semen with the spurting of blood from a wound in the direction of its inflictor." The imagery of wounding continues as the mind is "wounded"

---

72. See Graziano 1997, 156n95. With a slightly different emphasis, Barton (1993, 95–96) writes: "There is among the ancient Romans an insistent connection, and even identification, of the genitalia with the aggressive and prophylactic eye, and with the *fascinum*, the object that caught and defended the eye. . . . The source of the identification of the eye with the genitals (especially the phallus) was that the genitals shared with the eyes the excruciating paradox of exceptional vulnerability and power." Dickie and Dunbabin (1983), in their exploration of the visual imagery of *invidia*, suggest that the phallus represents the same aggressive component as the evil eye itself, which supports the suggestions made above.

73. See the discussions of the erotic gaze in Brown 1987; cf. 72: "for, like weapons, simulacra too are physical projectiles, which are thrown from objects and strike the eyes of the recipient." Useful also are Walters 1998; and Williams 1999, 61.

74. On the liquefying rather than penetrative force of the loved one's emissions, see Walker 1991.

(*saucia*) with love; women and beautiful boys "launch" (*iaculator*) their glances and their victims are "struck" (*feritur*).[75] Surely it is no coincidence that Lucretius, in the same book of his poem, treats vision as both hunger and sexual behavior: these are the three main instances in which bodily boundaries break down to admit or produce external matter, at least according to ancient ways of thinking, and looking and lovemaking especially breach the integrity of the body.

Absent the erotic context, the eye may be figured once again as the *source* of attack, so that it is now the corpuscular emissions from the eyes of the person doing the looking rather than from the body of the beloved that may be described as metaphorical weapons—spears or missiles or blows. This is a far more common trope in the Greek context than in the Latin, so that descriptions of the gaze as a weapon in Greek poetry (for example, *belos, toxeuma*) outnumber any Latin metaphor of the blow or striking force of the emission from the eyes (though *ictus* is used of the gaze at *Aetna* 349).[76] However, the terminology of the *acies oculorum* would suggest that the gaze could be conceptualized as a (sharp-edged?) beam or ray. When weakened, this beam was described as literally blunt, *hebes*;[77] when necessary, it could be sharpened like a knife or sword.[78] And the eyes remain a locus for hostile agency to make itself felt: one can be tortured by the presence of another's gaze upon one's body ([Quint.], *Decl. Maior.* 19). An old crone can check the power of burning eyes (Pers. 2.34).[79] Augustus rejoices if a sharp look from him makes a man lower his head as if blinded by the sun's rays (Suet., *Aug.* 79.3). Pliny the younger praises Trajan because he quelled a battlefield by the casting of "threats and eyes" as well as weapons at his opponents (*Pan.* 17.3).[80] Not for nothing does

---

75. See the long list of citations of "the wound of love" in Brown 1987, 132–33.

76. "Abest species tantusque ruinis / impetus adtentos oculorum transfugit ictus."

77. Cf. similarly *contundo, praestringo, retundo*, as actions carried out on the gaze. The gaze's action can also be described in terms of scraping away surfaces like a sharp file rather than penetrating through the skin; see Hor., *Ep.* 1.14.37–38: "non istic obliquo oculo mea commoda quisquam / limat."

78. E.g., Pliny, *HN* 23.59, 24.99, 29.132.

79. "Urentis oculos inhibere perita." The scholiast comments that this is a reference to the evil eye— "merito, quia fascino urunt"—and then adds the conceit of eating as well, "tamquam consumunt."

80. "Nec modo telorum tuorum, sed oculorum etiam minarumque coniectum." On the gaze as an implement of torture, see Rakoczy 1996, 33–35. Rakoczy sensibly notes the connection

Varro seem to have claimed (*Ling.* 6.80) that the verb *videre*, "to see," was derived from *violare*, "to violate."[81]

In perhaps the most fascinating example of this way of thinking, the fourth-century CE commentator on Plato's *Timaeus*, Chalcidius, ends his discussion of Stoic theories of vision with a metaphor that evokes both contagion theory and the idea of the gaze as a reptilian force invading the body: when the cone of vision carries back its information to the mind by striking against it, "[t]he experience [*passio*] is similar to that of those who are paralyzed by the contagion of the marine fish, if its slime creeps up the line and the reed and through the hands and penetrates into the innermost sense" (*SVF* 2.863).[82] "Penetretque intimum sensum" recalls, probably inadvertently, the description in Seneca's contemporary Persius, who dwells on the invaded body of the man who listens to bad poetry; the verse seems to penetrate him anally and titillate his innards ("cum carmina lumbum intrant et tremulo scalpuntur ubi intima uersu" [*Sat.* 1.20–21]), and *virus* can mean not only slime but also semen, providing the entire metaphor with a curious sexual charge. And perhaps with a philosophical charge as well: the most famous instance in antiquity of paralysis by a torpedo fish (electric eel) occurs in Plato's *Meno* 80a, where the young Meno compares Socrates to such a fish, which benumbs anyone who comes near it.

More often we find the gaze figured as a wild animal, or as something that feeds on its victim, especially if the victim is in pain and the viewer is enjoying the sight. This dimension of viewing has been examined by Helen Morales (1996), who notes the existence of both an *assaultive* gaze and a *reactive* gaze to

---

between the prevalence of emission theory and the ubiquity of this kind of imagery. See also Barton (2001, 248–50) on "visual assassination," and Morales (1996) on the "assaultive gaze." On the connections between seeing and stoning, see Steiner 1995, 193–221. In a rather gross application of the idea that reading is a form of taking-in via the eyes, Sen., *Ep.* 84.6–7, compares reading to eating: if you have to empty your bowels immediately afterward, no profit has been absorbed. Cf. *Ep.* 2.2, where switching from book to book is described as a form of diarrhea.

81. A mistaken etymology, of course, but revelatory of how the Romans thought. See Rakoczy (1996, 62), relying on the emendation of Stiewe 1959. On sight as the most piercing of the senses, see also Pl., *Phdr.* 205d.

82. "Similisque eius passio est eorum, qui marini piscis contagione torpent, siquidem per linum et harundinem perque manus serpat virus illud penetretque intimum sensum."

scenes of violence in art or in reality: the one ravishes or feeds upon what it sees, the other is harmed by it.[83] The citizens of Syracuse want to feed their eyes on the torture and punishment of a pirate chief; Petronius' Encolpius is happy to do the same as he watches his rival getting soundly thrashed; the emperor Vitellius boasted that he wanted to feed his eyes on the public death of a usurer.[84] Caligula's gaze is itself a form of torture in Seneca's *De ira* 3.19.1, where it comes as the climax to a long list of torture devices. As Morales (1996, 205) puts it, "The spectator colludes in the assault — *spectator* is *particeps*. Imagined in paradigmatic relationship to the instruments of torture, the gaze itself is a figurative weapon." Paradoxically, in many of these examples the gaze "eats" or "is fed on" what it sees rather than "penetrates" it, so that the eye acts as receptor but maintains its aggressive valence.[85] Indeed, the play on which way the traversing of bodily boundaries is actually going forms the point to Martial's epigram 1.96.11–13, in which a man "devours" well-endowed fellows at the bath with his eyes, while his lips simultaneously twitch in anticipation.[86]

The hostile gaze at Rome, then, seems oddly defracted into two conceptual fields, not so much divided according to the emission or reception of physical material by the eyes (as we might guess), but rather according to the usual Roman emphasis upon agency versus being acted upon. The powerful gaze can either emit the noxious rays that give the evil eye its particular power, or it can assault its victims by figuratively eating or consuming them; the weak gaze is

---

83. On the aggressive gaze in a philosophical context, see Napolitano Valditara (1994, 57), who suggests that Plato characterizes the *falsi sapienti* as having the gaze of the envious.

84. In order: Cic., *Verr.* 2.5.65.12, "cum eius cruciatu atque supplicio pascere oculos . . . vellent"; Petr., *Sat.* 96.4, "ego autem alternos opponebam foramini oculos / iniuriaque Eumolpi velut quodam cibo me replebam"; Suet., *Vit.* 14.2.6, "coram interfici iussit, uelle se dicens pascere oculos."

85. On feeding one's eyes on the suffering of others, see also Livy, 24.14.2; Nepos, *Eum.* 11.2.2; Quint., *Maj.* 7.10.20, 7.18.10; Calp. Flacc., *Decl.* 4.9; Suet., *Vit.* 14.2.6; Tac., *Hist.* 1.44.2; Cic., *Mil.* 58.9; Cic., *Verr.* 2.65.12; Cic., *Phil.* 11.7–8; Val. Max., 9.2.1. See also Leigh (1996, 171–97) on the "cannibal eye" of Roman tyrants and with additional citations. Leontius at Pl., *Resp.* 439e–f, famously damns his eyes for filling themselves on the sight of dead bodies. Feeding one's eyes on a loved one is an equally common conceit; in Achilles Tatius, 1.5, 5.3, and 6.1, the sight of the loved one is equated to dinner, with no gastric sadism in sight. Cf. also Ov., *Am.* 3.2.5–6; Ter., *Phorm.* 85; Petr., *Sat.* 131.11.3. On voyeurism as a form of eating, see Barton 1993, 96.

86. "Una lavamur: aspicit nihil sursum, / Sed spectat oculis devorantibus draucos / Nec otiosis mentulas videt labris." Eating, seeing, and sex here and elsewhere share conceptual boundaries in Roman thought that are evinced in Martial and Juvenal in particular.

averted, elided, or wounded by the object of love. These fields could be, and were, manipulated and reversed to drive home Roman commentary on Greek cultural givens. As we have seen, the familiar trope of the power of the sight of the loved one upon the lover receives its greatest Latin emphasis in Lucretius' atomist poem, where the devastating power of the *simulacra* emitted by the beloved (whether in a dream or in everyday life) strip such agency from the lover, who instead of being the wise *erastes* of the Greek tradition becomes a hollow pit of yearning, a man whose putative superiority in age or sex vanishes before the object whose emissive particles penetrate *him*. Here superiority on the battlefield of love, couched in the appropriate military terminology, is incongruously handed over to the beautiful woman or young boy, whose *simulacra* "shoot" the lover and render him paradoxically passive. For when ejaculation (a manly feat) becomes a gushing wound (as befits the penetrated victim), all hierarchies must come under question.

SENATORIAL SAFEGUARDS

We have discussed two paradigms of viewing in Roman culture, elite self-display and penetrative viewing (what Matthew Leigh [1996] has called the "cannibal eye"). Here we look at one arena in which these two threatened to merge already in the republic, asking why they did not do so. How could forms of self-display before the assembled gaze of the civic audience damage and effeminize some males but leave their elite brethren unscathed? Why do we hear nothing of orators and officeholders threatened by the evil eye despite their enviable rank and status?[87]

The paradigmatic figures here are perhaps the actor and the orator, each at a different end of the spectrum of class, vulnerability, and *virtus*—though not of self-display. In Greece, there was little or no space on this spectrum: the actor and the citizen were one, and appearing on the tragic or comic stage bore no stigma for the elite citizen. The actor's position at Rome could not have

---

87. Modern readers might ask at this point: where is the woman in these economies of the gaze? The answer is that in the Roman context, she is absent. For the most part, Roman women are the seen rather than the seers, the judged rather than the judging. They share this with *pathici*, actors, and other members of Roman society whose main function was to be the subject rather than the author of ethical sermonizing.

been more different. As the Roman biographer Cornelius Nepos noted, in comparing Roman mores to Greek, it was not considered shameful for a Greek citizen to appear on the stage and be a spectacle for the people ("populo esse spectaculo" [*Vir. illust.* proem.1.5.2]),[88] while for the Romans, this involved disgrace and the loss of citizenship rights: no flexibility was allowed. For a senator to even become too *like* the actor would be to assimilate himself to the members of the lowest rank in the Roman social hierarchy, the *infames*: actors, slaves, prostitutes, gladiators, and, at least in theory, citizen men who had let their body be used "like a woman." This despised group had no claim on the freedom from corporal punishment that was the privilege of the Roman citizen.[89] Likewise, they had no recourse against being beaten by magistrates on the streets, and this seems to have led to the association of the *infames* with vulnerability to all forms of bodily invasion. (Indeed, the sexual assault of an actor, a slave, a prostitute did not constitute a crime.)[90]

Actors especially seem to have been characterized as being sexual effeminates, as having bodies "broken" or emasculated (*fracti*) by softness; their gestures in particular were effeminate and indecent.[91] They were thus constitutionally unable to be the "real men" demanded by politics and oratory. When Seneca the Elder fulminates against the dandies among contemporary Roman youth, he bids his interlocutor good luck in finding an orator "in those plucked and hairless types, who only in their lust merit the name of men" (*Controv.* 1.pr.8–9); Aulus Gellius tells us similarly that the great orator Q. Hortensius was slandered as resembling not only an actor but also a dancing girl because of his dandified appearance and delivery (*NA* 1.5.2). We might fairly hypothesize that this pervasive charge of sexual unmanliness was due to

---

88. "Magnis in laudibus tota fere fuit Graecia uictorem Olympiae citari, in scaenam uero prodire ac populo esse spectaculo nemini in eisdem gentibus fuit turpitudini. quae omnia apud nos partim infamia, partim humilia atque ab honestate remota ponuntur."

89. On the connection between freedom from corporal punishment and the concept of *libertas*, see Roller 2001a, 229–33; Saller 1994, 140.

90. See Edwards 1997b, 73–75. On the *infames* as a class, and with several further categories mentioned, see *Dig. Iust.* 3.2. Suet., *Aug.* 45.3–4, and Tac., *Ann.* 1.77, attest that actors could be beaten by magistrates.

91. See, e.g., Quint., 1.10.31; Tac., *Ann.* 15.1; Pliny, *Pan.* 46.5, etc. On the effeminacy of actors, see Edwards 1993, 129–31; and Edwards 1997b. This effeminacy, of course, provided another reason for orators to avoid assimilation to the theater. On rhetoric and gender at Rome, see Gunderson 2000, 59–86; Richlin 1997; for the second sophistic, Gleason 1995.

interlocking causes: the actor's body was vulnerable to corporal punishment and thus automatically unmanned by its openness to the assault of the other; the theater itself was "a hotbed of pathic activity" (Taylor 1996–97) where prostitutes (male and female) often plied their trade (not a few actors sold their body as well);[92] and male actors played female parts on stage and were thus forced to dress up in unmanly attire (although not, apparently, in the mime). This seems to have been the factor that most upset the younger Seneca's contemporary Columella, who chastised the Romans in the preface to his farming manual for clapping at the antics of men in drag rather than going to plow their fields: "All of us, as Marcus Varro complained already in the times of our ancestors, though we are heads of households, have crept within the city walls, sickle and plow abandoned, and we busy our hands in the circuses and in the theaters rather than among the crops and the vines; and, stunned, we admire the gestures of effeminate men as with womanly movement they falsely adopt a sex denied to men by nature and deceive the eyes of the spectators" (*Rust.* 1.pr.15).[93]

Most important, the act of appearing on stage, of showing oneself to a crowd of onlookers, seems to have been ipso facto associated with deviancy. This is why the Roman satirist Juvenal (2.117–20) can compare the disgrace of a male citizen who acts as a gladiator before a crowd to the disgrace of his being another man's "wife": both of these activities represented the breaching of the citizen's body, whether by the eyes or by the phallus, as well as the submissive position of being the provider of pleasure. Jonathan Walters (1998, 364) has noted of this passage: "For a man's body to be sexually penetrated, used 'like a woman' by another man, and for his body to appear as spectacle in the arena were both conceptualized as paradigms of the state of being in the power of another. . . . It is not solely the sexual use of his body by another man that lowers a man's status; it is any use of his body by other men for their pleasure."[94]

---

92. Pliny the Elder mentions several gentlemen who died while in extremis with the pantomime actor Mysticus (*HN* 7.184), and several sources mention Maecenas' affair with a male actor (Tac., *Ann.* 1.54; Dio Cass., 54.17.5). On this topic, see also Edwards 1997b.

93. I thank Jim Dobreff for bringing this passage to my attention.

94. As Williams (1999, 141) has similarly hypothesized, "Roman readers were likely to conceive of effeminacy as a disorder or a disease that manifested itself not only in the desire to be sexually penetrated but also in a desire to put oneself on display, even to sell oneself, for the purpose of entertaining others."

Walters goes on to point out that Hostius Quadra, too, brings together deviancy and desire as he makes a spectacle of himself and accepts (and provides) penetration in front of his mirrors (362–63). Seneca's pun that these mirrors, and Hostius' desire to be the watcher of his own acts, result in *obscenitas in scaenam producta*, making a scene of ob-scenity (*Q Nat.* 1.16.1), underscores the deviancy inherent in self-display even on a metaphorical stage; in Hostius' case, it is all the more shocking because he is not *infamis* but a member of the elite. No wonder, opines Seneca, that Augustus deemed Hostius unworthy of revenge when his own slaves murdered him; ideally, he should have been torn apart in front of his own mirrors—the ultimate *fractus* body on display.[95]

A final reason for the cultural effeminization of the actor and of the body on display might lie in the well-attested connection of the theatrical experience to the sensual pleasure, *voluptas*, of the audience. For *voluptas* was precisely what the *ludicrae artes*, especially the pantomime, offered their viewers; as Justinian's *Digest* 38.1.7.6 notes, the actor is a fabricator of pleasure, a *uoluptatis artifex*. And *voluptas* was itself suspect as a force that unmanned those who reveled in it; it was "enervated and rouged and soft" (Sen., *Vit. Beat.* 7.3), "a thing *infamis*" (Sen., *Ep.* 59.2) that brought disgrace and was diametrically opposed to the practice of *virtus* (Quint., *Inst.* 5.10.83).[96] In this dynamic, then, it is not only the taking of money for services rendered that links the actor to the prostitute, it is the commonality of the sensual pleasure they provide.[97] We might even wonder whether presenting one's body as a spectacle was considered to invite not only metaphorical but also physical invasion of the body.[98] As we have seen, forms of the gaze that are *like* a weapon, *like* a wild animal, that cause metaphorical wounds and real sickness, are clearly conceptualized as

---

95. Fredrick (2002b) cautions against the binarism of Walters's model, arguing that there are more forms of corporeal assault than the two on which Walters focuses (sexual penetration and beating). Also at issue are personal boundaries, physical needs, access to privacy, and the control of information in one's environment.

96. On the effeminizing effect of *voluptas* in general, see Sen., *Ep.* 84.11, 92.10, etc.; also Wistrand 1990, 32–34.

97. Edwards (1997b, 85) points out that the Romans used sexual language as a metonymy for the pleasure purveyed by men who were *infames* and simultaneously the object of the uninhibited public gaze; these bodies had no dignity, were used for financial gain, and served the pleasures of others.

98. On the effeminacy of those in the performing arts, see especially Edwards 1993, 98–136; Parker 1999; Walters 1998; and Williams 1999, 139–42.

having a penetrative force that has a physical effect upon the object (much as the erotic gaze does). If the bad poetry Persius rants against in his first satire can be characterized as penetrating an audience to whom it is being recited, would it be too fanciful to suggest that the ravenous gaze was seen as a form of attack that also unmanned the violated body upon which it fed or whose boundaries it transgressed?[99] Roman sexual terminology often overlaps with the language of attack; as J. N. Adams (1982, 145) notes, "one of the largest semantic fields from which metaphors for sexual acts were taken in Latin is that of striking, cutting, and the like." Thus, *caedo, battuo, ferio* (all versions of "strike" or "beat"); *dolo, scalpo, scindo* (verbs of hewing and cutting); and the idea of wounding someone with your "spear" (for example, Mart. 11.78.6, Priap. 3.8) all occur as violent or satiric descriptions of what a man might do to his wife—or more often, another man.[100] In other words, the vulnerability of the *infames* to bodily attack overlaps lexically, and I would argue conceptually, with vulnerability to sexual attack, and these two semantic fields in turn share much with the idea of visual violation against the abject body on view.

The actor, then, was despised; in legal fact, in everyday life, and in the metaphorical language of the unnaturally sexed body, he represented the opposite of the elite citizen, with the latter's regard for exemplary appearances, unquestioned masculine dominance, and self-modeling on tradition.[101] And yet, Roman elites acknowledged that the orator's position was uncomfortably akin to that of an actor. Cicero's strictures to ensure that the former distinguish himself carefully from the latter are well known, and a series of sources both point out this similarity and offer warnings against it: not only the

---

99. Parker (1999, 166) toys with this idea, but does not state it outright, when he remarks that "The *infamis*—actor, gladiator, or whore—are [*sic*] those who are and can be penetrated; left open to the weapons, touch, gaze of others." The breaching of the body and the subsequent effeminization of the victim can also take place aurally; the most notorious example is probably Pers., 1.20–22, cited above. But I do not address these rare instances in this book, as it is only vision that is overtly combined with philosophical, ethical, and regulatory functions at Rome.

100. For a full list of examples, see Adams 1982, 145–52. In a tragedy of Accius (according to Varro, *Ling.* 6.80) Actaeon is said to violate Diana with his eyes, a usage whose indirection Varro compares to violating a virgin—*violavit* for *vitiavit.*

101. Rhetoric played a role in shaping this truth as well, of course. In contrast, note Cicero's concern for the opinion of the theater-going public in the *Pro Sestio.* Their political reading of the theatrical renders the theater a site of commentary upon current events here and elsewhere (see Bartsch 1994, chap. 3). In these instances, the voluptuary effect of the stage is subordinated to its ability to provide an indication of the pulse of the people.

role-playing, but also the gestures and vocal inflections of the actor were to be avoided.[102] The orator faced the double bind of being persuasive and vehement while having to avoid the gestures and intonations of an actor; part of his instruction in the art of politics inevitably involved reminders of how to "walk like a man," in Maud Gleason's phrase (1995, 60). Cicero, for example, waxes negative on the hasty gait (*Off.* 1.131), as did Demosthenes before him (*Or.* 37.52, 55; *Or.* 45.77).[103] Quintilian warns his pupils to avoid all feminine mannerisms (such as tilting one's head to the side)—concerns as urgent in their day as in the period of Gleason's study, the Second Sophistic.

Despite this, however, adult upper-class Romans under the republic seem to have been comparatively unconcerned with the coexistence of what may seem to us two noncompatible ideologies of seeing (aggressive and exemplary), and there was little friction at the places where these cultures of viewing might have made an abrasive connection, such as the situation of self-displaying elite males who provide a spectacle for the people. We might wonder why the orator's body (despite caveats against effeminate behavior) is never felt to be assaulted by the combined gaze of a crowd, and why senators were consistently impervious to the indignities that befall actors (that is, unless the former too literally mounted the stage and performed for a crowd). We might find it interesting that no *contiones* before the people have been recorded as provoking anxiety about the evil eye. Or we might wonder whether the funeral procession, with its use of lowly actors to wear the distinguished *imagines* of the dead, or the triumph, so often described in the language of theater, might not provoke a sense of the uneasy proximity between the glory and the danger of being on view in specifically stagelike environments.[104] If, as Holt Parker (1999, 167) points out, "the tension

---

102. Actors similar to orators: see, e.g., Aul. Gell., 1.5; Cic., *De Or.* 1.128–30, 3.214; Cic., *Brut.* 200, 290; Cic., *Div.* 1.60; Cic., *Off.* 1.129–30; Val. Max., 8.10.2. Need to be careful not to be like orators: Cic., *De Or.* 3.220–21; Quint., 1.8.3, 1.11.1–3, etc. See Dupont 1985, 31–34, 95–110; Edwards 1993, 117–19; Edwards 1997, 79–81; Gleason 1995, 105–7, 114–16; Dupont 1985, 95–110; Gunderson 2000, 111–48; Richlin 1997, 99–105. As Corbeill (2002, 189) remarks, "Too close a resemblance to acting could also endanger the masculine status of the speaker." Axer (1989) discusses Cicero's modeling of several speeches to evoke and benefit from his audience's experiences in the theater or the arena.

103. Corbeill (2002, 203) notes in the context of politicians speaking at the *contio*, "Appeals to the masses create a nearly inescapable double bind: the politician becomes his demeanor, the demeanor denotes his politics."

104. In Macrob., *Sat.* 2.7.5, we read that the audience at Laberius' mime-performance all stared at Julius Caesar, whose hasty act of putting Laberius on the stage they felt was "stoned" by Laberius' wit. Here is an occasion with some striking reversals of the prevalent visual paradigms.

between the [need for] inviolability from the gaze and the necessity to be seen is at its most extreme for the most visible of all: orators and politicians," why do the written sources have so little to say about this tension?[105]

There is no magically complete answer to this question, only several factors that must have helped the Roman elite maintain what usually seemed to them a self-evident distinction. None of these reasons will surprise us; most of them have already been discussed in this chapter. One site of tension is clearly visible: the similarity of the orator to the actor, and the necessity that the former avoid inadvertently falling into impropriety by gestures or intonations that are not fit for an elite speaker. Yet clear differentiating factors are at work here: the elite orator (unlike the actor, who mouthed another's words, wore another's clothing, and had to elide his own persona in the interest of the character's) spoke what he had written, and did so in his own voice and of his own volition. The oratory, political participation, and self-display of the senatorial elite had real effects and took place in the real world, however theatrical such performances might seem. The actor's world was purely fictive. He was associated with deceit, with makeup, and hence with the immoral. His world was that of leisure, not work.[106]

Obvious, too, is the importance of the *purpose* of any given act of self-display: is it to educate (as the elite would characterize their own speeches, exempla, and parades) or to please (as with the actors of the theater and the mime)? Unlike the actor, the purpose of the elite citizen's self-display was not to entertain others, but to instruct them; to provide a demonstration of *virtus* rather than a *frisson* of *voluptas*. We have seen that the theater and the amphitheater were associated with pleasures that were problematically sensual in nature, as were other forms of viewing born of *luxuria*. Theater itself could be a manifestation of *luxuria*, like the ostentatious temporary building of M. Aemilius Scaurus in 58 BCE, whose aedileship (according to Pliny the Elder, *HN* 36.1113)

---

105. The more important you are, the more scrutiny you face: Apul., *Flor.* 9.1–12. Also: "The shame of 'making a spectacle of oneself' runs counter to an even more important Roman cultural imperative: to be 'the observed of all observers.'... The Romans found themselves in a culturally determined double bind: to be the object of others' sight was to be open to attack, yet to be publicly observed was proof of power" (Parker 1999, 167).

106. At the moment when the orator most closely resembles the actor—when he is engaging in *prosopopeia*, the adoption of another person's voice and character—Quintilian both encourages and warns against the descent into histrionic talents, *Inst.* 1.8.3, 6.1.25.

"perhaps wrecked morals more than any other." In contrast, although a Roman audience might thrill to a display of *virtus*, to an orator on the podium, or to a general riding in triumph, there is no suggestion that these sights provided a quiver in their loins. In Roman ideology, virtue is not sexy; its absence is.

Furthermore, unlike the actor or the pantomime, the elite Roman was fully clothed in the traditional garb of the toga; his body was never on display but, on the contrary, remained carefully circumscribed by the nature of his garment and by the strictures of tradition.[107] This may explain the predominance of ithyphallic imagery in the baths, discussed by John Clarke (1996): here was one of the rare sites at which the elite body was disrobed and, hence, vulnerable.[108] Also unlike the actor, the elite Roman was protected by his rank. As discussed above, the *infamis* was automatically vulnerable to bodily violation, the citizen was protected from it by law. Nor can it have been insignificant that actors at Rome were from the birth of the theater aliens and slaves, so that the institution was indelibly stained by the servile origins of its participants. A Roman citizen had control over himself and such other people, and maintaining control over the nature and meaning of self-representation was key to whether he felt he profited from, or risked being exploited by, his position at the center of vision. As Parker (1999, 168) puts it, the elite Roman "must be the giver of images, never the object of others' interpretations." The elite Roman on view was following his own volition, rather than obeying the whim of another, or working for his money. (In contrast, the actor/gladiator received payment, another form of debasement, according to Juv., *Sat* 8.192–210.) When Julius Caesar forced Laberius the playwright to mount the stage in c. 46 BCE, it was precisely his equestrian rank that caused the scandal reported by Macrobius (*Sat.* 2.7).

Finally, we should take into account that slaves and actors were not in a position to provide an audience to the free in any institutionalized sense. It is uncertain whether slaves were even allowed in the theater in the late republic

---

107. See, e.g., Quint., *Inst.* 11.3.83, on unmanly shrugging, and 1.11.19, on avoiding gestures too much like an actor's. For these issues in the second century CE, see Gleason 1995.

108. Clarke suggests (1996, 192) that the humorous laughter provoked by these images was thought to dispel the evil eye. In a later work, he also suggests that the outré and/or woman-on-top paintings of the Apodyterium in the Suburban Baths at Pompeii are there to evoke laughter from the bathers and in so doing, protect them from the evil eye (Clarke 2002).

(the only evidence in favor of their presence at an earlier date is provided by the prologue to Plautus' *Poenulus*). Certainly the evidence of Cicero's *Har. Resp.* 26 suggests that they were excluded from the theater during the games celebrated by Gaius and Appius Claudius. And their mass presence during the theatrical entertainments of the *ludi Megalenses* of 56 BCE is an impetus for horror and outrage on Cicero's part (*Har. Resp.* 21–26). According to his inflammatory account of what happened on this occasion, as the initial ceremonies were getting under way, an unruly throng of slaves suddenly rushed into the theater, all incited by P. Clodius, and took command of the proceedings. In an offensive reversal of the dynamics of power and the gaze, these slaves took over the roles of viewer and of director—"Slaves gave these games, slaves watched them" (hos ludos servi fecerunt, servi spectaverunt [*Har. Resp.* 24])—and dared both to infiltrate the audience as new spectators, where they did not belong, and to exert power over the original spectators, leading Cicero to declare that the games had been irrevocably polluted (*Har. Resp.* 25).[109]

To assert the presence of a distinction here is not to deny that elite weak spots, as it were, could and can be identified in this ideology of the gaze. The upper-class subject was not always safe. For one, although he was usually inured to the effect of the subordinate's gaze, he might yet fall prey to the weakness of his own visual hunger for inexemplary sights and corrupting pleasures; contrary to all expectations, the object rather than the subject of the gaze could bring the viewer down to his own level of abjection, or at the very least, threaten the viewer's moral character and masculinity.[110] So it is that actors, spectacles, and other forms of self-indulgent viewing could unman their audiences, supplying, as they did, the tainted coin of *voluptas*. "There is nothing so injurious to good character as sitting idly at some spectacle, for then the vices

---

109. And in the end, perhaps we should also include a less obvious factor: the simple force of habit For a people ingrained from birth with the utmost respect for the authority and genealogy of the senators, such comparisons may simply have seemed unfeasible or ridiculous, the crossing of a line that no one questioned despite the common ground on both sides—like comparing drugs for mental illness and hallucinogenics, or foie gras and monkey brains. The bias of our upper-class sources may also be at work here. Such sources may well have been unlikely to report instances in which a member of the nobility showed an unmanly anxiety about the hostile force of the gaze.

110. The idea of the spectator damaged by the spectacle, and many of the examples that follow, were pointed out to me by Andrew Feldherr in his response to a lecture at Dickinson College, 30 September 2000.

creep in more easily by means of pleasure" (*Ep.* 7.2), opines Seneca.[111] Cicero (*Har. Resp.* 26) tells his audience that Clodius has *violati oculi*—perhaps because of his lustful habits in general, or perhaps because he has been an indecent spectator of the *Megalensi* (we are left to guess). Still worse, the desire for this kind of pleasure-through-viewing could run amok, like other forms of *luxus* or *incontinentia*: Seneca (*Ep.* 90.45) laments of the amphitheater that men now kill each other for the sake of spectating alone (this, as he condemns the other lusts of *luxus*: gold, silver, and precious stones).[112] Even too much attention to a polychromatic fish in a jar could wreak havoc on a senatorial audience: in a bit of bravura rhetoric, Seneca (*Q Nat.* 3.18.4–7) relates the invidious effect of the surmullet, which turned brilliant shades of vermilion in its death-throes; this empty, even sadistic pleasure captivates Seneca's contemporaries, who now never go to the deathbed of a dying friend or father, or to the funeral of a family member. These lost men are all appetite—even in their eyes ("oculis quoque gulosi sunt").[113] The assaultive gaze can harm a viewer, too.[114]

---

111. "Nihil vero tam damnosum bonis moribus quam in aliquo spectaculo desidere; tunc enim per voluptatem facilius vitia subrepunt." The context here makes it clear Seneca is talking about gladiatorial games. Wistrand (1990) proffers the interesting argument that in general Seneca and Pliny approved of gladiatorial fights; where Seneca seems to damn them, he is criticizing only "mass executions of criminals without any educational value" (17–18). However, I am not sure I am convinced, given that Seneca says it would have been criminal (*nefas*) to train such men to fight (i.e., make gladiators of them), let alone send them naked and unarmed into the arena (*Ep.* 95.33). Wistrand meets this objection by simply saying, "The strong expression *nefas* should not be taken too literally" (1990, 37n17). Another piece of contradictory evidence is offered in Cic., *Tusc.* 2.41. The gladiatorial games may have built character in the past, but not so in the present: Cicero himself longs for the good old days when gladiatorial games built character; many now find them merely "crudele . . . et inhumanum." However, as Leigh (1997, 280) and Wistrand (1990, 33n10) point out, Seneca's use of gladiatorial imagery in metaphors throughout his corpus contrasts with his negative assessment of the effects of spectatorship. Note that the willpower and sense of dignity of the gladiator who suffocated himself with a toilet-plunger rather than fight (*Ep.* 70.20–21) come in for Seneca's praise. On pleasure linked with actors and games (*voluptates* again), see Sen., *Ep.* 88.22.

112. This brings to mind, of course, the famous example of Augustine's friend Alypius, who opened his eyes at a gladiatorial show and "was struck by a deeper blow in his soul than the gladiator in his body" (*Conf.* 6.8). Tertullian's *De spectaculis* makes the same point with a number of arguments.

113. See also *De tranq.* 2.13–14 on *oculi luxuriosi*; and similarly Arrowsmith (1966, 315) on Echion in the *Satyricon*: "The man Echion is literally brutalized by what he sees and what he eats. . . . 'Bread and circuses' are merely diverse expressions of the same fact."

114. Benton (2002) analyzes Seneca's *Troades* in terms of its audience's assaultive gaze—but also in terms of senatorial identification with the captive women stripped of their class.

Only in rare contexts could this destruction of the moral fiber and masculine mores of the viewer be a laudable thing; in a comment that recalls the autocrat Aristodemus' distribution of mirrors and combs to the youth of Cumae (Dion. Hal., *Ant. Rom.* 7.9.4), Seneca suggests that letting a tyrant indulge in actors and prostitutes is a good idea: these things will soften his nature.[115]

A more strictly philosophical animus directed against the corrupting activity of the eye can be traced as far back as Plato's story of Leontius in *Republic* 4, who damned his eyes for wanting to sate themselves on the sight of dead bodies. As we have seen, the failure of the rational part of the soul to control forms of desire or disruption for which the eye is the pathway recurs in moralizing Roman texts as well.[116] In the context of philosophy, Aulus Gellius (*NA* 10.17) tells the story of how a Greek philosopher, Democritus, blinded himself to stop the delights of seeing from interfering with his mental concentration. But the Roman version of this interdiction often manages to impart a sexual dimension to the success or failure of the self to regulate its forms of seeing, as with Seneca's amphitheaters and surmullets. When the same Aulus Gellius (*NA* 3.5) tells an anecdote about *mollities oculorum*, effeminate "softness of the eyes," the point is wholly sexual, and the joke rests on the bon mot that the philosopher Arcesilaus delivered against a man who, though dolled up to the nines, was *a stupro integer* (whole, not anally penetrated). No matter, quoth Arcesilaus, seeing his fancy hairdo and his eyes full of enticement and kinky pleasure: "It makes no difference if you're a *cinaedus* in your back parts or your front."

Likewise, the issue of control over the *meaning* of the gaze, inevitably, could not always be regulated in as clear-cut a fashion as the paradigms in this chapter suggest; indeed, one of my points here has been that to some degree, the cultural barriers between *exemplum* and *voluptas* are more the product of senatorial ideology than of natural distinction. Pliny the younger, in his desperately flattering panegyric of the emperor Trajan, would rely on just this flexibility to draw a distinction between the gladiatorial games put on by the dead Domitian and those of the new man in power. He notes of a recent

---

115. Sen., *Ben.* 7.20.3: "Si pro magno petet munere artifices scenae et scorta et quae feritatem eius emolliant, libens offeram." See similarly Tac., *Germ.* 19.1; Sen., *Vit. Beat.* 11.4.

116. Cf. also Publius Syrus, *Sent.* N 2: "Nihil peccant oculi, si animus oculis imperat"; and [Quint.], *Decl. Maj.* 15.12.21: "Sed imperare oculis, sed animum regere non possum."

performance that "[w]e saw a spectacle then that was neither effeminate nor debauched, nor the sort that softens men's minds and breaks them, but the sort to set us afire for beautiful wounds and contempt of death, since even in the bodies of slaves and the guilty the love of praise and the desire for victory could be discerned" (*Pan.* 33.1).[117] In so doing, he evokes the games' dual potential for corruption and for edification: Trajan's viewers came away strengthened by the exemplary deeds put on in the amphitheater, while the dangerous *voluptas* of Domitian's games—or theater, it is not clear—unmanned the same audience. Essentially, Pliny tries to elide that the spectacle can be interpreted either in terms of an ethical model *or* in terms of the violation of the viewer. In a different manifestation of visual instability, and as Morales (1996) has pointed out, the reactive gaze (damage to viewer) can coexist with the aggressive gaze (damage to thing viewed) at one and the same act of spectatorship; the very sight that a Roman aggressively consumes with his eyes can corrupt and effeminize him.[118]

Elsewhere in our Roman texts, it seems at least possible that the bias of elite authors themselves may have been responsible for lack of attention to the vulnerability of elite bodies to lower-class gazes. One of the rare situations in which the exemplary male did take precautions against becoming victim rather than model was on the occasion of the triumph, when, as we saw above, the phallus hanging under his chariot was intended to protect him from the evil eye at this greatest moment of his glory. This is only mentioned, however, in Pliny the Elder's vast and curious *Naturalis Historia*, a compendium of factoids about geography, horticulture, medicinal herbs and products, metallurgy, and minerals. Tacitus tells us that the emperor Tiberius denounced Piso for displaying Germanicus' naked corpse to the public for the crowd to "handle" or violate with their eyes ("contrectandum vulgi oculis" [*Ann.* 3.12]). Cicero professes—in a speech he never delivered—that the corrupt governor of Sicily,

---

117. "Visum est spectaculum inde non enerue nec fluxum, nec quod animos uirorum molliret et frangeret, sed quod ad pulchra uulnera contemptumque mortis accenderet, cum in seruorum etiam noxiorumque corporibus amor laudis et cupido uictoriae cerneretur."

118. Robin (1993) and others link the senatorial elite's relative powerlessness in the empire to a feminized position in which anxiety about bodily vulnerability is rife; this is an effect of the hierarchal confusion of the early empire (as Fredrick [2002a, 16] points out). In addition, the senators' wealth contributes to undermining their masculinity: "As competition drives the elite into the arms of *luxuria*, it is increasingly difficult to see them as the masters of their own appetites. Conspicuous pleasure penetrates the penetrators" (Fredrick 2002a, 17).

Verres, should be ashamed to feel the hostile gaze of the multitude at his trial
("quae nunc te animo iniquissimo infestissimoque intuetur" [*Verr.* 2.5.144]);
and of course this same Cicero's head and hands met with a horrible fate after
his murder, mounted on the rostra for viewing by whoever wanted to gloat. But
these examples are few, and should, of course, be distinguished from anxiety
about the gaze of one's *peers*, which was more often acknowledged—though
never in terms of the evil eye.[119]

Perhaps, at ancient Rome as in many cultures, class and popular superstition
were inversely proportionate, so that the paucity of our evidence reflects an
issue that may have been of less concern to senators and equestrians than to
some of their poorer or more rural countrymen. Still, the absence of anxiety
about one's exposed stance at the rostra does seem a puzzling feature in the
sources, and there does, accordingly, remain a rift between the two dominant
paradigms of viewing in republican Rome, the one a source of power for the
man at the center of an audience, the other a source of his degradation. This
situation would change: in the early empire, Roman senators and equestrians
seem to have lost a sense of precisely these "natural" safeguards against the
violation of their status and persons at the same time that they lost their sense
of providing a model to their peers.

THE PHILOSOPHER'S BODY

Actors, slaves, and prostitutes: for these unfortunates, the symbiotic relationship between foreignness, self-display, not being one's own master, and low social class renders their position on the Roman totem pole of penetrability at
least predictable. A group whose sexual debasement we might find more surprising are the philosophers themselves, whose standing at Rome—from the
elite Seneca to the vagabond Cynics—seems to have likewise suffered from

---

119. The hostile gaze of one's peers: see, e.g., the informers under Trajan's reign despised and
sneered at by the watching senators (Pliny, *Pan.* 33.4); or Cicero, in a letter to M. Varro, expressing his desire to avoid the gaze of his enemies (*Fam.* 9.2.2). On the destructive gaze at Rome, see
Barton 2001, 204–7, 246–49. On the constraints felt by emperors under the gaze of their subjects
(often during games or in the theater) see Bartsch 1994, chap. 3. A near-comical example of elite
eyes "violated" by what they see is provided by Dio's account of Livia, who had to save a group
of naked men from the death penalty after their bodies inadvertently impinged upon her gaze
(Dio Cass., 58.2.4).

imputations of effeminacy, role-playing, and deceit. Here we can see how curious a fate the marriage of eros and philosophy (so familiar to us from the *Phaedrus*, the *Symposium*, and the *Alcibiades* I) suffers in its transition to a different cultural ground.[120] If, in fifth-century Athens, the elite philosopher's relationship to desire and to the *eromenos*'s body could be cast in terms of a search for beauty that could sublimate itself into a desire for the Forms, or for self-knowledge, no such role is reserved for same-sex sexuality in the Roman metropolis. It is true that sexual desire and the philosopher are still linked—but now as invective located *outside* philosophical texts rather than as practices endorsed *within* those texts. The Greek identification of the philosopher with same-sex desire seems to have loomed large and dangerously for the Romans, even as philosophers took care to dissociate themselves from the charges lobbed against them in the popular literature—that under their austere exteriors they hid the soft flesh and perverted longings of men who (by Roman standards) were not men at all.

Our starting point may be the curious fact that in a surprising number of popular texts, the philosopher at Rome in the early imperial period is associated with sexual behavior of the kind most despised in the aggressively masculine culture of the ancient Mediterranean, where the gender categories in play were not male and female so much as active and passive.[121] We can search in vain for texts that introduce the beneficial presence of the philosopher-lover and his arousal by the embodied beauty of a young boy. Instead, we find eros entering through the back door, where it is instantiated not as a means to wisdom but as the lie that the philosopher's practice conceals: the philosopher himself is now associated with the unmanly role of the *eromenos*, and though an adult, he has taken on the despised role of the one penetrated. Consider the following epigram of Martial, addressed to such a philosopher (*Epigrams* 9.47):

> You prattle about Democritus, Zeno, and enigmatic Plato,
> And any grubby figure shown hairy on a bust—
> As if you were successor and heir to Pythagoras!

---

120. On the continuing popularity and influence of Plato's *Phaedrus* in the first century and beyond, see Trapp 1990.

121. On the basic dichotomy of "active" and "passive," see especially Parker 1997; and Williams 1999, 160–224.

And sure, your beard is just as long as theirs.
But you have something those goaty, hairy types abjure:
That stiff-with-dirt beard over a baby-soft bottom!
You who know the origins and arguments of the schools:
Tell me, Pannychus, what's the dogma on buggery?[122]

In another epigram, Martial advises the wild divorcée Galla to be careful if she dates a philosopher: they look stern and hairy on the outside, but under the rustic appearance lurks a *cinaedus*, a "pansy-boy" who only wants to be penetrated by other men (*Epigrams* 7.58). The would-be philosophers are represented as perverts: under the rugged exterior, they are said to engage in the practices that Roman sexual ideology depicted as the most debased. Juvenal too rails against such false philosophers (*Sat.* 2.8–13):[123]

One can't rely on men's faces: every street overflows with
Austere-visaged perverts. How can *you* reprove immorality,
Most notorious man-hole among the Socratic pansy-boys?
Your hairy limbs and the stiff bristles on your arms
Promise a stern soul, but the doctor has to mock you
As he cuts the swollen piles from your depilated anus.[124]

The point of this distasteful diatribe is precisely the emphasis on the self-depilation and violated masculine integrity of the apparent philosopher, whose ascetic exterior hides a collection of unmanly desires and practices. Only our man Chrestus of *Epigram* 9.27 is *visibly* depilated as well as the owner of secretly hairless genitals—but even he tries to conceal his condition by jabbering about the

---

122. "Democritos, Zenonas inexplicitosque Platonas / quidquid et hirsutis squalet imaginibus, / sic quasi Pythagorae loqueris successor et heres. / praependet sane nec tibi barba minor: / sed, quod et hircosis serum est et turpe pilosis, / in molli rigidam clune libenter habes. / Tu, qui sectarum causas et pondera nosti, / dic mihi, percidi, Pannyche, dogma quod est?"

123. The second-century CE satirist Lucian is also well known for his satirical portraits of the philosophers of his day: see, for example, *Lives for Sale; The Resurrected, or, The Fisherman;* and *Menippus.*

124. "Frontis nulla fides; quis enim non uicus abundat / tristibus obscenis? castigas turpia, cum sis / inter Socraticos notissima fossa cinaedos? / hispida membra quidem et durae per bracchia saetae / promittunt atrocem animum, sed podice leui / caeduntur tumidae medico ridente mariscae."

Curii, the Camilli, the Quinctii, other Roman heroes "and anything to do with the bristly men [that is, philosophers] we read about anywhere."[125]

Why is the philosopher figured in these texts as a man with deviant sexual mores; why, under the bristly beard that stands in Roman thinking for the mark of the philosopher, is he said to have the soft and hairless skin associated with self-depilating deviants? Literally, of course, the expression *Socraticus cinaedus* makes no historical sense: even the most critical reading of the physical practices behind Platonic pederasty would still attribute to Socrates and the other philosophy-laden lovers of these texts the active rather than the passive role; it was the *eromenos*, the young man, who was at danger of losing his qualification for citizenship by allowing himself to be anally penetrated. But Juvenal's and Martial's claimants to philosophy are nonetheless blasted here with the worst possible of Roman insults, the charge of being adult penetratees. Even the established Roman philosopher Seneca comes in for slander in the later sources, when Dio Cassius tells us that he was given over to the love of mature men, and taught Nero to like the same; that far from acting out traditional Roman masculinity, he liked to fellate other men (61.10.4).[126] It seems that not even the flood of Senecan writing about the practices of the good Stoic could defend him from the sexual suspicion attached to the adoption of an ascetic persona.

To some degree, this same charge was also leveled against the Epicureans, whose writings (if misunderstood) might lead critics to damn them as voluptuaries.[127] A famous anecdote recorded by Diogenes Laertius suggests that Stoics figured themselves as *masculine* in comparison to the Epicureans already in the time of Arcesilaus: according to Diogenes, Arcesilaus explained the defection of other philosophers to the Epicurean camp, and the lack of

---

125. "Curios Camillos Quinctios Numas Ancos / et quidquid usquam legimus pilosorum / loqueris" (9.27.6–8). Persius' fifth satire offers a distinctive spin on this notion: here, it is the satirist himself, portrayed as a student of Stoic philosophy, who casts himself in the role of the young *eromenos* who "submits" (in both senses) to his teacher Cornutus ("me tibi supposui. teneros tu suscipis annos / Socratico, Cornute, sinu. tum fallere sollers" [5.36.37]).

126. Contrast this to Seneca's tantalizingly short reference to charges that he played the active role with younger men (*Vit. Beat.* 27.5).

127. On this topic, see Edwards 2005, on whom I base much of this paragraph. However, Warren (2004, chap. 4) suggests that Cicero (and some modern critics) understate the degree to which Epicureanism is compatible with invulnerability. See also Gill (forthcoming).

defection in the opposite direction, by saying that though it was possible for a
man to be turned into a eunuch, no eunuch could ever become a man (Diog.
Laert., *Lives* 4.43). Epictetus, himself a Stoic, is said to have deemed Epicurus a
cinaedologos (Diog. Laert., *Lives* 10.6); Cicero referred to the common belief
that Epicureans "do everything for the sake of pleasure" (voluptatis causa
[*Cael.* 40–41]); and Seneca famously denounced the linkage of virtue and the
pleasant life endorsed in Epicurus' *Letter to Menoecus* 132. For Seneca, virtue
may be found in the Forum, the Senate, the army; pleasure (*voluptas*) lurks
around the bath-houses, "soft, drooping, oozing wine and cologne, either pale
or painted and done up for burial with cosmetics" (*Vit. Beat.* 7.3). As Edwards
(2005, 86) points out, "There is a strong association between effeminacy and
susceptibility to pleasure in Seneca's writing"—and pleasure itself can be
figured in terms that are curiously evocative of bodily penetration. "Voluptas . . .
flows in through every opening and softens the soul with its blandishments
and it launches an attack from one side and other to harry all or parts of our
souls" (*Vit. Beat.* 5.4).[128] Nothing could be more different from the aggressive,
priapic sex of the sort deemed appropriate to Roman men, where, if anything
flowed, it had to be outward into another body rather than inward from
another body.[129]

This association of the philosopher and his desire for a younger boy (whatever its social reality) had a life that extended from the classical period as far as
the Greek erotic narratives of the first centuries CE. To quote the wonderful line
of Ps.-Lucian that opens Simon Goldhill's book *Foucault's Virginity*, "Male
lions don't desire male lions, because lions don't do philosophy."[130] For
Ps.-Lucian's speaker here, the love of (free-born) boys is the only true option
for the philosopher; as for Plato, it produces a form of procreation that is intellectual rather than (literally) infantile. And as the narrator Lycinus concludes,
"Everyone should get married, but pederasty is to be allowed only to the

---

128. Gordon (2002) traces the Roman charges of effeminacy against the Epicurean school to
the nonaggressive and nonacquisitive nature of their philosophy. As she points out of Lucretius'
treatment of sex in *De rerum natura* 4: "For Lucretius, erotic desire is dangerously allied with
illusory visual pleasures and the grasping and striving that the Garden rejects." Epicureanism is
thus effeminate in that it avoids the aggressive form of desire characteristic of the real *vir*.

129. See, e.g., Richlin 1992a, passim.

130. Goldhill 1995, ix, citing Lucian, *Erotes* 36.

wise."[131] (Of course, one might protest that the association of a sublimated form of pederastic desire with the genre of ancient Greek philosophy is a problematic claim; inasmuch as pederastic practice seems to have been understood as a habit of the educated elite in ancient Athens, Plato's texts could simply point to the refinement of a practice not associated by his peers with philosophy per se.[132] But the association was made by the Romans themselves, regardless of its sociohistorical truth content.)

Perhaps not surprisingly, then, the role of eros in Roman philosophical texts—in contrast to the metaphorical and literal content of several of Plato's dialogues—is virtually nil. From the outside, philosophers were mocked as men who were so unable to control their desires and urges that under the façade of the philosopher they engaged in the most shameful form of male-male sexuality in both Greek and Roman eyes: the passive role, the role of the free adult male who yielded his body to penetration by others and liked it all too well.[133] From the inside, Seneca's repeated attempts to masculinize Stoic philosophy by implicit contrast to Epicureanism and by the replacement of bodily impenetrability with mental fortitude can seem a mute acknowledgment of how pervasive these charges might actually have been. But why?

Most practitioners of philosophy at the turn of the first century CE at Rome were, of course, Greeks themselves, and as such they were automatically tainted with what the Romans thought of as "Greek practices" by association.[134] Yet we find Roman philosophers coming in for the same criticism (as with Dio's comments on Seneca), while the usual criticism of Greek philosophers in the republic is addressed toward their fascination with logic rather than their sexuality (cf. Cic., De Or. 1.47–50, 1.104). Indeed, serious-minded

---

131. διὸ δὴ γαμητέον μὲν ἅπασι, παιδεραστεῖν δὲ ἐφείσθω μόνοις τοῖς σοφοῖς (Erotes 51). See also the discussion in Foucault 1986, 211–27.

132. As Danielle Allen points out to me. Moreover, texts such as Plato's Laws contain apparent stipulations against pederasty as "unnatural." See especially Goldhill (1995, 46–111) for a discussion of phusis and same-sex eroticism.

133. Anathema in both Greece and Rome, of course; for the Greek world, and the delicate position of the citizen eromenos who could not show pleasure at his subjection to his older citizen lover, see especially Halperin 1986.

134. On "Greek practices" see, e.g., Polyb., 31.25.3; Cic., Tusc. 4.70 and 5.58; as well as MacMullen 1982. When Cicero has C. Aurelius Cotta comment, in De natura deorum, on his own appreciation for young Greek boys—a sentiment he holds "with the concurrence of the philosophers of old"—Cotta does so on the defensive (Nat. D. 79).

Romans, in their depiction of the virtues of a Socrates, chose to develop Plato's depiction of the philosopher as a shibboleth for sexual abstinence rather than deal with the implications of pederasty with freeborn boys as a method of philosophical self-advancement. In a clear reference to Plato's *Symposium*, for example, the rhetorician Quintilian praises Socrates (*Inst.* 8.4.23) for refusing to do what Alcibiades wanted of him, and even in the randy context of Petronius' *Satyricon*, a novel focusing precisely on the homoerotic misadventures of several lower-class figures from the Roman underlife, the sexy young Giton has this bitter comment to make, after a passionless night with his older lover, Encolpius: "Thanks, Encolpius, for loving me with such Socratic zeal. For not even Alcibiades spent the night in his teacher's bed as unmolested as I" (128.7).[135]

A literalist reader of Martial, Juvenal, and our other sources might explain away the existence of the charges we are discussing by claiming that practitioners of philosophy in early imperial Rome (Romans and Greeks alike) were in fact to the best of our evidence *cinaedi*, passive adult participants in same-sex liaisons, to the last man. I doubt that such an explanation could be taken seriously, but it is worth noting, nonetheless, that our Roman philosophical texts offer wholesale condemnation of the practice of pederasty, and are critical of same-sex eros in general—let alone any mention of a passive role for the older man. If we follow within a single dominant school, that of the Stoics, the development in attitudes toward same-sex love from the Hellenistic period to early imperial Rome, a clear shift is visible from the tolerant, even encouraging doctrines of a Zeno or a Chrysippus to those of Musonius Rufus and Seneca. The Greek founders of Stoicism, Chrysippus and Zeno, seem to have supported the "philosophic" love of boys. Thus, in examining the Hellenistic Stoic response to the tensions present in philosophic homoeroticism, Martha Nussbaum (1995) has delineated the contrast between its beneficial or educational purposes and the fear of falling under the control of lust or losing oneself in love. Stoic doctrine held, on the one hand, that all *pathe* (passions) should be extirpated, but on the other hand, that the wise man could—and would—love

---

135. A similar usage crops up in Achilles Tatius, *Clitophon and Leucippe*, of which Goldhill (1995, 98) remarks: "At crucial points in this narrative . . . 'to be a philosopher,' *philosophein*, means 'to be committed to sexual chastity and its supporting arguments.'"

virtuous and beautiful young men. Although this "love" was specified to be love of "friendship" rather than of "intercourse," Roman philosophers did not afford the idea a warm reception.[136]

A more interesting explanation of the association of the Roman philosopher with the role of the pathic, I hold, emerges from the ideological underpinnings of Roman Stoicism itself. To begin with, the texts of Seneca and Epictetus propound a philosophy whose main focus is that the mind and the soul should remain free from dictates of the body; indeed, much of the content of this philosophy—and of the daily *meditatio*—was aimed at dulling our instinctive sense that the body must be protected and pain avoided as an evil. Roman Stoics were to drum into their minds a sense of the perishability and the worthlessness of the body; they were to inure themselves to future ills not only by making them familiar but also by stressing that the only harm they could do would be to a humble and rotting fleshly casing of the soul. One of Seneca's favorite topics in such self-address was the bodily harm that a tyrant (or an emperor, or a torturer) could inflict upon the good Roman; one could prepare against this by reminding oneself that neither death, nor whips, nor swords, could do one any harm (*Ep.* 82.7–8). Similarly,

If a man sees flashing swords without lowering his gaze and knows that it makes no difference whether his life exits through his mouth or through his throat, call him happy; so too if he denounces the tortures of the body—both those which happen by chance and those that occur through the injustice of a more powerful man, and if he hears without anxiety about bondage and exile and the empty fears of human minds, and says: "Maiden, no new form / of toils, no unexpected ones, rise up before my face; / I have forestalled everything and considered it in my mind" [Verg., *Aen.* 6.103–5]. You today threaten me with these: but I have always threatened myself with them and have presented myself as a man before human fate. The blow [*ictus*] of a disaster is gentle when it has been prepared for by meditation. (*Ep.* 76.33–34)

---

136. For a good discussion of the different attitudes toward eros in Greek and Latin Stoic texts, see Gaca 2003, 59–116. Gaca concentrates on heterosexual eros, but even here draws strong distinctions between the more permissive views of the Greek Stoics and the Senecan and Epictetan opposition to sex for pleasure.

Here and elsewhere, the body is discussed in terms of its expendability; its tra-
vails bear no relation to the health of the soul. As Seneca chides an addressee
(*Constant.* 15.1–2): "Stop asking, 'Won't it hurt the wise man, if he is beaten, if his
eyes are dug out?' . . . You guess at the nature of a noble soul based on your own
weakness, and when you have reflected on how much you yourself can bear, you
put the endurance [*patientia*] of the wise man a little further on." For the wise
man can lose nothing, even as he leaves a trail of body parts in his wake: "We do
not deny that it is inconvenient to be lashed and shoved and to lose a limb, but
we deny that all those are injuries" (*Constant.* 16.2). Epictetus, himself once a
Roman slave, has a particularly winning expression of this attitude: as he puts
it, if you take a wise man, flog him soundly, imprison him, and finally behead
him, he suffers no harm, so long as he bears it all in a noble spirit (4.1.127).
Offering advice to a man whose leg was wounded, the same Epictetus sternly
advises him to stop fussing: When the man laments, "Alas, I am lame in my leg!"
Epictetus can only respond with: "Slave, do you invoke the universe because you
are lame in one stupid leg? Why don't you make a free gift of it to the world?
Give it up!" (1.12.24). And Seneca chimes in with the expendability of a hand or
eye (*Ep.* 9.4): "If a disease or an enemy lops off the wise man's hand, or if some
disaster knocks out an eye or both, what's left will satisfy him and he'll be as
happy with his mutilated and amputated body as he was when whole."[137]

As we have seen, there is no evidence that pre-Senecan forms of the meditation included such a focus on pain and suffering. This teaching seems to owe
more to the influence of Plato than the Greek Stoics, in whose philosophy body
and soul, the physical and the psychic, are closely integrated. The Stoic doctrine
of "total blending" (*krasis di'holou*) held that two substances can occupy
the same space, even though each is continuous and contains no void; thus
pneuma, breath that was a particular combination of air and fire, was seen as
both constituting the *psyche* (which was corporeal itself) *and* as penetrating all
the tissues of the body (cf., for example, *SVF* 2.366–68; Gal., *PHP* 3.1.10–12;
and even in the second century CE Hierocles, *El. Eth.* 4.38–53).[138] On the traditional Stoic view, then, spirit (*psyche* or *logos*) and matter (*hyle*) were seen as

---

137. "Si illi manum aut morbus aut hostis exciderit, si quis oculum vel oculos casus excusserit,
reliquiae illi suae satisfacient et erit imminuto corpore et amputato tam laetus quam [in] integro
fuit."

138. For a more detailed treatment, see Long 1982.

conjoined rather than separate; one did not act as a container for the other. (Similarly in the macrocosm of the world, the god of the Stoics was understood as a breath penetrating and unifying the whole of the universe.) It is true that a specific part of this psyche was called the *hegemonikon*, or center of command, and worked as the seat of sensation, assent, impulse, and reason. But even from this center there extended seven breaths to the eyes, ears, mouth, nose, and skin to convey the incoming stimuli from the entirety of the body (Sandbach 1975, 83). According to this system, at least, the role of the body is not as a mere casing for the *psyche*.

In contrast, the vivid renunciations of the body-as-shell, the notion that the human body is a prison for the soul, or a set of chains around its soul, are ideas more familiar to us from Plato and the Platonic school than from Greek Stoicism; it is hard to think of Socrates awaiting death in the *Phaedo* without recalling his famous line of consolation to his friends: "What is purification but . . . the release of the soul from the chains of the body?" In fact, Socrates says, philosophy is itself nothing other than the study of dying and being dead (*Phd.* 64a), and when the soul leaves the body and the deceptions that it practices, the soul is finally free to seek what is eternal. In *Phdr.* 250c, the body itself is denigrated as "this thing we are carrying around now, which we call a body, locked in it like an oyster in its shell"; elsewhere, the body is compared to a cloak for the soul (*Phd.* 87b) or a structure built around it (*Ti.* 69c).[139] These analogies are repeatedly echoed in Seneca. The body is here the clothing of the soul (*Ad Marc.* 25.1), or, worse, a temporary and makeshift dwelling (*Ep.* 70.16–17) that is gloomy, dark, unpleasant (*Ep.* 65.17), a prison in which the soul is housed (for example, *Ad Marc.* 23.2). It is falling down and decrepit (*Ep.* 58.35), a chain around the soul's freedom (*Ep.* 65.21, *Ad Marc.* 24.5), and altogether unworthy of it (*Ep.* 120.14).[140] Seneca hastens to remind us that we consist of a putrid and perishable casing; how can we hope that from this we might give birth to anything solid and eternal? Clearly, he says, this is the meaning of the ancient

---

139. On the similarities, see Natali (1992, 508), who agrees that "in Seneca we find a clear difference from the Stoic position in which the body is a natural component of the soul and indivisible from it."

140. Respectively: "uestes aliaque tegimenta corporum"; "Nemo nostrum cogitat quandoque sibi ex hoc domicilio exeundum"; "animus in hoc tristi et obscuro domicilio clusus, quotiens potest, apertum petit"; "aegre has angustias ferunt"; "prosiliam ex aedificio putri ac ruenti"; "vinclum aliquod libertati meae circumdatum"; "nec domum esse hoc corpus sed hospitium."

command *Know thyself:* it reminds us that the body is merely an earthenware vessel that breaks when it is shaken, a thing unable to bear cold or heat, doomed to decay, quick to sicken and to rot (*Ad Marc.* 11.1). (Epictetus even compares the body to a shoe [*Ench.* 39] and a donkey [*Disc.* 4.1.79]!)[141] In all these cases, the body is simply a flesh casing for the soul, not something through which the soul is evenly distributed.[142] Well might we exclaim, with the philosopher: "Behold this clogging burden of a body, to which nature has fettered me!" (*Ep.* 24.17).

Seneca (and later Epictetus) shows us, then, a deliberate and apparently proscriptive change in the valorization of the body that is particularly conspicuous among a small group of thinkers and writers in the early imperial period; it is a way of thinking that sets itself apart from the literary, cultural, and even philosophical models this group might have. Most important, it is far removed from traditional Roman ideas about the elite body. In this culture, the body's inviolability to assault or even to display for the pleasure of others was crucial to citizenship status. The very concept of liberty, or *libertas*, as Matthew Roller has argued, seems to have meant for the Romans a particular kind of freedom—freedom from the force that a master could use against a slave, specifically his right to inflict corporal punishment.[143] This may seem odd to us, as we associate "liberty" so often with political rights, forms of constitutions, or abstract ideals; at Rome, however, the many examples of the terminology of *libertas* cited by Roller (2001a) suggest that it was conceptualized in far more concrete terms. Further, this inviolability of the citizen body marked not only the *free* man, but the free *man*: Since one's status as a man was based on one's "perceived bodily integrity and freedom, or the lack of it, from invasion from the outside" (Walters 1997, 30), the impenetrability of the body, either at Rome or anywhere else, plugged into gender constructs as well as issues of social status among the male elite. The term *vir*, "man," is not applied to just any adult male: not only must he be a freeborn Roman citizen; not only must he be

---

141. On Epictetus' negative attitude toward the body, see Long 2002, 149, 157–62.

142. For a full list of images of the body as prison or as a set of chains in Seneca, see Armisen-Marchetti 1989, 154, 78 (on the imagery of the weapons with which fortune threatens man), 164–65 (on torture instruments).

143. Roller 2001a, especially 220–33. On the Roman bias against the mutilated body, and on the imperial mutilation of elite Romans, see Vlahogiannis 1998.

biologically a male; but he must demonstrate the requisite dominant behavior in the sexual, physical, and political spheres.[144] Indeed, there is a strong connection at Rome between sexual activity and literal assaults on the body, such as whipping or beating, for example. Both were conceptualized under the same rubric: a violation of the body that signified, metaphorically, a violation of the citizenship status of the free male. As such, it is clear that under some circumstances at least, "sexual penetration and beating, those two forms of corporeal assault, are in Roman terms structurally equivalent."[145]

The Stoic body, in contrast (even though its practitioners included the Roman elite) is willingly surrendered, at least in theory, to all sorts of violation. This is not to say that Seneca thinks of the philosopher as weak or unmanly in the Roman sense, or that he himself assimilates the philosopher to those of low status; rather, as the philosopher gives up his body, it is his *mental* impenetrability that is figured as the new sign of masculinity. For mental impenetrability it is; curiously enough, Seneca puts to use the same literal language of bodily penetration and violation to describe the mental detachment of the good Stoic, to whose mind none of these weapons can pose any threat: "Therefore I assert that the wise man is vulnerable to no injury: therefore it does not matter how many spears are hurled at him, since he is penetrable [*penetrabilis*] by none. As the hardness of certain stones is impervious to steel, and adamant cannot be cut . . . just so the spirit of the wise man is impregnable" (*Constant.* 3.5).[146] One must surround oneself with philosophy, as if it were a suit of armor, or a fort; fortune will not be able to breach it, even as she hurls her weapons at it (*Ep.* 82.5). Within the safety of this protection, the mind can laugh at those who would seek to harm it: "How glorious it is for the mind, impenetrable, as it were, to every weapon [*nulli penetrabilem telo*], to despise all injuries and insults!" (*Ira* 3.5.8).

Valor in battle, the inaccessibility of a fortress, the safety of a *quadrato* formation on the march, an impenetrable suit of armor: these metaphors, all

---

144. For the aggressive quality of Roman sexual humor, see Richlin 1992b, especially 57–80.

145. Walters 1997, 39. Fredrick (2002b, 238) argues that all forms of violation could be figured as penetration. "This vulnerable self is the true locus of penetration." He also stresses, correctly, a nonbinary, sliding scale of "penetrability" affected by the complications of mobility of Roman class and economic system.

146. "Hoc igitur dico, sapientem nulli esse iniuriae obnoxium; itaque non refert quam multa in illum coiciantur tela, cum sit nulli penetrabilis. Quomodo quorundam lapidum inexpugnabilis ferro duritia est nec secari adamas aut caedi . . . ita sapientis animus solidus est."

taken from the sphere of military action, are what Seneca relies upon to describe the invulnerability of the philosopher's mind.[147] In turn, it is this impenetrable mental state, rather than the inviolability of the body, that is figured as "male" in contrast to other philosophies (*Constant.* 1.1):

> I might say, and not without reason, Serenus, that there is as much of a difference between the Stoics and others who profess wisdom as between woman and men, since each group contributes just as much to human society, but one group has been born for obeying, and the other for commanding. Other wise men cure sick bodies gently and with coddling, just like servants and house-doctors, not by the best and quickest method but as it is permitted. The Stoics, on the other hand, taking up the virile approach [*virilem . . . viam*], do not worry that it should seem pleasant to those who enter upon it, but that it should snatch us away as soon as possible and lead us to that high peak which so rises up above the range of every weapon that it towers over fortune.

Elsewhere Seneca relies on gladiatorial imagery to describe the fearlessness and impregnability of the Stoic soldier:

> You have promised that you will be a good man, which is the strongest chain for a good mind, and you swore a soldier's oath. If anyone tells you that military service is soft and easy, he will be making a joke: I don't want you to misunderstand. Those words—"to be burned, bound, and killed by the sword"—are characteristic of the most honorable contract and the most shameful one as well. Let those who rent their strength to the arena and eat and drink what they will pay back in blood take care lest they suffer all that while unwilling: you, take care that you suffer willingly and with good will. To gladiators it is permitted to put down their weapons and try for the pity of the people; you will neither put them down nor plead for your life: you must die erect and unconquered. Moreover, what can a few days or years win you? We are born without the possibility of discharge. (*Ep.* 37.1–3)

---

147. See further Wilson 1997.

Or, using another metaphor of hardness and insensitivity, Seneca imagines Socrates' reaction to insults, suggesting he is like flint, which hurts the man who strikes at it, or like a stony crag in the sea, which is unable to feel the waves lashing on either side (*Vit. Beat.* 27.2–3). To be a stone: a form of passivity that paradoxically (as Seneca would have it) proves itself more destructive to the one striking it than the strikes it sustains.[148]

When Seneca, then, defines self-knowledge as "know how fragile you are," he introduces an element into a long historical tradition of philosophical self-inspection that has a very different emphasis from the Greek concept of *sophrosyne* as, in part, knowing one's limits. For Seneca, knowledge of the body's frailty goes hand in hand with knowledge of its lack of importance in the philosophical shape of things; and the purpose of the Senecan *meditatio* renders it an exercise to induce the *proficiens* to let go of that which his class and his history as a Roman have taught him is most important: the integrity of his citizen body. Yet, as we saw in the case of Seneca's emphasis on an internal rather than an external spectator in this quest, here too the philosopher relies on the traditional republican imagery of *virtus* to "launch" the student (as Roller puts it) into consciousness of a very different sort of *virtus* altogether.

However, even as Seneca claims for the practitioners of Stoic philosophy a Superman-like impenetrability, it seems likely that this revolution in attitudes toward the body might draw mixed reactions from an audience of Romans. Seneca and his kind pride themselves on their impenetrability, but their passive attitude about the boundaries of their own bodies suggests a kind of insouciance about this category that assimilates them to the despised ranks of the actors, gladiators, slaves, and effeminates so despised in Roman culture— the ranks of the *infames*, men without citizenship rights. The new assessment of the value of the body could lead to such striking stories as Seneca's heroicizing anecdote about the German captive who killed himself by swallowing a toilet plunger rather than appear in the arena as a gladiator (*Ep.* 70.20)—a story that only makes sense in the Stoic context, since a formerly unimaginable form of death, and indeed one suited to a slave, is here elevated to the level of an exemplum for philosophy. A shameful form of bodily violation here

---

148. Being like a stone also has literary antecedents: see, e.g., *Il.* 16.33–35, and *Aen.* 6.620, though in both places it is opposed to being human (and thereby being able to be touched by emotion).

becomes a badge of pride—both in this anecdote and for the philosopher himself, if he can merely think aright.[149]

Consider the character of Scaeva in Lucan's *De bello civili,* a work also penned under Nero by an author with Stoic leanings and a fascination with the mutilation of the body. Scaeva emerges from this epic as a poster-boy for the Stoic attitude toward the body, fighting so fearlessly in battle that his body (Lucan tells us) is pierced over and over again by the spears and arrows of the enemy. As he continues to receive wounds, however, the multitude of weapons sticking out of him eventually grows so dense that further weapons cannot get to him, but bounce off his hedgehog-like exterior: "Nothing blocks his naked innards now / except the spears sticking deep into his bones" (tempora, nec quicquam nudis uitalibus obstat / iam praeter stantis in summis ossibus hastas [*BC* 6.194–95]). "He faces them alone, carrying a dense forest in his chest, now with weary steps" (solus obit densamque ferens in pectore siluam / iam gradibus fessis [*BC* 6.205–6]). Astonishingly, ultra-penetrability has become ultra-impenetrability here. Scaeva's willingness, even eagerness, to be skewered innumerable times at the hands of the enemy is precisely what renders him impervious to their bows and arrows at the end of the scene: none of them can actually pierce through to him any longer.[150] In metaphorical terms, his willingness to completely relinquish his body to abuse has made him immune to that abuse; like the Stoic, his only path to happiness (*virtus*) is in giving up the traditional elite Roman's concern for the inviolability of his physical body.[151]

As in this metaphor, for Seneca the protective armor of philosophy and the frame of mind it can foster must step in for the bodily impenetrability of the elite Roman male. In a reversal of the linkage between freedom from abuse and the status of the citizen, it is no longer the former that is associated with the

---

149. One might object that Roman heroes were always praised for their indifference to bodily suffering, as the long tradition on (say) C. Mucius Scaevola makes clear. But this was never elevated to the level of a philosophy before Seneca's writing; nor would such examples of heroism normally extend to slaves swallowing toilet plungers, even with the ethnographic tradition of the hardy Germans attested to by Tacitus.

150. Cf. Sen., *Constant.* 19.3, on the wise man: "iniurias uero ut uulnera, alia armis, alia pectori infixa, non deiectus, ne motus quidem gradu sustineat."

151. Edwards (1999) notes Seneca's use of metaphors of bodily sickness and suffering for cases of mental weakness; as she points out, this kind of imagery is especially developed and vivid in Seneca.

word *libertas*; it is philosophy that brings liberty. Even servitude to philosophy is a form of liberty, as Seneca puts it paradoxically in some of his formulations: "You ought to serve philosophy, so you can attain real liberty" (philosophiae servias oportet, ut tibi contingat vera libertas [*Ep.* 8.7–8]).[152] This liberty stems from a paradox: that a complete submission to the violation of the body renders the elite citizen free from the danger of "real" violation. The despised body, precisely by means of being despised, is the way to ultimate happiness, or at least Stoic happiness, which John Henderson (1991, 127) has called "the fantasy-ideology of an absolute control of Self as the boundary and teleology of human freedom."

This linguistic and conceptual revolution finds corroboration in an interesting coincidence of philosophical and sexual terminology that forms around the word *patientia*, "endurance," so common in these philosophical texts. The *patientia* of the wise man, his endurance or willingness to suffer, was what enabled this abandonment of the body, the goal to which the Stoics aspired. As Seneca puts it, the goal of this philosophy is that the wise man might protect himself from all injury by his *patientia* and *magnitudo* (*Constant.* 9.4, cf. 15.2); this refrain is heard before him in Cicero and after him in Aulus Gellius, always invoking this same terminology. Zeno, in the *Tusculan Disputations*, is thus made to say that he does "not deny that pain hurts—otherwise why would bravery be necessary?—but that overcoming pain is called *patientia*, if such a thing exists. And if it does not, why do we beautify philosophy, and why do we take pride in its name?" (*Tusc.* 2.33; cf. Aul. Gell. *NA* pr.2.1, 2.1.1, of Socrates).[153] In these texts, at least, *patientia* is a particularly philosophical form of endurance that can be associated with traditional forms of Roman valor, such as bearing up under suffering, even in military contexts such as battle.[154]

---

152. On the liberty brought by philosophy, see further Sen., *Ep.* 26.10: "'Meditare mortem': qui hoc dicit meditari libertatem iubet. Qui mori didicit servire dedidicit; supra omnem potentiam est, certe extra omnem"; also *Ep.* 37.4, 65.15–21, 104.16.

153. "Non ego dolorem dolorem esse nego—cur enim fortitudo desideraretur?—sed eum opprimi dico patientia, si modo est aliqua patientia; si nulla est, quid exornamus philosophiam aut quid eius nomine gloriosi sumus?"

154. On this meaning, see Kaster (2002) with citations. As is well known, Seneca also borrows metaphors from the arena to describe the philosopher's endurance of pain and his stalwart will; see, e.g., *Tranq.* 11.4–5, *Constant.* 16.2. The figure of the gladiator engages some of the same contradictions of class and *virtus* to be found in the notion of philosophical *patientia*; on this topic, see especially Barton 1993; Gunderson 1996, 133–49; and Wiedemann 1992, 35–40.

However, the word *patientia* had a rather more sinister sense in Latin as well.[155] It was the noun that described the sexually submissive role of a man having sex with another man, and was used in the condemnation of such men as *infamis* and effeminate.[156] It occurs in precisely such a sense in Seneca himself, who invokes the word to excoriate the notorious Hostius Quadra (see chapter 2). This man represents for Seneca the reverse image of the philosopher, inasmuch as he uses the mirror not for self-knowledge, as Seneca recommends, but for self-titillation (*Q Nat.* 1.16.7)—and for precisely the kind of deviant behavior that would be paradoxically associated with the philosopher himself by Martial, Juvenal, and Dio Cassius. His *patientia*—his sexual penetration by another male (the term is used three times in *Q Nat.* 1.16.5–9)—forms the shocking kernel of this story about a man whose life represented everything a philosopher's should not be.[157] As Robert Kaster (2002, 134) has astutely written of Hostius and his apparent opposite, the Roman hero Mucius Scaevola who stoically burned his own hand: "They both seem to occupy opposing poles of existence, the one taken to embody the extremes of physical and moral hardihood, the other summoned up as the ultimate in physical and moral degradation. And yet, in Roman terms, they are united by exemplifying precisely the same quality: *patientia*."

In other words, *patientia* is on the one hand the self-ennobling standard of the Roman philosopher, who prided himself, under the dangerous and arbitrary rule of such emperors as Nero, on his capacity to endure the violation of his body—if it came to that—with an unflinching will and with devotion to the principles he had spent his adult life endorsing. But, on the other hand, *patientia* is also the mark of the un-man, of the Roman who is forced to accept the aggression of the other; the mark of the stage-actor, the man without citizenship, the unmanly *cinaedus* and his ilk. It is, for the Roman citizen, the mark of the absence of aggressive male sexuality.[158] At the center of this paradox the

---

155. On *patientia* and its meanings, see especially the excellent treatment of Kaster 2002.

156. *Oxford Latin Dictionary, s.v.*1b: submission to unnatural lust, pathicism. Cic., *Verr.* 2.5.13.§ 34; Sen., *Q Nat.* 1, 16, 5; Sen., *Vit. Beat.* 13, 3; Tac., *Ann.* 6, 1; Petr., 9 and 25; *Mos. et Rom. Leg. Coll.* 5, 3, 2. See also Adams 1982, 189–90; and Williams 1999, 174–75, on *patientia* as the receptive role in a penetrative sexual act.

157. On Hostius Quadra's relation to the rest of this Senecan text on meteorology, see the excellent article of Leitao 1998.

158. As Kaster (2002, 138) points out, it is often used in Tacitus' writing to refer to the slavery of the upper classes under the emperor—another form of emasculation. Cf. *Agr.* 2.3, *Hist.* 2.29, *Ann.* 3.65, etc.

philosopher takes his stand, in a place where eros as we know it is absent but its violating force is well and alive—a force no longer figured as the caressing inflow of one gaze into the eyes of the other, but rather as an assault comparable to a blow against body and mind that gives us no Socrates, but rather turns both Plato's beloved and his lover into a single figure of the isolated and violated Roman *sapiens*.

Let us return, in closing, to Juvenal's lines from Satire 2 limning the odd relationship between the hypocritical philosopher and his smirking doctor. The doctor's smile as he cuts away the *mariscae* from the philosopher's depilated hindquarters confirms his amusement at the gap between ascetic exterior and unmanly interior. But to drive home his point, Juvenal plays on the double meaning of such surgical intervention: the verb *caeduntur* here (the piles "are cut out") points to the equivalence in Roman thinking between cutting and sexual activity, as well: the philosopher is getting it up the rear even as the results of this activity are being operated on.[159] Is Juvenal too playing with the connection between beating, sexual activity, and the body of the philosopher? Perhaps. But at any rate, this much seems clear: a multitude of social and historical factors render the Roman philosopher a man in a dangerously liminal position. If satiric writers of the early empire make a connection between the philosopher and the sexually passive man, we may look not only to these factors but also to an additional possibility: while Seneca and his ilk pride themselves on their impenetrability, their passive attitude about the boundaries of their own bodies renders them, in the eyes of others in their culture, models par excellence of unmanly penetration. In other words, give up one kind of defense against the violation of the body—its immunity to violence—and in a leap of thought, for your Roman audience, you've given them all up: the philosopher is a *cinaedus*.

We are left here, not for the first time, with a series of problematic binaries in Roman culture, all of them undercut by a slipperiness in usage or practice that seems only tangentially acknowledged by our sources. The proximity of the actor and the orator is one exception; here the presence of uncomfortable overlap is documented by our ancient sources. But the proximity of positively and negatively evaluated forms of self-display, of performance and

---

159. See Walters 1998 on this passage.

role-playing, strength and vulnerability, endurance (*patientia*) and submission (*patientia*), map onto an endemic instability in Roman culture *not* shared by the Greeks. To what degree aspects of this can be laid at the social class of actors, the suspicion directed at the practice of philosophy, or the culture of exemplarity is a question perhaps impossible to answer. In the following two chapters, however, I reveal some of the increasing tensions operative in these binaries by turning to Seneca's own development of "the mirror of the self" in imperial Rome.

4 The Self on Display

In 55 or 56 CE, when Seneca wrote the *De clementia* (On Mercy) and addressed it to his former pupil, the eighteen-year-old Nero, the new *princeps* had not yet made a mockery of his own professions of respect for tradition and for the Senate. But Caligula, who exiled Seneca to Corsica in 51, and Claudius, who recalled him in 54, had already provided the bulk of Seneca's experience of the imperial court: both were leaders unpopular with the Senate, the former incestuous and probably insane, the latter perceived as the pawn of his own freedmen and suspiciously eager to try senatorial cases all by himself (worse still, he had notoriously restored the trials for *crimen maiestatis* in 39 CE). Nor was Nero quite untarnished: the murder of his half-brother Britannicus, if politically necessary, provided a harbinger of things to come.

When Seneca addresses Nero at the beginning of the *De clementia*, then, his ostensible purpose may be to set up a *speculum principis* that will show the emperor a version of himself, but it is hard not to feel that the figure in the mirror seems already distorted by history and foreknowledge:

> I have resolved to write about mercy, Emperor Nero, so that I might serve the function of a mirror, in a way, and show you to yourself as one who

will attain the greatest pleasure [*voluptatem*] of all. Although the true fruit of deeds done rightly is to have done them, nor is there any worthy reward for virtue that lies outside virtue, it is pleasant to inspect and survey a good conscience, then to cast one's eyes upon this huge multitude—discordant, factious, uncontrolled, ready to fling itself into its own ruin and that of others alike if it should break its yoke—and to speak thus with oneself: "Did *I* of all mortals find favor and was *I* chosen to carry out the offices of the gods on earth?" (*Clem.* 1.1–2)

This mirror for a prince shows us little that is familiar from the specular tradition.[1] In Seneca's adaptation of the mirror-as-adviser, Nero is not exhorted to consider either his appearance or the expectations raised by it, for better or for worse. He is not to be scared out of moments of *akrasia* by the maniacal figure in the mirror. There is no talk in this essay of self-knowledge in the Platonic tradition, as a form of knowledge that brings the viewer that much closer to divinity by engaging him in a dialectic of the soul. Instead, what the "mirror"— Seneca's text—shows back to him is a Nero whose ideal self seems imminent on the horizon, here at the beginning and throughout the *De clementia*, without the necessity of any explicit alterations in behavior. Quite the contrary: *this* mirror encourages its viewer to self-congratulation rather than self-correction. For Nero has already been selected by the gods to be their regent on earth, and he has already shown the behaviors required of him as ruler—or he soon will.

The terminology of this opening paragraph is deeply problematic. What the mirror of the text promises to show Nero, if he succeeds in ethical rulership, is not self-knowledge—however pleasant it may be to inspect a good conscience— or a profitable estrangement from the self, but rather *voluptas*, a term that is distinctly sensual in its connotations. The only other occasions on which this word is employed in Latin texts in connection with a specular image are in Seneca's treatment of the orgiastic Hostius in the *Naturales quaestiones* and by the author of Justinian's *Digest*—when he dismisses the mirror as a tool for pleasure.[2] We recall that Hostius, too, felt only pleasure at his aggrandized reflection in the mirror—what we might call a physical, rather than metaphorical, reminder of

1. For a historical and political contextualization of the *De clementia*, see Griffin 2000, 532–45.
2. Here we are instructed as to how "lust condemns no instrument for providing pleasure [*voluptas*]" (1.16.1; cf. *Dig.* 33.7.12.16).

his superiority over other men. In both these Senecan examples, the mirror of self-knowledge returns not a Platonic truth or an ethical exhortation, but a distorted view that brings pleasure and that confirms the viewer in, not dissuades him from, his willfulness. The more usual form of viewing that produces *voluptas*, as we have seen, is the gaze trained upon the body on display, the actor's body—an entirely pernicious activity that threatens to unman the viewer even as he revels in the sensual pleasure of this form of spectatorship.

In introducing this terminology, then, Seneca has mingled two mirror traditions: he has introduced the erotic pleasure of the mirror of vanity into the corrective usage of the mirror of self-improvement.[3] And he has done so even though elsewhere he is usually careful to distinguish between *gaudium*, the sober joy born of philosophy, and *voluptas*, whose pleasures are fleeting and of this world.[4] This *voluptas* in the spectacle of the self seems more characteristic of a tyrant—a Caligula, delighting himself by making terrifying faces in the mirror, rather than a philosopher or even the good ruler.[5] And Nero's power is described that way in the second paragraph. As his imaginary, mirror-inspired monologue continues:

I am the arbiter of life and death for populations; the nature of each man's fate and situation is held in my hand; what Fortune wants for each man, she pronounces through my mouth; from my response the people and the cities feel reason for happiness; no part of the world flourishes unless I want and foster it; these so many thousands of swords, which my peace suppresses, will be drawn at my nod; it is in my power to decide what nations will be utterly destroyed, which will be transplanted, to which liberty will be granted or snatched away, which kings will become

---

3. He may also be drawing on the catoptric tradition of the mirror as predictor of the future.

4. As Seneca specifies in *Ep.* 23.4–5, "true *gaudium* is a serious matter"; it comes from philosophy, from knowing what is in one's power and what is not, from despising death and welcoming poverty. At *Ep.* 59.1–4 he acknowledges the common usage of *voluptas* to mean any pleasure, but points out that the Stoic meaning of this term is sharply distinguished from that of *gaudium*: "we consider *voluptas* to be a fault." For *gaudium*, unlike *voluptas*, results from self-knowledge: "it is the exaltation of a soul that trusts in its goods and its truths." This contrast is drawn throughout *De vita beata*; see also *Tranq.* 2.4. At *Ep.* 4.1, however, he uses both terms, apparently interchangeably; at *Ep.* 12.5 his usage (as A. A. Long points out to me) is positive. On this topic, see also Asmis 1990; Foucault 1986, 66; also *Ep.* 13.1 and 72.4; Epict., 2.11.22–25; Marc. Aur., *Medit.* 6.16; and the texts gathered in Long and Sedley 1987, 63.

5. "He made his face savage on purpose (although it was by nature horrid and ugly) by practicing all sorts of terrible and fearsome expressions in front of a mirror" (Suet., *Calig.* 50.1).

slaves and which should have their heads crowned, what cities should be destroyed and which should rise. (*Clem.* 1.1.2)[6]

In place of any mention of self-knowledge, what we see here is the absolute power of the gazing subject. The only exemplum the mirror evokes for the self-contemplating Nero is that of Nero himself. What will really bring him pleasure in the end? We can read optimistically so that all this suggests a vision of Nero's power to rule a discordant world well; but we can also read with hindsight, and recognize here that only the sight of his own power will provide Nero with *voluptas*. This is the man who, in the language of republican exemplarity we once saw applied to Scipio Africanus, is meant to stand as a visual model for all (*Clem.* 1.21.2). But to prescribe a happy use of power is not, after all, to predict it. We can see a similarly impotent use of a kind of *speculum principis* in Seneca's optimistic observations at *Polyb.* 6.1–3 and *Clem.* 1.8.4. In both places, he claims that the actions of the powerful are constrained by their knowledge of their position in the public eye. Yet Seneca seems to mention this only when actually *addressing* the powerful (Nero and Polybius), as if hoping that saying makes it so. His purpose in addressing Claudius' powerful freedman Polybius, after all, was to win a return from exile; why not, then, invoke the old language of exemplarity in an attempt to both praise and constrain the man?

It is striking that Nero's reaction of pleasure and self-satisfaction at the image of his power suggests more the *Medea* of Seneca's drama—whose emotion at killing her children is also *volputas* (*Med.* 991)—than the Stoic *proficiens*, the student of wisdom. The original purpose of this *speculum principis* may have been to praise Nero for his self-restraint despite this boundless power, and by so doing to encourage him to adhere to it, but already in this cursory reading, we can see how the distorting pressures inherent in offering ethical advice to an absolute ruler could transform old ideas almost beyond recognition. No specular tradition suggests that being reminded of one's absolute power by the reflected image in the mirror (or text) induces in the viewer a reluctance to exert that power. Instead, we are left with something closer to Carlin Barton's (1993, 56–57) description of the tyrant in his gilded cage: "the supreme example of the

---

6. As Griffin notes (2000, 537), "His power is compared not only to that of the gods, but to that of a father . . . and to that of a slave-owner. This is clearly the 'irresponsible rule which none but the wise man can sustain,' as Chrysippus characterized kingship (D.L. VII.122)."

solitary creature in a world that is identical with himself. . . . His world, insulated by flattering sycophants, becomes a mirrored prison, like the mirrored halls of the portico in which Domitian paced" (cf. Suet., *Dom.* 14.4).

Nero's "mirror" in *De clementia* turns out to be no less distorting than that of Hostius, and for all Seneca's protreptic efforts in the rest of the essay, its corrective effect upon the ruler seems to have been negligible. As Seneca's mirror gains in depth, it develops, after all, into a mirror that shows Nero not only his own glory, but his reflection in the eyes of the citizens, who turn to him, as to the sun, for their model:

> *Our* actions are felt only by a few; we can go out and return home and change our appearance without the public noticing; it's *your* lot to no more be able to hide away than the sun. There is a great light around you, all eyes are turned to it—you think you leave the house? You *rise*. You cannot talk without your voice being heard wherever there are nations; you cannot get angry without everything trembling, because you cannot afflict anyone without everything around him quaking too. Just as light-ning bolts falling from the sky are a danger to few, but cause fear in all, so too the punishments dealt by great powers terrify more widely than they harm, and not without reason. (*Clem.* 1.8.4–5)

Nero's comparison to the sun, the reverberations of the entire world around his every action, cast him as a natural force to be reckoned with, a man whose actions are echoed in nature (*omnia*) and whose rage crashes earthward like celestial lightning. If the good Stoic acts in conformity with nature, here nature seems rather to act in conformity with Nero. But not with Nero's ancestors: when Seneca exhorts him to keep Augustus in mind, the philosopher reverts to more traditional forms of mirroring, turning away from the mirror of omnipo-tence and reminding the young Nero of the many acts of clemency engaged in by the *princeps*. Our philosopher invokes both the old mirror and the new, though neither would be successful in curbing what Nero would become.

These unsuccessful textual mirrors reaffirm the conclusions Seneca draws in another passage on mirroring, part of which we considered briefly in chapter 1. As we have seen, Seneca tells us in *De ira* that the angry man who sees his dis-torted visage in the mirror will be shocked back into a more reasonable frame of mind—once again stressing the idea that the mirrored image of self has a normative and ethical force upon the individual. Yet even here, his continued exploration of the topic of the self-improving mirror ends up redirecting the volition to change into the hands of the self-examiner and undermining the force of that "communal" gaze on the self. As he addresses the objections of an imaginary interlocutor, he comments: "You say no one has really been frightened out of anger by a mirror? No matter: Any man who came to the mirror to change himself was already changed."[7] The mirror does little, after all: the frame of mind of its user has already been set. As for the rest of the self-spectators, the distressing fact is that while men remain angry, they look beautiful to themselves—that's how they *want* to look, just as enraged as they are ("qualesque esse etiam videri volunt" [2.36.3]). Since here only the individual who approaches self-reflection with the prior intention of changing himself is on the path to self-improvement, Seneca has altered, or rather undone, the traditional account by stressing the intention of the viewer and by validating the idea that catching sight of (even a distorted) self in a mirror can bring delight ("nulla est formosior effigies") rather than self-alienation. If Nero's mirror has no protreptic ability to make him want to change the image he sees in its reflective surface, it seems that he too, like the angry man, would have to have changed *before* he came to the mirror—or at least he would have to be ready to disbelieve its message that he was already the best possible ideal for himself. But the *De ira* suggests that our philosopher himself is skeptical about the power attributed to self-speculation. Indeed, this movement away from the shaping force of oneself-viewed-as-another is not isolated to a few passages in the *De clementia* and the *De ira*. On the contrary: as this chapter and the next will argue, such a movement can be shown to inform the vast body of Seneca's writing, where Seneca seems to be moving away from the visual paradigm we explored in chapter 3 and moving toward a novel position on the observable self—partly informed by Stoicism, partly by the remaining force of Roman tradition.[8]

As we shall see in what follows, the question of what might be the *right* mirror in which to see the self drives much of the philosophical inquiry of Seneca's

---

7. "Speculo quidem neminem deterritum ab ira credideris: quid ergo est? qui ad speculum uenerat ut se mutaret, iam mutauerat" (*De ira* 2.36.3).

8. I do not mean to suggest here that all Senecan invocations of the *gnothi sauton* include reference to the specular. On the contrary, the "know your limits" tradition of the earliest texts that refer to self-knowledge continues to be cited into Seneca's day and beyond. See, e.g., Sen., *Tranq.* 6.3; Juv., *Sat.* 11.27–45.

work. Part of Seneca's difficulty, of course, was that the demise of the republic and its traditional forms of self-display, approbation, and censure, together with the ascension to power of one man and his imperial court, warped the most traditional senatorial mirror of all, that of their peers and their admiring public. This process had already started in the Julio-Claudian period, when the fall of the republic after decades of civil war brought with it a new political position, that of *princeps*. What the Roman senatorial classes seem to have bristled against particularly in this new regime—especially after Augustus' death, when even the appearance of adhesion to the traditional forms of the republic became more transparent—was precisely the demise of those traditions of self-display in which and through which senatorial glory, reputation, and authority were maintained. Those republican institutions that represented the power of elite self-promotion were slowly stripped of power; in their place stepped the emperor, his court, his freedmen, and his friends. Werner Eck (1984) has decisively collected the evidence for the gradual suppression of autocratic self-display, starting with Octavian's refusal in 28 BCE to let Licinius Crassus dedicate the *spolia opima* in the temple of Jupiter Feretrius (Dio Cass., 51.24.4, *PIR²* L186). The last Roman senator with no relation to the imperial family who was allowed a public triumph of the sort mentioned in chapter 3 was L. Cornelius Balbus, in March of 19 BCE; after that, far less spectacular grants of the *ornamenta triumphalia* were proposed, and by Augustus himself.[9] Senatorially financed building activity, and the inscriptions that go along with it, stopped in Rome for public edifices (although this practice continued in the provinces) after the early years of the Augustan principate. A number of the proceedings of the standing law courts were transferred to the Senate, where they took place under the watchful eye of the emperor.[10] Similarly, the debates that had shaped foreign and domestic policy were eventually taken over by the *concilium principis*. The Senate, most public of places for display, became, in the cynical view of Tacitus and other historians, simply a gallery for imperial flattery. Senatorial representations on coinage disappeared.[11] And even the

---

9. See, e.g., Dio Cass., 50.10.3.

10. On the emperor's role in the Senate, see especially Talbert 1984, 163–84.

11. "The names of the *triumviri monetales*, which had reappeared on coins minted in Rome in about 20 BC, disappear again before the end of Augustus' reign" (Eck 1984, 154n16 with bibliography).

senatorial *imagines*, the domestic masks brought out for funerals, were seen less often in public, as their public display was largely usurped by the imperial family. Pliny the Elder tells us that the use of the *imagines* had all but died out in his time (*HN* 35.6–7); what now graced the atria of noblemen were luxurious artworks by foreign artists.[12] As John Bodel (1999, 271) concludes in his study of the Augustan cooptation of the *funus publicum*, the final privatization of the elite funeral had taken place by the end of the first century CE: "monopolization by the emperor of particular modes of self-display result[ed] in a diffusion of the traditional forms to new venues outside the city and an internalization in private domestic contexts of themes and . . . behaviors previously associated with the public civic spaces of Rome."[13]

The imperial monopoly on such forms of display inevitably eroded the traditional republican practice of exemplary viewing. From the Battle of Actium to the death of Nero, the imperial family simultaneously monopolized the forms of popular display typical of the senatorial elite and claimed for itself a new standard in morality and *virtus*. It was a period characterized by all sorts of bitter reversals, at least in the eyes of the ousted elite: as several senatorial sources lament, the imperial gaze turned upon them was invidious rather than emulatory, and the sense of personal danger must have severely compromised the former bodily dignity and status of this old class. The metaphor that springs into use at such a time is that of the actor: if, under Julius Caesar, the equestrian Laberius was forced to degrade himself by playing in a mime under Caesar's vengeful eye (Macrob., *Sat.* 2.7), later senators would complain instead that this imperial gaze turned them into performers outside the theater as well. Under the watchful eye of a Tiberius or a Nero, this new class of actors swallowed its anger and dissimulated its disgust.[14] So it is that Tacitus' *Annals*, with

---

12. On the decline of private *imagines*, see Bodel 1999 and Gregory 1994, 92. Flower (1996, 256–60) argues in some detail that the use of the *imagines* did not die out in the early empire, although "changes in electoral practice and the growing influence of the *princeps* removed much of the basic function of *imagines* as advertisements aimed directly at the electors" (256). Contra, see Bodel 1999, 273: "Evidence for the appearance of ancestral portraits at private funerals effectively ends with Tiberius; the practice may have continued for some decades after that time, but its significance was greatly dimished."

13. Augustus and Tiberius granted such funerals freely, but they curbed the level of pomp allowed and assigned the funeral oration to a leading senator rather than a family member (Bodel 1999, 272).

14. The topic of Bartsch 1994. In Tac., *Agr.* 45, the trope is taken further when Domitian is cast as even more abusively observant than Nero: "Nero at least averted his eyes and though he ordered crimes, he did not watch them; but it was a special part of our misery under Domitian to watch and to be watched, that time when our sighs were taken note of, when that savage and ruddy face,

its cynical denunciations of bowing and scraping senators, each more cowardly than the last, could profitably be read as a new historical experiment: the exposure of the *anti-exemplum*.[15]

This new dynamic of the gaze spurs the development of a political environment in which some members of the Roman elite reacted by creating new standards for *virtus* and by seeking to dispense with the community at large as a locus of approval or shaming.[16] The change goes so far as to recast the public *persona* as a form of self-presentation that is now sullied with the taint of performance, rather than being the normative self on view of the Roman citizen in the public eye. This impetus seeks further to negate the imperial eye, reinstall self-respect in the shamed senatorial class, and restore *libertas* to a group that had lost much of its former prerogatives. But it does not find a voice among the entire class of displaced Romans; rather, it achieves fullest expression in the work of one man, Seneca, himself one of the most problematic figures of the century.

SENECA'S WITNESS

The prose work of Lucius Annaeus Seneca—Stoic philosopher and imperial adviser, millionaire, and enforced suicide—demonstrates a pervasive concern with practicing and proselytizing about a self-directed transformation of the individual's relationship both with himself and with the social world around him. Most of his letters and essays treat different manifestations of one overriding goal: to set the other members of his elite group upon the path to accepting and internalizing a related family of philosophical truths largely taken from Stoicism.[17] His readers are to turn their gaze upon themselves; to hunt out their own weaknesses; to set in motion a set of self-administered

---

with which he fortified himself against shame, sufficed to mark down the pallor of so many men." See also Barton 2001, 248–50.

15. As Feldherr (1998, 218–19) puts it: "Tacitus' *exempla* . . . have nothing to do with state-building. On the contrary, good examples are now those that illustrate how the smaller social units that define each Roman individual, the family and personal freedom of will that enables disasters to be boldly faced, can preserve their integrity even when challenged by the hostility of the state." (And such good examples are comparatively rare.)

16. On Seneca's changes to Roman ethical terminology, see Roller (2001a, 97–108), arguing that for Seneca the moral category *virtus* was recast to refer not to the display of martial valor, but to a mental disposition. Roller (88–97) also discusses how Seneca engages with the problem of "assessing an agent's moral state on the basis of (potentially misleading) observable actions and other signs" (92).

17. Although some of Seneca's examples feature such lowly figures as gladiators and slaves, the examples themselves seem to be directed at his literate peers.

corrections that will render them true *proficientes*, that is, practicing Stoic acolytes. In these texts, Seneca is much less concerned with the logical and cosmological aspects of Hellenistic Stoicism than with the *gnothi sauton*: the imperative to know oneself. In his hands, to know oneself becomes to know the nature of one's *libertas*: the wise man can and will be free from the constraints of political exigency, from the fear of pain or torture, from anxiety about death. His goal is to practice a kind of freedom that privileges the ability of his thoughts to think what they will, over and despite the fate of the body. This type of freedom allows him to consciously choose what he will and will not consider important in life, even what he will and will not desire. In the absence of addiction, at least, it is a viable option.

This transformation depends upon a set of techniques that look to what I would call the ultimate end of Roman Stoicism—the inviolability of the self (rather than, with Foucault, the "care of the self" [le souci de soi]). As a set of meditative practices in the form of self-exhortation toward particular goals, the repetition of philosophical maxims, the keeping of a diary, and the daily review of one's actions and thoughts, these techniques (*meditatio* in Latin, *askesis* in Greek) were to help the Roman Stoic develop the ability to inure himself to the slings and arrows of emotional loss and political stress, and to do so by cultivating an extreme priority of mind over matter.[18] Seneca himself would cast this ability as the reevaluation, by the *hegemonikon*, of pleasure and gain as indifferents rather than goods, and also as the cultivation of physical or emotional analgesia in the face of suffering.[19] As in the *Alcibiades* I, then, Stoic self-shaping, at least *in part*, has to do with the cultivation of rationality within the human soul.[20] In practice, however, the process of Stoic *meditatio* has much more to do with self-witnessing than with seeing oneself in a divine mirror: both the "philosophical" and the erring parts of the soul are conceptualized as being in dialogue, and the judgments of the former on the latter provide the major impetus toward self-improvement.

---

18. On the history and practice of the *meditatio*, see Hadot 1995, 92–125; Hadot 1969; Hijmans 1959; Newman 1989; Sorabji 2002, 211–52.

19. "When your *hegemonikon* is in good shape it judges rightly as to the good, and this judgment flows smoothly into *horme*, or impulse, and so into action" (Campbell 1985, 328). On Seneca's psychological dualism, see Fillion-Lahille 1984, on *De ira*; Gill (forthcoming); Inwood 1993; and Nussbaum 1994, chap. 11. On the *praemeditatio malorum*, see Rabbow 1954, 169–70; Hadot 1969, 60–61.

20. For thoughtful reflections along these lines, see Long 2001.

The practice of *meditatio* as Seneca describes it, accordingly, often relies on hortatory self-communion in the form of a dialogue held by the self with the self to rid the soul of the passions and the fear of death, and to rekindle in it a sense of duty.[21] In such communion, the speaker addresses himself as an alter ego, with the questioning voice taking up the role of a superior or an ethical better as it quizzes the agent self about its activities or chastises it for slips of equanimity: "Why should I fear anything from my mistakes, when I can say: 'See to it that you don't do that any more; I forgive you this time. In that argument you spoke too aggressively. . . . You rebuked that man more frankly than you should have, and so you didn't mend him, you offended him'" (*De ira* 3.36.3–4). Seneca likes to review his day before falling asleep (and once his wife has piped down for the night), and he reports that his teacher Sextius would do the same at bedtime: "This was Sextius' practice: at the end of the day, when he had retired for his night's rest, he would question his soul: 'Which of your bad habits did you cure today? Which vice did you resist? In what respect are you better?' . . . What is finer than the habit of examining the whole day?" (*De ira* 3.1).[22] Sextius was the head of an independent school of thought that apparently was influenced by both Stoicism and Pythagoreanism. The practice of self-review did not come into existence with Roman Stoics; on the contrary, it has long roots in a number of philosophical schools: Stoicism, Pythagoreanism, Epicureanism, Skepticism, and even in the way of life of Plato's Socrates.[23] In all, the emphasis seems to have been on a form of self-mastery

---

21. For a focus on the written aspect of this practice (such as produced the *Epistulae morales*), see Edwards 1997a; Henderson 1991, 129. For self-dialogue in Epictetus and Marcus Aurelius, see Hadot 1995, 195–202.

22. For another sampling of what Seneca says "si mecum loquor," see *Ep.* 8.4–5. In general, the content of most of the epistles constitutes what Seneca might say to himself, although addressed here, of course, to the absent Lucilius.

23. Cicero says he practices Pythagorean *askesis*, but the focus here seems to be on exercising the memory rather than shaping the self. See *Sen.* 9.38: "Multum etiam Graecis litteris utor Pythagoreorumque more exercendae memoriae gratia quid quoque die dixerim audierim egerim, commemoro vesperi." Diog. Laert., 8.19.21 (on Pythagoras), shows the kind of dialogue with oneself one might hold; see also Diog. Laert., 9.64 (on Pyrrho the skeptic), 6.6 (Antisthenes), 7.171 (Cleanthes). See also Foucault 1986, 50–51. Hadot (1995, 87–89) and Rabbow (1954) discuss the history of meditation upon aphorisms; in Epicureanism, see Epicurus, *Letter to Menoecus* 135.5–8 and 123.1–2; for Pythagoras, Diog. Laert., 8.17–18. For the influence of Socratic dialogue, see Hadot 1995, 89–101; and Long 2002, 67–96. For the influence of popular exhortation and moral injunctions, see Hadot 1969, 10–22.

that privileged a philosophically informed perspective of the insignificance of societally driven values and mores in the face of more universal truths and in the path to happiness (however that might be defined).[24] So one might say to oneself: "I warn you, now, not to drown your soul in that worthless anxiety. Wrest it from your private case to a general one. Tell yourself you are a mortal and fragile body, and that suffering can arrive from more sources than a wrong done to you or from more powerful men" (*Ep.* 25.16). Practitioners of this method talked themselves into the correct state of mind via repetition and rhetoric, eventually replacing the dominance of one set of opinions in their perspective with another; diligent attention, says Seneca, can make even the curved beam straight again, and how much more pliable is the soul (*Ep.* 50.6)! A special area for attention in this regard, especially in Stoicism, was the human fear of bodily suffering, and here too the repetition of maxims designed to minimize its force was supposed to inure the philosopher to the prospect of torture or death down the road.[25] Poverty, humiliation, loss of life: as Seneca puts it in *De ira*, "There's nothing so difficult and demanding but that the human mind cannot overcome it and constant *meditatio* make it familiar."[26]

We will return to Roman Stoic forms of the *meditatio* in chapter 5, but for now I would like to point to one way in which the employment of this practice in Seneca (and to a lesser degree, Epictetus) differs from its philosophical precedents. In Seneca, a large part of the *meditatio* is given to the idea that we should live as if we could be seen by an ideal viewer; in other words, it relies heavily on the visual dynamic characteristic of Roman political and social life.[27] Seneca's project of self-transformation depends significantly on the eth-

---

24. The Pythagoreans and the Stoics recommended that a few moments be set aside in the morning and evening for this self-examination, although we find Epictetus zealously recommending questioning one's judgment at all times of day (*Disc.* 3.10.1–5).

25. See Newman (1989, 1480): "This type of internal dialogue lends itself to employing repetition, which is the best means of persuasion and of effecting a real change in the ruling faculty; constantly repeating the correct opinion will eventually drive out the corresponding false opinion. Rhetorical devices, such as contrasting words or phrases or the use of paradoxes, also enhance the persuasive capabilities of this type of dialogue."

26. *De ira* 2.12.3. Hadot (1969, 105) stresses the necessity not only of self-education but also of the active deployment of one's intellectually acquired wisdom in daily life for the successful practice of philosophy: *Übung* makes the man. See similarly Hijmans 1959, 67.

27. This feature is absent in Musonius Rufus, who is less of an innovator here as in other respects.

ical force of the gaze—or at least, he frames his injunctions to his readers and to himself around this traditional source of approval and censure.[28] In so doing he borrows from the kind of self-observation that most Romans found necessary to maintain their public *persona* in front of an audience—the kind that kept an orator, for example, from gesticulating too wildly in front of an audience.[29] Its source, however, can no longer be clearly mapped onto elite values.

To some degree, this stress on visuality engages a common philosophical metaphor. Like Plato before him, Seneca in his philosophical language often relies on tropes of vision and light to express the process of coming to knowledge and the nature of the Good; man uses the eyes of the soul to contemplate the truth, and this truth, along with philosophy and virtue, is described as forms of light or radiance.[30] Consider *Ep.* 115.6, where Seneca uses the metaphor of impeded vision to describe the difficulty of *seeing* virtue (here buried deep in the body, a most un-Platonic touch): "No one, I tell you, would not burn with love of virtue if it befell us to see it; now as it is many things impede us and either drive back our eyesight [*aciem nostram*] with excessive brightness or detain it with darkness. But if, just as our eyesight can be sharpened and cleansed by means of certain medicines, so too we want to free the sight of our soul from its impediments, we will be able to perceive virtue even buried in the body, even with poverty in the way, even with lowliness and disgrace lying in our way."[31]

In Seneca, however, the shine of virtue adapts itself as well to a more mundane and more earthly form of seeing, the gaze of one's compatriots upon one's actions. Seneca reverts to a very Roman way of thinking about the performance of virtue; for him, it is also the presence of a judging gaze and of a

---

28. Much of the discussion of the Senecan internal viewer that follows in this section reiterates points already made in print by Edwards (1997a), and especially Roller (2001a), whose insightful book came out while I was still finishing up my own work. I hope that the ends to which I will use these (preempted) observations will justify their inclusion here.

29. See, on oratorical self-mastery, Gunderson (2000, 87–110), though there is more here in the way of theory from Lacan and Butler than of concrete examples from antiquity.

30. On this imagery, see Armisen-Marchetti 1989, 131–32, 174–76; and Solimano 1991, 92–103. On Sophocles' use of light and knowledge metaphors, see Bernidaki-Aldous 1990.

31. Solimano (1991, 78) remarks on this Senecan "ossessionante ripetizione" of terms belonging to the semantic field of vision.

witness (*testis*) that propel us to ethical behavior.[32] We have seen already how an entire tradition imagines that to know oneself is to react to the self that one sees mirrored in the eyes of others, to develop from solipsism into ethical responsibility. In employing the metaphor of the mirror as an aid to self-knowledge, the popular traditions of self-reflection discussed in chapter 1 also advocated the training of one's gaze upon oneself: yet what one saw reflected in the mirror, ideally, were the judgments that a community of peers would pass upon one's behavior. To enable this kind of imagining, of course, the self-examining individual would already be familiar with the ethical standards, models, and expectations of that community, which would limit the subjective element in this turn to the self.[33]

As we will see, however, Seneca's concern is not so much with the traditional sources of this gaze at Rome: the censors, the officeholders, and the fellow elite; the *imagines* of one's noble house; the people who flocked to funerals, triumphs, and law-cases. It is no longer they who will provide a mirror to the self, but the individual himself. The idea is not completely novel in Roman philosophy; Cicero too speaks of the need to be honest without a witness.[34] But never before has it been hammered into the would-be *sapiens* with such insistence. Indeed, the community, in Seneca's day, can actively be the source of negative models, like a mirror that renders beautiful what is ugly: we arrange our life according to the example of the majority and we look to what is usual, not what is fitting, he complains in *Ep.* 99.16–17.[35] As he warns us, the majority's

---

32. One searches the older Greek Stoic fragments in vain to find a similar emphasis on the visual nature of self-governance, as Tobias Reinhardt remarked in response to a talk of mine at Corpus Christi, Oxford, in March 2000.

33. Even if the individual's understanding of the values of his community might depend to some extent upon the nature of his education and life experience, I think it is fair to project a basic conformity, especially within a particular class with a highly developed tradition of the *mos maiorum*. The ideal of the man whose internal witness renders him trustworthy even if no one can see him is well expressed in Cic., *Off.* 3.19.78, where Gyges is, of course, blameworthy for sinking into crime as soon as no one could see him.

34. An honorable person is honest even in the dark (*Off.* 3.78); a shameful thing is shameful even when hidden (*Leg.* 1.50–51); you need to be good without a witness (*Tusc.* 2.26.63–64).

35. As Roller (2001a, 88) has noted, "Seneca's rejection of traditional, external moral evaluation also calls into question that most familiar and ubiquitous form of Roman moral argumentation, the use of exempla." See also the examples collected in Solimano 1991, 61n135. Grimal (1989, 973) notes this withdrawal from public judgment. Nor, he says, is Seneca much impressed by Panaetius' accommodations to Roman life: on the contrary, Seneca represents "the moment in which Stoicism turns inward . . . and rediscovers interiority" (979).

choice is the worse option when it comes to following the good life (*Vit. beat.* 2.1–4): "When the happy life is under debate, there will be no use for you to reply to me, as if it were a matter of votes: 'This side seems to be in a majority.' For that is just the reason it is the worse side. . . . Therefore let us find out what is best to do, not what finds favor with the rabble, who are the worst possible exponents of the truth." And lest we think he is talking about the lower classes only, he specifies: "By the rabble I mean no less the servants of the court than the servants of the kitchen; for I do not regard the color of the garments that clothe the body. In rating a man I do not rely upon eyesight. . . . Why do I not rather seek some real good—one which I could feel, not one which I could display?"[36] In a distinct move away from the prestige-oriented and highly visible political traditions of the republican elite, the opinion of one's peers is said to be completely irrelevant; a just man will even derive pleasure from a bad reputation earned by doing good ("mala opinio bene parta" [*Ep.* 113.32]). Seneca goes so far as to warn his correspondent Lucilius that if he sees him applauded by the populace, if the whole state is singing his praises—he deserves nothing but pity (*Ep.* 29.12).[37] It is true, he acknowledges, that the force of the majority's judgment is difficult to resist, and even a Socrates, a Cato or a Laelius might have lost hold of their moral character before such an onslaught of praise or blame. But he reminds us that our options are not only to imitate or loathe the world, but also to ignore it: to recede into oneself and select with great care those with whom one associates (*Ep.* 7.6–8).[38] He stoutly reiterates the theme at the beginning of epistle 10: "I do not change my opinion; avoid the many, avoid the few, avoid even the individual. I know of no one with whom I should be willing to have you shared. And see what an opinion of you I have; for I dare to trust you with your own self [*te tibi credere*]" (*Ep.* 10.1).

---

36. "Vulgum autem tam chlamydatos quam coronatos uoco; non enim colorem uestium quibus praetexta sunt corpora aspicio. Oculis de homine non credo. . . . Quin potius quaero aliquod usu bonum, quod sentiam, non quod ostendam?" For the translation and interpretation, I have used the Loeb edition by John W. Basore.

37. On Seneca's attitude toward the opinion of the majority, see further Grimal 1989; Motto and Clark 1993; and *Ep.* 94.55, 68; 99.17.

38. "Recede in te ipse quantum potes; cum his versare qui te meliorem facturi sunt, illos admitte quos tu potes facere meliores." On Epictetus' treatment of the difficulty the Stoic faces in regard to the force of public opinion, see Hijmans 1959, 99–100. Epictetus too stresses the importance of discounting outside judgments and the outside gaze: we are to be the watchers and the watched ourselves, all in one person. Cf. Epict., *Disc.* 4.6; and Citroni-Marchetti 1994, 4584.

Seneca's injunctions on acquiring self-knowledge, then, would usually have us *turn away* from the assessing gaze of the community at large, and reject the observation and judgment of the community in general as a source of ethical self-shaping.[39] Such a movement away from public judgment mirrors on a small scale his larger comments in the *De otio* on the proper role of the philosopher in a corrupt political community, namely, that he should abstain from public life altogether (*De ot.* 3.3).[40] The replacement for gaze and judgment of one's political peers is the adoption of a personal gaze on the self; the witness here is one with the witnessed, and it is the task of the former to deploy Stoic philosophy to shape the latter.[41] This is the path to proper self-knowledge: self-scrutiny rather than public scrutiny, philosophy rather than the *cursus honorum*, interiority rather than display. Seneca advises his correspondent Lucilius accordingly: "Shake yourself out and scrutinize and observe yourself in various ways; but look to this before anything else, namely, whether you have made progress in philosophy or in life itself. Philosophy is no trick for the people, nor is it acquired by display; it consists not in words but in deeds" (*Ep.* 16.2–3).[42] If Livy points to the role of a general such as M. Porcius as an observer and judge of bravery in battle (*AUC* 42.34.7), Seneca borrows this military vocabulary to accentuate the role of the individual in his personal struggles. "Are you doing battle against some illness?" he asks Lucilius, using the martial imagery

39. See similarly *Ep.* 94.55, 94.68, 99.17; *Constant.* 11.2, 13.2–3; and Citroni-Marchetti 1994, 4564. We are to reject, as well, the exempla provided by such a community: alas, "quia frequentius, sequimur quasi honestius" (*Ep.* 123.6). This idea occurs earlier in Cic., *Tusc.* 2.63–64, where, too, the judgment of the multitude is denigrated in favor of that of the individual: "Nullum theatrum virtuti conscientia maius est." I do not claim, then, that the notion is unique to Seneca, but rather that the stress placed on it by the later author shows a shift in the relative importance of this idea to the rest of his work.

40. As Schofield (1999, 770) puts it, "the claims of citizenship of the universe come to dwarf those of the existing societies in which we find ourselves: the cosmic perspective increasingly overshadows the vantage point of ordinary life." See also *Ep.* 8.1, where Lucilius asks: "Are you telling me to shun the public, to withdraw and be content with my own conscience? Where are those teachings of your school, which bid one to die while actively at work?"

41. Edwards (1997a) views the project of letter-writing in terms of a self-revelatory activity, which is clearly correct: Seneca shows himself to Lucilius, and claims of him that he, too, "mihi ostendis" (*Ep.* 40.1). Of course, the turn toward introspection that Edwards identifies here is characteristic of several of the other prose works as well.

42. "Excute te et varie scrutare et observa; illud ante omnia vide, utrum in philosophia an in ipsa vita profeceris. Non est philosophia populare artificium nec ostentationi paratum; non in verbis sed in rebus est."

more traditionally suited to the winning of *gloria* than to tossing in bed sick. In that case, "[y]our task awaits: fight bravely with the disease. If it forces you to nothing, if its appeals produce nothing, it is an outstanding exemplum that you provide. O what huge material there would be for glory, if we should be watched while we were sick! You yourself be the watcher; you yourself offer yourself praise" (*Ep.* 78.21).[43] Here is the new hero: he hands down to posterity not an exemplary deed, but an exemplary—nothing; it is his very inaction, his Stoic lack of response to the painful demands of his illness, that is laudable. And he endures, not under the gaze of a Porcius, but of himself; he is the arbiter of his own glory.

In the same way, the irascible man can cure himself if only he takes up the task of being a *speculator sui*, a *censor de moribus* for one man alone: "Anger will cease and become more controllable if it finds that it must appear before a judge every day. Can anything be finer than examining the whole day? And how delightful the sleep that follows this self-examination—how tranquil it is, how deep and untroubled, when the soul has either praised and admonished itself, and when this secret examiner [*speculator sui censorque secretus*] and critic of self has given report of its own character!" It is all too easy to see another's faults, Seneca often notes, but one's own can only be detected by a conscious examination of the self, a *respectus nostri* (*De ira* 2.28.8; cf. *Ep.* 98.4, 26.4–5).[44] In this reflexive dynamic of the gaze, even the most hallowed of republican symbols, the ancestral *imago*, loses its prescriptive powers and becomes, for Seneca, a simple reminder of the meaninglessness of wealth and station: it is not your *imagines* that make you good or noble, but your soul (*Ep.* 44.5; cf. *Ep.* 76.12; *Ben.* 3.28.2).[45]

As should be clear, the philosophical practice Seneca adopts is still tinted with the distinct shade of the Roman elite, couched in the language of the regulatory gaze and the presence of a censor—what Foucault has called the "disciplinary

---

43. "Habes quod agas: bene luctare cum morbo. Si nihil te coegerit, si nihil exoraverit, insigne prodis exemplum. O quam magna erat gloriae materia, si spectaremur aegri! ipse te specta, ipse te lauda."

44. On using a friend to help in the project of self-improvement, see Cic., *Off.* 1.91; Cic., *Amic.* 7.23; Hor., *Ep.* 11.25–26; Hor., *Sat.* 1.4.129, 1.3.35, 1.6.65.

45. This usage is not, however, consistent, and Seneca sometimes reverts to a traditional perspective on the value of the *imagines*; cf. *Ep.* 64.9 and *Helv.* 12.7.

gaze" in his treatment of the history of penal institutions.[46] Here as elsewhere, as Matthew Roller (2001a, 87) has put it, Seneca "chooses to present the evaluative structures of Stoic ethics precisely *in terms of* the 'commonsense' evaluative structures of traditional Roman ethics, a fact that sometimes leads to contradictory strains in his philosophy." Much of Seneca's imagery, both in the discussion of self-examination and in his treatment of the regulatory gaze in general, is also influenced by the language of the law courts as well; not only the presence of a *testis*, but also the language of self-control and self-possession. The accusation of one's vices, the examination of what one did during the day, the presence of the wise man as judge, as Armisen-Marchetti (1989, 155–57) documents, are all procedures that gesture toward the establishment of an internal court of judgment that depends upon a previously extant institutional setting.[47]

Accordingly, while Seneca will sometimes represent the practice of self-speculation in the more traditionally Roman terminology (familiar to us from the mirror tradition) of living up to the expectations and norms of one's social equals, far more often this other is an idealized figure rather than a real one, so that the actual practice of exemplary viewing is largely an imaginative or indeed impossible interaction. Here too, there is some continuity with tradition: after all, the gaze of the *imagines* was also an imaginary form of surveillance. But Seneca's internalized viewer, when not described in terms of a doubling of the self, or a splitting of the ego into an exemplary watcher and the occasionally faltering object of his gaze, is almost always no longer a living figure. Sometimes he invokes the Roman great men of the past, and at other

---

46. See Foucault 1979, 174.

47. See also Barton 2001, 60n31; Courcelle 1975, 54; Edwards 1997a; and Foucault 1986, 206–7. *Ep.* 28.10 offers an excellent example: in evaluating his own behavior, the individual must put himself on trial and play the parts of accuser, judge, and intercessor alike. And the law court explains some of Seneca's odder turns of phrase; as Cancik (1998) remarks, "The formula 'suum esse' is juridical language; it evokes personal property, which is inviolable and permits free disposal according to the owner's will and power" (e.g., *Ben.* 7.4.1–5, 7.6.2). Epictetus, too, relies on the language of the trial for some of his imagery of observation and judgment; cf. 2.5.29 and 3.18.7. See *Ench.* 48.3, where we are told watch over ourselves like an enemy lying in wait. In general it is safe to say that many (but not all; see chapter 5) of Seneca's themes and exercises are taken up by the later author. Epictetus repeats that for the Stoics, reputation is an indifferent (Epict., 1.29.10, 3.24.68–69). For him too, God is figured as internal judge and guardian who is constantly present (Epict., 1.14.12–14). See Long (2002, 165–66) for a good discussion of Epictetus' internalized daimon, and Kamtekar (1998, 147–52) on Epictetus' treatment of roles.

times the founders of the philosophical schools whose precepts Seneca has borrowed, such as Epicurus or Socrates. In so doing, he claims to follow the advice of Epicurus himself, who told us (Seneca says) to take "some man of high character, and keep him ever before your eyes, living as if he were watching you, and ordering all your actions as if he beheld them" (*Ep.* 11.8–10). Choose therefore, Seneca continues, a Cato or a Laelius (men of high character—and dead), and "picture him always to yourself as your protector or your example."[48] The choice of a dead Roman hero is even represented as a concession, a preliminary to relying on the internal *speculator*, as if Seneca were well aware that the move to self-reliance would come less naturally to a Roman than reliance on the imagined surveillance of a Cato. He specifies (*Ep.* 25.6), "When you have progressed so far that you have also respect for yourself, you may send away your attendant; but until then, set as a guard over yourself the authority of some man, whether your choice be the great Cato or Scipio, or Laelius—or any man in whose presence even abandoned wretches would check their bad impulses. Meanwhile, you are engaged in making of yourself the sort of person in whose company you would not dare to sin."[49] When Laelius and Cato are not being asked to lend their ghostly presence from the past, Epicurus himself is a favorite.[50] Thus Seneca bids Lucilius to pretend to be constantly under this philosopher's gaze: "I must insert in this letter one or two more of [Epicurus'] sayings: 'Do everything as if Epicurus were watching you'" (*Ep.* 25.5).[51] Seneca sometimes arrogates this role to himself: "Live as if I will hear of whatever you do—no rather, as if I will see it," he urges the same Lucilius (*Ep.* 32.1).[52] But this

48. "Elige eum cuius tibi placuit et vita et oratio et ipse animum ante se ferens vultus; illum tibi semper ostende vel custodem vel exemplum."

49. "Cum iam profeceris tantum ut sit tibi etiam tui reverentia, licebit dimittas paedagogum: interim aliquorum te auctoritate custodi aut Cato ille sit aut Scipio aut Laelius aut alius cuius interventu perditi quoque homines vitia supprimerent, dum te efficis eum cum quo peccare non audeas."

50. Cato's stern morals and disapproving gaze are often invoked by the Roman satirists, who make apotropaic gestures in his direction; cf. Mart., 1.pr.; and examples collected in Richlin 1992b, 5–6.

51. "'Sic fac' inquit 'omnia tamquam spectet Epicurus.'" No wonder the household philosopher of Lucian, *De mercede* 41, who sees all the domestic goings-on, is finally dismissed!

52. "Sic vive tamquam quid facias auditurus sim, immo tamquam visurus." What seems to please Seneca most here is that he has had no news of Lucilius whatsoever; his correspondent is not being ostentatiously philosophical in front of the common herd, a habit Seneca rails against in *Ep.* 29.12.

is a rare case of a contemporary witness as imaginary other.[53] Although Seneca
tells Lucilius that we can select our guides from both the living and the dead
(*Ep.* 52.7–10), no such living *exemplum* is offered as a possibility; Marcia's
father may be watching her, but he is gazing down from above, poor man.[54]

As a result, the more traditionally figured aspects of Seneca's project could
only work in the presence of an imaginary community of *similes* with figures
from the past, dead philosophers, or doubled self. (As he tells Lucilius in *Ep.*
32.2, while exhorting him to pretend Seneca is watching him, it is dangerous to
associate with people unlike yourself.) And yet as Seneca himself attests, there
was no such community in Neronian Rome. He must have been a lonely man,
isolated by his position at court from those who might share some of his philosophical leanings, like the so-called Stoic opposition. For the actual Romans
who surrounded him—and in particular the *vulgus* and its opinions—were to
be completely discounted, as he warns us again and again; what they honor are
merely "simulacra rerum honestarum et effigies" (copies and imitations of
what is good; *Ep.* 81.13.3; cf. 72.7.7, 99.17) and to find honor in their eyes is no
mark of *virtus* (for example, *De ira* 3.41.2; *Ep.* 29.10–11).[55] Indeed, we need a
guardian to *protect* us against their praise (*Ep.* 94.55).[56]

God, of course, is alive, and in Seneca's economy of virtue he too can keep
watchful guard on us. "God is near you, he is with you, he is inside you. I mean
this, Lucilius: a holy spirit lives inside us, an observer and guardian of our good
and bad deeds" (*Ep.* 41.1–2).[57] This notion is not inconsistent with Stoic
thought, but it is significant that elsewhere, when Seneca identifies this internalized other with God, he nonetheless ends up squarely with the self watching

---

53. Although in *Ep.* 62.2 Demetrius of Sunium, a Cynic banished by Nero, comes in for high
praise. Seneca occasionally speaks in general terms of how friends can see the faults you are blind
to (a common enough ancient maxim); cf. *De ira* 2.28.8.

54. *Cons. ad Marc.* 25.3.1. Edwards (1997a, 30) discusses this Senecan focus on an ideal watcher.
See also Citroni-Marchetti 1994, 4564–68; Solimano 1991, 35–36.

55. See especially Motto and Clark 1993.

56. This idea is not entirely new; Cicero too comments that "[t]here is no theater greater than
the consciousness of one's own virtue" (*Tusc.* 2.64). But the constant emphasis on this idea and the
intensity with which it is preached is wholly Seneca's. See also the discussion in Barton 2001,
280–86.

57. "Prope est a te deus, tecum est, intus est. Ita dico, Lucili: sacer intra nos spiritus sedet, malorum bonorumque nostrorum observator et custos." On Senecan citations to the effect that God
is watching, see Solimano 1991, 35nn55, 56. Epicurus too informs his students that they have a divinity within; see, e.g., Epict., *Disc.* 1.14.11–14, 2.19.26–27; and Long 2002, 176–77.

the self. Consider the oscillations of the following example: "We should live as if we lived in plain sight, and we should think as if someone could look into our innermost heart. For someone can. What use is it for something to be hidden from man? Nothing is hidden from God. He is present in our minds and intervenes in the middle of our thoughts. . . . Therefore, I will do as you bid, and I will gladly write to you about what I am doing, and in what order. I will observe myself continually and (this is most useful) I will review my day. It is this that makes us bad—that no one turns his gaze on his life" (Sen. *Ep.* 83.1–2). We travel here from the notion of the watching community, to that of an all-knowing God, and end up with the self-observant self—with Seneca, rather than God, as the endpoint.[58] It is worth remarking how un-Platonic this notion is, and how far removed from the ideas of the *Alcibiades* I. For one's godhood is not reflected in the eyes of the other; instead, the visual dimension of self-evaluation devolves once again here upon the individual and his capacity for an internal splitting into agent and viewer.[59]

Seneca, then, introduces a twist on one of the oldest injunctions in classical philosophy; his understanding of the *gnothi sauton* is that to know oneself is to watch oneself, to engage in an act of self-scrutiny that judges personal choices and activities in disregard of the opinions of one's peers.[60] Like Socrates, Seneca would see himself as listening to an ethical voice from within (if it is fair to call the *daimonion* an internal force; it is not figured as such by Socrates himself, cf. *Ap.* 39e–40c); unlike Socrates, Seneca's voice was not a nay-saying *daimonion* but a second self that observed the actions of the agent and took over responsibility for the judgment and guidance of this alter (observed) ego. The emphasis has shifted to the observer and its dialogic engagement with the agent self. This is a very different configuration from the Socratic stance, however ironic that may be, which focuses on the agent's surprise and ignorance before the prohibitions of the *daimonion.* Given Seneca's particular emphases, he does not reprise Socrates' role as civic gadfly but focuses more on

---

58. A similar progression prevails at *Ben.* 3.1.17, where the bad man is said to be punished by knowing that he is under the gaze of the community—then of God—then of himself.

59. Epictetus, some decades later, stressed many themes similar to Seneca's: the notion of a God within, the pitting of self-knowledge against the gaze of the community, the self as both pupil and teacher to itself.

60. For a modern critique of the relevance of self-observation to proper self-knowledge, see Myers 1986.

self-improvement than on improving the citizens around him; Seneca's own "elenctic" is often an internal dialogue rather than a spoken one. The Senecan *gnothi sauton*, finally, is addressed to the judging self, the viewing self, the one who turns its gaze to the figure in the mirror; the agent self is subjected to its questioning and expected to render account of itself in terms this self can approve. We might contrast Cicero's treatment of the topic at *Tusc.* 1.22.52, where he discusses the Delphic *nosce te* very much in terms derived from the *Alcibiades* I: the force of Apollo's precept is that the soul sees itself by means of the soul itself, and "know thyself" means "know thy soul." The body is just a receptacle. Cicero's treatment, in other words, does not involve a folding of the self upon the self without the explicit intermediary of another living soul.[61]

Now, if the observer self is not to derive its ethical values from the corrupted imperial society that surrounds it and that it has replaced, whence its source of moral authority?[62] The answer, of course, is from the precepts of Senecan Stoicism, however much this may be influenced by and merged with enduring Roman ideals.[63] Adapting this visual tradition to the exigencies of a practice of self-knowledge, however, produced inconsistencies in Seneca's development of the ethical gaze that are themselves worth exploring. Most strikingly, as Matthew Roller has perceptively demonstrated and as we have seen above, Seneca denigrates community judgment, yet more than once he indicates that the mark of the truly good man is the ability to live as if in a glass house.[64] Indeed, he claims that a good conscience wants to enter the public sphere and

---

61. At *Tusc.* 5.25.70 the focus is again on the mind's knowledge of itself as a path to union with the divine mind. For a full discussion of Cicero's usage of the *gnothi sauton* and his certain acquaintance with the *Alcibiades* I, see Courcelle 1975, 28–29; and Wilkins 1917, 67–70.

62. To be sure, deliberately imagining an audience is not original to Seneca; it crops up as an injunction and a practice especially in military contexts, such as Caes., *BGall.* 6.8.4, where Caesar's army is told to imagine that he himself is present and watching them (cf. similarly at 7.62.2). But this is different. The audience that Seneca most privileges is not only idealized, but also (usually) dead.

63. As Bernard Williams (1993, 100) has remarked, the internalized other never consists purely of *either* societal values *or* a projection of the self's values and desires; the two are too difficult to separate. Here their intertwined nature seems most evident in Seneca's combination of the visual preoccupation of Roman ethical habits and a feature more directly connected with Stoic practice per se—namely, the *meditatio* that we have seen the good man was to carry out at the end of the day.

64. I made observations similar to Roller's (2001a), but not as well developed, in an article (Bartsch 2001) that came out at the same time as Roller's book.

be seen, or actively invites the crowd in to see it. "What's the use of hiding one-self and avoiding the eyes and ears of men? A good conscience invites in the crowd, a bad one is anxious and troubled even in solitude. If what you do is honorable, let everyone know; if shameful, what does it matter if no one knows, when *you* do? What a wretch you would be, if you scorn this witness!" (*Ep.* 43.5).[65] If the value judgments of this community are so meaningless, it's hard to understand why Seneca would care much for its presence—and if it offers approval, what of his warning to Lucilius that this very response means he has gone astray?[66] Seneca here tilts the emphasis toward a perspective on the self that he abjures elsewhere; similarly so at *Ben.* 3.17.2, where he opines that public disapproval is the worst punishment for the man who does wrong.[67] In a further example discussed by Roller (2001a, 86), Seneca juxtaposes these views without much regard to their seeming inconsistency (in Roller's termi-nology, for the sake of getting his Stoic views "off the ground" [77] by dressing them in traditional Roman garb). At *De vita beata* 20.4 he tells us, "I do noth-ing for the sake of opinion, and everything for the sake of my conscience." But in the very next sentence: "I will pretend that whatever I do deliberately takes place with the public as my audience."[68] As Thomas Rosenmeyer has remarked of this phenomenon, "Again and again the moralist seems to be recommending self-reliance and autonomy, but it is clear also that the old shame-consciousness of the culture inevitably calls for the approving presence of others. Without their express sanction, the achievement of the solitary agent would forfeit its value."[69] In such passages is clearly visible the tension between cultural and philosophical norms about the good man.

In the majority of examples, however, Senecan self-knowledge depends on the division of the self into a morally enabled guard watching over a wayward agent

---

65. On wanting to be seen: Sen. *Ep.* 97.12, "But a good conscience wants to go out and be seen." On the philosopher's glass house compared to the panopticon, see Foucault 1979, 249.

66. For analyses of self-understanding as a product of social interaction, see especially Burkitt 1994, Gergen 1977, Giddens 1991, Laing 1965, Rzepka 1986, and Mead 1934.

67. But note that Seneca goes on to include the gaze of the gods and of the self as part of the reproving audience.

68. See also *Q Nat.* 4.pr.18a; *De ira* 1.14.3.

69. Rosenmeyer 1989, 52. Roller (2001a, 63–126) has an excellent discussion of such ethical inconsistencies in Seneca. Our conclusions will differ, but my thinking has been much influenced by his powerful exposition of the Senecan language of interiority.

in such a way as to enable the enactment of judgments upon that self, and the subsequent training of the agent self to identify itself with that volition. "Make progress, and take care above all else to be consistent with yourself [*ut constes tibi*]. Whenever you want to find out if you have accomplished something, see if you want the same things today that you did yesterday; a change of your will shows that the mind is fluctuating. . . . That which is fixed and well founded does not wander; this quality falls to the perfect wise man, and to some degree to the *proficiens* making progress" (*Ep.* 35.4). The success of this procedure is not always guaranteed; Seneca admits to trying and failing, and emphasizes the role of practice and repetition. As he concedes in *Ep.* 71.30, "It is a mistake to make the same demands on the wise man and the learner. I still exhort myself to do that which I recommend, but my exhortations are not yet followed." Yet any aspiring Roman who can already formulate what is happening within him in these terms is already a *proficiens*; the process of looking at the self, judging it, and engaging it in dialogue advances a man from folly to wisdom.

These examples show a shift in the locus of the republican regulatory gaze: in turning to imaginary viewers, Seneca seems to suggest that whatever forms of surveillance are still exant in the early empire are no longer provided by the exemplary men of the community, but by those who stand outside the (ideal) community by dint of their closeness to the imperial court, or by the emperor himself. In Seneca's own day, the circular orbit of the gaze of the good citizen, who shapes himself by watching a Cato or a Laelius even as he feels their gaze upon him, is short-circuited into a one-way gaze only: that of a Nero or Sejanus upon the man whose fate he holds in his hands. Here is the presence of a very different gaze altogether: the abusive, performance-demanding gaze of power, the gaze that leads Seneca to urge, over and over again, that the good Stoic should never change his expression, because a Caligula, or a Sejanus, or an informer might be watching.[70] Living under a tyrant is vividly described in terms of the corruption of the gaze of one's peers, which no longer represents

---

70. A phenomenon common to many repressive regimes, and even to others. (On Rome, see Bartsch 1994.) As Jay (1993, 383) remarks of the work of Althusser and others, "Not only could vision be damned for its construction of an ideological notion of the ego, it could also be deemed complicitous in the complementary apparatuses of surveillance and spectacle so central to the maintenance of disciplinary or repressive power in the modern world."

the ethical gaze, but rather a malevolent surveillance.[71] "You are wrong," Seneca warns Lucilius, "if you trust the faces of those you meet in the street: they have the likenesses of men, but the minds of wild animals." Worse still: while animals kill from fear or hunger, men alone destroy others for pleasure.[72] Crimes that used to hide away from the eyes of men now flaunt themselves before the fearful gaze of those few honest men who are left (*De ira* 2.9.1–2). The possibility of exemplarity seems largely to have vanished. It can remain alive in the internalized audience inherited from an era with greater political potential, but in the present that audience's values cannot be seen to shine too brightly.

In Seneca's Rome, only God, it seems, is not the source of a corrupted surveillance.[73] Seneca may exhort his philosophical fellows to take up the role of conscience to society: the good citizen can be of use politically, he reminds them, "by being seen and heard, by his expression, his nod, his silent resistance and by his very gait."[74] But there seem to have been few such men. The only answer to such a problem in a society where ethics had its basis in the reflected gaze is, perhaps, the doubled self; the self that provides its own watcher, its own interlocutor. This practice led not only toward the development of the perfect Stoic (a goal that Seneca himself, like Chrysippus, acknowledged to be near impossible) but also to a perspective on the world that allowed the substitution

---

71. On the danger of the informer's gaze upon the philosopher, see Citroni-Marchetti 1994. On the informer's gaze in general, Tacitus writes most eloquently; see, e.g., Bartsch 1994. Ears as well as eyes can figure in this surveillance, obviously; cf. *Clem.* 1.26.2: "Everything is gloomy, scared, disordered; the very pleasures are feared; men do not go carefree to dinner parties, in which even the drunkards' tongues must be carefully guarded, nor into the games, where material for criminal charges and danger are sought."

72. "Erras, si istorum tibi qui occurrunt vultibus credis: hominum effigies habent, animos ferarum, nisi quod illarum perniciosus est primus incursus: quos transiere non quaerunt. Numquam enim illas ad nocendum nisi necessitas incitat; [hae] aut fame aut timore coguntur ad pugnam: homini perdere hominem libet" (*Ep.* 103.2).

73. Matthew Leigh (1997, 30) elegantly shows how Lucan's gods are said to watch the humans fighting below them as if they were gladiators—the result of this would normally be *voluptas* for the theater audience. Where, he asks, does Stoic imperturbability end and cruel pleasure begin? Lucretius' Epicurean gods don't care—nor does the imaginary viewer at the beginning of his book 2, who derives pleasure (*voluptas*) from seeing men in a stormy sea, so long as he is safe. Seneca's gods, in contrast, enjoy watching Cato's opposition to tyranny (*cum magno gaudio, libenter*) because it provides a moral exemplum (*Prov.* 2.12.9–12).

74. "Numquam inutilis est opera ciuis boni: auditus uisusque, uultu nutu obstinatione tacita incessuque ipso prodest" (*Tranq.* 4.6.4).

of a new source of ethical authority (the philosophical self) for the traditional role of the people and the Senate.

THE PHILOSOPHER'S THEATER

Seneca's ethical theater is a private place. On it, one man performs for his own gaze, or for that of an idealized other. His behavior matches, or comes to match, the prescriptions of Stoic doctrine, and he follows his path with disregard for public opinion. At other times, though not often, the public is allowed in to perform some helpful task in guiding the *proficiens* to virtue. But there is a third possibility for the role of the gaze that we have not yet considered: that the gaze of the other stimulates the emergence of a self that is felt to be *untrue* to its ethical potential—the emergence, that is, of what one might call a *persona* in the Senecan, rather than traditional, sense of the term (I will come back to this very charged word later). This is because the gaze that Seneca describes (internal or external) is not always salubrious, and because bad choices of *testis* or *custos* can be made. Here, as with the old anxieties about the proximity of the orator to the actor, we find that self-display is doubly charged, and that the philosopher's theater (for such it is) is a very confusing place. Worse still, it can create inappropriate forms of behavior rather than suppressing them.

Seneca warns Lucilius about this possibility in several of the letters. "See," he remarks, "how a person lives in one way for the public, and in another for himself. . . . When the witness and the spectator are absent, the vices whose profit lies in being pointed out and being gazed at subside."[75] Here our philosopher is talking about the enjoyment of wealth and power, but it seems that the same is true of how we feel grief:

How few men [he says] are sad in their own company! They groan louder when they are heard, and although they are silent and tranquil in private,

---

75. Sen. *Ep.* 94.69: "Aspice, quanto aliter unusquisque populo vivat, aliter sibi. . . . Ubi testis et spectator abscessit, vitia subsidunt, quorum monstrari et conspici frutus est." This is what ailed Maecenas, in Seneca's diagnosis (*Ep.* 114.4): "Quomodo Maecenas vixerit notius est quam ut narrari nunc debeat quomodo ambulaverit, quam delicatus fuerit, quam cupierit videri, quam vitia sua latere noluerit." As Solimano (1991, 38) notes, "Man wants a spectator, a witness of his own wealth, power, talent, refinement, even of his philosophical leanings, of his vices, and of his sorrow." The idea is echoed in Mart., 1.33.4: "He who grieves without a witness is grieving truly."

whenever they see anyone they are spurred to new floods. Then they lay violent hands on their own persons, which they would have been able to do more easily if no one were there to stop them; then they pray for their own deaths, then they roll off their beds; without a spectator, grief goes away. (*Ep.* 99.16)[76]

In one's own troubles, too, one ought to behave so as to cede to grief what nature, not convention, demands. Many men shed tears to make a show, and have dry eyes whenever a spectator is absent, judging it shameful for tears to be missing when everyone is weeping: so deeply has this bad habit of depending on the opinion of others taken root that even the simplest thing of all, grief, has crossed over into pretense [*in simulationem*]. (*Tranq.* 15.6)

To add to the complications inherent here, this performative excess is not just the pernicious effect of the (nonphilosophical) external audience provided by the community: strikingly, it can also be the effect of *our watching of ourselves*. This is the content of Seneca's chastisement of Lucilius in *Ep.* 63.3, as his correspondent grieves for his dead friend Flaccus: "As soon as you stop observing yourself grieving, the picture of your unhappiness will go away; for now, you yourself are the guardian of your own grief [*custodis dolorem tuum*]": the metaphor is that of the internalized other who keeps watch, and for whom Lucilius, willy-nilly, is now performing *as if* it were the community that was watching. It seems that the presence of an audience, even when it is internalized, can corrupt the behavior of the subject under observation. And yet, for Seneca, self-knowledge and self-improvement involve precisely such observation. In other words, one paradox of Senecan identity is the ambiguous status of the subject under view as the site of authenticity: to act before an assessing gaze is often precisely that—to act, to put on a show—and yet this assessing gaze is crucial to the development of a better self.[77]

---

76. People even lose their appetite for fancy foodstuffs when an audience is missing (*Tranq.* 7.2.6). Other vices fall away as well: "Ambition and luxury and lack of self-control want a witness: you'll cure all those faults, if you hide them" (*Ep.* 94.71).

77. "Stoic heroism . . . achieves its full meaning only if it draws attention to itself as the central spectacle in a crowded arena" (Rosenmeyer 1989, 48). See also Leigh 1997, 182–83, on Vulteius' craving for an audience.

This same oscillation crops up elsewhere in Seneca's work as well. The idea of having to play a role, for example, is represented now as leading to an inauthentic self that straitjackets itself to satisfy community standards, now as the means to a specifically Stoic authenticity that relies on the shaping force of a role to reform the character who plays it. In a passage from his essay *On Tranquility* that links self-observation to precisely such role-playing, Seneca observes that "[c]onstant observation of oneself is tortuous, and one fears to be caught out of one's usual role. Nor can we ever relax, when we think we're being assessed every time we're looked at; on the one hand, many chance occurrences can bare us against our will, and on the other, even granted that all this effort over oneself is successful, it's not a pleasant life, nor one free from anxiety, to live constantly wearing a mask" (*Tranq.* 17.1).[78] Here assiduous self-observation is linked not to a positive but to a negative self-formation; it is a self-spectatorship that looks to the assessment of the community to such a degree that the agent performs constantly for the assessing other, presumably trying to live up to a set of standards that are exhausting to fulfill. It seems safe to conclude that here, at least, Seneca refers to the real political community of Neronian Rome, and to the kinds of fears about inadvertently disclosing how one really feels that I have delineated elsewhere.[79] But in other cases this kind of public role-playing is depicted as potentially positive. In the *Consolation to Polybius*, Seneca urges the emperor Claudius' powerful freedman to control his grief for his dead brother: people, after all, are watching him. The unanimous will of the people has imposed upon him a great role (the Latin word is *persona*), and this role must be maintained. Polybius must accordingly don an expression that belies his grieving *animus* in the interest of providing a model for his audience (*Polyb.* 5.4–5). Of course, Polybius need not fear the retribution of those who watch him; Seneca here uses republican standards of living up to the community's judgment precisely to this ex-slave whom such standards would flatter.)

To play one's role well, and consistently, to the end is a central Stoic metaphor for the business of being alive, and even Stoic theorizing about identity is couched in the language of the four *personae*, or roles, that a person must ful-

---

78. "Torquet enim assidua obseruatio sui et deprehendi aliter ac solet metuit. Nec umquam cura soluimur, ubi totiens nos aestimari putamus quotiens aspici. Nam et multa incidunt quae inuitos denudant, et, ut bene cedat tanta sui diligentia, non tamen iucunda uita aut secura est semper sub persona uiuentium."

79. See Bartsch 1994.

fill.[80] The life of the Stoic student is seen as the struggle to play a role well—the role of himself. All that matters is to stick to it, or, as Seneca puts it in another striking formation, to "be consistent with yourself" (*Ep.* 35.4).[81] "It is a great achievement," he reminds us, "to play the part of just one man; no one can do it except the wise man; the rest of us take on too many different appearances. Now we seem worthy and serious, now wasteful and silly; we change our mask suddenly and put on a contradictory one. Demand from yourself therefore that you play that same role to the end in which you first presented yourself; and if you can't be praised, at least make sure you can be recognized"—and here again the verb is *agnoscere*, linking the consistent playing of one identity to a term Seneca uses to mark an identity that has reached its full potential.[82] Finally, even the "theatricality" of role-playing is put into question: what was initially a role can through force of habit become the authentic person. So it is that we read in the *De ira* that the conscientious playing of a role—in this case, the role of a man who is not irascible—can affect for the better the reality of who one is: Train yourself not to show the emotions you feel, Seneca advises his readers, and eventually your insides will learn to conform with your outsides.[83]

Is the difference between this positive role-playing and the kind that Seneca calls "tortuous" based on the distinction between the gaze of an idealized other and that of the community at large? One might think so, but even this distinction fails to hold: the virtues that struggle for outside show among the populace at large are sometimes worthy ones, sometimes mere plumage, and both varieties are strengthened over time by this public exposure (*Tranq.* 1.3). On the other hand, the philosopher *qua* philosopher must often moderate his urge to put his

---

80. On the four *personae*, see especially Gill (1988) and the discussion in chapter 5. On the metaphor of life as theater in Stoic philosophy, see further *Ep.* 74.7, 76.31, 77.20, 108.6–8, 115.15; *Marc.* 10.1; *Vit. Beat.* 2.2; *Ben.* 1.2.4, 6.30.6; and the collection in Armisen-Marchetti 1989, 166–67. The metaphor of the arena in particular is discussed by Wistrand (1990) and Armisen-Marchetti (1989, 124–26). See also Suet., *Aug.* 99.1.

81. The role of life is played before a general audience, and yet the most important thing is still "ut constes tibi." Cf. *Ben.* 2.17.2 on the behavior of a Cynic philosopher: "hanc personam induisti; agenda est."

82. "Magnam rem puta unum hominem agere. Praeter sapientem autem nemo unum agit, ceteri multiformes sumus. Modo frugi tibi videbimur et graves, modo prodigi et vani; mutamus subinde personam et contrariam ei sumimus quam exuimus. Hoc ergo a te exige, ut qualem institueris praestare te, talem usque ad exitum serves; effice ut possis laudari, si minus, ut adgnosci" (*Ep.* 120.21–22). For a similar use, see Cic., *Acad.* 1.3.9.

83. Sen., *De ira* 3.13.2. Cf. Gal., *Aff. Dig.* 5.20–21.

good works and his self-regulation on display.[84] Naturally, if he seemed unduly self-indulgent, the public would be quick to carp at him; Seneca apes such complaints at *Vit. Beat.* 27.4: "Why is this philosopher living so prodigally? Why does he dine so richly?" But even the display of virtuous behavior could be seen as antithetical to the philosophical project of a self-sufficient rejection of the judgment of the (elite and nonelite) community. So Seneca warns the would-be philosopher to keep a low profile even in his rejection of elite trappings. "But I advise you not to do anything unusual in your dress or in your mode of life, like those who don't want to make progress but to be conspicuous; rough attire and an unshaved head and an unkempt beard and an open hatred of silver and a bed laid on the ground and whatever else perversely tries for gaining attention— avoid it. . . . Let everything be different on the inside, but let the outside conform to the public" (*Ep.* 5.1–2). Similarly, when Epictetus describes the practice of *askesis* in *Disc.* 3.12, he reminds his student that this self-shaping must involve no ostentation of display; once one seeks external praise, one has turned outward to seek the approval of the spectators, and in so doing one has already failed in the purpose of the exercise (*Disc.* 3.12.16; again at 3.14.4–6). Instead, he invokes the practice of Euphrates, who hid his status as a philosopher from others to keep his motives for self-improvement pure (*Disc.* 4.8.17–18).[85] Indeed, too ostentatiously neglectful an exterior might actually mark a philosopher as a fraud.[86] As the author of the *Minor Declamations* would remark of philosophers: "What can you find in them besides a fabricated self-presentation and perpetual leisure and a certain authority assumed from arrogance?"[87]

---

84. As Barton (2001, 219) puts it, "One needed to be self-controlled, but one also needed to reveal to others the cost of that control." Caizzi (1994) addresses the issue of self-display among the Hellenistic philosophers; the Stoics and Cynics in particular were known for their public poverty and dirtiness.

85. See here Long 2002, 121–25. On self-display in the Second Sophistic, see Gleason 1995.

86. On fraudulent philosophers who parade a stern exterior, see the examples in chapter 3, as well as Pers., *Sat.* 1.8–11, 5.115–18; Juv., *Sat.* 2.8–14; Quint., 1.pr.5; Mart., 1.24. Such fraudulence is sometimes linked to sexual passivity, as I discuss in chapter 5. On the difficulty of the *proficiens* in the face of public opinion, see also Epict., *Disc.* 1.22.18; Hijmans 1959, 99–100.

87. [Quint.], *Minor Decl.* 286.13: "Quid in his deprehendas praeter fictam frontem et perpetuum otium et quandam ex adrogantia auctoritatem?" And yet, the same old pull to visual self-fashioning would persist among philosophers well into the future; as Zanker (1995, 259–60) notes of the second century CE, "It is remarkable how the philosophers of the period talk about their clothing, hair, and beards as never before, probably because in a society in which the visual image played such a dominant role, they too needed recognizable symbols to establish their identity and to reaffirm the considerable authority they had recently acquired."

These phenomena point to a tension in Roman stoicism between the various possibilities for role-playing: as a mark of self-control, as an outward display of inward values, as a form of dissimulation, as a form of self-training, as a desire to please—all rather different possibilities for one form of behavior. In turn, this tension allows us to better understand aspects of Seneca's thought that are hard to explain with any unitary model. One such passage would be the account, in *De ira*, of the encounter between Caligula and a Roman knight named Pastor:

> When Gaius Caesar had jailed the son of a distinguished Roman knight because he was offended by the son's elegant appearance and ornate hairdo, the father then asked Gaius for his son's safety as a favor. But as if Gaius had been reminded to punish the son instead he ordered for him to be executed immediately. In order not to be completely inhuman to the father, however, he invited him to dinner on that same day. Pastor came with no reproach in his face. Caesar drank a toast to him and set a guard to watch him: the wretched man carried through with it, and drank as if he were drinking his son's blood. Caesar sent him perfume and garlands and gave orders to see whether he took them: Pastor took them . . . all the while not shedding a single tear, not allowing his grief to burst forth in any respect. (*De ira* 2.33.3–4)

Pastor comes; he drinks the toast that Caligula proposes and puts on the garlands and unguents Caligula has supplied; he shows no sign of reproach whatsoever, but rather smiles, laughs, makes merry, and in general, says Seneca, "acted as if he had obtained the pardon he had sought for his son. Do you ask why? The answer is: he had a second son" (2.33.4). Although Pastor's actions are aimed at pleasing the judgment of his viewer, the interchange, of course, is hardly philosophical; rather, given the corrupt nature of his judge, Pastor must compromise his own ethical beliefs in the interests of saving the life of his second son.

The general framework of *De ira* 3 is a discussion on how to refrain from lashing out against others with anger, a framework that is devoted more to the powerful than to the victims until this point. We expect blame for Caligula rather than praise for Pastor, and we might be predisposed to see Pastor's form of acting not as a praiseworthy control of one's anger, but rather as a cowardly denial of one's opinions; Tacitus, after all, would surely rank Pastor with the terrified but carefully blank-faced audience that saw Nero poison his brother

Britannicus. Yet Seneca does not condemn this behavior: "Injuries from the more powerful must be borne with a cheerful face, not just with endurance; they will do it again if they believe they've done it once" (*De ira* 2.33.1).

What has troubled readers of this passage is that Seneca seems to be endorsing a form of slavery, a cowardly kowtowing to the powerful, that hardly seems Stoic even if Pastor does save the life of his second son. The conscious use of self-control and the contrary act of playing a role out of fear blend into each other here, and Seneca's description seems to fit two opposed models of behavior: the political exigency of saving oneself and one's loved ones under the imperial gaze, and the Stoic designation of "freedom" as perfect detachment and self-control in times of stress.

In theory, it should not matter if the Stoic changes his expression in the face of a tyrant: after all, the so called Stoic opposition made reactions clear, and Seneca elsewhere is full of praise for the freedom signified by the wise man's changes of expression. The Senecan chorus in *Hercules Oetaeus* calls that person "happy" who can change his expression as the circumstances demand, who can tolerate alike being a slave or a king—resignation renders all fortunes alike ("felix quisque novit famulam regemque pati / vultusque suos variare potest" [*Her. Oet.* 227–28]). Pastor's frozen smile, then, is the opposite of *libertas*; it is where Stoicism shows itself as a dissembling technique to deal not only with the vagaries of fortune but also with the abuses of power and how to survive them: it is *complicit*, not defiant, in the dynamic between tyrant and subject. Faking equanimity under the eyes of the powerful viewer provides a moment where Stoic theory, at least in Seneca, *relinquishes* the control of the self by the self. And it may be fair to say that Roman Stoicism is constantly caught up in this constitutive instability between self-control and self-betrayal; its lessons can be learned in order to defy power, or in order to survive it.[88] It is quite possible that Seneca, unlike Socrates, was less interested in changing his world than in adapting himself to it.

An illustration of this is provided by a very similar passage in book 3 of *De ira* whose interpretation by Seneca falls precisely under the rubric of cowardly kowtowing—here a disgraceful act that shows the underside of Stoic complacency. A member of Cambyses' court, one Praexaspes, has the misjudgment to advise the drunk Cambyses to abstain from further alcohol. Enraged, Cambyses

---

88. For an analysis of this passage that focuses on its nature as a negative exemplum for imperial-aristocratic relations, see Roller 2001a, 163–64.

vows to prove just how steady his hands still are, and has Praexaspes' son dragged up: "Then he drew his bow and pierced the very heart of the youth (for he had said he was aiming at it) and having cut open the chest he showed the arrow sticking in the heart itself, and looking back at the father he asked him if his hand was sure enough. And the father said that Apollo could not have made a surer shot. May the gods ruin such a man, more of a slave in soul than by rank! He praised an action it were already excessive to watch. And he thought that the chest of his son, cut in two, and the heart quivering with its wound, provided an occasion for flattery!" (*De ira* 3.14.2–3). No kind words from Seneca for the bereaved father this time around, whom he condemns as a slave and a flatterer.[89]

We can contrast Pastor's "stoic" behavior with still other acts (in both senses) which come in for Senecan praise. As with Pastor, often having a poker face rather than having the freedom to emote is the sign of psychic *libertas*. Socrates himself, under the Thirty Tyrants, never changed his expression, we are told (*Ep.* 104.28; *Helv.* 13.4.4).[90] Cato didn't either, even as the republic fell around his ears (*Ep.* 104.30). No matter what happens to him, says Seneca, the Stoic never lets himself visibly react: "Facing the torture machines of horrific men he holds his gaze steady; he changes nothing in his expression whether difficult or favorable outcomes are shown to him" (*Constant.* 5.4). This is a form of Stoic freedom, but the difference from Pastor's case could not be clearer: Socrates' self-control, and Cato's, do not arise from fear. Nor do they aim at any advantage; they are not trying to *please* a tyrant, as is Pastor; if anything, such behavior made it possible that they would suffer the more. By praising Pastor in the same language usually reserved for these other figures, and by damning Praexaspes so thoroughly, Seneca unwittingly puts his finger on the very spot where Stoic theory bumps up against societal praxis, and where freedom and slavery merge.

The Senecan model of the performance of selfhood, then, is one that jostles side by side with Roman social and literary practices in which the same elements recur: subjection to a gaze, the notion of a dialogue with the self, a concern with the playing of roles. And yet these other practices abjure any

---

89. At *De ira* 3.14.5, he does acknowledge that some people might argue that Praexaspes wanted to protect his other loved ones — the very perspective Seneca himself used for Pastor at *De ira* 2.33.4.

90. For an excellent study of Socrates' reception in Hellenistic philosophy and beyond, see Long 1988. On Socrates' influence on Seneca's thought, see now Gill (forthcoming). On Socrates and Epictetus, see Long 2002, chap. 3; and Gill (forthcoming).

concern with authenticity or immutability. Those who participate in them are more concerned to please the audience than themselves, and they role-play accordingly; the regulatory gaze of a Cato exists only to be mocked. One is tempted to suggest that Seneca's project—amid all this writing on spectatorship and identity, which, as we have seen, is not always internally coherent—is to reestablish the sense of some authentic core of non–socially determined selfhood in the turbulent culture of the first century CE. It was a culture in which, socially and politically, this core self seemed to be less stable than ever before. But Seneca's attempts represent a project rather than a reality; and, it seems, that is exactly what they would remain.[91]

THE METAMORPHOSIS OF *PERSONA*

As his treatment of the visual dynamic behind Roman elite ethics and the stance of the good man before the tyrant illustrates, Seneca's writings leave room for a conflict between ideal behaviors and necessary behaviors, the former driven by Stoic theory, the latter by political necessity, but both perhaps easy to confuse from the outside. Seneca's focus on the performativity of the self and the possibility he acknowledges of being *false* to one's potential for a fully developed selfhood, sometimes because of the pressure to act in front of

---

91. Is Stoic philosophy guilty of Zimmerman's (2000) charge that it teaches people to rationalize their suffering? Zimmerman's comments in his critique of Harry Frankfurt pinpoint the problem of happy victimhood, which Seneca's views could be taken to support. We can render ourselves so free from our intrinsic desire not to suffer that we are in essence complicit with those who hurt us, and indifferent to a situation we would normally wish to change. In this scenario, those who intentionally free themselves from the desires that their circumstances prevent them from fulfilling (Zimmerman names slaves, battered housewives, and sweatshop workers) "succeed in rendering themselves more autonomous than they would have been if they had done nothing but suffer under the constraints imposed by their tormentors" (2000, 40). Inwood (2003, 94–97) responds that this is not a correct reading of Senecan Stoicism. It does not, he argues, "teach us to rationalize in this way, to reshape our characters and beliefs to help us cope with constraint and coercion" because we are only rationalizing "when we hold beliefs pertinent to our situation which we would never have held *if not for* the motivation provided by unsatisfactory external circumstances. . . . But if we have reasons to hold this view independently of our own personal and unpleasant circumstances . . . then it won't count as rationalization if we preserve our happiness by coming to hold this view" (2003, 97). Inwood is right to some degree. However, the smack of rationalization still lingers, because we could argue that much of the bodily focus of Roman Stoicism is spurred by senatorial anxieties under the empire. Who can say that Seneca did not turn to Stoicism because of his life situation? No one turns to a philosophy *ex nihilo*.

an assessing gaze, find corroboration in a perhaps unlikely place: his use of the term *persona*, a word that carries an important ideological load both in Stoic philosophy and in Roman civic life. Whether used in a political or a philosophical context (as in Cicero's *De officiis*), the *persona* generally referred to a Roman citizen's behavior in his publicly acknowledged role(s). A man in office was expected to live up to the expectations generated by his rank, to engage in decisions and actions that were *digna* of his role and that demonstrated the proper decorum. In so acting, he won praise: the potential difference between this set of behaviors and who he might "really" be away from his role was not at issue, and superior performance of the *persona* did not lead to any perception of a gap between a "true" self and the *persona*.

In Seneca, however, the term undergoes a subtle shift, borrowing from the metaphor of the theater (where it originated) to connote a political world in which the performance of the *persona* entailed the donning of a false mask. No longer an unambiguous way to describe the naturalness of a public identity (an identity conceived of both as assumed *and* as not-false), the *persona* is often put to use in Seneca to represent a form of self-performance that is marked as inauthentic: for example, an agent's behavior when coerced by unequal power dynamics or by the hostile gaze of an untrustworthy audience of peers. As a result, the *persona* is no longer fully appropriate to the Stoic emphasis on the necessary propriety of the role one picks in life; as we shall see, the behaviors it can mark in Seneca are both inappropriate and false to Stoic truths; they constitute a betrayal of the self in ways that suggest, by Seneca's time, an alteration in the axis along which the Romans evaluated *persona* in the first place.

Persona has itself been a loaded term where studies of selfhood are concerned, partially because Cicero uses it to discuss the Stoic philosopher Panaetius' notion of the appropriate roles a person should play in life; accordingly, some scholars of antiquity have wanted to suggest that in Cicero's discussion of the four Stoic *personae*, the seeds of something like a modern self are to be found.[92] Cicero's account in *De officiis* attributes to each individual four

92. For Cicero's debt to Panaetius here, and for discussion of the possibility that the third and fourth *personae* are Cicero's own invention, see Gill 1988; de Lacy 1979, 163–65; and Dyck 1996, ad loc. On the four-*personae* theory as containing the seeds of a modern notion of personal identity, see De Lacy 1977, 166; and Rist 1969, 186–89. On the links between *persona*, property ownership, and *oikeiosis*, see Long (1997), who further suggests that Stoic *oikeiosis* was fundamental to a notion of personal identity and possibly personality.

personae, a doctrine whose purpose, according to De Lacy (1977, 170), was "to provide a formula for discovering for any given person in any given situation the appropriate act, *quid deceat*." Of the first two of these *personae*,

> One is universal, because of the fact that we are all endowed with rationality and with the superiority by means of which we are better than animals; from this comes everything honorable and fitting, and the means of discovering our duty. The other *persona*, however, is assigned to individuals in particular. Just as there are large differences in bodies, and we see that some men are good at speed in running, others in strength for wrestling, and just as likewise dignity is inherent in some bodies, charm in others, thus too in our souls there exist even more varieties. . . . Each man must hold on to his own characteristics [*sua cuique*], not the corrupt ones, but the ones that are properly his, so that that propriety, which we are investigating, may be retained. (*Off.* 1.107, 110)

Of the remaining two *personae*, one is dictated to us by the circumstances that bring us high birth, wealth, or their opposites; the fourth relies upon our own choices in life, such as the selection of one career over another (*Off.* 115). To live well is then to bring all four *personae* into harmony (Panaetius, frags. 96, 109 Van Straaten).[93]

The second *persona* has garnered the most critical interest, for two reasons. First, Cicero seems here to point to a concept of the person in which room is made for individual gifts and aptitudes, thereby (presumably) adding a unique ingredient to the more standard fare of rationality, career, and circumstance. Still, there is no suggestion that the second *persona* is one in which the individual forms himself in a manner not influenced by social norms and expectations; the goal is still a shared standard of decorum, and it is not a singular claim to say that a man who tends toward obesity should not devote himself to professional gymnastics. Nor is the second *persona* privileged over the others, or a source of conflict with them. What is unique here, then, is "the idea that it is for each person to gauge for herself how to correlate the ethical claims

---

93. On the four Stoic *personae*, see De Lacy 1977; Gill 1988; Gill 1994, 4603–16. De Lacy suggests that Cicero's four-*personae* theory is an attempt to reconcile two strands in Stoic thought: the idea of the wise man as template, versus the notion that one's own strengths should determine one's *persona*.

represented by the four *personae*. . . . Taken in the context of the communal (and conventional) framework being presupposed, this idea does not lead to the more radical ethical individualism that we find in modern thinkers such as Nietzsche or Sartre" (Gill 1994, 4607). Instead, as Gill points out, a normative ethical understanding is provided by ideas such as "the community of the wise" or "the city of gods and humans": "such ideas are taken as providing an (objective and ultimate) framework on which to ground ethical life in conventional states" (Gill 1995, 59).

This passage has also attracted interest for what it suggests about the concept of *persona* itself. In developing the notion of the second *persona*, Cicero turns to a theatrical metaphor to point out that just as actors pick the role on stage best suited to their talents, so too should we pick such a role in life (*Off.* 1.114):[94] "Let each man know his own nature and show himself a keen judge of his good points and vices, lest actors seem to have more wisdom than we do. They choose, not the best plays, but the ones best suited to them. . . . We will therefore work in those areas in particular to which we are best suited."[95] Having stressed, then, the notion of role-playing in real life by this analogy to the stage, Cicero later consolidates that suggestion by pointing out that for the good of others we will occasionally have to assume in public emotions we do not (and should not) actually feel, such as anger. If a man needs to be reproved, "we should perhaps use more emphasis in our voice and a more cutting weight in our word, and even act so that we seem to be angry. But just as we turn rarely and unwillingly to cauterizing and surgery, so too to this kind of castigation, and never unless it is necessary and no other cure can be found; but let anger be absent, in which nothing can be done rightly or thoughtfully" (*Off.* 1.136). And public value is to be found in the *simulacra* of virtue (1.46) as well as in

---

94. The metaphor of life as theater is a common one in antiquity. It can be found in philosophical writing from Plato to the Stoics Musonius Rufus, Seneca, Epictetus, and Marcus Aurelius, as well as in Suetonius' *Lives of the Caesars*. In this case, it is likely that the Cynics' analogy of agents to actors influenced Panaetius. For a complete list of Senecan analogies between life and theater, see Armisen-Marchetti 1989, 166–67, 1991n240. The analogy is also to be found in Ariston of Chios, Cicero, Petronius, Marcus Aurelius—and in Suet., *Aug.* 99.1, as the last words of Augustus ipse. In general, see Dupont 1985 and 2000. For an example of an actor picking a role well suited to his talents, see Fronto, *Eloq.* 2.253.17, on Aesopus.

95. "[Suum] quisque igitur noscat ingenium acremque se et bonorum et vitiorum suorum iudicem praebeat, ne scaenici plus quam nos videantur habere prudentiae. Illi enim non optumas, sed sibi accomodatissimas fabulas eligunt. . . . Ad quas igitur res aptissimi erimus, in iis potissimum elaborabimus."

the real thing. The same privileging of role over reality (a misleading turn of phrase, but I leave it for the moment) crops up in the *Commentariolum* by Cicero's brother Quintus, in which the public behavior of a candidate for office must be his most crucial concern; Q. Cicero urges him to simulate whatever qualities he lacks as he presses the flesh around town (42).

The analogy of the second *persona* to an actor's role lends itself to two extremes of interpretation, both, I think, equally misguided. The first would argue that—excluding the factors of human rationality, the influence of chance, and our career decisions represented by the other *personae*—the Romans felt that the selves we perform as social animals are precisely that, feigned performances rather than authentic manifestations of selfhood. The analogy to the theater in particular may suggest that one think in terms of an authentic Fred, say, buried under his playing of the role of King Lear, or Spiderman. And the very terminology of *persona* may help us in this (incorrect) deduction, since its original meaning of "mask" suggests a concealing cover or surface that may be peeled off. The second extreme would be to say that the *persona* and its "interior" were for the Romans identical: that "there is no difference between comporting oneself as a virtuous individual and actually being one," with the result that speaking of the person in any terms besides that of *persona* is to be nonsensical.[96] The closest one comes to such a formulation in antiquity is, I think, in the idea that the assumption of a role may alter the individual who performs it so as to bring him closer to the *persona* he plays (as noted in chapter 3; cf. Sen., *De ira* 3.13.3). Cicero claims that both the actor and the orator will be moved by their own fictive emotion (*De or.* 2.191–95; cf. Quint., 6.2.35). Galen believes that to address the manifestation of anger is to eventually address anger itself (*Aff. Dig.* 20–21).[97] Even Ovid opines that "pretending makes it so" for the fevered lover who assumes indifference (*Rem. Am.* 497–504)—and in reverse, as well! (*Ars Am.* 1.615–16).

These two extreme views are difficult to map onto Roman culture because they map *persona* onto a true/false axis in mind rather than understanding it in terms of propriety and impropriety, or in terms of Roman civic performativity. As David Burchell (1998, 7–8) correctly notes, "Cicero's image of this second *persona* is not that of the interior personality of modern psychological common-sense, an integrated selfhood from which one becomes dissociated by traumatic forces bearing

---

96. Burchell (1998, 114), who refers to medieval and Renaissance authors who read Cicero this way.
97. See the discussion in Hankinson 1993, 200–201.

from outside. Rather it is of a finished artifact which has to be deliberately fashioned out of the uneven raw material of our impulses . . . and capacities (*Off.* 1.111). Nothing is more conducive to *decorum*, he tells us, than 'an evenness [*aequabilitas*] both of one's whole life and of one's actions.'"[98] The *persona* was neither felt to be the whole of the individual (to begin with, the possibility of four would then be nonsensical), nor was it usually felt to be *fake*, a semblance that concealed the truth of who one was. Instead, it seems that in the late republic the normative usage of the term *persona* outside the literal context of the theater and its actors was to indicate a public role that formed part and parcel of the individual's identity. There is no contrast in our sources from this period between the *persona* and the "real person"; inasmuch as an individual's social and political roles constituted an important part of that real person, the *persona* represented an aspect of being rather than either an exposition or a dissimulation of that person. Most often it seems to refer to someone in his role as a public official. The usage is common in Cicero and his peers; for example, Cicero writes to a friend in 46 BCE that he has decided to lay aside that *persona* with which he has often won even Caesar's approval and bury himself in writing (*Fam.* 7.33.2); in another letter Servius Sulpicius reminds Cicero, on the occasion of Tullia's death, to remember the behavior that is worthy of his *persona* (*Fam.* 4.5.5). Again, Cicero, in his defense of Cn. Plancius, tells us that Plancius so loved him that he refused to let Cicero leave for Asia when Cicero wished to, "tossing aside his *persona* as *quaestor* and taking up the one of a friend" (abiecta quaestoria persona comitisque sumpta [*Planc.* 100]). Here it is not that his *persona* as *quaestor* was false, but that he chose in this crisis to act in a manner more befitting the role of a friend than of an official.[99]

Both in its technical Stoic usage, then, as in Cicero's discussion of the four Stoic *personae*, and in its normative Roman examples, there is no reason to think that a *persona* should represent *false* role-playing in any way. And the same is true of the terminology of *persona* in rhetorical and grammatical texts. In the latter, its meaning is far removed from any strong association with role-playing; thus, when Varro defines "the triple nature of *persona*" (*Ling.* 8.20), he divides it into "the person who speaks, the person to whom speech is directed,

---

98. What if two of the *personae* embody contradictory tendencies? Cicero raises this possibility at *Off.* 1.150; cf. Gill 1994, 4633.

99. As Nédoncelle (1948, 298) points out (and he excepts Seneca, to whom we shall return), "The *persona* is neither one's intimate subjectivity nor the mask that covers it. It is, or it tends to be, the individual who strolls in the street and whom you see when you open your eyes."

and the person concerning whom the speech is," a division that Fuhrmann (1979, 94) speculates was inherited from the Alexandrian scholars.[100] In rhetorical terminology and practice, we find Cicero classifying *persona* and *negotium* as sources of *inventio* (*Inv. Rhet.* 1.34; cf. 2.16); more to the point, it is also used to designate the person in whose voice one might speak when delivering an oration or the introduction of fictitious characters as a way of moving an audience.[101] In a well-known example in the *De oratore* where Cicero stresses the need for a good orator to feel the emotions he expresses, Antonius tells his interlocutors that in his peroration for Manius Aquilius, when he (Antonius) was moved by his emotions, he was not the *actor* (here both speaker and actor are connoted) of someone else's role but of his own (*De Or.* 194).[102]

Some of the importance attached to the correct performance of one's *persona(e)* comes through in the emphasis Cicero places upon consistency. "If propriety is anything at all, it is nothing more than consistency both in one's whole life, and in one's individual actions. You cannot maintain it if, in imitating someone else's nature, you abandon your own" (*Off.* 1.111). The *persona*, then, is not readily interchangeable without a lapse in seemly public behavior, and it seems that to copy someone else's *persona* is, in a sense, to act falsely toward one's own. Cicero's advice to know your own nature in the selection of an appropriate second *persona* ("suum quisque igitur noscat ingenium" [*Off.* 114]) recalls the principle of *gnothi sauton*, but here in a way that is oriented toward propriety in one's role in life. The roles that Cicero then mentions as available are those that are standard in Roman society—and require the approbation of society.

This same emphasis on consistency turns up in nonphilosophical asides on one's life as a role; for example, when Cicero defends his action against Catiline, he says he simply maintained the *persona* imposed upon him by the republic— as was seemly under the political circumstances (*Mur.* 6).[103] Here and elsewhere

---

100. "Cum item personarum natura triplex esset, qui loqueretur, \<ad quem\>, de quo" (ed. R. Kent, 1938).

101. Cf. *De Or.* 2.102: "tris personas unus sustineo . . . meam, adversarii, iudicis"; *De Or.* 3.205: "personarum ficta inductio vel gravissimum lumen augendi."

102. Cicero will also use the term to designate the speakers in a written dialogue; speaking of his *Cato Major*, he writes, "induxi senem disputantem, quia nulla videbatur aptior persona" (*Fam.* 6.6.10, speaking of Cato).

103. "Illam vero gravitatis severitatisque personam non appetivi, sed ab re publica mihi impositam sustinui, sicut huius imperi dignitas in summo periculo civium postulabat." Cf. Tac., *Agr.* 2.45: "Grave est enim nomen imperi atque id etiam in levi persona pertimescitur."

(unless he is speaking of stage actors), Cicero's usage of the term, which usually refers to the proper performance of a public office or career, often occurs with *sustinere*, to maintain or sustain the *persona* in the presence of stress or adversity and thereby avoid impropriety and show oneself worthy of one's public position.[104] Also necessary is consistency of one's current behavior with that manifested in the past, such as at *Phil.* 12.17, where Cicero points out how inappropriate it was for his *persona* to be the one to negotiate a peace with Mark Antony's faction.[105] Even dramatists know how to imbue their characters with speech and actions appropriate to what we know of their traditional roles: as Cicero comments, "We say that the poets preserve that which is fitting when what is said and done is worthy of each *persona*, so that if Aeacus or Minos were to say 'Let them hate, so long as they hear' or 'The parent himself is a tomb for his children' it would seem inappropriate, because tradition has it that they were righteous men; but when Atreus says it, applause is provoked, because his lines are worthy of the *persona*" (*Off.* 1.97).[106] At the risk of repetition, then, what is most significant about this formulation is that it nowhere plays into some common modern assumptions about the performance of a role—assumptions perhaps best summed up by Jung's dictum that "the *persona* is a complicated system of relations between individual consciousness and society, fittingly enough a kind of mask, designed on the one hand to make a definite impression upon others, and, on the other, to conceal the true nature of the individual."[107] At Rome, in contrast, the word *persona* itself may have had its origins in an originally Etruscan word for "mask," but its normative republican usage away from the actual practice of drama almost always points to a public role that is *not felt to be a concealment* of some truer or inner private self.[108] Cicero, for example, may feel obliged to perform the public responsibilities invested in his role as a Roman official, as he does at *Har. Resp.* 61.7, but there is no

---

104. This is in harmony with the observations of Fuhrmann 1979.

105. Cf. also Val. Max., 6.2.5, on Cato Uticensis; this is not unlike the emphasis on consistency that turns up in *De officiis*.

106. Seneca's Medea certainly takes these words to heart.

107. Jung 1966, 305.

108. On the history and context of the term *persona* outside its Stoic usage, see Bettini 2000; Carrithers 1985; Dupont 1985, 80–81; Fuhrmann 1979; Rorty 1990. I have not here paid much attention to Mauss's distinction between the *personne* and the *moi*, since he conflates Stoic and Christian views of the latter. On *prosopon*, see Frontisi-Ducroux 1991; and Frontisi-Ducroux 1995, 57–75.

connotation that the *persona* and role the Roman people have assigned to him
to sustain (*sustinere*) represent an inappropriate or deceptive form of behavior.

The corresponding Greek term is, of course, the word *prosopon*, whose development should not be confused with that of *persona*. *Prosopon* in Greek originally
meant "face," and as such had no connotations of something placed *over* the face,
as the Latin word originally did, although it too was used to designate "mask"
by Aristotle and a few other sources (and is used by Polybius for the Roman
imagines [6.53.5]).[109] Oddly, one development of *prosopon* was toward the sense
of "moral character," especially in the ethical writings of Epictetus.[110] The term
persona may have shed its masklike connotations near the start; Frontisi-Ducroux
(1995, 61) has argued that this word, although it initially meant "mask" in
Etruscan, must have already been used to designate character as of its introduction into Latin, since at that point the Roman theater did not employ masks; and
that this development in turn similarly influenced the Greek word *prosopon*.[111]

Now, Seneca's usage of the term *persona* can be quite ordinary. In *De beneficiis*,
he will remind us throughout to keep in mind the *persona* of the person bestow-
ing or receiving a favor or a gift; it is relevant to the meaning of the gesture (for
example, *Ben.* 2.15.3).[112] As we have seen, in writing to Claudius' powerful
freedman librarian Polybius, he invokes Polybius' important office as a reason
for keeping a stiff upper lip. Polybius has to remember he is an exemplum to his
political audience; he has had a grand *persona* put on him that he must sustain
(*Polyb.* 6.1). This sounds much like what Cicero says of himself with typical
understatement in the eighth *Philippic*: "O ye immortal gods! How great a thing
it is to guard one's *persona* in the republic!—a *persona* which should serve
not only the souls, but even the eyes, of the citizens" (O di immortales! quam

<hr />

109. For the probably false etymology of *persona* from *personare*, "to sound through," see Aul.
Gell., *NA* 5.7. On the development of the term from the original meaning of "mask," see especially
Fuhrmann 1979.

110. Epict., *Disc.* 1.2.4; Epict., *Ench.* 17 and 37.

111. On the comparative development of *persona* and *prosopon*, see Frontisi-Ducroux 1991 and
1995; Nédoncelle 1948. For *prosopon* as character, see Plutarch's usage, passim; and the discussion
in De Lacy 1977, 164. De Lacy cites instances in which Plutarch refers to the ethos of the *prosopon*
(e.g., *Quaest. Conv.* 7.8.1), and others in which he uses it in the political sense of *persona* (e.g., *An
seni respublica gerenda sit* 785C, where he says it is shameful for the older statesman to change his
political *prosopon*). But De Lacy is wrong to suggest that this latter usage refers to "an appearance
that misrepresents the reality."

112. Normative usage: *De ira* 3.6.6, 3.40.2; *Marc.* 1.2, 6.1, 7.4; *Helv.* 19.2; *Ep.* 81.16; *Ben.* 1.12.3 (and
often in this dialogue).

magnum est personam in re publica tueri principis! quae non animis solum
debet, sed etiam oculis servire civium [*Phil.* 8.29]).[113] Unsurprisingly, the philosophic usage occurs in Seneca as well: in *De clementia,* he invokes the common
idea of harmony between the virtues, and, in a phrase reminiscent of the *De
officiis,* points out that certain virtues are better suited to certain *personae* than
to others ("cum autem virtutibus inter <se sit> concordia nec ulla altera melior
aut honestior sit, quaedam tamen quibusdam personis aptior est" [*Clem.* 1.5]; it
turns out Nero's *persona* is perfect for clemency).[114]

Often in Seneca's writing, however, the *persona* becomes a thing to be held
up for public inspection, but *unnaturally* so: sustaining it is an effort, being
caught without it is a fear, and truth lies *underneath* the mask, not in the performance of it. The usage seems to mesh the salient features of the *persona*-
mask (not an authentic person, but an actor) and the *persona*-public character
(not an actor, but a role in society). Now we have a role in society, but one that
is not true to one's self and necessitates wearing a mask; this wearing of a false
persona is an exhausting, and ultimately unsustainable, defense under dangerous forms of scrutiny.[115] In Seneca's description of the situation in *De tranquil-
litate,* he seems to catapult us, as we have already seen, into a kind of Foucaldian
scopic regime in which Seneca's fellow elite themselves people the panopticon:
"Constant observation of oneself [*obseruatio sui*] is tortuous. . . . [I]t's not a
pleasant life, nor one free from anxiety, to live constantly wearing a mask [*sub
persona*]" (*Tranq.* 17.1). In *De clementia* we come across the astonishing comment, directed at Nero, that covering up one's true nature in public is nearly
impossible: "No one can wear a mask for long; the feigned characteristics quickly
lapse back into what is natural. Under them lies the truth, and everything that is

---

113. On *persona* as political role, see Fuhrmann 1979, 89–91.

114. Asmis (1990, 225–31) suggests that Seneca's definition of the happy life ("convenies naturae
suae") is influenced by Panaetius' second *persona.* Cicero's advice not to fight your nature (*Off.* 110)
is echoed in Sen., *Tranq.* 6.3.

115. Barton (2001, 120) writes in a related vein, though with more emphasis on honor and
shame: "The face became a facade. The *persona* went from being primarily expressive to primarily
defensive. The Romans donned, as it were, the armor of hypocrisy, to borrow a phrase from Samuel
Dill. As it was for Livy's Brutus under Tarquinius or Suetonius' Claudius under Caligula, the mask,
even a dishonorable one—or I should say especially a dishonorable one—was a relief and an
assuagement for embarrassment and humiliation, a defense against an unbearable 'now' that
would crush you. When Tacitus' Nero poisons his rival Britannicus, Octavia looks upon the death
throes of her brother with a brazen face that hides her anguish and protects her life (*Annales* 13.16).
The 'thick-skinned' would survive."

based, as it were, on something real" (*Clem.* 1.1.6).[116] Nero, fortunately, does not have to worry about this effort, as his nature is all goodness, but the senators who are more vulnerable to performing under his gaze may well have felt the strain. We have moved from an iteration of the theory of *De officiis* to a more sinister world in which adopting an inappropriate *persona* is no longer just unproductive, or a sign of lack of self-knowledge. It is a deliberately false self-representation to the world, one driven by evil or necessitated by fear.

Elsewhere, the *persona* is invoked in all its theatrical context as a metaphor for life, but in a way that makes clear the falsity and mutability of what a *persona* is as well as the ideal need for a single and sustained *persona*.[117]

> The cheerfulness of those men who are called happy is feigned, or their sadness is heavy and festering, all the more so because in the meantime it is not permitted for them to be sad in public, but they must act the happy man while eating up their very heart amid their sorrows. I must often use the following example, and this mime of human life is more effectively expressed by no other, this mime which assigns us the roles we play badly. That fellow who strides pompously on the stage and says, with his nose in the air, "Look, I rule over Argos," is a slave, and he earns five measures of grain and five denarii. . . . You can say the same about all those fops whom the litter suspends over the heads of men and over the crowd: all of their happiness is role-playing [*omnium istorum personata felicitas est*]. (*Ep.* 80.6–8)

Such an emphasis on the false *persona* is rare before the early empire. The notion of playing a role false to oneself in the way we might understand it is designated in these texts, not by *persona*, but by such terminology as *simulatio* or *dissimulatio*.[118] Only on one occasion might Cicero's usage seem to suggest

---

116. "Nemo enim potest personam diu ferre, ficta cito in naturam cuam recidunt; quibus veritas subsit quaeque, ut ita dicam, ex solido nascuntur."

117. Cf. *Ep.* 76.31: "Not one of those men whom you see wearing purple is happy, no more than those who are given a scepter and a cloak on the stage in a drama."

118. Cf. *Verr.* 2.1.39, 2.4.6; *Red. Pop.* 21.7 and passim. In Cic., *Part. Or.* 55, *fictae personae* refer to the orator's dramaturge-like assumption of different voices in a case, as with *personarum ficta inductio* (*Or.* 3.205, cited above). Cf. Quintilian's technical terminology at 6.1.25: "His praecipue locis utiles sunt prosopopoeiae, id est fictae alienarum personarum orationes." A similar usage occurs also in Seneca: "Simul tu intelleges quanto minus negotii habeas cum fastidio tui quam ii quos, ad professionem speciosam alligatos et sub ingenti titulo laborantes, in sua simulatione pudor magis quam uoluntas tenet" (*Tranq.* 2.5; as well as *Brev.* 18.6 on the charms of Caligula).

the performance of an untrue and inappropriate role—ironically, when he criticizes the philosophical aspirations of Epicurus, whose school he here holds in little regard (*Tusc.* 5.73.3). According to Cicero, Epicurus has only put on the *persona* of a philosopher, rather than actually being one ("induit" [*Tusc.* 5.73.3]).[119] Seneca similarly comments that a philosopher must wear the mask of his discipline and not seek monetary handouts ("Indixisti pecuniae odium; hoc professus es, hanc personam induisti: agenda est. Iniquissimum est te pecuniam sub gloria egestatis adquirere" [*Ben.* 2.17.2]); presumably Epicurus' perceived focus on pleasure is what disqualifies him from his *persona* in Cicero's eyes.

In Seneca, however, the emphasis on the false *persona* is sustained. The idea is that one can strip the public mask from people to see who they really are. Perhaps like the false appearances associated with the desirability of great wealth, or the fear of pain or death, the masks that people wear lead Seneca to challenge us to see beyond them, beyond the false front of reality and its terrors: "But remember this above all, to remove the confusion from things and to see what is in them; you will realize that there is nothing terrible in them besides fear itself. What you see happening to boys also befalls us slightly older boys; if they see those whom they love, to whom they are accustomed and with whom they play, wearing masks [*personatas*], they are terrified: one must remove the mask not only from men but also from things, and restore their own appearance" (*Ep.* 24.12–13). It is a theme we find also in Lucretius, who urges us to see through appearance to the reality of things as they are. But his famous phrase, "the *persona* is torn off, the reality remains" (eripitur persona, manet res [3.58]), is limited in its relevance to the fear of death (and other superstitions) that forms only part of Seneca's broader concerns; Lucretius refers here to the mask of rationality that humans maintain until the moment when danger and "the black of death" overcome their civilized exterior.

With Seneca's emphasis on the falsity of the public *persona*, it is hard to imagine what a sustained propriety would look like, or the congruent harmony of all four *personae* from Cicero's *De officiis*. Seneca describes the importance of the second *persona* at *Tranq.* 6.1–4 in language that is completely Ciceronian:

---

119. Fuhrmann (1979, 91) would still refer this usage to a typology of social *personae*, and compares it to *Pis.* 71; *Arch.* 3; and *Caecin.* 14.

Above all, it is necessary for a man to evaluate himself because generally we think we have greater abilities than we do: one man slips up by trusting in his eloquence, another demands more from his fortune than it can bear, a third oppresses a weak body with a toilsome duty. The modesty of some men is ill-suited for government, which needs a strong façade; the haughtiness of others will not do for court; some do not have their anger under control, and any provocation drives them to rash words; some do not know how to check their urbanity or to abstain from risky jokes. For all of these a quiet life is more useful than public service. A fierce and impatient nature should avoid all incitements to a freedom of speech that will harm him.

And Seneca, also like Cicero, emphasizes the need for internal consistency in a man's behavior. It is the unwise soul who will differ from himself; one must strive, if not to be praised, at least to be recognized (*adgnosci* [*Ep.* 120.21–22]). This idea that the man of consistent *persona* can be recognized will prove important for us when we turn to Senecan drama. In the meantime, we may note that Seneca says little, in his remarks about consistency, about the other constraints upon our *personae*: the world into which we were born, the choices that shape our lives. Perhaps with reason. For it is hard to see how a position in Nero's court would allow any form of ideal Stoic self-consistency, nor do we have any evidence that Seneca was the man to show it.

Despite the undesirability of any form of theatrical stain upon the activity and conduct of the Romans of the upper classes, then, there were clearly areas in which the distinction between acting out one kind of *persona* (the public one of the republic) and another (the self-betraying one of the empire) threatened to become muddy. Senecan Stoicism, in its attempt to separate forms of performance that were philosophical in nature from forms that simply kowtowed to prevailing political necessities, acknowledged the problem rather than dismantled it. The slipperiness of the binary categories at play at Rome in this period continues unchecked despite the efforts of Stoics and senators alike. The notion of maintaining a poker face no matter what the circumstances could be harnessed both to the idea of resistance and to that of compliance; self-control could be now a form of strength, now a form of weakness; to play a role for an audience could be characteristic either of the *proficiens* or of the actor. At issue is not so much that Seneca himself, or other Stoics, or Roman senators under Nero, would find these sources of contradiction paralyzing in nature: they clearly did not. But these areas of ideological friction do reveal much that is fascinating about Roman Stoicism's evolution in a particular political context. It is clear that the turn of emphasis from the public eye to the self-generated eye—from the mirror of the community to a form of mirroring that relied upon a doubling of the self—generated as many problems in practice as it may have resolved in theory. Like Nero's mirror in the *De clementia*, what this mirror was meant to reflect, and what it did reflect, may not have been one and the same.

5 Models of Personhood

In this final chapter, I turn to a closer consideration of the qualities in Senecan philosophy and drama that support the idea that a new and more reflexive concept of the self was emerging in this author's work. In particular, I offer further arguments for a move away from the community-oriented, or "participant-observer," self visible in Greek literature and philosophy, and away from the models embedded in class, exemplarity, and political performance that are familiar from republican Rome. Seneca's representation of the self, as I have suggested, relies on a model of self-witnessing that derives its normative values directly from the tenets of Stoic philosophy rather than from the judgments of one's peers.[1] But the Senecan self-in-progress also relies on forms of self-*dialogue.* Such dialogues invoke less strongly the idea of the visual witness, but maintain the distinction between a knowing self and a learning self. In them,

---

1. As such, Seneca offers theoretical versions of the kind of behavior represented in action by figures from his own day, such as Thrasea Paetus and Rubellius Plautus. Tacitus writes that Thrasea walked out of the Senate in 59 CE rather than offer thanks for Nero's survival of Agrippina's murder plot (*Ann.* 12.12; cf. *Ann.* 16.21). He continued to shun the Senate until his forced suicide in 66. On the danger of being a Stoic under Nero, see also Tac., *Ann.* 14.57, 16.22. On the no longer popular idea of a Stoic opposition per se, see Griffin 1976, 363–66.

one speaking voice takes on the role of the doctrinaire Stoic, while the other voice listens to (or protests at) the moral instruction of its interlocutor. In this "dialogic" self, then, ethical development is represented as the result of an intrapersonal dialogue (here too with an internalized other) in which one interlocutor holds all the moral cards, and the other is the recipient of advice and instructions. This form of internal dialogue can clearly be distinguished from the internal dialogues of heroic figures in Greek epic and tragedy, such as Hector or Odysseus. It is also distinct from the interpersonal philosophical dialogues of Plato's Socrates. To be sure, the model I describe rehearses some of the features of the mirrored self of the *Alcibiades* I: the idea, for example, that what one sees in the "mirror of the self" provides the individual with access to an unchanging realm of ethical values represented by the divinity, and that progress depends on the consideration and internalization of those values. But the Senecan mirror of the self shows far greater attention to reflexivity as constitutive of the process of coming to know oneself than does that of the *Alcibiades*. At the same time, Seneca's descriptions cannot simply be mapped onto post-Cartesian notions of selfhood; although reflexivity is present, the idea that we cannot have sure knowledge of the world outside our mind is not.

One of the main features of the self that I here call dialogic is its attention to what the philosopher Harry Frankfurt has described as "second-order" judgments and volitions: that is, the self's judgments about the self's own desires and wishes. Frankfurt identifies this feature as a necessary component of what distinguishes humans from other animals. Seneca's emphasis upon self-exhortation, self-address, and self-reproval as the tools of the *proficiens* means that the process of second-order reasoning and judgment is crucial to the *meditatio*, and this allows a close parallel between Seneca's terminology for what takes place within the self and that of Frankfurt. In both cases, there remains a judging self that is the source of the second-order evaluations and a judged self that is torn in two or more directions—for example, toward and simultaneously away from the desire to binge on chocolate éclairs, or to run from the scene of a crime. At the same time, neither Seneca's ethical writing nor Frankfurt's treatment of second-orderliness pays much attention to a dangerous potential latent in dependence on second-order reasoning as a source of ethical guidance: to privilege such a form of reasoning as a procedure for governing and controlling the first-order self is to underplay the ability of second-order reasoning to provide an impetus for evil as well as for good. Just as reflexivity can open the door to a form of ethical solipsism, so too second-order reasoning can provide a framework for judgment that itself has little to do with shared ethical norms. It may, after all, take a lot of self-command and self-exhortation to become an adulterer, or a thief—or a murderess.

One of our most famous ancient murderesses is, of course, Medea. In Seneca's play of the same name we can see some of the pitfalls of a philosophy that advances the idea that one should now ideally perform for oneself rather than for one's peers, that second-order thought provides the path to freedom, and that the soul conceals a potential for greatness that needs to be identified and developed. These are the features inherent in Seneca's version of Stoic selfhood that emerge strongly from this drama. In addition, Seneca's drama highlights the difficulties raised by a philosophy that both denigrates and acknowledges the importance of a judging audience and treats self-control as either a mark of *libertas* (as with Socrates, whose expression never changed under the Thirty Tyrants) or a mark of servitude (as with Pastor, who had to paste a grin on his grieving face). The self-critical tendencies of Seneca's tragic antiheroes suggest a form of criticism of Stoic philosophy that acknowledges the dangers, rather than the benefits, of the practice of self-formation. The power of mind over matter shown by Medea drives her deeper into evil rather than into wisdom, and her independence from the ethical values of her community introduces a form of self-reliance that stands as a marker of the danger of Stoic meditative procedures. In the end, Medea offers herself precisely as a reading of the Stoic philosopher—in a perverted mirror, but still clearly visible, and a fearsome sight indeed.

THE SECOND-ORDER SELF

Let us start with the complicated issue of Senecan selfhood and its relationship to ancient ethical thought. The Senecan alter ego we have examined in relation to ethical self-command stands at a significant distance from the communally mirrored self examined in chapter 1, but it is also at a clear remove from other historical and literary examples of the divided self in classical antiquity—what Christopher Gill (1996) has described as the "objective-participant self." Gill bases his important study of personality in Greek epic, tragedy, and philosophy on the distinction between ancient thinking about the relationship of self and community and our modern post-Cartesian notions linking selfhood to individuality and to personally generated (that is, Romantic) *or* categorical (that is, post-Kantian) notions of the Good. The latter models share a Cartesian emphasis on the individual subject as the locus of psychological and ethical life, which to us may seem second nature in any discussion of selfhood but is historically and socially dependent upon our own place in the history of philosophy. As Gill points out, not only is *self* a modern English term with no equivalent in Greek, but as we tend to use it, it reflects a particularly modern tendency to privilege such components as a unitary consciousness, personal individuality, self-discovery, and the uniqueness and worth of each individual self, a tendency that inevitably distorts our understanding of ancient notions of ethical selfhood and enourages the teleological perspective on the development of the modern self familiar from such important thinkers such as Bruno Snell and A. W. H. Adkins.

Ethical theorists critical of this modern tendency, such as Alasdair MacIntyre (1981) and Bernard Williams (1985), along with Gill himself, have suggested that a more appropriate way of understanding the normative ancient self (and its anticipation of new, non-Cartesian descriptions of selfhood in the present day) is to recognize the role of interpersonal and communal relationships in its formation and its moral judgments. Following this line of thought, Gill would reject what he calls the "subjective-individualist" tradition of thought about selfhood and substitute an "objective-participant" model. He seeks "to bring out the way in which Greek ethical thinking stresses the primary role of *participation* in interpersonal and communal relationships" and the way this participation is seen as prerequisite "for the acquisition of *objective* ethical knowledge" (1996, 10). There are several differences between the two models. The subjective-individualist conception entails self-consciousness as a unified I, the grounding of one's moral life in an individual stance, and a drive for "authenticity" in realizing one's unique selfhood. The objective-participant conception holds that to be human is to act on the basis of reason, and to engage with one's communal role in such as a way as to find the nature of the best human life. Most important for my purposes here, it is "to be the kind of animal whose psycho-ethical life (typically conceived as 'dialogue' between parts of the psyche) is capable, in principle, of being shaped so as to become fully 'reason-ruled' by (a) the action-guiding discourse of interpersonal and communal engagement and (b) reflective debate about the proper goals of a human life" (1996, 12).

Odysseus' monologue at *Il.* 11.404–10 provides a simple case of reasoning that is both objective-participant and leads directly to action. Isolated in the front lines of battle and facing the Trojan warrior Diomedes, Odysseus ponders within himself ("he spoke to his great-hearted spirit," his *thumos*) whether to flee or to risk death. He answers his own question: only cowards flee, while the best men stand their ground. For Gill, then, "Odysseus recognizes the priority of what is implied in 'being best' through engagement with the roles and practices in which such an ideal makes sense" and not through any abstract moral imperative (1996, 77–78).[2] Gill also supplies a conceptual apparatus for dealing with more complicated forms of internal dialogue in these characters, such as Odysseus' deliberation in *Od.* 20 on what to do with Penelope's arrogant suitors and the maids who are their bedmates. As Odysseus (still disguised as a beggar) lies awake in his bed, he hears the serving-women laughing as they go to join their lovers, and his spirit is roused to anger. At this point, as he wonders whether to kill them on the spot, Odysseus speaks to his heart (*kardia*) and tells it to wait: "Endure, O heart: for once you endured a thing more shameful still, on that day when the strong Cyclops ate my brave companions. But you endured that, until your cunning rescued you from the cave, though you thought you would die" (18–21). Odysseus' brief address here to his *kardia* involves not only a self-splitting in which a body part takes the function of an interlocutor, but also a choice between two forms of behavior (both communally sanctioned), immediate revenge versus a craftier and more profitable vengeance later. It thus "internalizes a version of the type of appeal which standardly forms part of Homeric interpersonal discourse: the appeal to suppress indignation in the short term, in order to achieve a desirable longer term goal" (1996, 187). It also involves a debate about choices, a decision about alternative courses of action, both of which seem attractive at the first-order level. Odysseus decides to wait based on what Frankfurt would call a second-order judgment about the desirability of one desire rather than the other.[3]

---

2. Or Hector trapped outside the walls of Troy, whose reasoning "is informed by ethical attitudes which are derived . . . from his engagement with his familial and communal role" (Gill 1996, 82).

3. Walsh (1990) has a wonderful discussion of internalized dialogue in the Polyphemus character of Theoc. 11, whose ability to eavesdrop on his own speech is the first step toward a therapeutic freedom from desire.

For Gill, this thought-as-inner-dialogue model is part and parcel of the objective-participant nature of selfhood in ancient Greek literature and philosophy. As he points out, "the idea embodied in the form of the Homeric monologues [is] that the formation of judgments, or decisions, is the outcome of an internal dialogue involving affirmation and assent. . . . The deliberative monologues represent an (exceptional) internalization of the interpersonal discourse which is central to the mode of living presented in the poem" (1996, 47, 59).[4] Gill would also claim that this is a characteristic of Platonic dialogical thought, in that the philosophically adept self is one that has learned to deliberate on the ethical principles of its community. "In the Republic, reflective reasoning seems to take the form of systematic dialogue or argument (*not introspection*) about the fundamental ethical principles of the community, conducted between those who are dispositionally and intellectually prepared to engage in this" (281; emphasis added)—that is, between the philosopher-rulers, whose reflective reasoning on the Good depends and builds upon principles whose validity can be recognized by members of their own community. And this holds true of Plato's philosophical mouthpiece as well, for otherwise Socrates' ability to lead his interlocutors to repudiate their former beliefs could not proceed logically (as it does) from those very beliefs.[5]

Gill's contribution to the understanding of Greek selfhood and ethics, the whole of which I cannot do justice to here, is invaluable both as an assault on

---

4. "The two voices represent the expression of standard ethical claims in interpersonal relationships, on the one hand, and the outcome of reflective debate on the basis of such claims, on the other. In these respects, these actual or quasi-monologues constitute a mode of articulating ideas which stem from . . . an interpersonal relationship, were it not for the figure's exceptional isolation. Thus the innerness of the form is interpreted here as the (exceptional) internalization of the modes of dialogue involved . . . , rather than as the emergence of an understanding of the person as a fundamentally inner (self-conscious, first-personal) entity" (Gill 1996, 183).

5. According to Gill's study, the philosophers of Plato's *Republic* are acting within an objectivist-participant framework in that they care about the welfare of their community and are in communication with that community (cf. the famous "return to the cave"). In addition, "the achievement of the normative human state depends on the person's having participated effectively in interconnected forms of interactive and reflective discourse. Whether or not this is so . . . does not depend wholly on the person herself, as an individual" (Gill 1996, 449). He argues (454) that book 9 of the *Republic* "cannot negate the earlier indications that the ideal psycho-ethical pattern cannot be achieved, or even grasped, fully without the prior existence of the ideal state and the educational programme that this provides." In contrast, Kant is objectivist-individualist because he "combines a focus on the (individual) moral agent with the idea that the agent, when acting properly, subordinates herself to universal, objectively valid laws" (446).

our preconceptions in approaching the ancient self, and as a tool for understanding ancient philosophical approaches to self-formation and ethical behavior. At the same time, I suggest that the developments of Roman Stoicism, and in particular the thought of Seneca, innovate in ways that cannot ultimately be contained within the model he sets out for ancient Greek philosophy and literature (perhaps not surprisingly). Seneca too "launches" his arguments using imagery and terminology familiar to his Roman readers: the idea that *virtus* depends on an audience, the importance of maintaining a solid *persona*, the desirability of military *virtus*, and the "impenetrability" of the elite citizen. Certainly, the desirability of honor and integrity play into his viewpoint. But he borrows these desirables in the service of ideas that are not readily reconcilable with their more usual definition: that *virtus* can be attained in the absence of military or political service; that life under an emperor can have dignity and integrity; that the gaze of the public, and even of one's peers, can be a force for corruption rather than exemplary action. Indeed, Seneca's "community" largely consists of characters who are dead, imaginary, or divine, and while the values of a Laelius or a Cato mesh well with the traditional ethical stance of the senatorial class, it would be difficult to claim that Seneca represents his moral thinking as based on dialogue with members of his own class and in his own time—the exception, of course, being his correspondent Lucilius, who is already a Stoic *proficiens*, plus a few other like-minded senators. Others from his class may shunned him as too close to Nero. In other words, Seneca's immediate community in the imperial court may suggest that the objective-participant model that works so well for Gill's case studies may not be fully appropriate for the formation of Roman Stoic selfhood as represented by Seneca's writings.

Let us turn to another possible model I have mentioned for thinking about imperial Stoics, the one developed by Frankfurt. In a famous article written in 1971, Frankfurt located the difference between persons and animals in the human ability to form second-order desires, desires about which first-order desires to have. He then proceeded one step further and defined freedom of the will as the *freedom to want what one wants to want*, even if one is prohibited from carrying it out in action. Finally, he pointed out that one can act in accordance with a first-order desire *despite* a conflicting second-order desire (most commonly in the case of addiction). Second-order desires that the agent desires to translate into action are known as second-order volitions, and they are the mark of the person (as opposed to the merely human): "Someone has a desire of the second-order either when he wants simply to have a certain desire or when he wants a certain desire to be his will. In situations of the latter kind, I shall call his second-order desires 'second order volitions.' . . . It is having second-order volitions, and not having second-order desires generally, that I regard as essential to being a person" (6). In an extreme case, someone whose actions simply translate his first-order desires into being without any second-order reflection upon their desirability can be described, in Frankfurt's terminology, as a "wanton," a human little different from an animal: "When a *person* acts, the desire by which he is moved is either the will he wants or a will he wants to be without. When a *wanton* acts, it is neither" (1971, 14; original emphasis).[6]

Gill also devotes space to Frankfurt's theories, although he finds them problematic when applied to Greek philosophical characterizations of human psychological functions. It is not so much that Gill's terminology is framed in terms of reasoning, and Frankfurt's in terms of desires, but that Frankfurt, unlike Gill's subject cases, takes second-order functions as *the* key feature in distinctively human psychology, rather than as *a* key feature (Gill 1996, 418). Also problematic for Gill is that Frankfurt's theory is itself shaped by the kind of post-Cartesian reasoning Gill and others have warned us to stay away from. That is, it "presupposes the capacity for self-awareness that has often been taken as central in post-Cartesian thinking," in that one's capacity to have guiding second-order desires smacks of Kant's notion of autonomy "as the capacity to detach oneself from one's existing desires and inclinations and to legislate for oneself rules which have overriding force (which are effective in determining action)" (419–20). Finally, Frankfurt's model focuses on the individual himself, while the Greek texts Gill treats "presuppose engagement with an (ethical and dialectical) community" (1996, 418). Nonetheless, I shall claim that precisely these features of Frankfurt's thought make his model a particularly appropriate one for discussing Seneca's writing, where the capacity for second-order functions is explicitly treated as the crucial step on the way to full (Stoic) selfhood, while the post-Cartesian aspects of the model reflect to some degree

---

6. "Acting on a second-order desire [i.e., desires *about* desires], doing something to bring it about that one acquires a first-order desire, is acting upon oneself just as one would act upon another person: one *schools* oneself, one offers oneself persuasions, arguments, threats, bribes, in the hopes of inducing oneself to acquire the first-order desire" (Dennett 1976, 193; quoted in Gill 1996, 186).

the reduced role of the community in Seneca's philosophizing, as well as its heightened attention to reflexivity.[7]

In Frankfurt's article, as in Seneca's presentation of Stoicism, it appears to be a normative assumption that a person's second-order volition will usually function so as to align him with the "higher" (that is, communally, ethically, or religiously sanctioned) of two first-order desires.[8] For example, Frankfurt writes of a drug addict who wishes to quit but also wants to get high: "The unwilling addict identifies himself . . . through the formation of a second-order volition, with one rather than the other of his conflicting first-order desires. He makes one of them more truly his own and, in so doing, he withdraws himself from the other. It is in virtue of this identification . . . that the unwilling addict may meaningfully make the analytically puzzling statements that the force moving him to take the drug is a force other than his own" (1971, 13).[9] That is, the drug addict feels as if the second-order desire to *not* take drugs represents the truth of who he is, and whatever (addictive) force drives him to act upon the wrong first-order desire, despite his second-order volition to act upon the other one, is somehow alien to this "true him." This is not an uncommon phenomenon in ancient philosophy as well, where what would correspond to the first-order volition that we decide against is described as being pushed down into the realm of an inferior or dissenting voice, or (in the case of the Platonic soul) into a part of the psyche that is not representative of rational thought. Plato's Leontius in *Republic* 4 damns his eyes because he wants to look at a stack of corpses but also doesn't *want* to want

---

7. Inwood (2000) has been of much use to me, especially in helping me to reformulate some of my ideas about what exactly is original in Seneca. In a later work, Inwood (2003, 94) suggests that Seneca's concern with second-order intentional states is not dissimilar to that of Frankfurt; exercising one's will is "having beliefs and desires about one's beliefs and desires—a necessary condition for any project of self-improvement or self-shaping." Both Frankfurt and the Stoics are vulnerable to the charge that "they stoop to rationalization where a more detached rationality might naturally be preferred" (a charge with which Inwood disagrees).

8. In a footnote Frankfurt (1971, 13n6) abjures the identification of second-order volition with a necessarily "higher" ethical stance by stating that "I do not mean to suggest that a person's second order volitions necessarily manifest a *moral* stance on his part towards his first-order desires." Nonetheless, the article proceeds as if this is the most common case. As Zimmerman (2000) has suggested, Frankfurt's first- and second-order levels seem to map onto Seneca's (occasional) mind-body dualism quite nicely: the first-order volitions have to do with the latter, the second-order with the former.

9. Watson (2003) reads Frankfurt to be defining second-order volition as the second-order desire that *does* get translated into action, but the case of the unwilling addict's second-order volition in this paragraph seems to argue against his interpretation. Accordingly, it is important to stress the "would" in Frankfurt's definition (1971, 8): The notion of will is "the notion of an *effective* desire—one that moves (or will or would move) a person all the way to action."

to look, and his second-order judgment that the latter desire is better makes him feel alienated from the part of him that wants to look—in this case, a part that he both anthropomorphizes *and* locates in a physically delineated organ. Hence his strangled cry: "There, you wretches—fill yourself with this fine sight!" His eyes, not him, are in this formulation the guilty party.[10]

How does this phenomenon manifest itself in Seneca's writing? Here too, in stressing a hierarchy of desires about desires, Seneca's Stoic project of self-improvement is represented as one in which the would-be philosopher, like the Frankfurtian "person," is characterized as forming ethically correct second-order volitions about his first-order desires. When the *proficiens* makes this desire to not desire material goods, or to not fear death, into his will (via a long process of self-command, exhortation, imagery, and all the other elements of the *meditatio*),[11] he is in essence acting out Frankfurt's distinction between first- and second-order selves on his path to wisdom.[12] In Seneca, this second-order deliberation on first-order desires is consistently couched in terms of a dialogue the self holds with the self, not unlike the much less frequent examples from the *Iliad* and from tragic drama. Here, however, there is no trace of "what will the community think if . . . ?" Instead, the second-order part of the dialogue is attributed automatically to the more Stoically principled of the deliberating voices. Little attention is wasted on the first-order self that might want the bet-

---

10. *Resp.* 439e–440a. Cf. Campbell 1985, 331: "If some sorts [of action] are judged preferable to others, these aspects of the self which issue in the preferred sorts of action will be looked on with most favour. Thus arises the tendency to identify one's 'true' self with the favoured aspects, excluding the rest as alien."

11. I have used the charged term *will* here, but not as a sign of having taken positions on the debate on the will in Seneca. For a summary of the discussion and a well-reasoned mediary position, see Inwood 2000.

12. To repeat: Frankfurt's model makes the most explanatory sense when we are within the confines of a mind that has already accepted a particular ethical system; in Stoicism, one that emphasizes control of the appetitive and desiderative instincts above all. Otherwise, as Mele (1992) points out, an action's counting as continent or incontinent does not necessarily depend on having a *higher*-order desire at the time. An example is offered by the case of the would-be robber who fears being caught. In this case, his self-exhortation tells him to overcome his fear in order that he may carry out his plan, yet this self-exhortation, second-order though it may be, has nothing to do with an ethical higher order. This point need not trouble us in the context of Stoic philosophy, where second-order volition is *always* depicted as coming from the *testis* figure who is allied with *conscientia* and with the divinity. Watson (2003, 349) has also pointed to some problems with the Frankfurtian model, primarily in the claim that one's second-order self is always involved in the choice between two alternative courses of action. "In a case of conflict, Frankfurt would have us believe that what it is to identify with some desire rather than another is to have a volition concerning the

ter of the two choices, because Seneca's examples are consistently ones in which one choice is clearly wrong from a Stoic point of view (if not from a traditional elite point of view) and its voice needs to be lectured into right thinking by its dialogic partner.[13] At the same time, the first-order self is not shunted off into a body part, like Leontius' eyes; it remains a clearly personal voice.

The procedure is best summed up by Seneca's second-order opening lines to letter 61: "Let us cease to desire what we have desired [*desinamus, quod voluimus, velle*]."[14] Examples of how to do so are rife. Here, for example, is a dialogue Seneca imagines between himself and Lucilius (condensed from *Ep.* 20):

> "The greatest task and proof of wisdom is that your words and actions should match, that a man should be equal to himself under all conditions, and always the same."
>
> "But who can maintain this standard?"
>
> "Very few. So observe yourself and live by a single norm."
>
> "But who will support my household?"
>
> "You will learn the bounty of poverty, and you will know who your true friends are."
>
> "Can't you be rich and despise your wealth, instead?"
>
> "It is great to be poor amid riches."

---

former which is of higher order than any concerning the latter." There are two problems laid out here, if I read Watson correctly. First, why should second-order volitions have any special relation to "oneself"? (After all, there can exist third-order volitions, and so on.) Second, why claim second-order volitions even necessary for coming to a decision? "They do not (or need not usually) ask themselves which of their desires they want to be effective in action; they ask themselves which course of action is most worth pursuing" (350). Instead, they choose between independent sources of motivation. This is generally true. But it does not negate our use of Frankfurt with regard to Seneca. Frankfurt's description simply represents a subset of Watson's; in some situations, people do ask themselves which of their desires they want to be effective in action, and this necessitates stepping up to the second-order level. Because of the particular configuration of Senecan concerns, because of the involvement of ethical choices and ancient moralizing about the control of the appetites, and because of the set-up of Stoicism as involving self-control in such cases, Seneca's case does involve first- and second-order decisions.

13. Bakhtin (1984, 59) comments of humanity in general that "a man never coincides with himself. One cannot apply to him the formula of identity A = A. . . . The genuine life of the personality takes place at the point of non-coincidence between man and himself. . . . The genuine life of the personality is made available only through a *dialogic* penetration of that personality, during which it freely and reciprocally reveals itself. "

14. Epictetus is like Seneca in that for both, a chief concern is with desires and aversions; see Epict., *Disc.* 3.2.1, 2.2.1–7.

"But how could a rich man bear falling into poverty?"

"If you practice beforehand [*multo ante meditatus*], even poverty is pleasant."

The rich man who runs the risk of poverty smacks of Seneca himself, of course, as does the strain of consistency for a man in his position. Here we have the moral voice of the Stoic in dialogue with a Roman senator, or the Stoic Seneca with his less philosophical self. The Stoic shows his interlocutor that his judgments about what to desire and what to fear are wrong; that he needs to form himself according to a new set of desires. In this simple dialogic structure, the second-order voice is identical with that of a wise interlocutor or "second self" that we can trace, if we wish, to an internalization of God, or nature, or Zeno, Chrysippus, and "tota cohors Stoicorum" (*Ep.* 22.11).

In other examples of self-dialogue, both interlocutors are clearly alternating first-person voices of the meditating self:

"I will become a poor man."

"I'll have lots of company!"

"I'll be exiled."

"I'll pretend I was born wherever I'm sent."

"I'll be thrown in chains."

"So what? Are you free of chains now? . . ."

"I will die."

"You mean, 'I will *cease* to be able to get sick, to be bound, to die.'"

(*Ep.* 24.17)

Who are the speakers here? Both, of course, belong to the *proficiens*, or to Seneca. But inasmuch as it is his goal to believe the judgments of the internalized sage, the Senecan procedure for self-correction and self-knowledge depends on a form of self-address aimed at the final conversion of the agent to unity with the (here, always philosophically preferable) second-order voice, the one that tells him what to desire.[15] As Seneca puts it: "Whenever you want to

---

15. Inwood (2000, 51–52) notes that while Seneca is not unique in his attention to "the second-order quality of our mental lives," he stands out "for the frequency and explicitness of his interest." Occasional examples of this kind of thinking crop up in Cicero, here too couched in terms of a viewer: Cic., *Tusc.* 2.47–49, showing pain is base and disgraceful. So, says Cicero, "it remains for you to rule over yourself." This is accomplished in part via the *custodia* of friends and relatives.

know what one should flee and what one should pursue, look to the supreme Good, the goal of your whole life. For whatever we do ought to be consistent with this" (*Ep.* 71.2). Here and elsewhere, the first-order desire with which the second-order self chooses to identify itself is always the ethically superior one from a Stoic point of view because the second-order voice represents an ethical framework that is already in place and that already has his intellectual acceptance. *Akrasia* rarely rears its head in the letters, though it may have presented a problem in real life.[16]

Along this pathway, the Stoic had to develop skill in accepting or rejecting the appearances of things (*phantasiai*), which could lead the untrained mind to make incorrect evaluations of aspects of the world around him.[17] As Epictetus put it, "People are not made anxious by things, but by their judgments about things. Death, for example, is nothing fearsome (since it would have seemed so to Socrates too) but it is our opinion that death is fearsome that is the fearsome thing" (*Ench.* 5.1). The point is well made by Reydams-Schils (1998, 42–43): "If we learn to give our assent cautiously, to juxtapose contrasting representations, to examine our behavior in terms of consistency and ultimate happiness as opposed to immediate gratification, if we train ourselves by anticipating what we might consider upsetting and teach ourselves to accept calmly the inevitable; if we do all this, then, according to Epictetus we 'make correct use of our representations.'" Epictetus identifies the development of this skill as one of the three areas of *askesis*: the control of desire and aversion so as to avoid any form of passionate attachments; attention to duty, social obligations, and religious and familial ties; and the testing of mental judgments in assenting to sense-impressions (Epict., *Disc.* 3.2.1–6).[18] Another discourse on moral intention and the practice of virtue introduces the metaphor of "the wand of Hermes" to describe the importance of correct judgments on impressions (*phantasiae*): "Bring whatever you want and I will render it a good. Bring disease, bring death, bring poverty, bring slander, a death-penalty case—via

---

16. Generally defined, an action is akratic if the agent does A rather than B at a certain point in time while judging, at that same point in time, that it is better to do B, and while being perfectly free to either do or refrain from doing either action.

17. On Stoic *phantasia*, see especially Frede 1986; Inwood 1985, 42–101; Long 1991; and Sandbach 1971.

18. See Francis 1995, 17.

Hermes' magic wand, all these things will become benefits. 'What will you make death into?' What else but a means of glory for you, or the way to show by your own actions what kind of man follows the will of nature. . . . Everything you give me, I will transform into something blessed, happy, holy, enviable" (Epict., *Disc.* 3.20.12–15). In other words, the "wand of Hermes" exercise is another way of not being dominated by one's impressions.[19] Of course, one could only change *oneself* in this regard, not the world; both for Seneca and Epictetus, it was therefore crucial to focus on the distinction between what does and does not depend on us.[20]

Paradoxically, only the dialogic self, or the self that addresses and exhorts itself, can be identified as that of a *proficiens*.[21] The man who finally attains congruence between his commanding self (pick this desire! pick that judgment!) and the self that has conflicting first-order desires will finally have real *libertas*, freedom from unwanted desires and fears, freedom from the shifts of mind that characterize a man who knows himself.[22] No dialogue would be necessary anymore, and the split self that is so necessary to the *proficiens* can disappear.

The triumph of the second-order voice that would characterize a good Stoic thus represents a full integration or "fulfillment" of the self in some of Seneca's thought, which explains some of the peculiarities in his vocabulary in his correspondence with Lucilius. Most important, it clarifies the language of *recognition* that Seneca uses to address his interlocutor as the latter becomes more and more sagelike: "Agnosco Lucilium meum," as Seneca writes in *Ep.* 31.1: "I recognize my Lucilius! He is beginning to show the self of which he gave promise. Follow that impulse of the soul via which you were heading to everything that is best, with popular ideas of what is good trodden underfoot!" That is, Lucilius, on the way to becoming the (Stoic) Lucilius, is now readily recognizable as who he really is under all those false fears and false beliefs. We will return to this idea when we take up the *Medea*.

---

19. On the spiritual exercises of Stoic philosophy in general, see Hadot 1995, 81–125.

20. For Epictetus' views here, see especially Long 2002, chap. 6.

21. As Barton (2002, 223) remarks, "If a Roman had a sense of 'integrity' it was one built, paradoxically, on the dividing of the self."

22. Although I speak here and elsewhere of a "split self," it is important to recognize that the Stoics did not divide the soul into reasons and emotions, since for them even the emotions constituted judgments of a sort.

RETHINKING REFLEXIVITY

The features of the Senecan self so far examined may point to the dialogic nature of that self, but this alone does not necessarily serve a different model of self-understanding than the objective-participant one described by Gill. Any claim that Seneca's procedures point to a more reflexive notion of selfhood—one in which reflexivity is per se an essential feature of self-understanding—will need further illustration, especially in providing an answer to such questions as how Seneca's dialogic model differs from the mirroring self of chapter 1, the Alcibiadic self that looks to self-reflection in godhead, the self that has internalized a shaming viewer, or a self that debates within itself between one of two community-sanctioned alternatives.

We should start by observing several important features that seem to be unusually stressed in Seneca. The first is the *voluntary* nature of an individual's decision to adopt the internalized voice that answers the deliberating subject. We examined briefly the idea that in a culture based on the evaluative gaze of a community of peers, an actual audience does not have to be present and judging the actions of each member of that culture: instead, there develops what Bernard Williams has called "the internalized other," a part of the self that has so thoroughly adopted the values of the community that it itself acts as an audience to the actions of the individual. In such cases, however, the internalized other is always an *unconscious* development that seems to the individual who harbors it simply another ethical possibility that can find grounding in the attitudes of one or another subset (or indeed the whole) of the community of which that individual is a part. Hector debating with himself outside the walls of Troy does not need to willfully *create* a *thumos* he can address; Socrates' *daimonion* is not a product of his decision to provide himself with an ethical interlocutor; Cicero's conscience can plague him against his will.[23]

Yet in Seneca, the internalized other is a conscious product of the will of the Stoic individual. One *must set up* a Cato or an Epicurus in one's mind and pretend he is watching. One is answerable to a figure one has selected and installed for oneself: "Cross over to better men: live with the Catos, with Laelius, with Tubero. Or, if you like living with Greeks too, associate with Socrates and with Zeno: the one will teach you to die if it should be necessary; the other to die

---

23. On the Socratic heritage of Seneca's views, see, in general, Williams 1985, chap. 1.

before it should be necessary. Live with Chrysippus, with Posidonius: they will pass on to you things the knowledge of things earthly and divine; they will order you to keep busy and not to speak so elegantly and to pontificate for the pleasure of your audience, but to harden your soul and rise up against threats" (*Ep.* 104.21–22). One's progress toward normative Stoic virtue depends on the assumption of a set of guiding values that Seneca himself claims are no longer to be found within the community, but only in the writings of philosophers and the conduct of long dead exemplars—men whom one must select as one's dialogic partners or watching judges. Thus, the case is no longer that this internalized other operates automatically as an aspect of community-regulated ethics; rather, we are to self-consciously set it up as a second I that regulates our behavior from within. Even in the famous example from *De ira*, the angry man has to have changed *before* he comes to the mirror—simply seeing how he appears to the others around him is not enough. Can we still speak in terms of community-sanctioned ethics, when the community has shrunk to a number of idealized (dead) watchers, and when even this tiny community is absent barring an act of will?

Another innovation is Seneca's alternating identification of the philosopher (or his *hegemonikon*) now with one internal voice, now with the other. For example, Leontius allies himself not with his eyes and "their" first-order desire, but with the agent that struggles against them; he may damn the desire of his eyes, but there is no risk that he will identify himself with this dialogic partner, any more than Odysseus identifies himself with his *kardia*. Both these figures have the upper hand in addressing the desire of the part-that-is-not-they; or, as Aristotle puts it in *Ethics* 9.4, what we are most is the entity doing the watching (of the errant part). Seneca's writing, in contrast, generates a model of selfhood that, in splitting the I into (potentially errant) agent and (morally superior) witness, lets the identification of the self be as much with the *errant* as with the ethically sanctioned of the two selves—as it were, with the Odyssean heart rather than with his ego. For example, in the well-known letter in which an aging Seneca visits his family farm and feels rage at its shriveled trees and shriveled bailiff, he shows us his own folly at struggling against the passage of time before launching into the voice of the sage speaking to others who share his fears: "You say 'It's annoying to have death before one's eyes'? But . . . death should kept before one's eyes as much by the elderly as by the young" (*Ep.* 12.6). Or, in the opposite case, it is the voice of wisdom that speaks in the role of subject, as when it scolds: "Do you see those who praise your eloquence, who follow your wealth, who curry favor, who extol your power? All of them are your enemies, or—the same thing—can be" (*Vit. Beat.* 2.4). That is, in cases where I/you pronouns are used rather than I/I, the self with which the speaker identifies can be the errant or the adviser self. In terms of their pronominal identification, the roles of the internalized voices are fluid and not fixed, and the I can also be the you.

Another significant difference from the Greek literary model emerges here. Unlike Hector or Odysseus, and despite the flexibility in the identity of the speaking I, there is missing here any sense of a genuine *deliberation* as to which option might be the better. Because of the explicit outlines of Stoic teaching, there is no either/or: there is simply the morally superior watcher and the *proficiens* at whom the barrage of instruction and rebuke is aimed. So when the I (or in other cases, the you) says: "Whenever you want to know what one should flee and what one should pursue, look to the supreme Good, the goal of your whole life. For whatever we do ought to be consistent with this" (*Ep.* 71.2), there is no debate: the second-order I advises the first-order you, and the you would not dream of refusing.[24] And when the dialogue actually takes the form of a real debate or conversation, this imbalance does not disappear: the feeble objections of the errant self ("But I'm scared!") are contemptuously squashed by the all-knowing Stoically correct interlocutor, as we saw in *Ep.* 24.17—*exile, schmexile!*

Finally, the level of *linguistic* reflexivity in Seneca represents an innovation in literary Latin. Consider the following self-exhortations, culled from the many in the letters and essays, and addressed now by Seneca to Seneca, now by Seneca to Lucilius (but in a medium that makes it clear that the use of these statements can be as directions to the self by the internalized watcher):

Linger a while with yourself (*Ep.* 2.1).
Liberate yourself for yourself (*Ep.* 1.1).
Dare to entrust you to yourself (*Ep.* 10.2).
You flee from yourself, but you carry yourself with you (*Ep.* 28.2).

---

24. On Senecan self-command, see Star 2003. Edwards (1997a, 30) remarks of the constant use of the terminology of witnessing that "the self divides in order to play a variety of roles simultaneously—one part of the self scrutinizes the other—though with no sense of the rigid hierarchy of parts of the soul that one finds particularly in Plato." Yet there is a hierarchy, though not, evidently, a Platonic one.

Be worthy of yourself, be equal to yourself (*Ep.* 20.2).

Catch yourself (*Tranq.* 1.2).

You run from yourself, who are also your companion (*Ep.* 104.20).

You outstripped others—better still, you outstripped yourself (*Ep.* 15.10).

You will be perfect when you have yourself (*Ep.* 124.24).[25]

This pronominal usage is deliberately startling, catachrestic even. It is one thing to say, "Be still, my heart;" another to say, "Dare to entrust you to yourself." As Cancik (1998, 343) points out, while a few of these formulas were already extant in Latin, in Seneca the reflexive pattern reaches its peak.[26] This claim is supported by Traina (1974), who remarks that most of Seneca's usage is innovative; a few examples of this reflexivity can be found in earlier Latin literature, but nowhere to the extent found in Seneca.[27]

What are we to make of the fact that Seneca lets the same pronouns jostle side by side in a way that would surely have been striking to his readers, however much they may have been accustomed to Odysseus addressing his *thumos* or his *kardia*, or even to Socrates being bullied about by his nay-saying *daimonion*?[28] The effect of this, I think, and of several of the other features I have identified, is to highlight the potential identification of both dialoguing parts with the I rather than that of one of them with any *actual*, that is, worldly or extant other (God, one's parents, the laws, public opinion, a living Stoic tutor, a fellow philosopher). At the same time, one of those dialoguing parts is represented as already fully accomplished in knowing the (Stoic) truth about the

----

25. For a full list of these usages, see Traina 1974, 14–19, 52–65. Armisen-Marchetti (1989, 252–60) treats Senecan passages on "la pensée et le regard intérieur"; other examples are collected in Cancik 1998 and Traina 1974. The reflexive occurs in the accusative and in the dative; e.g., "relinqui sibi" (*Mar.* 24.5; *Ep.* 109.6). Does the language of doubling in the case of a man who wants to escape himself imply that even the *pre*-proficient self is split? I should point out that anyone who can already formulate his problem in these terms is, for Seneca, already a *proficiens*.

26. Cancik (1998), however, sees it as a sign of "the increasing interiorization of morals." See also Grimal (1992) on Seneca's interior-oriented vocabulary.

27. Cf. Lucr., 3.1068: "hoc se quisque modo simper fugit"; Hor., *Carm.* 2.16.19; Hor., *Ep.* 1.4.13. Cf. also Epict., *Disc.* 3.13.6: αὐτὸν ἑαυτῷ συνεῖναι; and several further examples in Traina 1974, 17–19.

28. In *Ben.* 5.7 Seneca denies that one can bestow a benefit upon oneself, and argues that we should not be misled by linguistic expressions such as "I am angry at myself" or "I am conversing with myself," for "there are many occasions on which habit divides us" (*Ben.* 5.7.6). But the expressions above are not reducible to mere linguistic habit, and their use of reflexivity is not normative but catachrestic.

world. Ethical responsibility thus lies squarely within the *self*. These elements do not add up to a Cartesian privileging of the mind's reflexive relationship to itself (*cogito me cogitare*) as the only infallible source of what *is* (because Stoic theory takes much of the place of that authority). Still, they take a step in this direction by letting the divided self's dialogue with *itself* stand in for the ethical benefits of an objective moral order, in a conversation where the I voice can represent that order or the person who struggles against it—though it is always internal. We can justly borrow Charles Taylor's language describing the *modern* subject: "a new localization, whereby we place 'within' the subject what was previously seen as existing, as it were, between knower/agent and world, linking them and making them inseparable" (1989, 188).[29]

Skeptics may protest: one of the internal voices, after all, represents the objective voice of Stoic philosophy. And given that Seneca, like Epictetus, argues for the presence of divinity within the soul, this direct pipeline to God suggests that we cannot, after all, claim a detachment from what Taylor calls "world" in the quotation above, especially since in Stoic theory world and God are both manifestations of rational *logos*. Seneca has simply interiorized the fundamental, objective, precepts of Stoicism and characterized them as a dialogic partner. The truth is therefore still ontic, and is not an idea of the mind. But there are several replies to be made. We have to acknowledge that the slipperiness of the terminology of I and you, as well as the self-contained nature of the dialoguing self in the *meditatio*, at least attenuates the sense that an objective world order exists outside the self. Theory aside, Stoic *logos* is an ephemeral form of the outside world. It is not insignificant that in Senecan drama, nature or *logos* tends to reflect the turmoil of the protagonists' souls rather than vice versa. In addition, the apparently voluntary nature of the adoption of the Stoic perspective highlights personal volition in the search for the ethical self. Although the Stoics believed that man naturally inclines toward the good, the Platonic notion that knowledge leads to virtue seems underplayed in Seneca's writing; knowledge leads to virtue only if you desire it to do so (Hostius is fully

---

29. To clarify Seneca's contribution to the development of the idea of the will, Inwood (2001, 59–60) brings into play many of the features I have noted in Seneca, such as his "interest in second-orderness in the form of talk about self-shaping and self-knowledge; the language of self-command; the focus on self-control, especially in the face of natural human proclivities to precipitate and passionate response; and the singling out of a moment of causally efficacious judgment or decision in the process of reacting to provocative stimuli."

aware of his philosophical misuse of the mirror). And if this is the case, a weakness appears in the Stoic claim for a mirroring cognitive link between the *logos* of the soul and that of the *cosmos*: one has to *choose* to live the life of wisdom.[30]

In addition, the heightened attention to reflexivity per se in Seneca's writing and his reflexive form of self-observation chimes closely with the philosophical division between self as judge and self, or disengaged self, which is one aspect of Cartesian reflexivity.[31] As Charles Taylor (1989, 159, 161–62) writes of the "disengaged" Cartesian self, "What this calls for is the ability to take an instrumental stance to one's given properties, desires, inclinations, tendencies, habits of thought and feeling, so that they can be *worked* on, doing away with some and strengthening others. . . . It involves taking a stance to ourselves which takes us out of our normal way of experiencing the world and ourselves." Taylor remarks of the focus on self-mastery in Descartes that it is "a moral view which is quite reminiscent of ancient Stoicism."[32] Descartes, unlike the Stoics, no longer thinks in terms of the cosmos as the embodiment of meaningful order. But he still places his reliance in a veracious God as the source of truth, a similarity that permits the comparison of the two models of reflexivity.

Consequently, I suggest that we might well approach Seneca's thought in terms of a shift toward the valorization of reflexivity that still dovetails with the traditional Stoic view on the cosmos, but that also suggests a privileged role for human consciousness contemplating itself for the access of the good. As Maria Antonaccio (1998, 84–85) has characterized such a model (she is speaking here of the relevance of Taylor's views for *modern* forms of *askesis*), "the reflexive model holds that consciousness or subjectivity is the inescapable *medium* for our access to moral sources, not that consciousness is

---

30. As pointed out by Antonaccio (1998, 76), although she makes the point as a criticism of the arguments in Hadot (1995, 283). Hadot argues, as I do, that "it is one's choice of life which precedes metaphysical theories. . . . We can make our choice of life, whether or not we justify it by improved or entirely new arguments."

31. See Cohen (1994, 10) and Danziger (1997) on this trend, including William James's "social self," C. H. Cooley's "looking glass self," and G. H. Mead's "taking the role of the other." The nicest parallels for a Senecan observation of self-by-self actually occur in Montaigne, where, as Jay (1993, 71n158) remarks, "The model is closer to the observation of an object by a subject than a purely specular subject looking at itself."

32. However, in Descartes the point is made in terms of the will. Cf. his letter to Queen Christina of Sweden, 20 November 1647.

identifiable with the source and content of the moral good. The claim of this model is that by turning inward, we discover not only our own powers but accede to a condition of thought that surpasses subjectivism." Seneca, too, claims to surpass subjectivism, of course (or rather, he never considers it): there is no suggestion of the development of an "original" self, and the *telos* of self-reflection is already set. But the self he describes can no longer be characterized, in Gill's terminology, as "objective-participant." It most resembles a category Gill does not discover in the ancient world, and that is "objective-individualist": a comparatively isolated self not predominantly embedded in the values of its community but nonetheless believing that its own values are objectively true.[33]

I have not said much here about the Stoic philosopher Epictetus, Seneca's near contemporary, whose *Discourses* parallel Seneca's concerns in many regards, especially the material on *askesis*, the attention to the ethical force of dialogue, the *praemeditatio malorum*, and the focus on second-order judgment. Here, too, arguments have been made for a shift in the nature of the representation of the self; most notably, A. A. Long has argued that Epictetus' treatment of *prohairesis*, ethical choice or volition, "is best interpreted ... as a new focus on consciousness, on the individuality of the perceiving subject, as the fundamental feature of the mental" (1996, 266). In emphasizing that our choices and judgments are up to us (ἐφ' ἡμῖν), and that our ability to form them cannot be constrained (for example, *Disc.* 1.17.21–28), Epictetus privileges our autonomy and our freedom as subjects, as well as our position at the center of impressions and judgments. As Long writes, "If my representations are up to me to interpret, accept or reject, there must be a 'me' to which they appear and an 'I' which reacts to them—a subject that is identifiable precisely

---

33. Of course, not all forms of senatorial control had disappeared; as Paul Allen Miller (1998, 177) points out, following Foucault, "What one sees in the early imperial period ... is not a complete dissolution of the isomorphic structures of power over the self, the members of one's household, and other members of the community ..., but a problematization of those relations as they are inserted into a new, more complex set of determinations in which local power remains a viable option but always within limits imposed by a larger structure that is itself discontinuous with the power relations of daily life." Roller (2001a) is, I think, completely correct to stress the connection between the adoption of Stoicism among some members of the elite and such sociopolitical factors as senatorial decline in military prestige, the corrupted nature of community judgment, and the absolute power of the emperor. Edwards (1997a, 33–38) likewise suggests that the political climate might be responsible for the fragmented and conflict-ridden Senecan self she sees behind the letters.

by the representations that it receives and by what it does with them" (1996, 276).[34] To evaluate Long's claim is beyond my abilities, but it is worth noting several differences in Epictetus' material as well. For one, Seneca's peculiar emphasis on reflexivity is far less in evidence in Epictetus; as Gill has argued, "Epictetus' own practice . . . indicates no such priority of inner, reflexive states over interpersonal discourse. Epictetus seems to regard it as equally appropriate to examine his interlocutor's impressions through dialogue as to urge his interlocutor to do so for himself" (Gill [forthcoming]; and see, for example, *Disc.* 1.11, 2.19.29–34.) The presence of pedagogic dialogues within the *Discourses* points to Epictetus' own rendition of internalized debates, but he is less interested in recommending isolatory tactics, such as the adoption of a nonliving judge and viewer. In addition—perhaps because of the vast gulf that separated an ex-slave from a member of the Roman elite (and Nero's court)—Epictetus' writing seems much less pregnant with the tensions I have identified in Seneca's presentation of Stoicism and much less liable to the charge of complicity with imperial power. Epictetus has no equivalent to Seneca's Pastor and none of the tension of Seneca's high-wire act. In the place of the man who toasts his tormentor to save his son's life, we are presented with individuals who, in Epictetus' formulation, value themselves *either* as ordinary cloth (and are willing to kowtow as necessary) *or* as the purple that sets off the senator's garment (and who scorn the tyrant's dictates accordingly; *Disc.* 1.2.17–18). Each man knows his own price, and knows what is appropriate to his proper character; there are cowards and there are brave men, but complicity and Stoic forbearance are not confused with each other. It is only in Seneca's writing that endurance (*patientia*) and victimhood (*patientia*) can meld into the same state.

Let me turn now to another theorist of ancient subjectivity, Michel Foucault. Foucault's writing in *The Care of the Self* and a series of related articles also posits a development of "technologies of the self" in the Stoic teaching of the first centuries CE. These, he claims, "permit individuals to effect by their own means or with the help of others a certain number of operations on their own bodies and souls, thoughts, conduct, and way of being, so as to transform themselves in order to attain a certain state of happiness, purity, wisdom,

---

34. On *prohairesis*, see also Long 2002, chap. 8. For a similar perspective to Long's, see Kahn 1988, 253. For a critique of this view, see Gill (forthcoming); and Engberg-Pedersen 1990.

perfection, or immortality."[35] For Foucault, this involves a series of practices—the *askesis*, physical exercises, reading, discussion, the practice of abstinence—that occupy not only the Stoic but also the Epicurean schools and "neo-Pythagorean circles" at Rome, and that has its roots in early Greek philosophical and medical sources.[36] Nonetheless, the main focus of his attention here is the "crisis of subjectivation" (1986, 95) in the early imperial period, which he partially attributes, as I have done here, to the restriction of elite action and responsibility in the public sphere.[37]

This turn toward the subject's work on himself (or less often, herself) was itself a surprising development in Foucault's late writing, given his earlier focus on the constitutive role of power in the formation of the subject, which appeared more or less at the mercy of the discursive or social mechanisms through which it was historically constituted. In two essays dating to 1982, however ("The Subject and Power" and "Technologies of the Self") he signaled the inclusion of "subjectification," or the process through which a human being "turns him- or herself into a subject," with other modes of objectification transforming human beings into subjects (1983, 208), so that now the subject was seen as having the ability to "subjectify" himself. This phraseology remains confusing, especially in elucidating the link between self-mastery and the constitution of the self as a a subject. Nonetheless, Foucault is obviously right to point to the Stoic writing of the first centuries CE as reflecting a new intensity "of the relations to self, that is, the forms in which one is called upon to take oneself as an object of knowledge and a field of action" (1986, 42).

---

35. Foucault 1988, 18. The two volumes, *The Use of Pleasure* and *The Care of the Self*, together span Greco-Roman antiquity, but I focus here on the claims of the second, especially in "The Cultivation of the Self" (39–68).

36. We should not assume complete continuity from the Pythagorean or Epicurean precursors of the *meditatio*. Roman Stoic *meditatio* is more focused on the consideration of evils and preparation for any turn of fortune (the *praemeditatio malorum*), not unlike Socrates' emphasis, in the *Phaedo*, on philosophy as a preparation for death. Epicurean *meditatio*, in contrast, seems to have devoted more attention to what is pleasant (cf. Cic., *Fin.* 1.17.55, 1.19.62; *Tusc.* 15.32–33). As Hadot (1995, 88) sums up: "The spiritual exercise of trying to live in the present moment is very different for Stoics and Epicureans. For the former, it means mental tension and constant wakefulness of the moral conscience; for the latter, it is . . . an invitation to relaxation and security."

37. It is beyond the scope of this chapter to discuss the developments that Foucault then discerns in the spheres of martial life, boy-love, and the body. For a cogent critique, see Cohen and Saller 1994.

I am sympathetic to Foucault's arguments, which provided the catalyst for a whole field of discourse, and certainly I share his interest in the connection between ethics and erotics. However, not all of his argument can be, or has been, readily accepted. To begin with, there are difficulties with his suggestion that this project of working on the self was essentially an aesthetic act of self-creation.[38] In his 1983 interview with Paul Rabinow and Herbert Dreyfus, entitled "On the Genealogy of Ethics: An Overview of Work in Progress," Foucault explicitly claims that the goal of Stoic *askesis* "was an esthetic one. . . . It was a personal choice for a small elite. The reason for making this choice was the will to live a beautiful life, and to leave to others memories of a beautiful existence" (1984, 341). Yet the aesthetic dimension of Stoic self-cultivation has little support in the sources, even if on a few occasions Seneca uses the language of molding or shaping the self into its more sagelike manifestation.[39] On the contrary, it seems clear that while allowances could be made for different personal strengths and aptitudes in the individual seeking to transform himself via a regimen of *meditatio*, the goal of this practice remained essentially the same for everyone who embarked on it: to align one's belief structures with the tenets of Stoicism so as bring to full fruition one's inherent capacity for rational agency.[40] As Gill (1994, 4635–36) puts it, "The kind of 'self-realization' urged by Seneca is that in which the *proficiens* goes as far as possible towards expressing the ethical objectives and correlated state of mind of the *sapiens*." And Hadot writes (1995, 206–7), "The description M. Foucault gives of what I had termed 'spiritual exercises,' and which he prefers to call 'techniques of the self,' is precisely focused far too much on the 'self,' or at least on a specific

---

38. Where Foucault speaks of aesthetics, other historians of the self have introduced "sincerity" or "authenticity" as the critical development of the modern self. As Gill (1994, 4631) points out in a brief discussion of Trilling's claim that "sincerity" is a concept of the late sixteenth and early seventeenth century, the self that such historians point to is invariably one that "involves commitment to values which run deeper than—and which therefore come into conflict with—the ethical values of normal social engagement." See also Rudd 1976, 145–81.

39. The verb used is *formare*, and cf. the use of *se fingere* in *Ep.* 18.12 and 31.11. In several places he calls the wise man an *artifex* (e.g., *Ep.* 85.41, 95.7) or describes him as a sculptor of his own self or another's, while the soul is described as material in *Ep.* 52.4. For similar examples, see Armisen-Marchetti 1989, 80.

40. A point well made by Beiner 1995; Hadot 1992; and Hadot 1995, 206–13. Beiner notes that for Foucault, the "Californian cult of the self" is not as radical as that of the Stoics, because the former is a search for the true self, while the latter is an untrammeled self-creation!

conception of the self."[41] The idea, as it were, of a "free-range" subjectivity whose self-fashioning component is pleasurable in nature and aesthetic in goal elides the normative background supplied by Stoic theory.

In addition, Foucault's emphasis on the institutional context of *meditatio*, which constituted "a true social practice" (1986, 51), seems overstressed in the case of Seneca, whose position at the imperial court made alignment with Stoic senatorial opposition to Nero somewhat difficult.[42] Even if Seneca's moral prescriptions borrow something from normative Roman ethics (and some overlap is inevitable, such as the focus on *continentia* or the shared use of figures such as Laelius and Scipio), the philosopher himself is explicit about the corruption around him. Even if he praises Cato in the same way as many eminent Romans had done since the republic, he could hardly do so in his addresses to Nero; and even if his stress on the visual origin of ethical behavior is common to Greco-Roman culture at large, the adoption of an imaginary other as constant companion cannot be matched in earlier literature. Seneca's reflective procedures are more or less alienated from any immediate group. Returning to Gill's terminology, we might say that the "objectivity" is there—supplied by the tenets of Stoic philosophy—but the "participant" aspect of the individual in his community is etiolated.[43]

The general trajectory of *The Care of the Self*, too, describes a very different arc from the one of this book. Where I have stressed the de-ethicalization of boy-love in the Roman world, Foucault goes further to argue that this shift in emphasis, along with the new technologies of the self, strengthened the

---

41. Cf. also Antonaccio 1998, 78–81; Black 1998, 52; Gill (forthcoming); and Nussbaum 1994, 5–6. As Gill comments, "To rephrase this criticism, Foucault's account of the care of the self in Hellenistic-Roman philosophy *seems*, at least, to reflect a 'subjective-individualist' approach to personality. This is so even though Foucault himself is far from endorsing the ideas of the post-Cartesian and post-Kantian tradition from which this approach typically derives." For evaluations of Foucault's treatment of classical antiquity, see, e.g., Cohen and Saller 1994; Cohen 1991, 171–202; Detel 1998; Halperin 1990b and 1994; Goldhill 1995; the essays in Larmour, Miller, and Platter 1998.

42. Note, however, that Foucault remarks in a later essay that the "exposé of one's soul which one makes to someone, who may be a [living] friend, an adviser, a guide" was more developed in Epicurean and medical circles than in Stoic ones (1993, 208).

43. The Senecan emphasis on the comparative isolation of the Stoic philosopher is, interestingly enough, taken up in the description of Socrates himself in Petron., *Sat.* 140.14, as a shunner of the crowd—an odd characterization of a man who actively sought to engage with others.

valorization of the marital bond in early imperial Rome *in general*, leading to "the existence of a 'heterosexual' relation marked by a male-female polarity, the insistence on an abstention that is modeled much more on virginal integrity than on the political and virile domination of desires; and finally, the fulfillment and reward of this purity in a union that has the form and value of a spiritual marriage" (1986, 228). This wide-ranging shift in sexual practices led, in his view, to "a great apprehension concerning the sexual pleasures, more attention given to the relation that one might have with them" (1986, 39). Here, Foucault's selection of classicizing Greek texts of the early imperial period that discuss the love of boys and contrast homoerotic love with heterosexual marriage (Plutarch and Pseudo-Lucian) allows him to stretch out a genealogy of sexuality that is, in its Roman manifestation, decidedly misleading, and his broad generalizations across Greco-Roman society fail to take into account the limited range of these practices. The net effect is a flattening of distinctions across genres, cultures, hierarchies, and political regimes; there is no mention, for example, of *mockery* of those with philosophical pretensions, despite Foucault's own interest in the intersection of the ethical and the erotic. Here is where this book takes its greatest departure from *The Care of the Self*: its sexual trajectory stalls at the transition to Rome in chapters 2 and 3, and abandons both pederasty and erotic sublimation at the gates of the city.[44]

MEDEA'S *MEDITATIO*

So far our attention has been directed almost entirely at Seneca's philosophy rather than his drama. And yet, the most strident representations of the subject in self-dialogue and the most striking display of the self exhorting itself to a path of action take place on the Senecan stage, and not in his letters and essays. Medea deliberating on killing her children; Phaedra struggling with her

---

44. Long (2001, 33–34) points out Foucault's excessive assimilation of Stoic practices with early Christian attitudes. Cohen and Saller (1994) offer a corrective to Foucault's stress on the new valorization of marriage in early imperial Rome. Beiner (1995, 359) criticizes Foucault's attention to pleasure as the outcome of Stoic self-control, though he should also note the care Foucault takes to separate *gaudium* and *voluptas* (in Foucault 1986, 66–67). Goldhill (1995, 44–45, 92–94, 91–102, 110–11) notes that Foucault ignores the ridicule, in genres other than the ones he privileges, of philosophical pretensions to virtue.

desire for Hippolytus; Thyestes seduced away from contentment with exile and poverty; Atreus, dramatist in his own right, setting the stage for his brother's unholy supper: these characters loom large against the etiolated philosophers of the prose, who practice their second-order judgments and strive to align themselves with a cosmos not much in local evidence.

The question of just what to do with these figures, and indeed with Seneca's drama in general, is a problem with a long pedigree. Once taken as a poor echo of their classical Greek precedents, his plays, whether or not they were ever performed, have more recently generated various interpretations of their meaning and intent. Political readings have found in them an avenue for Seneca to voice his discontent with the successive rules of Caligula, Claudius, and Nero; on this reading, he puts on stage a series of tyrants terrorizing their advisers, their siblings, and their subjects alike. Others read them as illustrations of Seneca's Stoicism, vividly staging what happens to men and women who have no self-control and who cling to power and wealth instead of understanding that this is a mark of philosophical slavery. Still others have suggested that they bear little relationship to Seneca's other writing, but instead mainly play with a literary tradition whose interest lies in its intertextuality.[45] These angles, productive though they all are, are limited in their engagement with the topic of Senecan selfhood, and it is this issue in particular that I take up here in an interpretation of a dramatic figure we might call the paradigm of the self-in-progress, and one of the most recognizable mythological figures of classical antiquity—Medea.

Let us start precisely with the question of recognition. At the very end of Seneca's drama, as Medea flies off in triumph on her serpent-yoked chariot and the play nears its horrific close, she shouts down to the earthbound Jason standing among the corpses of their children: "Raise your swollen eyes up here, Jason,

---

45. On the idea that tragedy could illustrate the meaning of a philosophical argument with particular intensity, and that Medea provides a negative exemplum for the audience to shy away from, see also Armisen-Marchetti 1989, 345–71; Egermann 1940; Knoche 1941; Pratt 1948 and 1983. Marti (1945 and 1947) suggests that the order of the plays is itself a demonstration of Stoic moral improvement; the *Medea*, which is an early play, shows the result of the defeat of reason by passion in the soul. Other scholars who argue that Senecan drama upholds the teachings of Senecan Stoicism are Henry and Henry 1985; and Rosenmeyer 1989. For Dingel (1974, 94–100) the tragedies serve as "Die Negation der Philosophie," but not as a commentary on it. On metatheatricality in Seneca, see especially Schiesaro 2003, which is very good on the *Thyestes*, as well as Fitch and McElduff 2002.

you ingrate: do you recognize your wife?" (lumina huc tumida alleva, ingrate Iason. / coniugem agnoscis tuam? [*Med.* 1020–21]).[46] Jason ignores the question; his only response is to bid her attest that her heaven-borne path proves that the gods do not exist, a conclusion that he finds indubitable after seeing a mother slaughter her own sons. But the question of recognition is not to be brushed aside. Whatever *Jason* may think has become of his wife, Medea herself feels she is finally recognizable as Medea.[47] If she was once a loyal wife, a good mother to her boys, and a potential member of Creon's Corinthian community—in hindsight, it was all an aberration. *This* is Medea: the madwoman with the bloody hands, the granddaughter of the Sun, the epitome of the most drastic form of vengeance. And while Jason may stare in horror, we in the audience nod in recognition: yes, this is the Medea we know; this is how the story goes.

But she has been becoming Medea ever since the first lines of the play. Faced with Jason's betrayal, she has already been planning her revenge in a way that repeatedly evokes the existence of her namesake in myth and literature. Her will to triumph permeates her conversation with her quaking *nutrix* (*Med.* 164–71):

NURSE: Return to Colchis; you cannot trust your spouse,
 And there is nothing left of all your wealth.
MEDEA: Medea is left, and in her you see land and sea
 And the sword, and fire, and the gods, and thunderbolts.
NURSE: The king must be feared
MEDEA: My father had been king
NURSE: Don't you fear his weapons?
MEDEA: Not even if they sprang from the earth.
NURSE: You will die.
MEDEA: I want to.
NURSE: Flee!

---

46. Nussbaum (1994, 443) points out the Platonic genealogy of this chariot. In using it, she suggests, Seneca reveals to us "the true nature of the erotic: the human agent is drawn along toward heat and fire by two scaly serpents, whose sinuous and ignoble movements mimic the movements of the two lovers' bodies in the grip of passion." Here again, perhaps, we see the repudiation of the erotic component of philosophy by a Roman philosopher. In a footnote to this passage, she reminds us how well known Plato's *Phaedrus* was to Roman Stoics.

47. This is indicated immediately by the next line ("sic fugere *soleo* . . .")—but, as we shall see, it has been coming for a long time.

MEDEA: I'm sick of flight.
NURSE: Medea—
MEDEA:—will I become.[48]

The tinge of metatheatricality here has been picked up by successive generations of scholars ever since Wilamowitz, who famously commented that Seneca's Medea had obviously read Euripides' play of the same name.[49] The third-person terminology Medea uses in this passage to announce her survival of the ruin around her ("Medea superest") and the repetition of the name "Medea" as the goal toward which she is striving suggest that the literary and legendary model of who "Medea" is stands before her eyes as well as ours. Medea names herself eight times in this play, in comparison to the single self-naming of Euripides' play.[50] Later, when she has murdered Creon and his daughter, she signals the end of the process of shaping herself to meet this "ideal" by her famous claim (and the last evocation of her name), "Now I am Medea: my nature has grown though evils" (910).[51] The announcement is premature; Medea will continue to struggle between opposing first-order desires until she has slaughtered both her children, but the metatheatrical implications are unavoidable. Christopher Gill (1987, 32) puts it well: "Medea . . . reinforces her resolve by self-allusion; at the same time, her words derive some of their impact from more or less overt allusions to other speeches of self-incitement earlier in this play or in earlier versions of Medea. . . . This process is clearest, and most potent, in the use of the

---

48. Nutrix: abiere Colchi, coniugis nulla est fides / nihilque superest opibus e tantis tibi. Medea: Medea superest, hic mare et terras vides / ferrumque et ignes et deos et fulmina. Nutrix: rex est timendus. Medea: rex meus fuerat pater. Nutrix: non metuis arma? Medea: sint licet terra edita. Nutrix: moriere. Medea: cupio. Nutrix: profuge. Medea: paenituit fugae. Nutrix: Medea— Medea: fiam.

49. Wilamowitz 1919, 3:162.

50. As Fitch and McElduff already point out (2002, 25). They continue: "Indeed, self-naming is often a way of defining who one *should* be, an index of the gap between one's present performance and one's ideal role."

51. Schiesaro (1997, 93, citing lines 52–53) suggests that "Medea seems to be aware of the essentially literary nature of her pursuit. Not only in the sense caught by Wilamowitz's dictum that she must have read Euripides' tragedy on herself, but also because she explicitly hopes for a future of *literary* recognition for her deeds: 'let your repudiation be told as equal to your wedding.'" See also Bäumer 1982, 147; Dupont 1995, 82–83; Henry and Walker 1967, 175–77. Fyfe 1983, 84: "Medea *triumphans* is, among other things, the fulfillment through language of Medea's own self-mythology." Rosenmeyer (1989, 48) and Schiesaro (2003, 14–16) address Senecan metatheatricality more generally.

personal name, especially in the line (910): 'Medea nunc sum; crevit ingenium malis.' "⁵² We might compare Atreus in Seneca's play *Thyestes*, who needs no prior versions of himself, but is similarly driven to match himself to a model: he has his family, whose precedent in the art of cooking children stands before him like a mockery of more traditional ancestral *imagines*. "Tantalus and Pelops— look to them," he exhorts himself, "my hands are summoned to match these models" (Tantalum et Pelopem—aspice; ad haec manus exempla poscuntur meae [*Thy.* 242–43]). The messenger, of course, will be less sanguine at such a sight, which is not a model for imitation in any normal universe: "haeret in vultu trucis / imago facti" (*Thy.* 636–37).⁵³

Medea's metatheatricality in particular has been the subject of much commentary, yet not all of its Stoic implications have been explored in earlier readings of the play. The mythological Medea may stand in her mind's eye as the model to which she must aspire, but both the presence of this model and the means by which the Senecan Medea manages to live up to it echo many of the themes and processes of Seneca's instructions on the self-observation and self-command of the *proficiens*. We might say that the very metatheatricality of her procedure makes possible the parallel between two kinds of identity: the "true nature" of a literary character as shown by the extant writings and mythology about that character, and the "true nature" of a philosophical character as that which is fulfilled once he (or she) becomes the fulfilled Stoic instantiation of him- or herself. Where the *proficiens* can look to the model of a Cato, or imagine what the sage would do in trying circumstances, Medea (and to some degree Seneca's other antiheroes, although here I concentrate on just one) seems to look to the history of her self and her family line. Seneca's manipulation of this parallel in the *Medea* raises the question of just what her self-transformation can be taken to mean.

---

52. Dupont (1995, 25) echoes this when she writes: "The hero must himself rediscover the *nefas* which his legend has always narrated. . . . The Roman spectacle interlaces itself with the Greek *fabula* and it is the tragic hero who is the master interlacer."

53. Other models won't do: "Tereus' home saw an unspeakable feast; I grant it is a huge crime—but it's already been done" (vidit infandas domus / Odrysia mensas; fateor immane est scelus / sed occupatum [*Thy.* 272–74]). The vision of Thyestes eating his children also stays before his eyes and offers a guiding *imago* to which to aspire ("tota iam ante oculos meos / imago caedis errat, ingesta orbitas / in ora patris" [*Thy.* 281–83]). Other Senecan antiheroes also look to exempla from their past for how they should behave; cf. *Herc. Fur.* 736, *Herc. Oet.* 554. Fitch and McElduff (2002) are good on this topic. See also Dupont 1995, 70, 100–101, 143.

To return to the play's conclusion: it is striking that at the dramatic dénoue-
ment of the *Medea* our (anti-)heroine feels that her actions are unfinished
without a horrified spectator to give them their full authenticity. Although
these accomplishments are acts of exemplary evil, rather than of exemplary
goodness, they are not carried out in seclusion. Medea deliberately postpones
the slaying of her second son until Jason is present: "This one thing was lacking: that man as spectator," she cries (deerat hoc unum mihi / spectator iste
[*Med.* 992–93]). As Florence Dupont (1995, 51) has described this final demand for her husband's attention, "Jason's miserable gaze is the mirror in
which she contemplates her triumph." The same is true of Atreus as the
Thyestes comes to a close over still more bodies of small children. Atreus wishes
he could retain the fleeing gods, so that they might see his handiwork—but he
compromises: "quod sat est, videat pater" (*Thy.* 895). The suffering gaze of both
fathers adds to the *frisson* of their children's murderers, of course, but the visual
quality of this climactic moment also renders two other facts evident. The first
is the simple truth that Medea, like Atreus, has no interest in concealing her
deeds: neither of the two cares about the negative judgment of their community or their peers. There is no sense that their actions might cause them shame
(unlike Gyges, who needed the cover of invisibility to carry out his antisocial
exploits). Neither of the two shows concern for any evaluation that is not self-
generated, and of course their final self-satisfaction *is* self-generated, for all
Medea's sarcastic self-address as she drags along one son's corpse to public
view: "Don't waste your virtue in obscurity—get approval for your deed from
the public!" (nunc hoc age, anime: non in occulto tibi est perdenda virtus;
approba populo manum [976–77]).[54]

The second outcome of the visual twist to the ending of both plays is that it
enables a crucial moment of recognition. But this is a far cry from the Aristotelian notion of *anagnorisis*: here, as in the *Poetics*, there is a change from
ignorance to knowledge, but the knowledge now consists in seeing through
new eyes someone whose identity you have known all along. "Do you recognize your sons at all?" Atreus asks Thyestes as the latter takes a look at his dinner leftovers (natos ecquid agnoscis tuos? [*Thy.* 1005]), but Thyestes is more
stunned by a different act of recognition, and replies: "I recognize my brother"

---

54. Why this statement should be taken as ironic will, I hope, be clear by the end of this
discussion.

(Agnosco fratrem [*Thy.* 1006]).[55] *This* is who Atreus gave promise of being all along. Having been recognized, Atreus can now, presumably, die content (*Thy.* 1096–99), providing a gruesome and paradoxical confirmation of the chorus's claim that death comes grievously to a man who, however prominent, "dies unknown to himself" (ignotus moritur sibi [*Thy.* 401–3]). The philosophical parallel to this act of recognition is the moment when Seneca recognizes the true (epistolary) Lucilius, who has been altered by his self-training: "Agnosco Lucilium meum" (*Ep.* 31.1). Medea's question to Jason, we can now see, engages the same set of issues. When she crows at 984, "Now I am a virgin again," she is looking back at her Colchian self, but she is also looking forward to the self she has talked herself into being. When she asks Jason if he recognizes his wife, we might think the expected answer is no—"My God, what has *happened* to you, Medea? You used to adore me, and the kids!"—but in fact the expected answer is yes.[56]

The result of the drama's attention to the question of recognition is that *personal* self-recognition and *literary* recognition necessarily coalesce here. For Medea to recognize herself as Medea is also for Medea to become recognizable as the Medea her Roman audience would know from a whole series of dramas by that name: not only Euripides' drama, but also Neophron's and Carcinus' tragedies by the same name, as well as Apollonius Rhodius' epic *Argonautica*; and closer to home, Ennius' Latin translation of Euripides' play, Varro of Atax's version of the *Argonautica* (which Seneca himself quotes at *Ep.* 56.6), *Heroides* 12 (probably not Ovidian), the account of Medea in book 7 of Ovid's *Metamorphoses*, and, probably most influential, his own now lost *Medea*.[57] Even Lucan had started to write a *Medea*. Tracing these influences is not the goal of this chapter, but I want to draw attention to a source that confirms Roman awareness of precisely the *literary* possibilities for *agnoscere*: according to the

---

55. In an interesting mirror-image of this case, Seneca's Hercules, as he is being consumed by the poison on his cloak, laments that only a broken body remains ("quid iam supersit") of his massive frame; his father could not recognize "Hercules" if he saw him (*Herc. Oet.* 1234). The main referents here are bodily, but there is also a sense that "what is left" of Hercules is unrecognizable because it no longer acts like Hercules either, but writhes in agony.

56. To be sure, Medea's murder of her brother at Colchis hardly suggests a sweet and loving nature, but the point is whether or not Jason recognizes her as the woman whose life revolved around him.

57. On the influence of Ovid's *Medea* on Seneca's, see Leo 1878, especially 166–67; on the authenticity of *Heroides* 12, see Knox 1986.

elder Seneca, Ovid explained his borrowings from Virgil by saying he had undertaken them not as secret pilferings but as open borrowings, with the intention that they should be recognized (*agnosci*; Sen. Rhet., *Suas.* 3.7).[58] Medea, too, is seeking to be recognized: as herself, as a literary character, as the endpoint of a process of self-development.

The Stoic notion of recognition I have introduced suggests that reconsidering the process by which Medea becomes recognizable might have more in common with Lucilius' progress than we might have suspected. Medea has been working to become herself ever since her promise "I will become Medea" ("Medea—" "Fiam" [171]), but already here, at the beginning of the play, it is notable that the formula "X fiam" echoes the practice of the Stoic *proficiens* in the *meditatio*; it is his job to imagine future possibilities for himself by such mantras as "exul fiam" or "pauper fiam" (for example, *Ep.* 24.17). More significant still, it has as another referent the Stoic individual who strives to *become* "himself" by embarking on a series of mental operations to bring himself closer to the status of a sage. As we have seen, the rarity of such men provokes Seneca's criticisms of the nonreflective, nonstriving souls he sees around himself. Such people can never be themselves, or, as he puts it, "Nemo sibi contigit" ("no one falls to his own lot," "no one coincides with himself" [*Ep.* 32.4]); elsewhere, he puts this as "how few people chance upon having themselves" (quoto cuique habere se contigit [*Ep.* 42.10]). Such coincidence with oneself is a necessary feature of consistency, of "acting like one man." Seneca suggests that we demand from ourselves that "you preserve to the end the character you presented yourself as at the beginning; see to it that you can be praised, or at least, that you can be recognized" (*adgnosci* [*Ep.* 120.21–22]). His usage emphasizes the importance of constancy as a feature of recognizability, and the necessity of harmony between public life and mental convictions. Having attained this harmony, one will coincide with one's best possible self, which it is up to the individual to mold out of his own raw material.[59]

As Medea prepares herself to become (a recognizable, consistent) "Medea" in her great final monologue, she continues to borrow from the arsenal of the

---

58. I thank Robert Germany for bringing this passage to my attention.

59. Similarly, Citroni-Marchetti (1994, 4567) argues that it is taking the *sapiens* as model that will allow us the possibility of coinciding with ourselves.

Stoic *proficiens*. Most notably, she turns several times to address herself and to deliberate on which of her desires is correct, echoing the self-exhortations and self-reprovals of the Stoic's second-order *meditatio*. Urging herself onward to the climactic murder of her sons, she starts with a reproof of her *animus* for shying away from the task: "Why, soul, do you falter? Follow up your successful attack!" (*Med.* 895). The self-exhortation to action we see here (and its earlier instantiations in the play) assimilates Medea again to the practice of the *proficiens*; one of Seneca's most common lines in the self-addressed protreptic that drives the Stoic to the Good is precisely a version of the question, "What are you waiting for [*Quid cessas*]?" Medean self-reprovals such as "Why do you now delay, my soul? Why do you hesitate, when you have the power to act?" (quid nunc moraris, anime? quid dubitas potens? [988]) or "Cut short your sluggish delay!" (Rumpe iam segnes moras [54]) ring with the sound of such Stoic rebukes as "Do we hesitate?" (Dubitamus? [*Ep.* 123.10.6; cf. 94.42]), or from the *animus*, "What are you waiting for? A real man doesn't fear sweat" (quid cessas? non est viri timere sudorem [*Ep.* 31.8]), or other injunctions against fear or delay in action: "Why are you anxious?" (Quid est cur perturberis? [*Ep.* 77.1.15]); "*This* is what you're scared of?" (Hoc est quod timebatur? [*Ep.* 18.5]).[60] So too, if Medea tells her *animus* to "follow this happy impetus" (sequere felicem impetum), she echoes Seneca's advice at *Ep.* 31.1.2 to "follow up on that impetus of your mind [*sequere illum impetum animi*]."[61] Even her final decision to follow the path of anger is a Stoic parody. When she proclaims, "Anger, where you lead, I follow" (ira qua ducis sequor [*Med.* 953]), it is impossible not to hear behind this the echo of Seneca's translation of four lines by Cleanthes (*SVF* 1.527) in *Ep.* 107.10, ending with "Fate leads the willing, but drags the unwilling [*Ducunt volentem fata, nolentem trahunt*]," as well as the many repetitions of this sentiment in Seneca's own writing.[62]

---

60 This language is repeated in the Stoic injunctions of the letters and essays. Cf. *Dial.* 11.2.2.1; *Ep.* 31.7.5, 64.4.3; *Cons. Polyb.* 2; *Brev.* 9.2; also *Ag.* 198.

61. Questions and imperatives, such as *quid mortem times, quid cassum times, (per)age, quid trepidas, titubas, moraris, dubitas, torpis, pendes, occupa, consurge*, are used by many of Seneca's tragic characters. Dupont (1995, 140) comments, without further detail: "These great enraged figures must struggle without cease, even Atreus, to conserve their *furor* intact, by a permanent askesis, a violent effort carried out upon themselves."

62. E.g., *Prov.* 5.4: "boni uiri . . . non trahuntur a fortuna, sequuntur illam et aequant gradus."

Indeed, as Medea continues to harangue herself into action and lays claim to coming into her own ("Medea nunc sum" [910]), she stiffens her resolve by a *meditatio*-like review of her actions to date:

Yes—I'm happy, happy to have ripped off
My brother's head, to have cut off his limbs
And to have stripped my father of his secret spoils,
I'm happy to have equipped daughters
For the murder of an elderly parent.
(911–14)[63]

The review of actions as part of her protreptic to further action has already occurred at several points in the drama; at *Med.* 129–36 she used her past crimes to urge herself onward: the theft of the Golden Fleece, her murder of Absyrtus, Pelias in his pot. Meanwhile, Medea's introductory formula here— "I'm happy to have done X," *iuvat* with the infinitive—is familiar as a component of the self-review, occurring even in the comments that Seneca puts in Nero's mouth at the beginning of the *De clementia* ("iuvat inspicere et circumire bonam conscientiam" [*Clem.* 1.1.1]). It appears frequently in the letters as a form of encouragement—"contemplatio futuri operis iuvat" (*Ep.* 76.28), "iuvat praeteritos dolores retractare" (*Ep.* 78.14), "iuvat protinus quae audias facere" (*Ep.* 108.7). All of these Stoic formulations in the drama add up to a form of self-preparation that smacks of the good Stoic's training in the service of an entirely different ideal. Medea is explicit about the training-like quality of what she has done before: "My grief was in early practice when I did those things; what great deed could untrained hands dare?" (907–9).

One of the rules that the aspiring Stoic (not unlike the Roman *vir*) must remember is to conduct himself in a manner worthy of himself. There seems to be some flexibility in terms of the behavior this might actually designate for a given individual, as shown by Epictetus' famous refusal to cut off his beard rather than lose his head (*Disc.* 1.2.29); conversely, a Roman Stoic might argue that all sorts of demeaning behavior are appropriate when it comes to preserving the integrity of mind over matter. More generally, however, the

---

63. "Iuuat, iuuat rapuisse fraternum caput, / artus iuuat secuisse et arcano patrem / spoliasse sacro, iuuat in exitium senis / armasse natas."

consideration of what befits each individual (*quid decet*) or what is worthy (*dignum*) of him or her serves as a guiding principle to the forms of behavior that suit the *persona* one has adopted, and this rule holds equally valid outside the dramas and within them.[64] Seneca bids Lucilius, essentially, to become worthy of himself (*Ep.* 20.1: "Te dignum putas, qui aliquando fias tuus") and reminds him that it befits the wise man not to fear ills; caution is appropriate to such a figure, but not fear ("non timebit illa sed vitabit; cautio illum decet, timor non decet" [*Ep.* 85.2.5]). In the *Medea*, as in the other plays, the question of what befits her often takes a metatheatrical character in that Medea may seem to look to prior versions of her own story to discover what exactly *decet* her *persona* or is *dignum* of it; she comments of her role as mother that "greater crimes befit me now, after childbirth" (maiora iam me scelera post partus decent [*Med.* 50]) in the same way that Oedipus, after putting out his eyes, remarks that "*This* face befits (an) Oedipus" (Vultus Oedipodam hic decet [*Oed.* 1003]) or in the same way that Atreus comments on his plan for child-cookery, "This is a crime that befits Thyestes—and befits Atreus" (Dignum est Thyeste facinus et dignum Atreo [*Thy.* 271]).[65]

The final point to be made here before we turn away from Stoic phraseology and toward the larger issue of second-order agency in the *Medea* is simply that at points in the drama our heroine's assertions cannot be distinguished, at face value, from those of a Stoic.[66] This is most striking in a stichomythic passage early in the play in which she and the *nutrix* duel in maxims, Medea's responses picking up and inverting the direction of the nurse's words. When the nurse bids her keep quiet in the face of the outrage done her, Medea responds boldly: "Fortune fears the brave and oppresses the weak" (159). And to each further comment, she has a Stoic reply:

---

64. Cf. *Clem* 1.5.3; and the discussion of *persona* in chapter 4. On Epictetus' treatment of how an individual determines *quid decet*, see Kamtekar 1998, 147–52; Long 2002, 232–44.

65. See *Phoen.* 202; *Herc. Oet.* 1482; *Oed.* 879. On *dignum*, see also Fitch and McElduff 2002, 30. Atreus lays claim to another striking feature of the Stoic sage: to be "constans sibi." Cf. *Ep.* 15.2: "Ergo hanc praecipue valetudinem cura, deinde et illam secundam; quae non magno tibi constabit, si volueris bene valere"; and *Thy.* 703–4: "Mouere cunctos monstra, sed solus sibi / immotus Atreus constat."

66. At times it is Seneca, instead, who seems to speak in the tones of his tragic characters. Dingel (1974, 119) suggests that *Helv.* 18.6 is modeled on the ending of the *Oedipus*. Fitch and McElduff (2002, 38–39) talk about the appropriation of heroic language (rather than Stoic language) for heroic deeds.

NURSE: Virtue should only be approved of when it has a place.

MEDEA: It's impossible that a place for virtue should ever be lacking.[67]

NURSE: No hope can show the path when the situation is grim.

MEDEA: He who cannot hope for anything, despairs of nothing.

(160–63)[68]

Elsewhere, she will defend her behavior by allusion to how far above circumstance her spirit stands, indomitable and unable to be crushed. To Jason: "Every turn of fortune has stood below me" (Fortuna semper omnis infra me stetit [520]). To her nurse: "Fortune can take my wealth but not my spirit" (Fortuna opes auferre, non animum potest [176]).[69] Like the good Stoic, Medea scorns the vagaries of fortune, believes that virtue should always be a guide for behavior, and recognizes the illusory pull of hope. Rich or poor, successful or a failure, what is important is her "spirit," the one thing that is in her control, ἐφ' ἡμῖν.[70] Indeed, in some ways she provides a fitting counterpart to Epictetus' criticism of tragic characters: "What else are tragedies but the sufferings of humans stricken by external circumstance, staged in a particular meter?" (*Disc.* 1.4.26).[71] Where the death of her children is concerned, Medea stands far above her own tragedy.

Of course, all of these coincidences of language and behavior fail to mask the

---

67. It has a place even in one's bed, says Seneca (*Ep.* 78.21).

68. Medea: "Fortuna fortes metuit, ignavos premit." Nutrix: "Tunc est probanda, si locum virtus habet." Medea: "Numquam potest non esse virtuti locus." Nutrix: "Spes nulla rebus monstrat adflictis viam." Medea: "Qui nil potest sperare, desperet nihil."

69. Fitch and McElduff (2002, 37) agree: "When Medea speaks of her own *animus* as superior to external Fortune [150, 176], her *sententiae* could be quoted with approval by a Stoic." Cf. Seneca at *Brev.* 5.3: "Quid enim supra eum potest esse qui supra fortunam est?" (What can possibly be above a man who is above Fortune?).

70. Even the hapless nurse or servant in these two dramas seems to emerge as a troubling inversion of the Stoic friend or sage, the Seneca who might mirror one's actions in their truest light. As Thyestes engages in stichomythic exchange with a courtier, or Medea with her nurse, the voice that urges caution and self-restraint is instead picked up, inverted, and mirrored by the angry antagonist. So it is that Thyestes' servant might caution: "When there is no shame, nor care for the law, no holiness, no sense of duty, no trust / the kingdom is unstable" (ubi non est pudor / nec cura iuris *sanctitas pietas fides*, / instabile *regnum* est), only to hear the mocking mirror of "Holiness, a sense of duty, and trust are private goods; kings may go where they want" (*sanctitas pietas fides* / privata bona sunt; qua iuvat *reges* eant [*Thy.* 215–19]).

71. Epictetus, of course, is scornful of Medea's sufferings; she would have been fine, he argues, if she had just realized her husband's love was not one of the things under her own control.

massive ethical difference that when Medea chastises the part of herself that she feels has gone awry, it is a first-order desire that conforms to the morality of her community, while the voice that urges her to select murder as her choice takes on the role of the traditionally ethical second-order agent.[72] Nonetheless, even in her self-reflection and self-address Medea seems like a student of Stoic philosophy; like Seneca, she, too, seems to believe that second-order processes are the best means of effecting a change in the ruling faculty. The famous monologue at *Med.* 893–977, which she speaks after her murder of Creon and his daughter and before the stabbing of her first son, provides the clearest illustration of this process, and like its counterpart in Euripides, has been carefully examined by several modern critics as an illustration of the pernicious power of the passions from a Stoic point of view. Of special interest are the alternating perspectives Medea adopts as she wavers between two courses of action here—killing her children to avenge herself on Jason, or sparing them as a mother's love dictates.[73] These are her two first-order choices, and while it should clearly be granted that they do not graph perfectly onto the axis of madness versus reason (maternal love is generally not a *rational* force), they can safely be said to represent, on the one hand, a choice that the morality of Medea's immediate community would abjure, and, on the other, a choice that they would consider both more humane and, indeed, more rational.

The monologue begins properly at 895 with Medea's address to her soul: "Why, soul, do you falter?"[74] However, this poetic apostrophe does not introduce a proper dialogue between ego and a center of emotion, or even ego and *animus*; the latter shades immediately into Medea herself, who is the object of the comment "You love him still, madwoman, if his being a widower is enough for you" (amas adhuc, furiose, si satis est tibi / caelebs Iason [997–98]).[75] The dialogue becomes thus an internal one between Medea and Medea, and in the

---

72. Christopher Star points out (2003, 7–8) that the only Senecan prose in which the address to the *animus* occurs is *Prov.* 1.2.10: Cato commands "aggredere, anime, diu meditatum opus, eripe te rebus humanis." It is significant that the person speaking this way should be one of the most famous paragons of Stoicism.

73. See especially Gill 1987; and Nussbaum 1994, chap. 12.

74. Gill (1987, 31–37) notes the non-Euripidean pattern of the apostrophe of passions and virtues in the drama (they are particularly frequent later in this monologue).

75. Rosenmeyer (1989, 187), however, would stress the use of terms such as *animus* as "part of the Senecan rhythm of heroic deflection. It is as if the heroes have to assure themselves of the vitality of a world external to themselves." I would suggest the opposite: that the heroes have, finally, no interest in the vitality of a world external to them. Note that Medea is unlike Leontius: she doesn't distance herself from a body part because she always sees herself as rational, no matter what side she's on.

imperatives that follow, as Medea commands herself to put aside delay and take up her greatest crime yet, it becomes clear that she is urging herself first to pick one out of two possible first-order desires, then the other. Throughout, the second-order quality of her desire is signaled by the need for self-command. "Medea, do this!" is akin to "Medea, you should want this option." But the Medea who judges each option is not judging them from the perspective of a single second-order framework. Her argument does not proceed along the lines of "Should I kill, or not kill? On the one hand, killing my children is evil. On the other hand, I really want to make Jason suffer. These two options, one bad but soothing to me, one noble but unsatisfying, are tearing me apart." *Nor* does she echo Euripides' Medea in saying: "I know that what I am about to do is evil, but my *thumos* [here, "rage"] prevails over my counsels." To feel thus would be to judge her potential choices still from the perspective of a single second-order framework ("I know X is bad, but I still really want to do X.") Instead, Medea alternates between two second-order frameworks: one in which killing the kids is a glorious act ("now, now I have regained my power, my brother, my father!" [982]) and one in which it is a terrible act ("what have I done, wretch, wretch that I am?" [990]). The framework within which Medea is deliberating changes back and forth between a commonly accepted one in which she shares and endorses the values of her community, and a framework unique to her alone in this play, in which betrayal is the worst thing a husband can do to his wife, and in which honor demands immediate, and drastic, revenge. Even after the act, there are two more shifts: one to shame, then one to joy.[76] And at this point, at the end of the play, we are to believe that she will shift no more.[77]

In suggesting this line of argument, I find myself close to the conclusions of Nussbaum (1994, 449–51), although in her analysis Medea's changes are

---

76. Henry and Henry (1985, 65) note the broader context of each new set of decisions: "What is Senecan at such a moment is the speaker's projection of impulses and assumption of an observer's role, so that when the choice of action/inaction is made, she can describe and judge herself by new criteria whose responsibility is not hers alone." These new criteria are the content of the second-order framework of values.

77. These movements of second-order judgment are readily traceable in the passage under discussion. For the second-order judgment "I don't want to want to kill my kids," see *Med.* 929–34, 944; for the second-order judgment "I do want to want to kill my kids," see *Med.* 934–36, 951–54. The passages are interlaced with expressions of first-order desire as well. Contrast Euripides, where Medea judges her own actions bad (1078) and does not shift from this second-order viewpoint.

characterized as turnings of the soul rather than shifts in second-order frame-work. Nonetheless, Nussbaum's observation that Medea's perspective looks right to her when she is *in* it is crucially important to my argument; Medea undergoes "an oscillation between two positions of the mind and heart, each of which represents a way in which Medea sees the world. . . . Her entire soul is tossed back and forth." It is incorrect to see this in terms of an oscillation between reason and emotion; again, Nussbaum notes that "the identity of emotion with belief or judgment is in fact prominently stressed. Medea's passions are not shown as coming from some part of her character to which the rational judging part is opposed. They are inclinations of her thought or judgment itself—of her whole personality, conceived of as housed in the rational part."[78] Medea in the grip of the "wrong" second-order self is comparable, say, to a murderer hesitating outside the house of his victim: "Get a grip on yourself!" he might say. "Be a man! Do the job, and don't act like a coward! Don't listen to the voice telling you to run away while you still can!"—an effort at self-control that entails urging the first-order agent to live up to the expectations of the second-order self even if that larger framework is (in normative ethics) questionable.[79] The temporal nature of this oscillation is a feature readily reconcilable with the Stoic emphasis on the unity of the soul and with the concept of repeated shifts in second-order frameworks. In a famous passage in the *Moralia*, Plutarch reminds us that the Stoics do not believe in a split self but rather in a temporal back-and-forthing of the soul:[80] "Emotion is no different from reason nor is there dissension and strife between these two things, but the

---

78. Cf. Berry 1996, 12: "Nowhere and at no time does [Medea] appear to be out-of-control, pulled unwillingly along by the riptide of emotion." Indeed, Medea *assents* to her anger, as at *De ira* 2.3.5. Cf. also Gill 1995, 10: "She has identified herself with these plans and the associated feelings, and renewed her resolve not to 'weaken' the hand that will carry out the act."

79. Gill (1997, 266) rejects the possibility that the *Phaedra* and the *Medea* "represent cautionary examples of the consequences of asserting to, rather than counteracting, pre-emotions." For him, the plays are more representative of the Chrysippean theory of pathos. "The dialogues in which the two figures refuse the advice of their more reasonable advisers, as they go deeper into their passions, can be taken as displaying the Chrysippan idea that a passion constitutes a (sometimes conscious) 'rejection' or 'disobedience' of a rationality whose validity they at some level recognize" (227). But I'm not sure if Medea can be said to see the rationality of one framework when in the grip of another.

80. Nussbaum (1993) distinguishes between two strands of Stoic thought on the passions: the Chrysippean (or "cognitive") view, which holds that emotions are judgments, and thus reasoned and evaluative, and the Poseidonian (or "noncognitive") one, which holds that emotions are nonrational, and as such are especially susceptible to movement by other nonrational forms (like poetry).

turning of one reason in both directions; this escapes our notice because of the swiftness and speed of the shift" (*Virt. Mor.* 446f–447a).[81]

The intricacies of Medea's case, and especially her oscillations between second-order frameworks, do raise some difficulties here that should be addressed. The first is her own avowal, at line 953, that she has chosen to follow anger ("ira, qua ducis, sequor"). As we have seen, the line itself is a parody of the resignation of the Stoic sage to fate; it also stands as a clear example of second-order volition. In addition, the line has a striking precedent in *Heroides* 12, where Medea's literary predecessor in outrage asserts that she will follow whatever path anger leads her on ("quo feret ira sequar" [*Her.* 12.209]). Yet it may seem problematic that it is a *passion* (even if still a form of judgment) that Medea declares her loyalty to. Can one declare that one will follow the path of anger, but not *feel* anger? If this seems unlikely, does the presence of emotion here nullify the second-order nature of the decision? This may not seem very Stoic, but aligning her second order decision to her first-order state of mind and becoming (temporarily) unified thereby is, after all, a goal to be desired under other circumstances (and one she seems to achieve permanently at the play's end). What, then, about the lines after this declaration, in which she signals presence of her brother's Furies (958–66)? Are we to believe Medea is mad? This is a difficult question to answer without knowing if the apparition is real or (like Orestes') the figment of her imagination. Or should we see here, too, the presence of Medea's "intertext"—namely, the Medeas who have preceded her? Given that Ovid's lost Medea was probably the strongest model for our protagonist in her quest to "become" herself, it is suggestive that one of our two remaining fragments from this play shows her mad indeed, carried hither and thither as if possessed by the god ("feror huc illuc ut plena deo" [Sen. Rhet., *Suas.* 3.5]). But it is also reasonable to see this stage, too, as one in a series of fluctuations that cease once Medea has "found" herself at the conclusion, a moment she marks with feelings of joy. "A great pleasure comes over me, though unwilling," she says at *Med.* 992—a suggestive echo of Nero's self-discovery in the *De clementia*, even as Medea is still struggling with the influence of her

---

81. Accessible in Long and Sedley 1987, 65G. Cf. Inwood 1993, 176: "The soul he describes is unitary; the complexity which Seneca introduces centres not on parts or powers, but rather on a *temporally* dynamic process." On the unitary soul and the involvement of the *hegemonikon* in every decision, see also Rist 1969, chap. 14; Annas 1992, 37–120.

penultimate framework (cf. *invitam*).[82] Unlike the Medea of the *Heroides*, there is no suggestion that *this* Medea may yet regret what she has wrought, and no sense that the hand has acted where the mind might have paused.

To worry about the problem of what Medea's behavior means is, of course, to take one's place in a discussion that extends as far back as the Stoic Chrysippus, who famously adduced the Euripidean Medea in a proof for Stoic belief in the unity of the soul and the involvement of the *hegemonikon* in all its decisions—that is, he read Medea's agonizing as having to do with judgment rather than passion.[83] Chrysippus apparently focused on Eur., *Med.* 1078–79, where Medea announces that she is aware of the evils she is about to do, but that *thumos* prevails over her counsels.[84] The point seems to have been that Medea's judgment involved the assent of her soul *as a whole*; the Euripidean passage showed how "her judgment may be wildly astray, but she still makes a judgment, and that involves an assent of her soul as a whole, not the overcoming of λογισμός (reasoning) by θυμός."[85] Ironically, Galen later cited this same passage in support for the opposite argument on the soul in *De placitis Hippocratis et Platonis*. For him, the lines demonstrated a Platonic rather than a Stoic perspective on psychology: the presence of an irrational element in the soul that could overcome reason. But Galen notwithstanding, it is significant for our purpose here that Epictetus would second Chrysippus; in his view, no one performs an act unless he believes it to be the best option available, and Medea therefore acts with full self-mastery (*Disc.* 1.28.7), albeit in self-deception, because she has consented to a wrong impression—that she has been the victim of one of the worst fates a woman can suffer.[86]

"Cannot someone think that something is beneficial to him, but not choose it?"

---

82. Focusing on *Med.* 951–66, Gill (1997, 217) suggests that even at the end Medea conceives of the infanticide as both crime and self-punishment, and thus fuses her moral and immoral responses to her own actions. But I wonder if her talk of this in this passage can be taken to reflect a continuous point of view up to the end, in such a shifting landscape.

83. On the Stoic *hegemonikon*, see Annas 1992, 37–120; Campbell 1985; Long 2002, 210; and Rist 1969, chap. 14.

84. καὶ μανθάνω μὲν οἷα δρᾶν μέλλω κακά, / θυμὸς δὲ κρείσσων τῶν ἐμῶν βουλευμάτων.

85. Dillon 1997, 217, 218n12, with bibliography on the continuing debate over the authenticity of these lines; Gill 1987; Gill 1996, 250; Nussbaum 1993, 142–45. Foley (1989) offers a gendered reading of Medea's passion in Euripides, along with an unusual interpretation of the two lines at issue (*kreisson* as "master of," *bouleuma* as "revenge plans").

86. On Epictetus, see also the discussion in Long 2002, 76–77.

"He cannot."

"What about the woman who says 'I understand the evils I am about to do, but my anger is greater than my counsels'?"

"This is because she considers gratifying her anger and punishing her husband more beneficial than saving her children."

"Yes, but she is mistaken!"

"Show her clearly that she is mistaken and she will not do it. But as long as you don't show her, what course of action can she follow if not what seems beneficial to her?"

But the Senecan Medea, in her relationship to Roman Stoicism, seems to me to raise additional questions, not so much about the unity of the soul, but about the process of second-order self-instruction that can shape and change the soul. As we have seen, Medea's attention to her own development, and the deliberate way in which she determines which of her desires she will choose to make her will, echoes with many of the themes of the self-shaping of the Stoic student. Her preoccupation with self-exhortation and self-analysis, and the sense that her identity is coterminous with the full development of a particular way of looking at the world (and the ensuing actions), all seem like an *inverted* version of the progress of the Stoic sage, or even a reflection of the Stoic emphasis on choice of action (*prohairesis*) as a mark of individuality.

Medea is of course no Stoic: she is a soul whose cognitively informed volition is that she identify with a first-order desire that her community does not endorse—the opposite, one might say, of the situation of the Stoic sage who does the same thing but with different results. Nonetheless, Medea does go through a process very like the Stoic's own self-training to actualize an ideal and "recognizable" self. In this regard, Seneca's writing seems to occasionally open the back door to a world in which an informed second-order volition has nothing to do with a willful movement toward virtue. Medea is not the only example; consider, for example, Hostius, who knows the illusory capacity of his pleasures and is happy to wallow in them anyhow. Hostius and Medea are not addicts, so we cannot excuse them as akratics: they act willfully by choosing a second-order framework that will permit the fulfillment of their first-order desires. They illustrate the consequences of a dialogic self whose second-order volition is not grounded in the values of its community—a dialogic self whose independence from objective-participant reasoning can run into problems that reasoning cannot cure. Medea becomes Medea by rejecting the values of her community.

Some of the isolation in which Medea is able to form her new second-order framework—an isolation that does not seem entirely different from that of the Stoic sage in Neronian Rome—is highlighted by several Senecan innovations in the play. For one, the chorus of the *Medea* is far less sympathetic to our Colchian exile than its Euripidean counterpart, generally deploring her behavior and singing, near the beginning of the play, the idealistic marriage-hymn for Jason and Creusa. And Seneca also innovates here, as in the *Phaedra*, by supplying his heroine with a nurse who represents the voice of reason, only to be rejected. As we saw, all of the nurse's rational advice to Medea is turned on its head by its passionate recipient; similarly, the traditionally acquiescent figure who in the Euripidean version advised Phaedra to *give in* to her passion is in Seneca's version of that play a more resistant interlocutor, one who might opine that "Nec me fugit, quam durus et veri insolens / ad recta flecti regius nolit tumor" (*Phaed.* 136–37) and who would counsel her mistress—at least at first—to practice self-control rather than self-abandon.[87] All for naught. Schmidt (1995, 292), noting the Stoic and Epicurean elements in the exchange between Phaedra and her nurse, rather nicely suggests that Seneca's purpose here is to show the difficulty of being Stoic adviser to a tyrant, and one imagines Medea's nurse could offer a similar illustration.[88] One could also see Medea's nurse, like Phaedra's, as a failed mirror; Dupont (1995, 109) notes that this counselor-as-mirror in the dramas represents the laws of civilized society, often by means of *sententiae* and maxims reflecting common morality.

Medea (and Phaedra) won't hear of such advice, of course. And for Medea, rejecting the mirror of social values is not enough; she must also reject her role as the member of a family, strip from herself the role of wife and also mother ("anger leaves, and the mother takes its place" [927–28]—and then the same thing in reverse). As Fitch and McElduff note (2002, 26), "The process of 'becoming Medea' . . . involves destroying the self-in-relationship, viz. as mother of Jason's children and therefore still connected to him." Her mono-

---

87. As Petrone (1984, 24–27, especially 24) has pointed out. Dupont (1995, 109) makes a similar point.

88. Schmidt (1995) notes several points of comparison between play and doctrine; see, e.g., *Phaed.* 132–35 = *De ira* 3.39.2; *Phaed.* 140–41 = *Ep.* 20.5 and 80.4. Seneca was well aware of the difficulty of speaking truth to power; see Sen., *Ben.* 6.32.

logues reveal her isolation, especially in comparison to her Euripidean fore-
bear: Gill (1987, 31) observes that when Seneca's Medea speaks, it is "much more
of a soliloquy; and the pattern of motivation for infanticide articulated in the
speech is one in which Medea responds to herself (especially to her character,
and her past) rather than the others immediately concerned, her children and
Jason." He adds elsewhere (1987, 36) that "this conflict centres on Medea's
thinking about herself (turning on the question of whether she can sustain
her image of herself as the perpetrator of ultimate evil) rather than on her
responses to others; and so the 'madness'—or solipsism—of 958 and following provides an appropriate context for its resolution."

Again, to say that Medea, like the Senecan Stoic, is responsible for getting
herself to a state where she can live up to her ideal is not to suggest that either
she or the sage will represent, at the culmination of their development, anything
like a self-originated creation along the lines of a Nietzschean Übermensch. Gill
(1996, 109–10) is quite right to stress that a modern treatment of Medea as an
evil but interesting and self-actualizing hero would be off the mark, especially in
its assumption that "the self-conscious realization of one's 'authentic' (that
is, autonomously conceived) personality is an inherent good." I agree with him
that a fusion of aesthetic and ethical categories (the creating of something unique as itself an aesthetic act) is not supported by our ancient texts. Thus, several
readings of Medea's development go too far.[89] But to say that the Medean self is
not self-actualizing because that would not be compatible with the objective-
participant understanding of ancient selfhood is itself a claim that needs to be
modified in the context of Seneca's thought, at least. Medea, like the sage, seems
to me to be an objective-individualist; her truths are objectively true (to her
mind, that is), but they are not shared by her community.

Medea lives in a solipsistic world by the end of the play, a world in which
her second-order framework is matched by no one else's. Such a situation
poses an important problem for ethical philosophy, because it is generally the
presence of a shared second-order framework that provides the impetus for
self-change sparked from the outside. When a second-order framework is
entirely personal, it will not suffice, for gaining virtue, to have one's first-order

---

89. When Fitch and McElduff (2002, 37) describe the shared goal of both Stoic *sapiens* and
figures such as Medea or Atreus as "radical self-definition," then, the term *radical* introduces too
strong a claim. Similarly for readings that see Medea going to a place beyond morality, such as
Henry and Walker 1967; Fyfe 1983.

desires under control of the second-order voice—like Medea, one can still be bad in the eyes of judges living under another framework (for example, a Stoic one). You have to feel something is wrong with you before you want to change. This means that one *already* has to feel Stoicism is the true path; for their students to pick the right second-order framework, the Stoics have to be preaching to the choir; as even Gill acknowledges (1996, 438): "the Stoic account of what constitutes a 'natural' ethical development for a human being . . . presupposes, if it is to be a fully intelligible and convincing account, an audience of people who have, to some extent at least, carried out this development themselves." Similarly Hijmans (1959, 68) points out that in order to learn something, one must want to learn it. "In principle, therefore, only those who already have a spark of the willingness, can set about exercising this 'will.'"[90]

 Can one solve the problem of what Williams calls "motivational solipsism"? For the Guardians of Plato's *Republic*, it is possible to argue, with Williams, that they do not need an internalized other "because they have internalized something else, and carry in them a paradigm of justice gained by their intellectual formation (more exactly, revived in them by it)" (1993, 99). But of course, there is no theory of anamnesis in Stoicism, and no educational program from childhood that will avert the possibility of a Medea or a Hostius.[91] What Stoicism does have is a model that stresses a natural affinity between the order of the cosmos and human rationality; some recent scholarship has found here the possibility that motivation toward the good can come from the agent's understanding that his or her own rationality is modeled upon that of nature,

---

90. Alford 1988, 200: "Just as Aristotle suggests that not every man, but only the good man, should love himself (*Nic. Ethics* 1169a10–15), so our considerations suggest that reconciliation between ego and ego ideal is good only when the content of the ego ideal is truly good." On a similar note, Campbell (1985, 332–37) explores the question of selecting bad *lekta* because assent has been formed by egocentric considerations. Cf. also Gill 1996, 459n173: the Stoics were "aware of the social and psycho-ethical difficulties that may counteract the work of this therapeutic discourse. Thus, they do not standardly claim that human beings are responsible, as individuals, for their success and failure in reaching the normatively human state by responding, or failing to respond, to such therapeutic discourse."

91. Hankinson (1993, 209–10) offers a particular way of formulating the problem about Stoicism derived from his discussion of Gal., *De plac. Hipp. et Plat.* For Galen, we have two choices. We can (a) show objectively that one kind of life makes you happier, or (b) demonstrate the philosophical truth that a certain life is superior—not *based on* the claim that it's better to live such a life, or that one will be happier living such a life, even though that will in fact be true.

and is thereby good.[92] A different perspective is offered by Seneca himself in *Ep.* 120, in which the question posed by this reading of *Medea* is confronted: How do we learn what is good? Seneca explains:

> Nature could not teach us this directly; she has given us the seeds of knowledge, but not knowledge itself. Some say that we merely happened upon this knowledge; but it is unbelievable that a vision of virtue could have presented itself to anyone by mere chance. We believe that it is inference due to observation, a comparison of events that have occurred frequently; our school of philosophy holds that the honourable and the good have been comprehended by analogy. . . . Kindly deeds, humane deeds, brave deeds, had at times amazed us; so we began to admire them as if they were perfect. Underneath, however, there were many faults, hidden by the appearance and the brilliancy of certain conspicuous acts; to these we shut our eyes. Nature bids us amplify praiseworthy things— everyone exalts renown beyond the truth. And thus from such deeds we deduced the conception of some great good [A story follows about C. Fabricius Luscinus, a Roman general who resisted bribery by Pyrrhus] . . . . These deeds and others of the same sort have revealed to us a picture of virtue.

We are here right back where we started: with the observation of virtues in the other. The ideal sage may not exist, but we have enough models in Roman history (and in philosophers gone by) to get us started; a little analogy and a little idealization carries out the rest.

Even here, however, the Stoics acknowledge that the correctness or error of the goal can be affected by the environment in which one has grown up. As Campbell (1985, 330) notes, "Corruption and temptation are factors having a distorting effect on the processes of thinking. They can be present and effective in thinking on either theoretical or practical questions. Where they are effective, they issue in assent to the wrong *lekta.*" This is the same problem for ethical psychology that Long identifies (1991, 115): on the one hand, one has a responsibility to resist unethical impulses; on the other, one's beliefs and representations are shaped by the world in which one lives. We could downplay

---

92. For a summation of the scholarship, which relies heavily on Cic., *Fin.* 3.20–21, see Gill (forthcoming).

the significance of this problem by pointing out that the Stoics favored the idea that one's character had a predisposition to goodness, even if it could be perverted by life (cf. Cic., *Tusc.* 3.2–3); Seneca, however, seems to have been less orthodox on this issue, suggesting in *De ira* 2.20.1 that environment and nature both play a role in making us tend toward anger, presumably meaning that one could start out less than ideal even without the corrupting influence of the outside world.[93]

Can we therefore lay aside the troubling questions raised by Medea? Perhaps she was a bad egg when she came out, or perhaps she was too damaged by her upbringing (Sen., *De ira* 2.5.4, on Hannibal, suggests that his childhood was responsible for his love of slaughter) to provide any real challenge to the tenets of Stoicism. But the problem remains that Stoicism can only appear attractive to those who already share its second-order framework; otherwise, even the methods of Stoicism can be used in the self-production of a monster-sage. Of course, we could call all such people *non*-people (though we would then have to chuck out the criteria used by Frankfurt). Wolf (1987), for example, introduces a new criterion for "freedom of the will": sanity, which she calls the connection of oneself to the world in a certain way—"a desire that one's self be *controlled* by the world in certain ways and not others" (1987, 55). Of characters like Medea she would presumably say: "Their deep selves lack the resources and the reasons that might have served as a basis for self-correction" (1987, 56). And she introduces us to the hypothetical JoJo, son of a tyrant, whose acts are demented, but who seems to himself quite free and happy (59): "In the case of these earlier victims, we were able to say that although the actions of the individuals were, at one level, in control of the individuals themselves, these individuals themselves, qua agents, were not the selves they more deeply wanted to be. . . . However, we cannot say of JoJo that his self, qua agent, is not the self he wants it to be. It *is* the self he wants it to be. *From the inside, he feels as integrated, free, and responsible as we do.* Our judgment that JoJo is not a responsible agent is one that we can make only from the outside" (emphasis added). JoJo and Medea and Hostius Quadra thus bear a certain similarity to each other, and we could avoid the whole problem of the way that figures like Hostius, Medea, and Atreus seem to throw negative light on the process

---

93. On this issue, cf. also *De ira* 3.26.4, "omnes mali sumus"; and see especially Stough 1978; also Nussbaum 1994, 420–21; Reydam-Schils 1998, 42–43; and Campbell 1985.

of self-becoming by simply labeling all three "insane." This, however, seems a dismissive approach, even if easy from the philosophical viewpoint. For one thing, it opens the door to labeling everyone as insane who is resistant to "being controlled by the world in certain ways" (Foucault has addressed this in his history of madness). In addition, it is unclear if the ancients—until Seneca—would recognize such a form of insanity, neither *akrasia* nor *ate*, but a massive overturning of the normative content of any societal or philosophical second-order framework. Finally, and as I have mentioned, *the rational cosmos itself* seems to be at the beck and call of Seneca's tragic heroine: the case is not so much that she has deviated from the benevolent order of a Stoic universe, but that the universe acts out her own internal reversal of Stoic eudaemonism, reversing itself at command. So it is that Medea, preparing her poisons in the play, summons water from dry clouds, repels the tides of the ocean, overturns the laws of the heavens, and reroutes the constellations of the sky; rivers flow back upon their sources, and the seasons are jumbled together (*Med.* 752–69). The *adynata* here are typical in their application to a witchlike character, and certainly to Medea (cf. Eur., *Med.* 410–14; Ov., *Met.* 7.199–200), but in the Stoic context of the play, their larger implication is undeniable: the Stoics identified their god with natural law as well as with rational *logos*, and here is Medea, inverting a natural order upon which is based much of their fragile enterprise of the rationalization of the Good. Her success *cannot* be simply dismissed as madness.

If Medea, at the end of the play, has fully adopted the perspective of the second-order framework she slipped in and out of earlier in the drama, we can presumably say of her, too, that from now on there will be no need for her to debate about her first-order choices; offered at any point the choice between praising or damning child-slaughter to take vengeance on a straying husband, she will praise the decision as (ethically) correct in this world of *quid pro quo*. She has accomplished a major goal of Stoicism: she has reached harmony between her first- and second-order voices. In this, she is like the man who becomes a philosopher at the end of that long path of *meditatio* and self-command and has no further need for internal dialogue or for the imaginary gaze of Epicurus. This man's seamless self has already been reduced to the level of automatic choice of the correct judgments, decisions, and actions for a Stoic *accompli*, and his first-order desires are identical with what his second-order volitions as a *proficiens* once were. In properly Stoic terminology, we might say that his judgments will now habitually and easily assent to what a Stoic would call true impressions; the witness self has merged with the agent self. This man has fulfilled the goal he set himself once long before: the goal of the daily *askesis*; the goal of all the dialogues Seneca engages in with himself, and which he urges Lucilius to undertake as well. But what Medea has become (from a normative perspective) is not a sage, but a monster. She has managed to cut herself off from the judgment of society; she has managed to shape herself by various forms of *meditatio* into a being that can follow unwaveringly the dictates of her second-order self; and she now no longer needs the guiding voice of that framework, because her first- and second-order perspectives have become one (as is the Stoic's ultimate goal).[94]

What are we to make, then, of this strange play, the *Medea*? One option is to say that it offers precisely a mirror to its audience, for whom the example of the protagonist will reaffirm the value of the correct second-order framework. Nussbaum (1993) argues that Senecan drama shows its audience negative exempla of the psychology of the passions; this is why its central characters are repellent. The evidence even for this efficacy is mixed; Nussbaum herself cites Seneca's various observations that poets are indifferent to ethical truths because they make us believe wealth is important (*Ben* 1.3.10, 1.4.5; *Marc.* 19.4; *Brev.* 16.5), but she also cites passages in which poetry is given a more significant role.[95] Most important for our purpose is Seneca's discussion at *Ep.* 108.8–10, in which Seneca follows Cleanthes in saying that poetry sharpens the meaning of what it has to say. He adds, however, the idea that drama can provide the viewer with a corrective mirror of his own sins.[96]

---

94. Dupont (2000, 227) suggests that Seneca's Medea becomes her mask by the end of the play—the sole moment of agreement between her voice and the mask is at the atrocious climax (presuming the play was performed).

95. For further scholarship on how the Stoics themselves saw the role of drama, see Armisen-Marchetti 1989, 345–71; Baümer 1982, 132–40; Nussbaum 1993, 128–30; and 1994, 443–44; Schiesaro 2003, 229–51; and Sorabji 2002, 76–92. Also see the various views expressed by Seneca himself at *De ira* 2.2.3–6, 3.9.1; *Ep.* 94.27, 108.7–10; *Tranq.* 17.10; *De brev.* 16.5; *Ad Marc.* 19.4.; *Polyb.* 11.5. For Pratt (1983, 76) they are negative exempla to "confront the 'patient' with the experience of his own symptoms, which is conveyed in the exemplum." This is the Poseidonian theory of catharsis, which Long (1986, 220) similarly links to Senecan drama.

96. Nussbaum (1993, 128–30) discusses the views of Plutarch and Epictetus, who suggest that tragic drama can prepare one for the misfortunes of life and teach one to avoid errors of judgment; cf. Plut., *Mor.* 35D; Epict., *Disc.* 1.24.16–18, 1.4.23–30, 2.26.31.

It is easy to rile up a listener to want what is right; for to all of us nature gave the foundations and the seed of the virtues. . . . Don't you see how the theater goers resound together every time things are said which we publicly recognize and unanimously avow to be true? "Poverty lacks much; greed lacks everything." "A greedy man is good for no one, but worst for himself." At these verses the most niggardly man claps and is happy that his vices are being reviled. . . . As Cleanthes used to say, "Just as our breath produces a keener sound when a trumpet lengthens it and pours it out through the narrow parts of its long tube which has a wider opening right at the end, so too the constricting rules of poetry render our experience keener too." The same things are heard more carelessly and make less of an impression when spoken in prose; but when meter is added and fixed feet constrain a striking idea, the same sentiment is hurled as if from a more violent throw.

Even the wicked, then, can respond to good exempla or moral maxims spoken at the theater, because nature has planted the foundations of goodness in all of us. A similar sentiment is voiced in Seneca's writing on anger: one must show the monstrous man to himself in order to cure him. "Therefore it is necessary to convict a man's foulness and savagery and to set before his eyes how much of the monster there is in him when he rages against another man, and with what an impetus he rushes on, destructive to himself as well as others and wrecking what he cannot sink without sinking himself too" (*De ira* 3.3.2). But there are, of course, two problems (at least) with such a salutary role for drama, aside from those identified by Nussbaum in her treatment of this issue (1993). As we have seen, both the *De clementia* and the *De ira* grapple with some of the issues raised by this reading, inasmuch as both leave the question of the self-satisfied self-viewer unresolved. Showing a flawed human being to herself does not necessarily induce in her the desire for self-improvement. Hostius in his mirror, the angry man in his, and even Caligula *like* what they see in their reflection; otherwise Stoicism could indeed win the adherents it wished to. In addition, it is not so clear that Medea can serve as sobering example to her viewers. Her triumphant state of mind at the end of the play may lead us to ask: did Medea indeed sink, or did she rise while wreckage was strewn around her, even if it was *voluptas*, not *gaudium*, that filled this un-sage with rapture?

It seems, then, that Seneca's internalization of the mirror of society and his revision of the values reflected in that mirror fail in his tragedies because there are no controls on second-order volition when there can be no sanctions imposed by one's ethical environment. This is why his dramatic characters run amok; this is the risk of what happens when the observer becomes internal: the methods of Stoic philosophy allow for the production of both saints *and* monsters who don't care about social sanctions. Gill comments of the problematic Homeric and tragic heroes that they "are presented as grounding their problematic actions in 'second-order' reasoning about the basic goals and principles that should govern human action" (117). But the Stoic Medea, the Senecan Medea, participates in a world in which the self takes shape via a form of second-order reasoning that does *not* engage with the first-order ethical imperatives of her society, or rather engages with them merely to subordinate them to second-order imperatives. In so doing she emerges as more than a problematic hero: in engaging in constant dialogue with herself about the desires she should or should not have, she is a hero who inverts the very basis of Stoic self-improvement and does so by the process the Stoic is supposed to aim at, the congruence of first- and second-order desires.

Like the murderer who exhorts himself to carry out the act, Medea and Hostius seem to present a problem for a philosophy that depends so vitally on the subject's judgment upon him- or herself. Both have full knowledge of their acts, both judge these acts to partake of depravity, and both wilfully and willingly commit them.[97] They illustrate, in the words of Williams (1994, 100), how without any regard for societal values, "the conviction of autonomous self-legislation may become hard to distinguish from an insensate degree of moral egoism." Medea's deformity, like that of the angry man in the mirror, shines back at her, and like him, she likes it—and her community of one is enough for her. So it is that Seneca's antiheroes provide us with a sobering counter-example to the exemplary mirror, the mirror of philosophic self-transformation. Indeed, none of the explanations to which Seneca points elsewhere solves the basic problem of a philosophy that claims to have an answer to the human passions, but so precariously places its trust in the mirror of the self.

---

97. Dillon (1997, 217–18) suggests that given the contemporary philosophical context of Euripidean drama, it is not inconceivable that "Euripides, in presenting Medea's dilemma in this form, and indeed in allowing Phaedra to made a speech of similar import in Hippolytus (373–87), is posing a direct challenge to the extreme intellectualist theory (associated with the name of Socrates) that it is impossible to do wrong willingly."

REFERENCES

Abrams, Murray H. 1953. *The Mirror and the Lamp: Romantic Theory and the Critical Tradition.* New York.

Adams, J. N. 1982. *The Latin Sexual Vocabulary.* Baltimore.

Agamben, Giorgio. 1993. *Stanzas: Word and Phantasm in Western Culture.* Minneapolis.

Alford, C. Fred. 1988. *Narcissism: Socrates, the Frankfurt School, and Psychoanalytic Theory.* New Haven, Conn.

Allen, David W. 1974. *The Fear of Looking; Or, Scopophilic-Exhibitionist Conflicts.* Charlottesville, Va.

Allen, R. E. 1962. "Note on *Alc. I*, 129b1." *American Journal of Philology* 83:187–90.

Alliez, Eric, and Michael Feher. 1989. "Reflections of a Soul." In *Fragments for a History of the Human Body*, vol. 2, ed. Michael Feher, Ramona Naddaff, and Nadia Tazi, 46–84. New York.

Anderson, William S. 1982. *Essays on Roman Satire.* Berkeley, Calif.

Annas, Julia. 1985. "Self-Knowledge in Early Plato." In *Platonic Investigations*, ed. Dominic J. O'Meara, 111–38. Washington, D.C.

———. 1992. *Hellenistic Philosophy of Mind.* Berkeley, Calif.

Antonaccio, Maria. 1998. "Contemporary Forms of Askesis and the Return of Spiritual Exercises." *Annual of the Society of Christian Ethics* 18:69–92.

Arendt, Hannah. 1971. *The Life of the Mind: Thinking.* New York.

Argyle, Michael, and Mark Cook. 1976. *Gaze and Mutual Gaze.* Cambridge, England.

Armisen-Marchetti, Mireille. 1989. *Sapientiae facies: Étude sur les images de Sénèque.* Paris.

Arrowsmith, William. 1966. "Death and Luxury in the *Satyricon.*" *Arion* 5:304–31.

Asmis, Elizabeth. 1982. "Lucretius' Venus and Stoic Zeus." *Hermes* 110:458–70.

———. 1990. "Seneca's *On the Happy Life* and Stoic Individualism." In *The Poetics of Therapy: Hellenistic Ethics in Its Rhetorical and Literary Context*, ed. Martha C. Nussbaum, 219–55. Special issue. *Apeiron* 23, no. 4.

Axer, Jerzy. 1989. "Tribunal-Stage-Arena: Modeling of the Communication Situation in M. Tullius Cicero's Judicial Speeches." *Rhetorica* 7:299–311.

Babut, Daniel. 1963. "Les stoïciens et l'amour." *Revue des études grecques* 76:55–63.

Bacon, Helen. 1958. "The Sybil in the Bottle." *Virginia Quarterly Review* 34:262–76.

Bader, Françoise. 1993. *Le Narcisse, les cigales, et les sirènes, ou les difficultés de la communication.* Testi linguistici 20. Pisa.

Bakhtin, Mikhail. 1984. *Problems of Dostoevsky's Poetics.* Ed. and trans. Caryl Emerson. Minneapolis.

Bal, Mieke. 1997. "Looking at Love: An Ethics of Vision." *Diacritics* 27:59–72.

Baldes, Richard W. 1975. "Democritus on Visual Perception: Two Theories or One?" *Phronesis* 20:93–105.

Balensiefen, Lilian. 1990. *Die Bedeutung des Spiegelbildes als ikonographisches Motiv in der antiken Kunst.* Tübingen.

Baltrusaitis, Jurgis. 1978. *Essai sur une légende scientifique: le miroir.* Paris.

Bann, Stephen. 1989. *The True Vine: On Visual Representation and the Western Tradition.* Cambridge, England.

Barbieri, Aroldo. 1983. *Poetica Petroniana: Satyricon 132, 15.* Rome.

Barton, Carlin A. 1993. *The Sorrows of the Ancient Romans: The Gladiator and the Monster.* Princeton, N.J.

———. 1994. "All Things Beseem the Victor: Paradoxes of Masculinity in Early Imperial Rome." In *Gender Rhetorics*, ed. Richard C. Trexler, 83–92. Binghamton, N.Y.

———. 1999. "The Roman Blush: The Delicate Matter of Self-Control." In *Constructions of the Classical Body*, ed. James I. Porter, 212–34. Ann Arbor, Mich.

———. 2001. *Roman Honor: The Fire in the Bones.* Berkeley, Calif.

———. 2002. "Being in the Eyes: Shame and Sight in Ancient Rome." In *The Roman Gaze*, ed. Fredrick, 216–35.

Bartsch, Shadi. 1994. *Actors in the Audience: Theatricality and Doublespeak from Nero to Hadrian.* Princeton, N.J.

———. 2000. "The Philosopher as Narcissus: Knowing Oneself in Classical Antiquity." In *Seeing as Others Saw: Visuality before and beyond the Renaissance*, ed. Robert S. Nelson, 70–97. Cambridge, England.

———. 2001. "The Self as Audience: Paradoxes of Identity in Imperial Rome." *Pegasus* 44:4–12.

———. 2005. "Eros and the Roman Philosopher." In *Erotikon*, ed. Bartsch and Bartscherer, 59–83.

Bartsch, Shadi, and Thomas Bartscherer, eds. 2005. *Erotikon: Essays on Eros, Ancient to Modern.* Chicago.

Bataille, Georges. 1986. *Eroticism*. Trans. Mary Dalwood. San Francisco.

Batinski, E. E. 1993. "Seneca's Response to Stoic Hermeneutics." *Mnemosyne* 46:69–77.

Baümer, Anne. 1982. *Die Bestie Mensch: Senecas Aggressionstheorie, ihre philosophischen Vorstufen und ihre literarischen Auswirkungen*. Bern.

Baumgarten, A. I., J. Assmann, and G. G. Stroumsa, eds. 1998. *Self, Soul, and Body in Religious Experience*. Leiden.

Beacham, Richard C. 1999. *Spectacle Entertainments of Early Imperial Rome*. New Haven, Conn.

Beiner, Ronald. 1995. "Foucault's Hyper-Liberalism." *Critical Review* 9:349–70.

Bell, Andrew J. E. 1997. "Cicero and the Spectacle of Power." *Journal of Roman Studies* 87:1–22.

Benedict, Ruth. 1947. *The Chrysanthemum and the Sword: Patterns of Japanese Culture*. London.

Benjamin, Jonathan. 1991. "Alice through the Looking-Glass: A Psychiatrist Reads Rorty's *Philosophy and the Mirror of Nature*." *Philosophy of the Social Sciences* 21:515–23.

Benton, Cindy. 2002. "Split Vision: The Politics of the Gaze in Seneca's *Troades*." In *The Roman Gaze*, ed. Fredrick, 31–56.

Beran, Zdenka. 1973. "The Realm of Sensory Perception and Its Significance in Petronius' *Satyricon*." *Ziva Antika* 23:227–51.

Berger, Anne-Emmanuelle. 1996. "The Latest Word from Echo." *New Literary History* 27:621–40.

Berger, John. 1972. *Ways of Seeing*. London.

Bergmann, Bettina, and Christine Kondoleon, eds. 1999. *The Art of Ancient Spectacle*. New Haven, Conn.

Bernidaki-Aldous, Eleftheria A. 1990. *Blindness in a Culture of Light: Especially the Case of Oedipus at Colonus of Sophocles*. New York.

Berry, Jon M. 1996. "The Dramatic Incarnation of Will in Seneca's *Medea*." *Journal of Dramatic Theory and Criticism*, 3–18.

Berryman, Sylvia. 1998. "Euclid and the Sceptic: A Paper on Vision, Doubt, Geometry, Light, and Drunkenness." *Phronesis* 43:176–96.

Bettini, Maurizio. 1991a. "Narciso e le immagini gemelle." In *La maschera, il doppio, e il ritratto*, ed. Bettini, 47–60.

———, ed. 1991b. *La maschera, il doppio, e il ritratto*. Bari.

———. 1999. *The Portrait of the Lover*. Berkeley, Calif.

———. 2000. "'Einander ins Gesicht sehen' im Antiken Rom: Begriffe der körperlichen Erscheinung in der lateinischen Kultur." *Saeculum* 51:1–23.

Biville, Frédérique. 1996. "*Et tu cum esses capo, cocococo*, Petron. 59,2: Métaphores et onomatopées animalières dans *Sat.* 57–59." *Latomus* 55:855–61.

Black, Joel. 1998. "Taking the Sex Out of Sexuality: Foucault's Failed History." In *Rethinking Sexuality*, ed. Larmour, Miller, and Platter, 42–60.

Blake, Marion E. 1941. *Roman Mosaics of the Second Century in Italy*. Memoirs of the American Academy in Rome 13. Bergamo.

Bloomer, W. Martin. 1997. "Schooling in *Persona*: Imagination and Subordination in Roman Education." *Classical Antiquity* 16:57–78.

Blumenberg, Hans. 1953. "Licht als Metapher der Wahrheit." *Studium Generale* 10:432–47.

Bodel, John. 1999. "Death on Display: Looking at Roman Funerals." In *The Art of Ancient Spectacle*, ed. Bergmann and Kondoleon, 259–82.

Bömer, Franz. 1969. *P. Ovidius Naso Metamorphosen Buch I–III Kommentar.* Heidelberg.

Borch-Jacobsen, Mikkel. 1991. *Lacan: The Absolute Master.* Trans. Douglas Brick. Stanford, Calif.

Borghini, A. 1978. "L'inganno della sintassi: il mito ovidiano di Narciso." *Materiali e discussioni per l'analisi dei testi classici* 1:177–92.

Braden, Gordon. 1970. "The Rhetoric and Psychology of Power in the Dramas of Seneca." *Arion* 9:5–41.

———. 1989. "Epic Anger: Milton and Seneca." *Milton Quarterly* 23:8–34.

Braun, Ludwig. 1981. "La forza del visibile nelle tragedie di Seneca." *Dioniso* 52:109–24.

Braund, Susanna Morton, and Christopher Gill. 1997. *The Passions in Roman Thought and Literature.* Cambridge, England.

Braund, Susanna Morton, and Paula James. 1998. "*Quasi Homo*: Distortion and Contortion in Seneca's *Apocolocyntosis*." *Arethusa* 31:285–311.

Brenk, Frederick. 1988. "Plutarch's *Erotikos*: The Drag Down Pulled Up." *Illinois Classical Studies* 13:457–71.

Brenkman, John. 1976. "Narcissus in the Text." *Georgia Review* 30:293–327.

———. 1977. "The Other and the One: Psychoanalysis, Reading, the *Symposium*." *Yale French Studies* 55–56:396–456.

Brennan, Teresa, and Martin Jay, eds. 1996. *Vision in Context: Historical and Contemporary Perspectives on Sight.* New York.

Brilliant, Richard. 1999. "Let the Trumpets Roar! The Roman Triumph." In *The Art of Ancient Spectacle*, ed. Bergmann and Kondoleon, 221–30.

Brisson, Luc. 2002. *Sexual Ambivalence: Androgyny and Hermaphroditism in Graeco-Roman Antiquity.* Trans. Janet Lloyd. Berkeley, Calif.

Brown, Robert D. 1987. *Lucretius on Love and Sex: A Commentary on* De rerum natura *IV, 1030–1287, with Prolegomena, Text, and Translation.* Leiden.

———. 1994. "The Bed-Wetters in Lucretius 4.1026." *Harvard Studies in Classical Philology* 96:191–96.

Bruell, Christopher. 1977. "Socratic Politics and Self-Knowledge: An Interpretation of Plato's *Charmides*." *Interpretation* 6:141–203.

Brunschwig, Jacques. 1973. "Sur quelques emplois d'ὄψις." In *Zetesis: Festschrift for Emil de Strycker*, 24–39. Antwerp.

———. 1996. "La deconstruction du 'Connais-toi toi-même' dans l'*Alcibiade majeur*." *Recherches sur la philosophie et langage* 18:61–84.

Brunschwig, Jacques, and Martha C. Nussbaum. 1993. *Passions and Perceptions: Studies in Hellenistic Philosophy of Mind.* Proceedings of the Fifth Symposium Hellenisticum. Cambridge, England.

Burchell, David. 1998. "Civic *Personae*: MacIntyre, Cicero and Moral Personality." *History of Political Thought* 19:101–18.

Burkert, Walter. 1977. "Air-Imprints or *Eidola*: Democritus' Aetiology of Vision." *Illinois Classical Studies* 2:97–109.

———. 1982. *Structure and History in Greek Mythology and Ritual*. Berkeley, Calif.

Burkitt, Ian. 1994. "The Shifting Concept of the Self." *History of the Human Sciences* 7:7–28.

Busche, Hubertus. 1997. "Hat Phantasie nach Aristoteles eine interpretierend Funktion in der Wahrnehmung?" *Zeitschrift für philosophische Forschung* 51:565–89.

Bychkov, Oleg. 1999 "Ἡ τοῦ κάλλους ἀπορροή: A Note on Achilles Tatius 1.9.4–5, 5.13.4." *Classical Quarterly* 49:339–41.´

Bynum, Caroline W. 1982. "Did the Twelfth Century Discover the Individual?" In *Jesus as Mother: Studies in the Spirituality of the High Middle Ages*, 82–109. Berkeley, Calif.

Cairns, Douglas L. 1993. *Aidos: The Psychology and Ethics of Honour and Shame in Ancient Greek Literature*. Oxford.

Caizzi, Fernando D. 1994. "The Porch and the Garden: Early Hellenistic Images of the Philosophical Life." In *Images and Ideologies: Self-Definition in the Hellenistic World*, ed. A. W. Bulloch, E. S. Gruen, A. A. Long, and Andrew Stewart, 303–29.

Callahan, John F. 1964. "Plautus' 'Mirror for a Mirror.'" *Classical Philology* 59:1–10.

Cameron, Averil. 1969. "Petronius and Plato." *Classical Quarterly* 19:367–70.

Camille, Michael. 1994. "The Abject Gaze and the Homosexual Body: Flandrin's *Figure d'Étude*." *Journal of Homosexuality* 27:161–88.

Campbell, K. 1985. "Self-Mastery and Stoic Ethics." *Philosophy* 60:327–40.

Cancik, Hubert. 1967. "Spiegel der Erkenntnis zu Ovid, *Met*. III 339–510." *Altsprachliche Unterricht* 10:42–53.

———. 1998. "Persona and Self in Stoic Philosophy." In *Self, Soul, and Body in Religious Experience*, ed. Baumgarten, Assmann, and Stroumsa, 335–46.

Cantarella, Eva. 1992. *Bisexuality in the Ancient World*. Trans. Cormac Ó Cuilleanáin. New Haven, Conn.

Carrithers, Michael. 1985. "An Alternative Social History of the Self." In *The Category of the Person*, ed. Carrithers, Collins, and Lukes, 234–56.

Carrithers, Michael, Steven Collins, and Steven Lukes, eds. 1985. *The Category of the Person: Anthropology, Philosophy, History*. Cambridge, England.

Carson, Anne. 1986. *Eros the Bittersweet*. Princeton, N.J.

Casali, Sergio. 1997. "Apollo, Ovid, and the Foreknowledge of Criticism, *Ars* 2.493–512." *Classical Journal* 93:19–27.

Chaplin, Jane D. 2000. *Livy's Exemplary History*. Oxford.

Chateauvert, J., and A. Gaudreault. 1996. "Le Corps, le regard, le miroir." *Semiotica* 112:93–107.

Cherry, John D. 1988. "Ethos vs. Persona: Self-Representation in Written Discourse." *Written Communication* 5:251–76.

Citroni-Marchetti, Sandra. 1994. "Il *sapiens* in pericolo: psicologia del raporto con gli altri, da Cicerone a Marco Aurelio." *Aufstieg und Niedergang der römischen Welt* 2.36.7: 4546–98.

Clarke, John R. 1993. "The Warren Cup and the Contexts for Representations of Male-to-Male Lovemaking in Augustan and Early Julio-Claudian Art." *Art Bulletin* 75:275–94.

———. 1996. "Hypersexual Black Men in Augustan Baths: Ideal Somatotypes and Apotropaic Magic." In *Sexuality in Ancient Art*, ed. Kampen et al., 184–98.

———. 1998. *Looking at Lovemaking: Constructions of Sexuality in Roman Art 100 B.C.–A.D. 250*. Berkeley, Calif.

———. 2002. "Look Who's Laughing at Sex: Men and Women Viewers in the *Apodyterium* of the Suburban Baths at Pompeii." In *The Roman Gaze*, ed. Fredrick, 149–81.

Claus, James J., and Sarah Iles Johnston, eds. 1997. *Medea: Essays on Medea in Myth, Literature, Philosophy, and Art*. Princeton, N.J.

Clavel-Lévêque, M. 1986. "L'Espace des jeux dans le monde romain." *Aufstieg und Niedergang der römischen Welt* 2.16.3: 2405–63.

Cleasby, Harold Loomis. 1907. "The *Medea* of Seneca." *Harvard Studies in Classical Philology* 18:39–71.

Cohen, David. 1991. *Law, Sexuality, and Society: The Enforcement of Morals in Classical Athens*. Cambridge, England.

Cohen, David, and Richard Saller. 1994. "Foucault on Sexuality in Greco-Roman Antiquity." In *Foucault and the Writing of History*, ed. Goldstein, 35–59.

Cohn, Dorrit. 1995. "Optics and Power in the Novel." *New Literary History* 26:3–20.

Conte, Gian Biagio. 1996. *The Hidden Author: An Interpretation of Petronius' Satyricon*. Berkeley, Calif.

Cooper, John M., trans. 1997. *Plato: Complete Works*. Indianapolis.

Corbeill, Anthony. 1997. "Dining Deviants in Roman Political Invective." In *Roman Sexualities*, ed. Hallett and Skinner, 99–128.

———. 2002. "Political Movement: Walking and Ideology in Republican Rome." In *The Roman Gaze*, ed. Fredrick, 182–215.

Courcelle, Pierre P. 1975. *Connais-toi toi-même: de Socrate à saint Bernard*. Paris.

Courtney, Edward. 1962. "Parody and Literary Allusion in Menippean Satire." *Philologus* 106:86–100.

Creighton, Millie R. 1990. "Revisiting Shame and Guilt Cultures: A Forty-Year Pilgrimage." *Ethos* 18:279–307.

Dalla, D. 1988. *Ubi Venus mutatur: Omosessualità e diritto nel mondo romano*. Milan.

Dällenbach, Lucien. 1989. *The Mirror in the Text*. Trans. Jeremy Whiteley. Chicago.

Danziger, Kurt. 1997. "A History of the Self." In *Self and Identity: Fundamental Issues*, ed. Richard Ashmore and Lee Jussim, 245–66. Oxford.

D'Arms, John. 1999. "Performing Culture: Roman Spectacle and the Banquets of the Powerful." In *The Art of Ancient Spectacle*, ed. Bergmann and Kondoleon, 301–20.

Daut, Raimund. 1975. *Imago: Untersuchungen zum Bildbegriff der Römer*. Heidelberg.

Davidson, Arnold. 1994. "Ethics as Aesthetics: Foucault, the History of Ethics, and Ancient Thought." In *Foucault and the Writing of History*, ed. Goldstein, 63–80.

Debray, Régis. 1992. *Vie et mort de l'image: une histoire du regard en Occident*. Paris.

De Lacy, Phillip H. 1977. "The Four Stoic *Personae*." *Illinois Classical Studies* 2:163–72.

Delatte, Armand. 1932. *La Catoptromancie grecque et se dérivés*. Paris.

Delvaux, Martine. 1995. "Le Moi et l'A/autre: Subjectivité divisée et unité culturelle." *Canadian Review of Comparative Literature* 22:487–500.

Dennett, Daniel. 1976. "Conditions of Personhood." In *The Identities of Persons*, ed. Rorty, 175–96.

Denyer, Nicholas, ed. 2001. *Plato: Alcibiades*. New York.

Denzin, Norman K. 1995. *The Cinematic Society: The Voyeur's Gaze*. London.

Deremetz, Alain. 1995. *Le Miroir des muses: poétiques de la réflexivité à Rome*. Villeneuve d'Ascq.

Detel, Wolfgang. 1998. *Macht, Moral, Wissen: Foucault und die Klassische Antike*. Frankfurt.

Devereux, Georges. 1973. "The Self-Blinding of Oidipous in Sophokles: *Oidipous Tyrannos*." *Journal of Hellenic Studies* 93:36–49.

De Vries, G. J. 1969. *A Commentary on Plato's Phaedrus*. Amsterdam.

DeVries, Keith. 1997. "The 'Frigid Eromenoi' and Their Wooers Revisited: A Closer Look at Greek Homosexuality in Vase Painting." In *Queer Representations*, ed. Duberman, 14–24.

Dickie, Matthew W. 1991. "Heliodorus and Plutarch on the Evil Eye." *Classical Philology* 86:17–29.

Dickie, Matthew W., and Katherine M. D. Dunbabin. 1983. "*Invidia Rumpantur Pectora*: The Iconography of Phthonos/Invidia in Graeco-Roman Art." *Jahrbuch für Antike und Christentum* 26:7–37.

Didi-Huberman, Georges. 1996. "L'image-matrice: Généalogie et vérité de la ressemblance selon Pline l'Ancien, *Histoire naturelle*, XXXV,1–7." *L'inactuel: Psychanalyse et culture* 6:109–24.

Diels, Hermann. 1934. *Die Fragmente der Vorsokratiker*. Ed. W. Kranz. Berlin. Cited as Diels-Kranz.

———, ed. 1965. *Doxographi graeci*. 4th ed. Berlin.

Dietz, Gunter, and Karlheinz Hilbert. 1970. *Phaeton und Narziss bei Ovid*. Heidelberger Texte. Didaktische Reihe, Heft 3. Heidelberg.

Dihle, Albrecht. 1982. *The Theory of Will in Classical Antiquity*. Berkeley, Calif.

Dillon, John A. 1997. "Medea among the Philosophers." In *Medea*, ed. Claus and Johnston, 211–18.

Dimundo, Rosalba. 1983. "Da Socrate a Eumolpo: Degradazione dei personaggi e delle funzioni nella novella del fanciullo de Pergamo." *Materiali e discussioni per l'analisi dei testi classici* 11:255–65.

Dingel, Joachim. 1974. *Seneca und die Dichtung*. Heidelberg.

DiSalvo, Marilyn. 1980. "The Myth of Narcissus." *Semiotica* 30:15–25.

Dobbin, Robert. 1991. "Προαίρεσις in Epictetus." *Ancient Philosophy* 11:111–35.

Dodds, E. R. 1951. *The Greeks and the Irrational.* Berkeley, Calif.

———. 1973. *The Ancient Concept of Progress and Other Essays in Greek Literature and Belief.* Oxford.

Dörrie, Heinrich. 1967. "Echo und Narzissus Ovid. *Met.* III: 341–510: Psychologische Fiktion in Spiel und Ernst." *Altsprachliche Unterricht* 10:54–75.

Dover, Kenneth James. 1974. *Greek Popular Morality in the Time of Plato and Aristotle.* Berkeley, Calif.

———. 1989. *Greek Homosexuality.* Boston, Mass.

Dowd, James J. 1995. "The Theatrical Self: Aporias of the Self." In *Alternative Identities: The Self in Literature, History, Theory,* ed. Linda M. Brooks, 245–66. New York.

Duberman, Martin, ed. 1997. *Queer Representations: Reading Lives, Reading Cultures.* New York.

duBois, Page. 1985. "Phallocentrism and Its Subversion in Plato's *Phaedrus.*" *Arethusa* 18:91–103.

———. 1998. "The Subject in Antiquity after Foucault." In *Rethinking Sexuality,* ed. Larmour, Miller, and Platter, 85–103.

Dumont, J.-P. 1994. "Sensation et perception dans la philosophie d'époque hellénistique et impériale." *Aufstieg und Niedergang der römischen Welt* 2.36.7: 4718–64.

Dunbabin, Katherine M. D. 1978. *The Mosaics of Roman North Africa: Studies in Iconography and Patronage.* Oxford.

Dupont, Florence. 1985. *L'Acteur-roi.* Paris.

———. 1987. "Les morts et la mémoire: l'image funèbre." In *Les morts, la mort, et l'audelà. Actes du colloque de Caen, 20–22 novembre 1985,* ed. François Hinard, 167–72. Caen.

———. 1990. "Der juristische und der tragische furor." In *Theater und Gesellschaft im Imperium Romanum,* ed. Jürgen Blänsdorf, Jean-Marie André, and Nicole Fick, 141–48. Tübingen.

———. 1995. *Les Monstres de Sénèque.* Paris.

———. 1997. "L'humain et l'inhumain dans *Médée* de Sénèque." In *L'humain et l'inhumain,* ed. Florence Dupont, Christine Berthin, Marie-Christine Bellosta, and Hans Hartje, 7–96. Paris.

———. 2000. *L'Orateur sans visage: Essai sur l'acteur romain et son masque.* Paris.

Durand-Sendrail, Béatrice. 1988. "Mirage des lumières: politique du regard dans les *Lettres persanes.*" *L'Esprit créateur* 28:69–81.

Dyck, Andrew R. 1996. *A Commentary on Cicero,* De Officiis. Ann Arbor, Mich.

Earl, Donald C. 1961. *The Political Thought of Sallust.* Cambridge, England.

Eck, Werner. 1984. "Senatorial Self-Representation: Developments in the Augustan Period." In *Caesar Augustus: Seven Aspects,* ed. Fergus Millar and Erich Segal, 129–67. Oxford.

Eco, Umberto. 1986. "Mirrors." In *Iconicity: Essays on the Nature of Culture: Festschrift for Thomas A. Sebeok on His Sixty-fifth Birthday,* ed. Paul Bouissac et al., 215–37. Tübingen.

Edwards, Catharine. 1993. *The Politics of Immorality in Ancient Rome*. Cambridge, England.

———. 1997a. "Self-Scrutiny and Self-Transformation in Seneca's Letters." *Greece and Rome* 44:23–38.

———. 1997b. "Unspeakable Professions: Public Performance and Prostitution in Ancient Rome." In *Roman Sexualities*, ed. Hallett and Skinner, 66–95.

———. 1999. "The Suffering Body: Philosophy and Pain in Seneca's *Letters*." In *Constructions of the Classical Body*, ed. James I. Porter, 252–68. Ann Arbor, Mich.

———. 2005. "Eros and the Roman Philosopher: Response." In *Erotikon*, ed. Bartsch and Bartscherer, 84–90.

Egermann, F. 1940. "Seneca als Dichterphilosoph." *Neue Jahrbücher für Antike und deutsche Bildung* 3:18–36.

Eitrem, Samson. 1935. "Narkissos." *Realencyclopädie der classischen Altertumwissenschaft*, vol. 16, 1721–33.

Eldred, Katherine O. 2002. "This Ship of Fools: Epic Vision in Lucan's Vulteius Episode." In *The Roman Gaze*, ed. Fredrick, 57–85.

Elkisch, Paula. 1957. "The Psychological Significance of the Mirror." *Journal of the American Psychoanalytical Association* 5:235–44.

Elsner, Jaś (John). 1993. "Seductions of Art: Encolpius and Eumolpus in a Neronian Picture Gallery." *Proceedings of the Cambridge Philological Society* 39:30–47.

———, ed. 1996a. *Art and Text in Roman Culture*. Cambridge, England.

———. 1996b. "Naturalism and the Erotics of the Gaze: Intimations of Narcissus." In *Sexuality in Ancient Art*, ed. Kampen et al., 247–61.

———. 2000. "Caught in the Ocular: Visualising Narcissus in the Roman World." In *Echoes of Narcissus*, ed. L. Spaas, 89–110. New York.

Engberg-Pederson, Troels. 1990. "Stoic Philosophy and the Concept of the Person." In *The Person and the Human Mind*, ed. Gill, 109–35.

———, ed. 1998. *The Emotions in Hellenistic Philosophy*. Dordrecht.

Fantham, Elaine. 1991. "*Stuprum*: Public Attitudes and Penalties for Sexual Offenses in Republican Rome." *Échos du monde classique* 35:267–91.

Feldherr, Andrew. 1998. *Spectacle and Society in Livy's History*. Berkeley, Calif.

Fenichel, Otto. 1937. "The Scopophilic Instinct and Identification." *International Journal of Psychoanalysis* 18:6–34.

Fillion-Lahille, Janine. 1984. *Le De ira de Sénèque et la philosophie stoïcienne des passions*. Paris.

Fitch, John G., and Siobhan McElduff. 2002. "Construction of the Self in Senecan Drama." *Mnemosyne* 55:18–40.

Fitzgerald, William. 1992. "Catullus and the Reader: The Erotics of Poetry." *Arethusa* 25:419–93.

———. 1995. *Catullan Provocations: Lyric Poetry and the Drama of Position*. Berkeley, Calif.

Flower, Harriet. 1996. *Ancestor Masks and Aristocratic Power in Roman Culture*. Oxford.

Foley, Helene. 1989. "Medea's Divided Self." *Classical Antiquity* 8:61–85.

Forde, Steven. 1987. "On the *Alcibiades* I." In *The Roots of Political Philosophy*, ed. Thomas L. Pangle, 222–39. Ithaca, N.Y.

Foucault, Michel. 1979. *Discipline and Punish: The Birth of the Prison*. Trans. Alan Sheridan. New York.

———. 1980. *The History of Sexuality: An Introduction*, vol. 1. Trans. Robert Hurley. New York.

———. 1983. "The Subject and Power." In *Michel Foucault: Beyond Structuralism and Hermeneutics*, ed. Hubert L. Dreyfus and Paul Rabinow, 208–26. Chicago.

———. 1984. "From the Classical Self to the Modern Subject." In *The Foucault Reader*, ed. Paul Rabinow, 359–72. New York.

———. 1985. *The Use of Pleasure: The History of Sexuality*, vol. 2. Trans. Robert Hurley. New York.

———. 1986. *The Care of the Self: The History of Sexuality*, vol. 3. Trans. Robert Hurley. New York.

———. 1988. "Technologies of the Self." In *Technologies of the Self: A Seminar with Michel Foucault*, ed. Luther H. Martin, Huck Gutman, and Patrick H. Hutton, 16–49. Amherst, Mass.

———. 1993. "About the Beginning of the Hermeneutics of the Self: Two Lectures at Dartmouth." *Political Theory* 21:198–227.

———. 2001. *L'herméneutique du sujet. Cours au Collège du France, 1981–1982*. Paris.

Francis, James A. 1995. *Subversive Virtue: Asceticism and Authority in the Second-Century Pagan World*. University Park, Pa.

Frankfurt, Harry G. 1971. "Freedom of the Will and the Concept of a Person." *Journal of Philosophy* 68:5–20.

Frappier-Mazur, Lucienne. 1996. *Writing the Orgy: Power and Parody in Sade*. Trans. Gillian C. Gill. Philadelphia.

Frede, Michael. 1983. "Stoics and Skeptics on Clear and Distinct Impressions." In *The Skeptical Tradition*, ed. Myles Burnyeat, 65–94. Berkeley, Calif.

———. 1986. "The Stoic Doctrine of the Affectations of the Soul." In *The Norms of Nature*, ed. Schofield and Striker, 93–110.

Fredrick, David. 1995. "Beyond the Atrium to Ariadne: Erotic Painting and Visual Pleasure in the Roman House." *Classical Antiquity* 14:266–88.

———. 1997. "Reading Broken Skin: Violence in Roman Elegy." In *Roman Sexualities*, ed. Hallett and Skinner, 172–93.

———. 2002a. "Introduction: Invisible Rome." In *The Roman Gaze*, ed. Fredrick, 1–30.

———. 2002b. "Mapping Penetrability in Late Republican and Early Imperial Rome." In *The Roman Gaze*, ed. Fredrick, 236–64.

———, ed. 2002c. *The Roman Gaze: Vision, Power, and the Body*. Baltimore.

Freedman, Barbara. 1991. *Staging the Gaze: Postmodernism, Psychoanalysis, and Shakespearean Comedy*. Ithaca, N.Y.

Freud, Sigmund. 1923. *The Ego and the Id*. Leipzig.

———. 1950. "Medusa's Head." In *Collected Papers*, ed. James Strachey, vol. 5, 105–6. The International Psychoanalytic Library, No. 37. London.

———. 1957a. "On Narcissism: An Introduction." In *The Standard Edition of Complete Psychological Works of Sigmund Freud*, ed. and trans. James Strachey, vol. 14, 73–102. London.

———. 1957b. "Mourning and Melancholia." In *The Standard Edition of Complete Psychological Works of Sigmund Freud*, ed. and trans. James Strachey, vol. 14, 237–58. London.

———. 1957c. "Three Essays on the Theory of Sexuality." In *The Standard Edition of Complete Psychological Works of Sigmund Freud*, ed. and trans. James Strachey, vol. 7, 130–243. London.

Friedländer, Paul. 1921. *Der grosse* Alcibiades: *ein Weg zu Plato*. 2 vols. Bonn.

Frontisi-Ducroux, Françoise. 1989. "In the Mirror of the Mask." Trans. Deborah Lyons. In *A City of Images: Iconography and Society in Ancient Greece*, ed. Claude Bérard, 147–61. Princeton, N.J.

———. 1991. "Senza maschera né specchio: l'uomo Greco e i doppi." In *La maschera, il doppio, e il ritratto*, ed. Bettini, 131–58.

———. 1995. Du masque au visage: aspects de l'identité en Grèce ancienne. Paris.

———. 1996. "Eros, Desire, and the Gaze." Trans. Nancy Kline. In *Sexuality in Ancient Art*, ed. Kampen et al., 81–100.

Frontisi-Ducroux, Françoise, and Jean-Pierre Vernant. 1997. *Dans l'oeil du miroir*. Paris.

Fuhrmann, Manfred. 1979. "Persona, ein römischer Rollenbegriff." In *Identität*, ed. Odo Marquard and Karlheinz Stierle, 83–106. Munich.

Fyfe, Helen. 1983. "An Analysis of Seneca's *Medea*." In *Seneca Tragicus: Ramus Essays on Senecan Drama*, ed. A. J. Boyle, 77–93. Berwick, Victoria.

Gaca, Kathy L. 2003. *The Making of Fornication: Eros, Ethics, and Political Reform in Greek Philosophy and Early Christianity*. Hellenistic Culture and Society, No. 40. Berkeley, Calif.

Galinsky, Karl. 1988. "The Anger of Aeneas." *American Journal of Philology* 109:321–48.

Gallistl, Bernhard. 1995. *Maske und Spiegel: Zur Maskenszene des Pompejaner Mysterienfrieses*. Studien zur Kunstgeschichte, No. 101. Hildesheim.

Gasché, Rodolphe. 1986. *The Tain of the Mirror: Derrida and the Philosophy of Reflection*. Cambridge, Mass.

George, Peter. 1974. "Petronius and Lucan *De Bello Civili*." *Classical Quarterly* 24:119–33.

Gergen, Kenneth J. 1977. "The Social Construction of Self-Knowledge." In *The Self: Psychological and Philosophical Issues*, ed. Theodore Mischel, 139–69. Totowa, N.J.

Gertler, Brie. 2003. "Self-Knowledge." In *The Stanford Encyclopedia of Philosophy*, ed. Edward N. Zalta. Spring 2003 edition. Available online at http://plato.stanford.edu/archives/spr2003/entries/self-knowledge/.

Giddens, Anthony. 1991. *Modernity and Self-identity: Self and Society in the Late Modern Age*. Stanford, Calif.

Gill, C. 1973. "The Sexual Episodes in the *Satyricon*." *Classical Philology* 68:172–85.

Gill, Christopher. 1983. "Did Chrysippus Understand Medea?" *Phronesis* 28:136–49.

———. 1987. "Two Monologues of Self-Division: Euripides, *Medea* 1021–80 and Seneca, *Medea* 893–977." In *Homo Viator: Classical Essays for John Bramble*, ed. Michael Whitby, Mary Whitby, and Philip Hardie, 25–37. Bristol, England.

———. 1988. "Personhood and Personality: The Four-*Personae* Theory in Cicero *De Officiis* 1." *Oxford Studies in Ancient Philosophy* 6:169–99.

———. 1990. "The Human Being as an Ethical Norm." In *The Person and the Human Mind: Issues in Ancient and Modern Philosophy*, ed. Christopher Gill, 137–61. Oxford.

———. 1994. "Peace of Mind and Being Yourself: Panaetius to Plutarch." *Aufstieg und Niedergang der römischen Welt* 2.36.7: 4599–4640.

———. 1995. *Greek Thought. Greece and Rome*, suppl. 25:1–97.

———. 1996. *Personality in Greek Epic, Tragedy, and Philosophy: The Self in Dialogue.* Oxford.

———. 1997. "Passion as Madness in Roman Poetry." In *The Passions in Roman Thought and Literature*, ed. Braund and Gill, 213–41.

———. Forthcoming. *The Structured Self in Hellenistic and Roman Thought.* Oxford.

Gleason, Maud W. 1995. *Making Men: Sophists and Self-Presentation in Ancient Rome.* Princeton, N.J.

Glei, Reinhold. 1992. "Erkenntnis als Aphrodisiakum: Poetische und philosophische *Voluptas* bei Lucrez." *Antike und Abendland* 38:82–94.

Goldberg, Benjamin. 1985. *The Mirror and Man.* Charlottesville, Va.

Goldhill, Simon. 1994. "The Naïve and Knowing Eye: Ecphrasis and the Culture of Viewing in the Hellenistic World." In *Art and Text in Ancient Greek Culture*, ed. Simon Goldhill and Robin Osborne, 197–223. Cambridge, England.

———. 1995. *Foucault's Virginity: Ancient Erotic Fiction and the History of Sexuality.* Cambridge, England.

———. 1996. "Refracting Classical Vision: Changing Cultures of Viewing." In *Vision in Context*, ed. Brennan and Jay, 15–28.

———. 1998. "The Reciprocity of the Gaze: Seducing Socrates' Girlfriends." In *Kosmos: Order, Individual and Community in Classical Athens*, ed. Paul Cartledge, Paul Millet, and Sita von Reden, 105–24. Cambridge, England.

———. 2001. "The Erotic Eye: Visual Stimulation and Cultural Conflict." In *Being Greek under Rome: Cultural Identity, the Second Sophistic and the Development of Empire*, ed. Simon Goldhill, 154–94. Cambridge, England.

Goldin, Owen. 1993. "Self, Sameness, and the Soul in *Alcibiades* I and the *Timaeus*." *Freiburger Zeitschrift für Philosophie und Theologie* 40:5–19.

Goldstein, Jan, ed. 1994. *Foucault and the Writing of History.* Cambridge, Mass.

Gordon, Pamela. 2002. "Some Unseen Monster: Rereading Lucretius on Sex." In *The Roman Gaze*, ed. Fredrick, 86–109.

Gosling, J. C. B. 1973. "Knowledge as Vision." In *Plato*, 120–39. London.

———. 1987. "The Stoics and ἀκρασία" *Apeiron* 20:179–202.

Gould, Thomas. 1963. *Platonic Love*. New York.

Gourinat, Jean-Baptiste. 1996. *Les stoïciens et l'âme*. Paris.

Grabes, Herbert. 1982. *The Mutable Glass: Mirror Imagery in Texts and Titles of the Middle Ages and the English Renaissance*. Trans. Gordon Collier. Cambridge, England.

Grant, Michael. 1975. *Eros in Pompeii: The Secret Rooms of the National Museum of Naples*. New York.

Graver, Margaret. 1990. "The Eye of the Beholder: Perceptual Relativity in Lucretius." In *The Poetics of Therapy: Hellenistic Ethics in Its Rhetorical and Literary Context*, ed. Martha C. Nussbaum, 91–116. Special issue. *Apeiron* 23.

Graziano, Frank. 1997. *The Lust of Seeing: Themes of the Gaze and Sexual Rituals in the Fiction of Felisberto Hernández*. Lewisburg, Pa.

Greene, Ellen. 1995a. "The Catullan Ego: Fragmentation and the Erotic Self." *American Journal of Philology* 116:77–93.

———. 1995b. "Elegiac Woman: Fantasy, *Materia* and Male Desire in Propertius 1.3 and 1.11." *American Journal of Philology* 116:308–18.

———. 1998. *The Erotics of Domination: Male Desire and the Mistress in Latin Love Poetry*. Baltimore.

Gregerson, Linda. 1993. "Narcissus Interrupted: Specularity and the Subject of the Tudor State." *Criticism* 35:1–40.

Gregory, Andrew. 1994. "'Powerful Images': Responses to Portraits and the Political Uses of Images in Rome." *Journal of Roman Archeology* 7:80–99.

Griffin, Miriam. 1976. *Seneca: A Philosopher in Politics*. Oxford.

———. 2000. "Seneca and Pliny." In *The Cambridge History of Greek and Roman Political Thought*, ed. Christopher Rowe and Malcolm Schofield, 532–58. Cambridge, England.

Griffith, Michael A. 1996–97. "Left-Hand Horses, Winged Souls, and Plato's *Phaedrus*: Sex and Philosophy." *Midwest Quarterly* 38:31–40.

Grimal, Pierre. 1963. *L'amour à Rome*. Paris.

———. 1979. *Sénèque ou la conscience de l'Empire*. Paris.

———. 1989. "Sénèque et le stoïcisme romain." *Aufstieg und Niedergang der römischen Welt* 2.36.3: 962–92.

———. 1992. "Le vocabulaire de l'intériorité dans l'oeuvre de Sénèque." In *La langue latine, langue de la philosophie: actes du colloque organisé par l'École française de Rome avec le concours de l'Université de Rome La Sapienza: Rome, 17–19 mai 1990*, ed. Pierre Grimal, 141–59. Rome.

Griswold, Charles L., Jr. 1986. *Self-Knowledge in Plato's Phaedrus*. New Haven, Conn.

de Grummond, Nancy Thomson, ed. 1982. *A Guide to Etruscan Mirrors*. Tallahassee, Fla.

Guidorizzi, Giulio. 1991. "Lo specchio e la mente: un sistema d'intersezioni." In *La maschera, il doppio, e il ritratto*, ed. Bettini, 31–46.

Gunderson, Erik. 1996. "The Ideology of the Arena." *Classical Antiquity* 15:113–51.

———. 2000. *Staging Masculinity: The Rhetoric of Performance in the Roman World.* Ann Arbor, Mich.

Habinek, Thomas. 1992. "An Aristocracy of Virtue: Seneca on the Beginnings of Wisdom." *Yale Classical Studes* 29:187–203.

———. 1998. *The Politics of Latin Literature: Writing, Identity, and Empire in Ancient Rome.* Princeton, N.J.

Hadot, Ilsetreut. 1969. *Seneca und die griechisch-römische Tradition der Seelenleitung.* Berlin.

Hadot, Pierre. 1992. "Reflections on the Notion of 'The Cultivation of the Self.'" In *Michel Foucault, Philosopher: Essays,* 225–31. Trans. Timothy J. Armstrong. New York.

———. 1995. *Philosophy as a Way of Life: Spiritual Exercises from Socrates to Foucault.* Trans. Arnold I. Davidson. London.

Haglund, Pamela E. 1996. "A Clear and Equal Glass: Reflections on the Metaphor of the Mirror." *Psychoanalytic Psychology* 13:225–45.

Hahm, David E. 1992. "A Neglected Stoic Argument for Human Responsibility." *Illinois Classical Studies* 17:23–48.

Hahn, Johannes. 1989. *Der Philosoph und die Gesellschaft: Selbstverständnis, öffentliches Auftreten und populare Erwartungen in der höhen Kaiserzeit.* Stuttgart.

Hallett, Judith P., and Marilyn B. Skinner, eds. 1997. *Roman Sexualities.* Princeton, N.J.

Halperin, David M. 1986. "Plato and Erotic Reciprocity." *Classical Antiquity* 5:60–80.

———. 1990a. "Why Is Diotima a Woman?" In *One Hundred Years of Homosexuality,* 15–40. New York.

———. 1990b. *One Hundred Years of Homosexuality and Other Essays in Greek Love.* New York.

———. 1992. "Plato and the Erotics of Narrativity." In *Innovations of Antiquity,* ed. Daniel Selden and Ralph Hexter, 95–126. New York.

———. 1994. "Historicizing the Subject of Desire: Sexual Preferences and Erotic Identities in the Pseudo-Lucianic *Erotes.*" In *Foucault and the Writing of History,* ed. Goldstein, 19–34.

———. 1998. "Forgetting Foucault: Acts, Identities, and the History of Sexuality." *Representations* 63:93–120.

Hankinson, James. 1993. "Actions and Passions: Affection, Emotion, and Moral Self-Management in Galen's Philosophical Psychology." In *Passions and Perceptions,* ed. Brunschwig and Nussbaum, 184–222.

Hannan, Maryanne. 1992. "A Psychoanalytic Interpretation of Ovid's Myth of Narcissus and Echo." *Psychoanalytic Review* 79:555–75.

Hannoosh, Michele. 1989. "The Reflexive Function of Parody." *Comparative Literature* 41:113–27.

Hardie, Philip. 1988. "Lucretius and the Delusions of Narcissus." *Materiali e discussioni per l'analisi dei testi classici* 20–21:71–89.

Havelock, E. A. 1963. *Preface to Plato*. Cambridge, Mass.

Henderson, John G. 1991. "The Pupil as Teacher: Persius' Didactic Satire." *Ramus* 20:123–48.

Henry, Denis, and Elisabeth Henry. 1985. *The Mask of Power: Seneca's Tragedies and Imperial Rome*. Warminster, Wiltshire, England.

Henry, Denis, and Bessie (Elisabeth) Walker. 1967. "Loss of Identity: *Medea Superest?*" *Classical Philology* 62:169–81.

Hershkowitz, Debra. 1998. *The Madness of Epic: Reading Insanity from Homer to Statius*. Oxford.

Hijmans, B. L. 1959. ΑΣΚΗΣΙΣ: *Notes on Epictetus' Educational System*. Wijsgerige Teksten en Studies 2. Assen, Netherlands.

———. 1994. "*Apuleius orator: Pro se de Magia* and *Florida*." *Aufstieg und Niedergang der römischen Welt* 2.34.2: 1708–84.

Hine, Harry M. 1996. *Studies in the Text of Seneca's* Naturales Quaestiones. Stuttgart.

———, ed. 2000. *Seneca: Medea*, with introduction, text, translation, and commentary. Warminster, Wiltshire, England.

Hook, Brian S. 2000. "Nothing Within Which Passeth Show: Character and Color in Senecan Tragedy." In *Seneca in Performance*, ed. G. W. M. Harrison, 53–71. London.

Housman, A. E. 1931. "Praefanda." *Hermes* 66:405–6.

Hubbard, Thomas K. 2002. "Pindar, Theoxenus, and the Homoerotic Eye." *Arethusa* 35:255–96.

Hugedé, Norbert. 1957. *La métaphore du miroir dans les épîtres de Saint Paul aux Corinthiens*. Neuchâtel.

Hunink, Vincent, ed. 1997. *Pro Se de Magia: Apologia, by Apuleius of Madauros*. Amsterdam.

Huskinson, Janet, ed. 2000. *Experiencing Rome: Culture, Identity and Power in the Roman Empire*. London.

Hutcheon, Linda. 1984. *Narcissistic Narrative: The Metafictional Paradox*. New York.

Hutchinson, A. C. 1982. "Petronius and Lucan." *Liverpool Classics Monthly* 7:46–47.

Ingenkamp, Heinz G. 1971. "Zur stoischen Lehre vom Sehen." *Rheinisches Museum* 114:240–46.

Inwood, Brad. 1985. *Ethics and Human Action in Early Stoicism*. Oxford.

———. 1993. "Seneca and Psychological Dualism." In *Passions and Perceptions*, ed. Brunschwig and Nussbaum, 150–83.

———. 1995. "Seneca in His Philosophical Milieu." *Harvard Studies in Classical Philology* 97:63–76.

———. 2000. "The Will in Seneca the Younger." *Classical Philology* 95:44–60.

———. 2003. "Reason, Rationalization, and Happiness in Seneca." In *Rationality and Happiness from the Ancients to the Medievals*, ed. Jorge Gracia and Jiyuan Yu, 91–107. Rochester, N.Y.

Irigaray, Luce. 1985. *Speculum of the Other Woman*. Trans. G. C. Gill. Ithaca, N.Y.

Jacoby, Felix, ed. 1923. *Die Fragmente der griechische Historiker*. Berlin.

Janan, Micaela. 1991. "'The Labyrinth and the Mirror': Incest and Influence in *Metamorphoses* 9." *Arethusa* 24:239–56.

Jay, Martin. 1993. *Downcast Eyes: The Denigration of Vision in Twentieth-Century French Thought*. Berkeley, Calif.

Johns, Catherine. 1982. *Sex or Symbol: Erotic Images of Greece and Rome*. Austin, Tex.

Johnson, Brian. N.d. "*Prosopology*: Epictetus on Individual Roles." Typescript.

Johnson, David M. 1999. "God as the True Self: Plato's *Alcibiades I*." *Ancient Philosophy* 19:1–19.

Jonas, Hans. 1982. "The Nobility of Sight: A Study in the Phenomenology of the Senses." In *The Phenomenon of Life: Toward a Philosophical Biology*, 135–52. Chicago.

Jonsson, Einar Mar. 1995. *Le Miroir: naissance d'un genre littéraire*. Paris.

Jung, Carl. 1966. *Two Essays on Analytical Psychology*. Trans. R. F. C. Hull. Princeton, N.J.

Kahn, Charles H. 1988. "Discovering the Will: From Aristotle to Augustine." In *The Question of "Eclecticism": Studies in Later Greek Philosophy*, ed. J. M. Dillon and A. A. Long, 234–59. Berkeley, Calif.

Kampen, Natalie B., Bettina Bergmann, Ada Cohen, and Eva Steh, eds. 1996. *Sexuality in Ancient Art: Near East, Egypt, Greece, and Italy*. Cambridge, England.

Kamtekar, Rachana. 1998. "ΑΙΔΩΣ in Epictetus." *Classical Philology* 93:136–60.

Kaplan, E. Ann. 1983. "Is the Gaze Male?" In *Powers of Desire: The Politics of Sexuality*, ed. Ann Barr Snitow, Christine Stansell, and Sharon Thompson, 309–27. New York.

Kaster, Robert. 1997. "The Shame of the Romans." *Transactions of the American Philological Association* 127:1–19.

———. 2002. "The Taxonomy of Patience, or When Is *Patientia* Not a Virtue?" *Classical Philology* 97:133–44.

Kellum, Barbara. 1996. "The Phallus as Signifier: The Forum of Augustus and Rituals of Masculinity." In *Sexuality in Ancient Art*, ed. Kampen et al., 170–83.

Kelly, Dorothy. 1992. *Telling Glances: Voyeurism in the French Novel*. New Brunswick, N.J.

Kennedy, George. 1978. "Encolpius and Agamemnon in Petronius." *American Journal of Philology* 99:171–78.

Keyser, Paul T. 1993. "Cicero on Optics *Att.* 2.3.2." *Phoenix* 47:67–69.

Kirby, John T. 1996. "Classical Origins of Western Aesthetic Theory." In *Languages of Visuality: Crossings between Science, Art, Politics, and Literature*, ed. Beate Allert, 29–45. Detroit.

Klassen, Norman. 1995. *Chaucer on Love, Knowledge, and Sight*. Rochester, N.Y.

Klebs, E. 1889. "Zur Composition von Petronius Satirae." *Philologus* 47:623–35.

Knoche, Ulrich. 1941. "Seneca's *Atreus*: Ein Beispiel." *Die Antike* 17:60–76.

Knoespel, Kenneth J. 1985. *Narcissus and the Invention of Personal History*. New York.

Knox, Peter. 1986. "Ovid's Medea and the Authenticity of *Heroides* 12." *Transactions of the American Philological Association* 90:207–23.

Kochhar-Lindgren, Gray. 1993a. *Narcissus Transformed: The Textual Subject in Psychoanalysis and Literature*. University Park, Pa.

———. 1993b. "The Obsessive Gaze: The Logic of Narcissism in Philosophy and Postmodern Fiction." *Dynamische Psychiatrie* 26:216–23.

Konersmann, Ralf. 1991. *Lebendige Spiegel: Der Metapher des Subjekts.* Frankfurt am Main.

Konstan, David. 1993. "Sexuality and Power in Juvenal's Second Satire." *Liverpool Classical Monthly* 18:12–14.

Konstan, David, and Martha Nussbaum, eds. 1990. *Sexuality in Greek and Roman Society.* Special issue. *Differences* 2.

Kraft, Kent. 1994. "Mind's Mirrors: Some Early Versions of Contemporary Specular Discourse." In *The Play of the Self,* ed. Ronald Bogue and Mihai I. Spariosu, 39–66. New York.

Kristeva, Julia. 1987. *Tales of Love.* Trans. Leon S. Roudiez. New York.

Kruger, Steven F. 1991. "Mirrors and the Trajectory of Vision in *Piers Plowman*: Medieval Epistemology and Transcendent Self-Exploration." *Speculum* 66:74–95.

Kubiak, Anthony. 1989. "Trial and Terror: Medea *Prima Facie.*" *Comparative Drama* 23:3–30.

Lacan, Jacques. 1978. *The Four Fundamental Concepts of Psycho-Analysis.* Ed. Jacques-Alain Miller. Trans. Alan Sheridan. New York.

———. 2004. "The Mirror Stage as Formative of the Function of the I as Revealed in Psychoanalytic Theory." In *Écrits: A Selection,* 3–9. Trans. Bruce Fink. New York.

Lahusen, Götz. 1982. "Statuae et Imagines." In *Praestant Interna. Festschrift für Ulrich Hausmann,* ed. B. von Freytag gen. Löringhoff, D. Mannsperger, and F. Prayon, 101–9. Tübingen.

Laing, Ronald D. 1965. *The Divided Self.* Harmondsworth, Middlesex, England.

LaPenna, Antonio. 1997. "*Fallit Imago*: Manilius and His Polemics against Vergil and Lucretius: Notes on '*Astronomica IV* 306.'" *Maia* 49:107–8.

Larmour, David H. J., Paul Allen Miller, and Charles Platter, eds. 1998. *Rethinking Sexuality: Foucault and Classical Antiquity.* Princeton, N.J.

Lawall, Gilbert. 1979. "Seneca's *Medea*: The Elusive Triumph of Civilization." In *Arktouros: Hellenic Studies Presented to B. M. W. Knox,* ed. G. W. Bowersock, 419–26. Berlin.

Layton, Lynne. 1985. "From Oedipus to Narcissus: Literature and the Psychology of Self." *Mosaic: A Journal for the Interdisciplinary Study of Literature* 18:97–105.

Leach, Eleanor. 1990. "The Politics of Self-Representation: Pliny's *Letters* and Roman Portrait Sculpture." *Classical Antiquity* 9:14–39.

Lear, Jonathan. 1994. "Plato's Politics of Narcissism." In *Virtue, Love and Form: Essays in Memory of Gregory Vlastos,* ed. Terence Irwin and Martha C. Nussbaum, 137–60. Special issue. *Apeiron* 36.

Lebeck, Anne. 1972. "The Central Myth of Plato's *Phaedrus.*" *Greek, Roman, and Byzantine Studies* 13:267–90.

Leigh, Matthew. 1996. "Varius Rufus, Thyestes and the Appetites of Antony." *Proceedings of the Cambridge Philological Society* 42:171–97.

————. 1997. *Lucan: Spectacle and Engagement.* Oxford.

Leisegang, Hans. 1937. "La Connaissance de Dieu au miroir de l'âme et de la Nature." *Revue d'histoire et de philosophie religieuses* 17:145–71.

Leitao, David D. 1998. "Senecan Catoptrics and the Passion of Hostius Quadra Sen. *Nat.* 1." *Materiali e discussioni* 41:127–60.

Lejeune, Albert. 1948. *Euclide et Ptolémée: deux stades de l'optique géometrique grecque.* Recueil de travaux d'histoire et de philologie, ser. 3, fasc. 31. Louvain.

————. 1957. *Recherches sur la catoptrique grecque d'après les sources antiques et médiévales.* Brussels.

Leo, F. 1878. *De Senecae tragoediis observationes criticae.* Berlin.

Levin, David M., ed. 1997. *Sites of Vision: The Discursive Construction of Sight in the History of Philosophy.* Cambridge, Mass.

Lewis, Eric. 1995. "The Stoics on Identity and Individuation." *Phronesis* 4:89–108.

Lilja, Saara. 1983. *Homosexuality in Republican and Augustan Rome.* Helsinki.

Lindberg, David C. 1976. *Theories of Vision from Al-Kindi to Kepler.* Chicago.

Littlewood, Cedric. 2002. "*Integer Ipse?* Self-Knowledge and Self-Representation in Persius *Satires* 4." *Phoenix* 56:56–83.

Lloyd, Antony C. 1964. "*Nosce Teipsum* and *Conscientia.*" *Archiv für Geschichte der Philosophie* 46:188–200.

————. 1978. "Emotion and Decision in Stoic Psychology." In *The Stoics*, ed. Rist, 233–46.

Lloyd-Morgan, G. 1982. "The Roman Mirror and its Origins." In *A Guide to Etruscan Mirrors*, ed. de Grummond, 39–48.

Long, A. A., ed. 1971. *Problems in Stoicism.* London.

————. 1982. "Soul and Body in Stoicism." *Phronesis* 27:34–57.

————. 1986. *Hellenistic Philosophy: Stoics, Epicureans, Sceptics.* Berkeley, Calif.

————. 1988. "Socrates in Hellenistic Philosophy." *Classical Quarterly* 38:150–71.

————. 1991. "Representation and the Self in Stoicism." In *Psychology: Companions to Ancient Thought II*, ed. Stephen Everson, 102–20. Cambridge, England.

————. 1993. "Hellenistic Ethics and Philosophical Power." In *Hellenistic History and Culture*, ed. P. Green, 138–56. Berkeley, Calif.

————. 1996. *Stoic Studies.* Cambridge. England.

————. 1997. "Stoic Philosophers on Persons, Property-ownership, and Community." In *Aristotle and After*, ed. Richard Sorabji, 13–31. *Bulletin of the Institute of Classical Studies*, suppl. 68. London.

————. 2001. "Ancient Philosophy's Hardest Question: What to Make of Oneself?" *Representations* 74:19–36.

————. 2002. *Epictetus: A Stoic and Socratic Guide to Life.* Oxford.

————. 2003. "Roman Ethics." In *A History of Western Ethics*, ed. L. C. Becker et al., 33–44. New York.

Long, A. A., and David Sedley, eds. 1987. *The Hellenistic Philosophers.* 2 vols. Cambridge, England.

Lutz, Cora E. 1947. "Musonius Rufus, the Roman Socrates." *Yale Classical Studies* 10:3–147.

MacGregor, Alexander P. 1989. "The Tigress and Her Cubs: Tracking Down a Roman Anecdote." In *Daidalikon: Studies in Memory of Raymond V. Schoder, S.J.*, ed. Robert F. Sutton, 218–27. Wauconda, Ill.

Machamer, Peter K., and Robert G. Turnbull, eds. 1978. *Studies in Perception: Inter-relations in the History of Philosophy and Science.* Columbus, Ohio.

MacIntyre, Alasdair. 1981. *After Virtue.* South Bend, Ind.

MacLachlan, B. 1993. *The Age of Grace: Charis in Early Greek Poetry.* Princeton, N.J.

Maclean, Robert M. 1979. *Narcissus and the Voyeur: Three Books and Two Films.* Approaches to Semiotics, No. 48. The Hague.

MacMullen, Ramsay. 1982. "Roman Attitudes towards Greek Love." *Historia* 31: 484–502.

Maier, Harry O. 1997. "Staging the Gaze: Early Christian Apocalypses and Narrative Self-Representation." *Harvard Theological Review* 90:131–54.

Makowski, John F. 1989–90. "Nisus and Euryalus: A Platonic Relationship." *Classical Journal* 85:1–15.

Manning, C. E. 1973. "Seneca and the Stoics on the Equality of the Sexes." *Mnemosyne* ser. 4, no. 26: 170–77.

———. 1994. "School Philosophy and Popular Philosophy in the Roman Empire." *Aufstieg und Niedergang der römischen Welt* 2.36.7: 4995–5026.

Manuwald, Bernd. 1975. "Narcissus bei Konon und Ovid." *Hermes* 103:349–72.

Marti, Berthe. 1945. "Seneca's Tragedies: A New Interpretation." *Transactions of the American Philological Association* 76:216–45.

———. 1947. "The Prototypes of Seneca's Tragedies." *Classical Philology* 42:1–16.

Mastrangelo, Mark. 2000. "Oedipus and Polyneices: Characterization and the Self in Sophocles' *Oedipus at Colonus.*" *Materiali e discussioni per l'analisi dei testi classici* 44:35–81.

Mauss, Marcel. 1985. "A Category of the Human Mind: The Notion of Person; the Notion of Self." In *The Category of the Person*, ed. Carrithers, Collins, and Lukes, 1–25.

Mayer, Roland. 1994. "*Personata Stoa*: Neostoicism and Senecan Tragedy." *Journal of the Warburg and Courtauld Institutes* 57:151–74.

McCarty, Willard. 1989. "The Shape of the Mirror: Metaphorical Catoptrics in Classical Literature." *Arethusa* 22:161–95.

McGlathery, Daniel B. 1998. "Reversals of Platonic Love in Petronius' *Satyricon.*" In *Rethinking Sexuality*, ed. Larmour, Miller, and Platter, 204–27.

McMahon, John M. 1998. *Paralysin Cave: Impotence, Perception, and Text in the* Satyrica *of Petronius.* Leiden.

Mead, George Herbert. 1934. *Mind, Self, and Society.* Chicago.

Melchior-Bonnet, Sabine. 2001. *The Mirror: A History.* Trans. Katharine H. Jewett. New York.

Mele, Alfred R. 1992. "Akrasia, Self-Control, and Second-Order Desires." *Nous* 26:281–302.

Miller, Paul Allen. 1998. "Catullan Consciousness, the 'Care of the Self,' and the Force of the Negative in History." In *Rethinking Sexuality*, ed. Larmour, Miller, and Platter, 171–203.

Milowicki, Edward J., and R. Rawdon Wilson. 1995. "Ovid through Shakespeare: The Divided Self." *Poetics Today* 16:217–52.

Misch, Georg. 1931. *Geschichte der Autobiographie.* Leipzig.

Mitsis, Philip. 1993. "Seneca on Reason, Rules, and Moral Development." In *Passions and Perceptions*, ed. Brunschwig and Nussbaum, 285–312.

Momigliano, Arnaldo. 1969. "Seneca between Political and Contemplative Life." In *Quarto contributo alla storia degli studi classici e del mondo antico*, 239–56. Rome.

Montserrat, Dominic, ed. 1998. *Changing Bodies, Changing Meanings: Studies on the Human Body in Antiquity.* London.

Moore, John D. 1973. "The Relation between Plato's *Symposium* and *Phaedrus.*" In *Patterns in Plato's Thought*, ed. J. M. E. Moravcsik, 52–71. Dordrecht.

Morales, Helen. 1996. "The Torturer's Apprentice: Parrhasius and the Limits of Art." In *Art and Text in Roman Culture*, ed. Elsner, 182–209.

Morris, H. 1994. "A Paternalistic Theory of Punishment." In *A Reader on Punishment*, ed. R. A. Duff and David Garland, 92–111. Oxford.

Morris, Phyllis Sutton. 1997. "Self-Creating Selves: Sartre and Foucault." *American Catholic Philosophical Quarterly* 70:537–49.

Moscovici, Claudia. 1991. "Blindness and the Quest for Truth in *Oedipus the King.*" *Maia* 43:185–87.

Motto, Anne Lydia, and John R. Clark. 1993. "Seneca on the *Profanum Vulgus.*" *Classical Bulletin* 69:35–39.

Mulvey, Laura. 1989. "Visual Pleasure and Narrative Cinema." In *Visual and Other Pleasures*, 14–26. Bloomington, Ind.

Murray, G. 1997. "Reviewing Vision in Sophocles' *Oedipus the King.*" *AUMLA, Journal of the Australasian Universities Language and Literature Association* 88:1–20.

Myerowitz, Molly. 1992. "The Domestication of Desire: Ovid's *Parva Tabella* and the Theater of Love." In *Pornography and Representation*, ed. Richlin, 131–57.

Myers, Gerald E. 1986. "Introspection and Self-Knowledge." *American Philosophical Quarterly* 23:199–207.

Napolitano Valditara, Linda M. 1994. *Lo Sguardo nel buio: metafore visive e forme grecoantiche della razionalità.* Rome.

Natali, Monica. 1992. "Gli Influssi del Platonismo sul neostoicismo Senecano." *Rivista di filosofia neo-scolastica* 84:494–514.

———. 1994. "Tra Stoicismo e Platonismo: Concezione della filosofia e del fine ultimo dell'uomo in Seneca." *Rivista di filosofia neo-scolastica* 86:427–47.

Nédoncelle, Maurice. 1948. "Πρόσωπον et *Persona* dans l'antiquité classique. Essai de bilan linguistique." *Revue des sciences religieuses* 22:277–99.

Nehamas, Alexander. 1998. *The Art of Living: Socratic Reflections from Plato to Foucault.* Berkeley, Calif.

Neumann, Harry. 1965. "Diotima's Concept of Love." *American Journal of Philology* 86:33–59.

Newman, R. 1989. "*Cotidie Meditare*: Theory and Practice of the *Meditatio* in Imperial Stoicism." *Aufstieg und Niedergang der römischen Welt* 2.36.3: 1473–1517.

Nicaise, Serge. 1991. "Je meurs de soif auprès de la fontaine: Narcisse, Echo et le problématique du double chez Ovide." *Études classiques* 59:67–72.

Nightingale, Andrea. 2001. "On Wandering and Wondering: *Theoria* in Greek Philosophy and Culture." *Arion* 9:23–58.

———. 2004. *Spectacles of Truth in Classical Greek Philosophy: Theoria in Its Cultural Context.* Cambridge, England.

Nilson, Herman. 1998. *Michel Foucault and the Games of Truth.* Trans. Rachel Clark. Basingstoke, Hampshire, England.

Nolan, Edward Peter. 1990. *Now through a Glass Darkly: Specular Images of Being and Knowing from Virgil to Chaucer.* Ann Arbor, Mich.

North, Helen. 1966. *Sophrosyne: Self-Knowledge and Self-Restraint in Greek Literature.* Ithaca, N.Y.

Nouvet, Claire. 1991. "An Impossible Response: The Disaster of Narcissus' Ovid." *Yale French Studies* 79:103–34.

Nugent, S. Georgia. 1990. "This Sex Which Is Not One: De-Constructing Ovid's Hermaphrodite." In *Sexuality in Greek and Roman Society*, ed. Konstan and Nussbaum, 160–85.

Nussbaum, Martha. 1986a. "Love and the Individual: Romantic Rightness and Platonic Aspiration." In *Reconstructing Individualism: Autonomy, Individuality, and the Self in Western Thought*, ed. Thomas C. Heller, Morton Sosna, David E. Wellbery, Arnold I. Davidson, Ann Swindler and Ian Watt, 253–77. Stanford, Calif.

———. 1986b. *The Fragility of Goodness: Luck and Ethics in Greek Tragedy and Philosophy.* Cambridge, England.

———. 1987. "The Stoics on the Extirpation of the Passions." *Apeiron* 20:129–76.

———. 1990. "Therapeutic Arguments and Structures of Desire." In *Sexuality in Greek and Roman Society*, ed. Konstan and Nussbaum, 46–66.

———. 1993. "Poetry and the Passions: Two Stoic Views." In *Passions and Perceptions*, ed. Brunschwig and Nussbaum, 97–149.

———. 1994. *The Therapy of Desire: Theory and Practice in Hellenistic Ethics.* Princeton, N.J.

———. 1995. "Eros and the Wise: The Stoic Response to a Cultural Dilemma." *Oxford Studies in Ancient Philosophy* 13:231–67.

———. 2002. "The Incomplete Feminism of Musonius Rufus, Platonist, Stoic, and Roman." In *The Sleep of Reason*, ed. Nussbaum and Sihvola, 283–326.

Nussbaum, Martha, and Juha Sihvola, eds. 2002. *The Sleep of Reason: Erotic Experience and Sexual Ethics in Ancient Greece and Rome.* Chicago.

Orlowsky, Ursula, and Rebekka Orlowsky. 1992. *Narziss und Narzissmus im Spiegel von Literatur, bildender Kunst und Psychoanalyse: vom Mythos zur leeren Selbst-inszenierung.* Munich.

Panayotakis, Costas. 1995. *Theatrum Arbitri: Theatrical Elements in the* Satyrica *of Petronius.* Leiden.

Papadopoulou, Thalia. 1997. "The Presentation of the Inner Self: Euripides' *Medea* 1021–55 and Apollonius Rhodius' *Argonautica* 3, 772–801." *Mnemosyne* 50:641–64.

Park, David. 1997. *The Fire within the Eye: A Historical Essay on the Nature and Meaning of Light.* Princeton, N.J.

Parker, Holt. 1997. "The Teratogenic Grid." In *Roman Sexualities*, ed. Hallett and Skinner, 47–65.

———. 1999. "The Observed of All Observers: Spectacle, Applause, and Cultural Poetics in the Roman Theater Audience." In *The Art of Ancient Spectacle*, ed. Bergmann and Kondoleon, 163–80.

Parsons, Michael. 1988. "Self-Knowledge Refused and Accepted: A Psychoanalytic Perspective on the *Bacchae* and the *Oedipus at Colonus*." *Bulletin of the Institute of Classical Studies* 35:1–14.

Pauly-Wissowa. 1894–1980. *Realencyclopädie der classischen Altertumswissenschaft.*

Payne, Michael. 1993. *Reading Theory: An Introduction to Lacan, Derrida, and Kristeva.* Oxford.

Pears, David. 1952. "The Incongruity of Counterparts." *Mind* 61:78–81.

Pearson, A. C. 1909. "Phrixus and Demodice: A Note on Pindar, *Pyth.* IV.162f." *Classical Review* 23:255–57.

Pellizer, Ezio. 1988. "Reflections, Echoes, and Amorous Reciprocity: On Reading the Narcissus Story." Trans. Diana Crampton. In *Interpretations of Greek Mythology*, ed. Jan Bremmer, 107–20. Totowa, N.J.

———. 1991. "Narciso e le figure della dualità." In *La maschera, il doppio e il ritratto*, ed. Bettini, 13–29.

Penwill, J. L. 1994. "Image, Ideology and Action in Cicero and Lucretius." *Ramus* 23:68–91.

Percy, William Armstrong, III. 1996. *Pederasty and Pedagogy in Archaic Greece.* Urbana, Ill.

Peterson, R. G. 1972–73. "The Unknown Self in the Fourth Satire of Persius." *Classical Journal* 68:205–9.

Petrone, Gianna. 1984. *La Scrittura tragica dell'irrazionale. Note di letture al teatro di Seneca.* Palermo.

Picard, Gilbert-Charles. 1981. "Les Grotesques: un système décoratif typique de l'art césarien et néronien." In *L'Art decoratif à Rome à la fin de la république et au début du principat*, 143–49. Collection de l'École Française de Rome, No. 55. Rome.

Platt, Verity. 2002. "Viewing, Desiring, Believing: Confronting the Divine in a Pompeian House." *Art History* 25:87–112.

Pohlenz, M. 1965. "Philosophie und Erlebnis in Senecas Dialogen." Anhang, "Ein römischer Zug in Senecas Denken." In *Kleine Schriften I*, 440–46. Hildesheim.

Porter, James I. 1997. "Aristotle on Specular Regimes: The Theater of Philosophical Discourse." In *Sites of Vision*, ed. Levin, 93–116.

Pöschl, Victor, Helga Gärtner, and Waltraud Heyke, eds. 1964. *Bibliographie zur antiken Dichtersprache*. Heidelberg.

Pradeau, Jean-François. 1999. *Alcibiade*. Translation and commentary. Paris.

Pratt, Norman T. 1948. "The Stoic Base of Senecan Drama." *Transactions of the American Philological Association* 79:1–11.

———. 1983. *Seneca's Drama*. Chapel Hill, N.C.

Price, A. W. 1989. *Love and Friendship in Plato and Aristotle*. Oxford.

———. 2002. "Plato, Zeno, and the Object of Love." In *The Sleep of Reason*, ed. Nussbaum and Sihvola, 170–99.

Rabbow, Paul. 1954. *Seelenführung. Methodik der Exerzitien in der Antike*. Munich.

Rabinowitz, Nancy S., and Amy Richlin, eds. 1993. *Feminist Theory and the Classics*. New York.

Raffel, Stanley. 1994. "Identity, Self-Reflection and the Problem of Validating Standards." *History of the Human Sciences* 7:65–81.

Rafn, B. 1992. "Narkissos." In *Lexicon Iconographicum Mythologiae Classicae*, VI.1, 703–11. Munich.

Rakoczy, Thomas. 1996. *Böser Blick, Macht des Auges und Neid der Götter: Eine Untersuchung zur Kraft des Blickes in der griechischen Literatur*. Tübingen.

Rank, Otto. 1971. *The Double*. Trans. Harry Tucker Jr. Chapel Hill, N.C.

Rappe, Sara. 1997. "Self-Perception in Plotinus and the Later Neoplatonic Tradition: A Hermeneutical Speculation on the History of the Philosophy of Reflection in Ancient Commentary." *American Catholic Philosophical Quarterly* 71:433–51.

Raucci, Stacie. 2004. "Gazing Games: Propertius and the Dynamics of Vision." Ph.D. diss., University of Chicago.

Rawson, Elizabeth. 1987. "*Discrimina Ordinum*: The Lex Julia Theatralis." *Papers of the British School at Rome* 55:83–114.

Reydams-Schils, Gretchen. 1998. "Roman and Stoic: The Self as a Mediator." *Dionysius* 16:35–62.

Richardson, T. Wade. 1984. "Homosexuality in the *Satyricon*." *Classica et Medievalia* 35:105–27.

Richlin, Amy, ed. 1992a. *Pornography and Representation in Ancient Greece and Rome*. Oxford.

———. 1992b. *The Garden of Priapus: Sexuality and Aggression in Roman Humor*. 2nd ed. Oxford.

———. 1993. "Not before Homosexuality: The Materiality of the *Cinaedus* and the Roman Law against Love between Men." *Journal of the History of Sexuality* 3:523–73.

———. 1997. "Gender and Rhetoric: Producing Manhood in Schools." In *Roman Eloquence: Rhetoric in Society and Literature*, ed. William J. Dominik, 90–110. London.

Richter, Gisela M. A. 1937. "Perspective, Ancient, Mediaeval and Renaissance." In *Scritti in onore di Bartolomeo Nogara*, ed. Roberto Paribeni, 381–88. Vatican City.

Riggsby, Andrew M. 1998. "Self and Community in the Younger Pliny." *Arethusa* 31:75–97.

Rimell, Victoria. 2002. *Petronius and the Anatomy of Fiction.* Cambridge, England.

Rist, John M. 1969. *Stoic Philosophy.* London.

———, ed. 1978. *The Stoics.* London.

———. 1989. "Seneca and Stoic Orthodoxy." *Aufstieg und Niedergang der römischen Welt* 36.2.3: 1993–2012.

———. 1998. "Platonic Soul, Aristotelian Form, Christian Person." In *Self, Soul, and Body in Religious Experience,* ed. Baumgarten, Assmann, and Stroumsa, 347–62.

Robin, D. 1993. "Film Theory and the Gendered Voice in Seneca." In *Feminist Theory and the Classics,* ed. Rabinowitz and Richlin, 102–21.

Rohde, E. 1876. *Der griechische Roman und seine Vorläufer.* Leipzig.

Roller, Matthew. 2001a. *Constructing Autocracy: Aristocrats and Emperors in Julio-Claudian Rome.* Princeton, N.J.

———. 2001b. Review of Jane Chaplin, *Livy's Exemplary History. Bryn Mawr Classical Review* (July 3). Available online at http://ccat.sas.upenn.edu/bmcr/2001/2001-07-03.html.

Rorty, Amelie Oksenberg, ed. 1976. *The Identities of Persons.* Berkeley, Calif.

———. 1990. "Persons and Personae." In *The Person and the Human Mind,* ed. Christopher Gill, 21–38. Oxford, England.

Rorty, Richard. 1979. *Philosophy and the Mirror of Nature.* Princeton, N.J.

Rosati, Gianpiero. 1983. *Narciso e Pigmalione: Illusione e spettacolo nelle* Metamorfosi *de Ovidio.* Florence.

Rose, Jacqueline. 1986. *Sexuality in the Field of Vision.* New York.

Rosen, Stanley. 1989. *The Ancients and the Moderns: Rethinking Modernity.* New Haven, Conn.

Rosenmeyer, Thomas G. 1989. *Senecan Drama and Stoic Cosmology.* Berkeley, Calif.

Rowe, C. J. 1987. *Plato*: Phaedrus. Warminster, Wiltshire, England.

Ruby, Jay. 1982. *Crack in the Mirror: Reflexive Perspectives in Anthropology.* Philadelphia.

Rudd, Niall. 1976. *Lines of Enquiry: Studies in Latin Poetry.* Cambridge, England.

Ruprecht, Louis A. 1999. *Symposia: Plato, the Erotic, and Moral Value.* Albany, N.Y.

Rushdy, Ara. 1993. "Cartesian Mirror/Quixotic Web: Toward a Narrativity of Desire." *Mosaic: A Journal for the Interdisciplinary Study of Literature* 2:83–110.

Rzepka, Charles J. 1986. *The Self as Mind: Vision and Identity in Wordsworth, Coleridge, and Keats.* Cambridge, Mass.

Saller, Richard. 1994. *Patriarchy, Property, and Death in the Roman Family.* Cambridge, England.

Sandbach, F. H. 1971. "Phantasia Kataleptike." In *Problems in Stoicism,* ed. Long, 9–21.

———. 1975. *The Stoics.* New York.

Schefold, Karl. 1940. "Griechische Spiegel." *Die Antike* 16:11–37.

————. 1957. *Die Wände Pompejis: Topographisches Verzeichnis der Bildmotive.* Berlin.

Schickel, Joachim. 1961–62. "Narziss: Zu Versen von Ovid." *Antaios* 3:486–96.

Schiesaro, Alessandro. 1997. "Passion, Reason, and Knowledge in Seneca's Tragedies." In *The Passions in Roman Thought and Literature*, ed. Braund and Gill, 89–111.

————. 2003. *The Passions in Play: Thyestes and the Dynamics of Senecan Drama.* Cambridge, England.

Schmeling, Gareth. 1994. "Quid Attinet Veritatem per Interpretem Quaerere? Interpretes and the Satyricon." *Ramus* 23:144–67.

Schmidt, Jens-Uwe. 1995. "Phaedra und der Einfluss ihrer Amme." *Philologus* 139:274–323.

Schmitt, Jean-Claude. 1996. "La Culture de l'imago." *Annales: histoire, sciences sociales* 51:3–36.

Schofield, Malcolm. 1999. "Social and Political Thought." In *The Cambridge History of Hellenistic Philosophy*, ed. Keimpe Algra, Jonathan Barnes, Jaap Mansfeld, and Malcolm Schofield, 739–70. Cambridge, England.

Schofield, Malcolm, and Gisela Striker, eds. 1986. *The Norms of Nature: Studies in Hellenistic Ethics.* Cambridge, England.

Schuller, Moritz H. W. 1989. "'Watching the Self': The Mirror of Self-Knowledge in Ancient Literature." Ph.D. diss., Yale University.

Schwaiger, Clemens. 2000. "Die Idee des Selbstdenkens in der römischen Philosophie— aufgezeigt am Beispiel Senecas." *Gymnasium* 107:129–42.

Schwartz, Hillel. 1996. *The Culture of the Copy: Striking Likenesses, Unreasonable Facsimiles.* New York.

Scott, Dominic. 1989. "Epicurean Illusions." *Classical Quarterly* 39:360–74.

Scott, W. O. 1988. "The Speculative Eye: Problematic Self-Knowledge in *Julius Caesar*." *Shakespeare Survey* 41:77–89.

Sedley, David. 1982. "The Stoic Criterion of Identity." *Phronesis* 27:255–75.

Segal, Charles. 1986. *Language and Desire in Seneca's* Phaedra. Princeton, N.J.

Selden, Daniel. 1992. "*Caveat Lector*: Catullus and the Rhetoric of Performance." In *Innovations of Antiquity*, ed. Selden and Hexter, 491–512.

Shanahan, Daniel. 1992. *Toward a Genealogy of Individualism.* Amherst, Mass.

Sheffield, Frisbee. 2001. "Psychic Pregnancy and Platonic Epistemology." *Oxford Studies in Ancient Philosophy* 20:1–33.

Shoemaker, Sydney. 1986. "Introspection and the Self." *Midwestern Studies in Philosophy* 10:101–20.

Siebers, Tobin. 1983. *The Mirror of Medusa.* Berkeley, Calif.

Siegel, Jerrold. 1999. "Problematizing the Self." In *Beyond the Cultural Turn: New Directions in the Study of Society and Culture*, ed. Victoria E. Bonnell and Lynn Hunt, 281–314. Berkeley, Calif.

Silverman, Allan. 1990. "Plato on Perception and 'Commons.'" *Classical Quarterly* 15:148–75.

Silverman, Kaja. 1992. *Male Subjectivity at the Margins*. New York.

———. 1996. *The Threshold of the Visible World*. New York.

Simon, Gérard. 1987. "Behind the Mirror." *Graduate Faculty Philosophy Journal* 12:311–50.

———. 1988. *Le Regard, l'être, et l'apparence dans l'optique de l'antiquité*. Paris.

Sinclair, Brent W. 1984. "Encolpius and Asianism *Satyricon* 2.7." In *Classical Texts and Their Traditions*, ed. D. F. Bright and E. S. Ramage, 231–37. Chico, Calif.

Skinner, Marilyn B. 1997. "*Ego Mulier*: The Construction of Male Sexuality in Catullus." In *Roman Sexualities*, ed. Hallett and Skinner, 129–50.

Skinner, Virginia. 1965. "Ovid's 'Narcissus'—An Analysis." *Classical Bulletin* 41:59–61.

Slater, Niall W. 1990a. *Reading Petronius*. Baltimore.

———. 1990b. "An Echo of *Ars Poetica* 5 in Petronius." *Philologus* 134:159–60.

———. 1997. "Vision, Perception, and Phantasia in the Roman Novel." In *Der antike Roman und seine mittelalterliche Rezeption*, ed. M. Picone and B. Zimmermann, 89–105. Basel.

———. 1998. "Passion and Petrifaction: The Gaze in Apuleius." *Classical Philology* 93:18–48.

Snell, Bruno. 1953. *The Discovery of the Mind*. Oxford.

Solimano, Giannina. 1991. *La Prepotenza dell'occhio: Riflessioni sull'opera di Seneca*. Genoa.

Sorabji, Richard. 1990. "Perceptual Content in the Stoics." *Phronesis* 35:307–14.

———. 2002. *Emotion and Peace of Mind: From Stoic Agitation to Christian Temptation*. Oxford.

Soulez-Luccioni, A. 1974. "Le Paradigme de la vision de soi-même dans l'*Alcibiade majeur*." *Revue de métaphysique et de morale* 79:196–222.

Stam, Robert. 1985. *Reflexivity in Film and Literature from Don Quixote to Jean-Luc Godard*. New York.

Stamm, Renate. 1975. *The Mirror-Technique in Seneca and Pre-Shakespearean Tragedy*. Bern.

Star, Christopher. 2003. "Action and Self-Control: Apostrophe in Seneca, Petronius and Lucan." Ph.D. diss., University of Chicago.

Steiner, Deborah. 1995. "Stoning and Sight: A Structural Equivalence in Greek Mythology." *Classical Antiquity* 14:193–221.

Stewart, Andrew. 1996. "Reflections." In *Sexuality in Ancient Art*, ed. Kampen et al., 136–54.

———. 1997. *Art, Desire, and the Body in Ancient Greece*. New York.

Stiewe, K. 1959. "Beintäge aus der Thesaurus-Arbeit." *Museum Helveticum* 16:162–71.

Stirrup, Barbara E. 1976. "Ovid's Narrative Technique: A Study in Duality." *Latomus* 35:97–107.

Stock, Brian. 1994. "The Self and Literary Experience in Late Antiquity and the Middle Ages." *New Literary History* 25:839–52.

Stough, Charlotte. 1978. "Stoic Determinism and Moral Responsibility." In *The Stoics*, ed. Rist, 203–31.

Sullivan, John P. 1982. "Petronius' *Bellum Civile* and Lucan's *Pharsalia*: A Political Reconsideration." In *Neronia 1977*, ed. J.-M. Croisille and P.-M. Fanchère, 151–55. Clermont-Ferrand, France.

Svenbro, Jesper. 1993. *Phrasikleia: An Anthropology of Reading in Ancient Greece*. Trans. Janet Lloyd. Ithaca, N.Y.

Talbert, Richard J. A. 1984. *The Senate of Imperial Rome*. Princeton, N.J.

Tarán, Leonardo. 1975. *Academica: Plato, Philip of Opus, and the Pseudo-Platonic Epinomis*. Philadelphia.

Tarrant, R. J. 1978. "Senecan Drama and Its Antecedents." *Harvard Studies in Classical Philology* 82:216–63.

Taylor, Charles. 1976. "Responsibility for Self." In *The Identities of Persons*, ed. Rorty, 281–99.

———. 1985. *Human Agency and Language*. Philosophical Papers, vol. 1. Cambridge, England.

———. 1989. *Sources of the Self: The Making of Modern Identity*. Cambridge, Mass.

Taylor, Rabun. 1996–97. "Two Pathic Subcultures in Ancient Rome." *Journal of the History of Sexuality* 7:319–71.

Thévenaz, Pierre. 1976. "L'Interiorità in Seneca." In *Seneca: Letture critiche*, ed. Alfonso Traina, 91–96. Milan.

Todd, Robert B. 1974. "Συνεντας, and the Stoic Theory of Perception." *Grazer Beiträge* 2:251–61.

Too, Yun Lee. 1994. "Educating Nero: A Reading of Seneca's Moral Epistles." In *Reflections of Nero: Culture, History, and Representation*, ed. Jaś Elsner and Jamie Masters, 131–49. Chapel Hill, N.C.

———. 1996. "Statues, Mirrors, Gods: Controlling Images in Apuleius." In *Art and Text in Roman Culture*, ed. Elsner, 211–24.

Torre, Chiara. 1995. "Il cavallo immagine del *Sapiens* in Seneca." *Maia* 47:371–78.

Toulmin, Stephen E. 1977. "Self-Knowledge and Knowledge of the Self." In *The Self: Psychological and Philosophical Issues*, ed. Theodore Mischel, 291–317. Totowa, N.J.

Tracy, Valerie A. 1976. "Roman Dandies and Transvestites." *Échos du monde classique* 20:60–63.

Traina, Alfonso. 1974. *Lo Stilo "drammatico" del filosofo Seneca*. Bologna.

Trapp, M. B. 1990. "Plato's *Phaedrus* in Second-Century Greek Literature." In *Antonine Literature*, ed. D. A. Russell, 141–73. Oxford.

Trilling, Lionel. 1972. *Sincerity and Authenticity*. Oxford.

van Hoorn, Willem. 1972. *As Images Unwind: Ancient and Modern Theories of Visual Perception*. Amsterdam.

Van Sickle, John. 1973–74. "Plat. Phaedr. 255d, 3–6." *Museum Criticum* 8–9:198–99.

Verene, Donald Phillip. 1997. *Philosophy and the Return to Self-Knowledge.* New Haven, Conn.

Vernant, Jean-Pierre. 1991. "In the Mirror of Medusa." In *Mortals and Immortals: Collected Essays by Jean-Pierre Vernant,* ed. Froma I. Zeitlin, 141–50. Princeton, N.J.

Versnel, H. S. 1970. *Triumphus: An Inquiry into the Origin, Development, and Meaning of the Roman Triumph.* Leiden.

Verstraete, Beert C. 1979–80. "Slavery and the Social Dynamics of Male Homosexual Relations in Ancient Rome." *Journal of Homosexuality* 5:227–36.

———. 1982. *Homosexuality in Ancient Greek and Roman Civilization: A Critical Bibliography with Supplement.* Toronto.

Veyne, Paul. 1981. "L'Homosexualité à Rome." *L'Histoire* 30:76–78.

Vinge, Louise. 1967. *The Narcissus Theme in Western European Literature up to the Early Nineteenth Century.* Lund.

Vizier, Alain. 1998. "*Incipit Philosophia.*" In *Rethinking Sexuality,* ed. Larmour, Miller, and Platter, 61–84.

Vlahogiannis, Nicholas. 1998. "Disabling Bodies." In *Changing Bodies, Changing Meanings: Studies on the Human Body in Antiquity,* ed. Montserrat, 13–36.

Vlastos, Gregory. 1973. *Platonic Studies.* Princeton, N.J.

Voelke, André-Jean. 1973. *L'Idée de volonté dans le stoicisme.* Paris.

von Arnim, Johannes, ed. 1964. *Stoicorum veterum fragmenta.* 4 vols. Stuttgart.

von Fritz, Kurt. 1953. "Democritus' Theory of Vision." In *Science, Medicine, and History: Essays on the Evolution of Scientific Thought and Medical Practice, Written in Honour of Charles Singer,* ed. Edgar A. Underwood, vol. 1, 83–99. London.

von Netoliczka, Oscar. 1935. "Katoptron." *Realencyclopädie der classischen Altertumwissenschaft,* vol. 11, 29–45.

von Staden, Heinrich. 1978. "The Stoic Theory of Perception and Its 'Platonic' Critics." In *Studies in Perception,* ed. Machamer and Turnbull, 96–136.

Wade, Nicholas J. 1998. "Light and Sight since Antiquity." *Perception* 27:637–70.

Waiblinger, Franz Peter. 1977. *Senecas* Naturales Quaestiones: *Griechische Wissenschaft und römische Form. Zetemata,* 70. Munich.

Walker, Andrew. 1992. "Eros and the Eye in the Love-Letters of Philostratus." *Proceedings of the Cambridge Philological Society* 38:132–48.

Walsh, George. 1990. "Surprised by Self: Audible Thought in Hellenistic Poetry." *Classical Philology* 85:1–19.

Walters, Jonathan. 1997. "Invading the Roman Body: Manliness and Impenetrability in Roman Thought." In *Roman Sexualities,* ed. Hallett and Skinner, 23–43.

———. 1998. "Making a Spectacle: Deviant Men, Invective, and Pleasure." *Arethusa* 31:355–68.

Warren, James. 2004. *Facing Death: Epicurus and His Critics.* Oxford.

Watson, Gary. 2003. "Free Agency." In *Free Will,* ed. Watson, 337–51.

Watson, Gerard. 1988. *Phantasia in Classical Thought*. Galway.

————. 1994. "The Concept of 'Phantasia' from the Late Hellenistic Period to Early Neoplatonism." *Aufstieg und Niedergang der römischen Welt* 2.36.7: 4765–4810.

Watson, L. 1982. "Apuleius, Apologia 16." *Liverpool Classics Monthly* 7:128–29.

Wesselski, Albert. 1935. "Narkissos oder der Spiegelbild." *Archiv Orientální* 7:37–63.

White, F. C. 1990. "Love and the Individual in Plato's *Phaedrus*." *Classical Quarterly* 40:396–406.

Whittaker, John. 1989. "Platonic Philosophy in the Early Centuries of the Empire." *Aufstieg und Niedergang der römischen Welt* 2.36.3: 81–123.

Wiedemann, Thomas E. J. 1992. *Emperors and Gladiators*. London.

Wilamowitz-Moellendorff, Ulrich von. 1919. *Griechische Tragoedien*. Berlin.

Wilkins, Eliza Gregory. 1917. *"Know Thyself" in Greek and Latin Literature*. New York.

Williams, Bernard A. O. 1985. *Ethics and the Limits of Philosophy*. London.

————. 1993. *Shame and Necessity*. Berkeley, Calif.

Williams, Craig A. 1997. "*Pudicitia* and *Pueri*: Roman Concepts of Male Sexual Experience." In *Queer Representations*, ed. Duberman, 25–38.

————. 1999. *Roman Homosexuality: Ideologies of Masculinity in Classical Antiquity*. Oxford.

Wilson, Emma. 1996. *Sexuality and the Reading Encounter: Identity and Desire in Proust, Duras, Tournier, and Cixous*. Oxford.

Wilson, Hugh R. 1991. "Shadows on the Cave Wall: Philosophy and Visual Science." *Philosophical Psychology* 4:65–78.

Wilson, Marcus. 1997. "The Subjugation of Grief in Seneca's 'Epistles.' " In *The Passions in Roman Thought and Literature*, ed. Braund and Gill, 48–67.

Wistrand, Magnus. 1990. "Violence and Entertainment in Seneca the Younger." *Eranos* 88:31–46.

————. 1992. *Entertainment and Violence in Ancient Rome: The Attitudes of Roman Writers of the First Century A.D.* Studia Graeca et Latina Gothoburgensia, No. 56. Göteburg.

Wolf, Susan. 1987. "Sanity and the Metaphysics of Responsibility." In *Responsibility, Character, and the Emotions: New Essays in Moral Psychology*, ed. Ferdinand Schoeman, 46–62. Cambridge, England.

Wyke, Maria. 1994. "Woman in the Mirror: The Rhetoric of Adornment in the Roman World." In *Women in Ancient Societies*, ed. L. J. Archer, S. Fischler, and M. Wyke, 134–51. London.

Zanker, Paul. 1966. "*Iste ego sum*: Der naïve und der bewusste Narziss." *Bonner Jahrbücher* 166:152–70.

————. 1988. *The Power of Images in the Age of Augustus*. Trans. Alan Shapiro. Ann Arbor, Mich.

————. 1995. *The Mask of Socrates: The Image of the Intellectual in Antiquity*. Trans. Alan Shapiro. Berkeley, Calif.

Zeitlin, Froma. 1971a. "Petronius as Paradox: Anarchy and Artistic Integration." *Transactions of the American Philological Association* 192:631–84.

———. 1971b. "Romanus Petronius: A Study of the *Trojae Halosis* and the *Bellum Civile.*" *Latomus* 30:56–82.

Zeitlin, Froma, John J. Winkler, and David Halperin, eds. 1990. *Before Sexuality: The Construction of Erotic Experience in the Ancient Greek World.* Princeton, N.J.

Zimmerman, David. 2000. "Making Do: Troubling Stoic Tendencies in an Otherwise Compelling Theory of Autonomy." *Canadian Journal of Philosophy* 30:25–53.

Zurcher, Louis A. 1977. *The Mutable Self: A Self-Concept for Social Change.* Beverly Hills, Calif.